Mark Jackson

12/2022

THE OXFORD ILLUSTRATED HISTORY OF THE

FIRST WORLD WAR

THE OXFORD
ILLUSTRATED HISTORY
OF THE
FIRST
WORLD
WAR

EDITED BY

HEW STRACHAN

Oxford   New York
OXFORD UNIVERSITY PRESS
1998

Oxford University Press, Great Clarendon Street, Oxford OX2 6DP
Oxford New York
Athens Auckland Bangkok Bogota Bombay
Buenos Aires Calcutta Cape Town Dar es Salaam
Delhi Florence Hong Kong Istanbul Karachi
Kuala Lumpur Madras Madrid Melbourne
Mexico City Nairobi Paris Singapore
Taipei Tokyo Toronto Warsaw
and associated companies in
Berlin Ibadan

Oxford is a trade mark of Oxford University Press

Published in the United States by
Oxford University Press Inc., New York

British Library Cataloguing in Publication Data
Data available

Library of Congress Cataloging in Publication Data
The Oxford Illustrated History of the First World War
Edited by Hew Strachan p. cm.
Includes bibliographical references.
1. World War, 1914–1918.   I. Strachan, Hew.
D521.087   1998
940.3—dc21   97—4497 CIP

ISBN 0 19 820614 3

1 3 5 7 9 10 8 6 4 2

Data captured by Jayvee, Trivandrum, India
Typeset by Oxuniprint
Printed in Great Britain by
Butler & Tanner, Frome, Somerset

CONTENTS

LIST OF COLOUR PLATES

LIST OF MAPS

NOTES ON CONTRIBUTORS

Samuel R. Williamson, Jr., is Professor of History and Vice-Chancellor of the University of the South, Sewanee. His books include *The Politics of Grand Strategy: Britain and France Prepare for War, 1904–1914* (2nd edn., 1990); *Austria–Hungary and the Origins of the First World War* (1990); and, with Steven Rearden, *The Origins of US Nuclear Strategy, 1945–1953* (1993).

Lancelot L. Farrar, an independent scholar, has taught most recently at Boston University and Brown University. He is the author of *The Short War Illusion: German Policy, Strategy and Domestic Affairs, August–December 1914* (1973); *Divide and Conquer: German Efforts to Conclude a Separate Peace, 1914–1918* (1978); *Arrogance and Anxiety: The Ambivalence of German Power, 1848–1914* (1981); and editor of *War: A Historical, Political, and Social Study* (1978).

Dennis E. Showalter is Professor of History at Colorado College. His books include *Railroads and Rifles: Soldiers, Technology, and the Unification of Germany* (1975); *German Military History, 1648–1982: A Critical Bibliography* (1984); *Tannenberg: Clash of Empires* (1991); and *The Wars of Frederick the Great* (1995).

David French is Professor of History and Head of the History Department at University College London. He is the author of a trilogy on British strategy in the First World War: *British Economic and Strategic Planning, 1905–1915* (1982); *British Strategy and War Aims, 1914–1916* (1986); and *The Strategy of the Lloyd George Coalition, 1916–1918* (1995).

Richard J. Crampton is Professor of East European History, Oxford University, and a Fellow at St Edmund Hall. His books include *Bulgaria 1878–1918: A History* (1983); *A Short History of Modern Bulgaria* (1987); and *Eastern Europe in the Twentieth Century and After* (1997).

Ulrich Trumpener is Professor Emeritus of History, University of Alberta, and has written *Germany and the Ottoman Empire, 1914–18* (1968).

David Killingray is Professor of Modern History at Goldsmiths College, University of London. He is the author of *A Plague of Europeans* (1973); and co-editor of *Khaki and Blue: Military and Police in British Colonial Africa* (1989). He has contributed to and edited several volumes on modern African history, including *Africa and the First World War* (1987) and *Africa and the Second World War* (1986).

Paul G. Halpern is Professor of History at Florida State University. He has written *The Mediterranean Naval Situation, 1908–1914* (1981); *The Naval War in the Mediterranean, 1914–1918* (1987); and *A Naval History of World War I* (1994); and edited *The Keyes Papers* (3 vols., 1972–81).

B. J. C. McKercher is Professor of History at the Royal Military College of Canada. He has written *The Second Baldwin Government and the United States, 1924–1929* (1984); and *Esme Howard: A Diplomatic Biography* (1989), as well as editing a number of volumes.

Hew Strachan is Professor of Modern History at the University of Glasgow. His books include *European Armies and the Conduct of War* (1983); *Wellington's Legacy: The Reform of the British Army, 1830–54* (1984); *From Waterloo to Balaclava: Tactics, Technology and the British Army, 1815–1854* (1985); and *The Politics of the British Army* (1997).

Gail Braybon manages the computing facilities for the Faculty of Art, Design and Humanities at the University of Brighton, and has written *Women Workers in the First World War: The*

British Experience (1981); and, with Penny Summerfield, *Out of the Cage: Women's Experiences in Two World Wars* (1987).

John Turner is Professor of Modern History and Politics, and Vice-Principal at Royal Holloway College, University of London, and is the author of *Lloyd George's Secretariat* (1980); *British Politics and the Great War: Coalitions and Conflict, 1915–1918* (1992); and *Macmillan* (1994).

Robin Prior is Associate Professor of History, Australian Defence Force Academy, University of New South Wales, and **Trevor Wilson** is Professor Emeritus of History, University of Adelaide. Together they have written *Command on the Western Front: The Military Career of Sir Henry Rawlinson, 1914–18* (1992) and *Passchendaele: The Untold Story* (1996). Prior is also the author of *Churchill's 'World Crisis' as History* (1983); and Wilson of *The Downfall of the Liberal Party, 1914–1935* (1966); and *The Myriad Faces of War: Britain and the Great War* (1986).

David Englander is Reader in History at the Open University. He has edited and contributed to a large number of books, and is the author of *Landlord and Tenant in Urban Britain, 1938–1918* (1983). His study of the social and political effects of military service in the two world wars will be published shortly.

David Stevenson is Senior Lecturer in International History at the London School of Economics and Political Science. He has written *French War Aims against Germany, 1914–1919* (1982); *The First World War and International Politics* (1988); *Armaments and the Coming of War: Europe 1904–1914* (1996); and *The Outbreak of the First World War: 1914 in Perspective* (1997).

J. M. Winter is Reader in Modern History at the University of Cambridge, and is a Fellow of Pembroke College. His books include *Socialism and the Challenge of War: Ideas and Politics in Britain, 1912–1918* (1974); *The Great War and the British People* (1985); *The Experience of World War I* (1988); and *Sites of Memory, Sites of Mourning: The Great War in European Cultural History* (1995).

John Horne is Associate Professor of Modern European History at Trinity College, Dublin; he has written *Labour at War: France and Britain, 1914–1918* (1991); and edited *State, Society and Mobilization in Europe during the First World War* (1997).

David Trask was Chief Historian at the United States Army Center of Military History. His books include *The United States and the Supreme War Council: American War Aims and Inter-Allied Strategy, 1917–1918* (1961); *Captains and Cabinets: Anglo-American Naval Relations, 1917–1918* (1972); with Mary Klachko, *Admiral William Shepherd Benson: First Chief of Naval Operations* (1987); and *The AEF and Coalition Warmaking, 1917–1918* (1993).

Holger H. Herwig is Professor of History, University of Calgary. He has written *The German Naval Officer Corps: A Social and Political History, 1890–1918* (1973); *'Luxury' Fleet: The Imperial German Navy, 1888–1918* (1980); and *The First World War: Germany and Austria-Hungary, 1914–1918* (1997).

John H. Morrow, Jr., is Franklin Professor of History at the University of Georgia. He has written *Building German Airpower, 1909–1919* (1976); *German Air Power in World War I* (1982); and *The Great War in the Air: Military Aviation from 1909 to 1921* (1993).

Timothy H. E. Travers is Professor of History at the University of Calgary. His books are *The Killing Ground: The British Army, the Western Front and the Emergence of Modern Warfare, 1900–1918* (1987); and *How the War Was Won: Command and Technology in the British Army on the Western Front, 1917–18* (1992).

Zara Steiner is an Emeritus Fellow of New Hall, Cambridge. She has written *The Foreign Office and Foreign Policy, 1898–1914* (1969); and *Britain and the Origins of the First World War* (1977).

Modris Eksteins is Professor of History at the University of Toronto. His books include *The Limits of Reason: The German Democratic Press and the Collapse of Weimar Democracy* (1975); and *Rites of Spring: The Great War and the Birth of the Modern Age* (1989).

Introduction

HEW STRACHAN

The war as cliché

This history's last chapter is on the memory of the First World War. Its author, Modris Eksteins, has examined entries made in the late 1980s in the visitors' books kept by the Commonwealth War Graves Commission. At the Bernafay cemetery, under the heading 'remarks', one Englishman entered 'none needed'. This pragmatic and yet pregnant response to the graves that trace a line through north-western Europe, from Ypres to Arras and on to Verdun and Belfort, is not one which historians have been able to share. The First World War has commanded a literature that is quite simply enormous. Furthermore, as the twentieth century closes, the rate of publication is expanding rather than contracting. Scholarship has deepened, and often revised and transformed, our understanding of what is familiar; it has also taken the history of the war in fresh directions, from campaigns and strategy to mentalities and culture. Indeed the range, quality, and diversity of current research on the war is one of the most obvious justifications for a synthesizing summary such as this.

Putting the war into words has never been easy, as the war poets themselves testified. Indeed the effort required may be one explanation for the publishing phenomenon that the war has generated. The need to comprehend, the urge to give shape to what can seem so inchoate and even irrational—these were, and still are, the most important impulses to writing. But the phrases which have resulted have too often not done justice to the scale of events, or to the emotional charge of the experience. Another recent visitor to the graves of the western front commented: 'I cannot find the words without breaking into clichés.' If those who wrote about the experience of the war were in large part responsible for the advent of modernism, as Samuel Hynes has argued in *A War Imagined: The First World War and English Culture*, it was precisely because they recognized that they needed a new vocabulary and a new style if they were to reflect adequately what the war meant.

Three epithets in particular are regularly used when describing what its contemporaries more simply, and with less attempt at relativism or at categorization, called the Great War. These are 'global', 'total', and 'modern'. They have each been employed in an effort to create a sense of the war's

1

scale, but each is ambiguous in its meaning and has itself become—if adjectives can become nouns—a cliché.

A world war

'Global' has the advantage of being geographically precise. But its use immediately raises objections on the score of accuracy. Not every country in the world had become a belligerent by the war's end. Furthermore, the fighting on land was largely confined to Europe, the Middle East, and parts of Africa, with brief outbreaks in central Asia and the Far East. But if the title 'global' is therefore rejected, the geographical descriptor which is substituted is 'European'. It began, after all, as the third Balkan war. Indeed, R. J. Crampton shows that Balkan tensions remained an extraordinarily self-contained element in the wider conflict that ensued. Some contemporaries called what followed the 'Great European War', and a few later historians have interpreted it as a sort of civil war, in which the continent's member states fell on each other in an orgy of self-destruction, in the process eliminating their collective hegemony.

This is far too limiting, in large measure precisely because of the very existence of that hegemony. Europe's global dominance, directly through the empires of its member states, and indirectly through its economic leadership, meant that a major war in Europe had inter-continental implications. Africa, as David Killingray makes clear in his chapter, was immediately involved. The Ottoman empire, still just in Europe after the two Balkan wars, felt compelled to fight in order to regulate its relationships with the other European powers. But since it was also an Asiatic and Middle Eastern power, the consequence was, as Ulrich Trumpener describes, to extend the war to the Caucasus, Iraq, and Syria. Moreover the Ottoman empire's status as the temporal leader of Islam gave it the authority to declare a holy war on behalf of muslims everywhere. Not many of the faith responded, but that does not mean that they were not forced to choose sides.

Such was the reach of the war that true neutrality became to all intents and purposes unsustainable. B. J. C. McKercher describes the pressures that economic warfare brought to bear on the neutrals bordering Germany. Outside Europe, where geographical distance meant that neutrals did not have to navigate between the Charybdis of the Central Powers and the Scylla of the Entente, they frequently found it easier just to opt for the latter. Indeed self-interest, as Japan in particular demonstrated, could make war a sensible option. Most significant of all, in 1917 the United States of America entered the fray not just because of Germany's adoption of unrestricted submarine warfare but also, as David Trask emphasizes, in pursuit of its own ambitions for a new international order. 'Global', therefore, is more, rather than less, helpful in describing the war.

A total war

The use of 'total' is much more problematic. Its implications are absolute but its application is relative: 'total war' remains, fortunately, an idea. Some of the battles of the First World War, pre-eminently those of the Somme, Verdun, and Passchendaele in the west, the twelve battles fought on the Isonzo in Italy, the wintry struggles in the Carpathians, carry connotations that help make the concept concrete. For the individuals who fought and died in such circumstances the experience was, at the risk of being platitudinous, 'total'. However, detachment, even at only one remove from the battlefield, created a different perspective. John Morrow nails the notion that the air war was a war of chivalry, where individual courage prevailed over the industrialization of war: by 1917–18 fighting in the air was considerably more dangerous than fighting on land, and the outcome was determined less by the resourcefulness of the aces and more by aircraft production. But high above the battlefields of the western front, the pilots could at least see, as the soldiers below them could not, how circumscribed the ground operations had become. Trench war had the effect of limiting the zone in which the physical dangers of war prevailed. Its effect was to create a protective barrier for all those behind it. The real threat to civilians arose only when that barrier was broken, when war became mobile, when soldiers plundered food stocks, and when fear and rumour gave rise to atrocity. For some, even the Turks' slaughter of the Armenians, to which Trumpener refers, can be explained in these ways.

For others, such rationalizations are inherently unacceptable. To place the massacre of the Armenians in the operational context of war is to relativize something which was awful in an absolute sense: what happened to the Armenians was a form of genocide, a precursor of the Holocaust. Certainly the fate of the Armenians confirms not only that the war impinged on civilians but that it did so in radically new ways. On the other hand the Armenian case was exceptional. The consequences of the war for civilians were rarely so physical, and more often psychological. The most important of these was totalitarian rather than 'total': it was the mobilization of men's minds through propaganda. At least until 1917 most official propaganda was directed overseas, principally towards neutrals who might be persuaded to become allies. But J. M. Winter sees this definition of propaganda as too limited: the mechanisms for manipulating opinion were very often in the hands of profit-making companies rather than those of the government, and the media that they used were far more diverse than the printed word. Visual images, at first posters, later films, but including banal souvenirs, picture postcards, and comic strips, had an immediacy and a universality that deepened the divisions of enmity. The need for belligerent governments to sponsor and develop these techniques was made clear by two phenomena which became evident in 1917. The first, discussed by David Englander, was mutinies at the front. The second, analysed by John Horne, was revolution at home. The former is often interpreted as a rejection not of the war's aims *per se*, but of the methods by which those aims were being pursued. The latter, because the Russians called for a peace without annexations and without indemnities, implied a rejection of the very purposes of the war. In reality the two currents could not stand apart: the Petrograd garrison carried revolution from the rear to the front; elements in the German army became vectors for socialism. This fusion of feeling between army and society was itself a product of the mobilization of mass armies, and one way at least in which the war was total.

The application of universal male conscription had another 'totalizing' effect. It stripped industrial production of much of its workforce. Gail Braybon warns against the perils of exaggerating the mobilization of women which followed. Many of those females engaged in munitions production were employed in other work before 1914. In peasant agriculture women were already integral to the rural economy; the loss of men to the army intensified an existing burden. The importance of the civil population to the output of war-related goods—and another way in which the war was total was that ultimately nothing could not be construed as at least indirectly relevant to the war effort—made it a legitimate target of warfare. In this war that would mean little more than material deprivation through maritime blockade: the loss of food, light, heat, and clothing. In the next, as air power strategists in 1918 already argued, the attack on cities would be direct.

A modern war

Thus war in the third dimension would edge nearer 'total' war. Technological sophistication enabled the development of the aircraft; the aircraft itself then became the means to hamper a nation's industrial mobilization. These two—technological sophistication and industrial mobilization—are the conditions on which industrialized warfare was predicated. But industrialized warfare is more than their sum. It also describes the manner in which they are employed—the fighting methods. To say that the First World War was a war between industrialized societies is not sufficient to warrant the conclusion that it was also a benchmark in the evolution of 'modern' war. Caveats are even more necessary when describing 'modern' than when describing 'total'.

To be sure, the new machinery of war usurped the rythmns of nature. Aerial observation forced men to manœuvre by night and lie low by by day; high explosive could literally move mountains—or at least hills. What set the soldier's timetable, not only of sleeping and waking, but of advancing and halting, was the artillery bombardment. Robin Prior and Trevor Wilson argue that by 1916 the sophistication and scale of artillery was the conditioning factor in war on the western front—a point confirmed by Tim Travers in his account of the allied victories in 1918. But the immediate effect of the tyranny of the gun was pre-modern. Men dug deep: trenches saved soldiers' lives, another way in which they rendered war less 'total'. The weapons that this troglodyte existence demanded were those of eighteenth-century siege warfare, mortars and grenades, and even of earlier forms of combat, clubs and axes. Primitivism, not modernism, was the first reaction to industrialized war.

But it was not the only reaction. Precision engineering applied to mass production produced light machine guns; chemical engineering developed new forms of explosives as well as phosgene gas; electrical engineering transformed the means of communication and made real-time intelligence, as well as accurate counter-battery fire, realizable ambitions. At the tactical level, the ultimate consequence of all this was the ability to reunite fire and movement, to reintegrate artillery and infantry. At the operational level of war, the ability of artillery to fire accurately but indirectly at long ranges and at high intensity over a short period gave the battlefield depth as well as linearity. The German victories were won, as Holger Herwig shows, by these techniques; the principles which they embodied subsequently became the conceptual bedrock of much in the practice of twentieth-century warfare.

The interface which conditioned 'modern' war, therefore, was that between tactics and technology. But that was not the interface which preoccupied general staffs in 1914. Their attention was directed to operations, the movements of armies within a theatre of war, with the campaign rather than with the battle. What concerned them before the war, therefore, was the relationship between operations and what we would now call grand strategy. Samuel Williamson does not accuse the generals of causing the war, but he does say that the mechanistic mobilization schedules which they had adopted narrowed the opportunities for diplomacy. Furthermore, once at war, the armies' focus was now manœuvre, as D. E. Showalter stresses, and this immediately elevated the operational level of war to the neglect of the tactical. Thus senior officers were, by virtue of existing doctrines and by the very nature of their own experiences in 1914–15, cut off from the immediate experiences and implications of trench warfare.

The direction of the war

These demarcations between the levels of war were not appropriate to the war at sea. Paul Halpern ranges as easily from tactics through operations to strategy and back again as did the British and German fleet commanders, Jellicoe and Scheer. At the battle of Jutland both of them were under fire; both could observe and respond to the tactical situation. But both were aware of the strategic implications of what they were about; above all, Jellicoe knew that a defeat in battle for the Grand Fleet could also mean defeat in the war as a whole for Britain.

One of the reasons that tactical and strategic direction collapsed in upon each other at sea was the advent of the wireless. Still too bulky for easy transport on land, it could be carried by every warship. The most obvious abuse of the new invention was excessive chatter; signals traffic enabled one side at the least to identify a ship's presence and—if in possession of the other's code books, as the British were of the Germans'—even to read its messages. But the temptation to which the British themselves succumbed was a different one: it was for those at the Admiralty in London to interfere directly with lower levels of command at sea. In 1914–15, Winston Churchill in particular, although a civilian minister, exploited wireless communications to orchestrate what were essentially operational matters, more than once with disastrous consequences.

The more generalized problem was that the distinction between what was properly an operational matter, to be settled by the armed services themselves, and what was a strategic matter, with political implications of national importance, was a very hard one to sustain in 'modern', 'total' war. The over-riding function of the belligerent states between 1914 and 1918 was the conduct of the war. For civilian politicians, as John Turner describes, this created a genuine and legitimate interest in how the war was fought, and in the objectives of particular campaigns. Broadly speaking, herein lay the kernel of civil–military friction in the liberal societies, such as France and Britain. For soldiers, on the other hand, the maximization of resources for the purposes of the war, in particular munitions production and manpower, gave them a reasonable professional interest in the running of the war economy. This was the point of entry for the German supreme command under Hindenburg and Ludendorff, from which they developed agendas which clearly exceeded any functional definition of their operational responsibilities.

When strategy became the supreme function of the state it was very difficult to subordinate soldiers to political control. In a sense the First World War underlined the point that what Clausewitz had said about the direction of war, that war was a 'true political instrument', was grounded more in philosophical abstraction than in reality. For much of the time the war became an end in itself, not a means to an end. The demands which it made on its participants elevated their expectations of what they wanted to achieve from it in almost inverse proportion to what they could realistically gain. As L. L. Farrar shows, those like Falkenhayn who urged the acceptance of compromise did so on the basis of military realities, but could not command political support. Nor, according to David French, were means and ends in any greater harmony on the side of the Entente. Lloyd George became prime minister in December 1916 determined to curb the generals and to reduce casualties, but he rejected the peace initiatives of that month and sought total victory with as much determination as Hindenburg and Ludendorff.

The purpose of the war

These two chapters, which provide a strategic overview of the war for the years 1914 to 1917, might lead to the conclusion that the war had lost all purpose—that it was, in the words of so many of Modris Eksteins's visitors to the western front, 'a waste'. David Stevenson, who, in discussing war aims, provides the third résumé of the war's direction, resists what is, after all, yet another cliché. He focuses on the political objectives of the war, and, while recognizing that the aims of both sides were too incompatible for successful negotiation, also argues that a 'peace without victory' could not have proved lasting.

That robust view is one shared by Zara Steiner, in her analysis of the Versailles settlement. The peace of 1919 proved short-lived not because of any inherent inadequacies in its terms but because of the subsequent failure of the great powers to enforce it. The luxury of hindsight, with the Second World War now half a century distant and the Cold War over, can enable us to take this upbeat assessment one stage further. The political consequences of the war and the peace which followed it are still being played out. In terms of its consequences it was not a futile struggle.

First, four autocratic empires collapsed. One of these, the German, seemed young and dynamic in 1914. Opinions on the second, the Russian, were divided: for some the incipient clash between tsarism and revolution promised domestic disintegration, for others there was a latent strength which was reflected in Russia's importance to great power calculations in 1914. The other two—the Austro-Hungarian and the Ottoman—were both deemed to be in terminal decline for much of the nineteenth century. Not the least of their weaknesses was their multi-ethnic composition in an age of assertive nationalism.

The victors at Versailles took nationalism as one of their guiding principles, and in so doing incorporated in international relations a reality of domestic politics, thus creating an enduring, if not always easy, foundation for great power relations in the rest of the century. Of course the application was flawed. Within Europe ethnic divisions did not necessarily conform to territorial boundaries; the consequent frictions in eastern Europe were ones only kept in check by another multinational empire, the Soviet Union. Outside Europe the principle of national self-determination was not recognized—at least not fully and not then. But, as within central and south-eastern Europe, so in the Middle East, much of the political map of the modern world took shape in 1919.

Secondly, the Versailles settlement incorporated a vision of liberalism and even of democracy. This was the fruit of the United States' entry to the war. Between 1914 and 1917 liberalism took a battering. Domestically, as John Turner argues, traditional definitions of liberalism were forfeit to the incursions of the state. Internationally, tsarist Russia's membership of the Entente sapped the ideological purity of the alliance's war effort. The triumph of Bolshevism, even if it meant Russia's withdrawal from the Entente, did not ease the British and French positions in intellectual terms as it presented a more dynamic challenge to liberalism, not least when it espoused the idea of peace. Woodrow Wilson's messianic commitment to a new international order revivified the ideological underpinnings of the war. Many who had joined up in 1914 had done so because they believed even then that the First World War was 'the war to end wars'. Wilson gave them renewed hope that that would be the case. In the short term the Senate's refusal to ratify the Versailles agreement, the collapse of the League of Nations, and then the Second World War suggested the collapse of the liberal international order. But in the long term the conclusion of the Cold War, with the demise of the Soviet Union, serves to point up the continuity in Wilsonian rhetoric. Armistice day was a cause for celebration before it was a cause for commemoration.

One task for the historian is to place events in perspective. The danger with war, and particularly with the First World War, is that such contexts rationalize and so reduce the enormity of events—that the historian has to deny his or her own humanity. But consider only one way in which the First World War is deemed to be 'total' and possibly even 'modern'—its length.

The length of the war

7

Many of the contributors to this volume refer to the pre-war expectation that the war would be short and that what happened between 1914 and 1915 was a process of disillusionment on this score. The implication is that what followed was a 'long' war. But neither 'short' nor 'long' is itself a clear definition of time. The obvious yardstick in 1914 was the wars of German unification in 1866 and 1870, which were measured in terms of weeks. And yet pre-war planning spoke of months, and no chief of the general staff was truly confident of the outcome even then; some informed commentators reckoned on a war of two or three years. In terms of popular expectations these professional calculations were visions of a 'long war'; in terms of what actually happened, if judged from the perspective of 1918 or 1919, these predictions were too 'short'.

For the historian of 'modern' war, the First World War should not be remarkable for its length. Given its scale and its consequences, its duration of fifty-two months is not evidence in itself of any form of 'totality'. The Second World War would of course be longer, but that lay in the future. From the perspective of those who fought in 1914–18, the Thirty Years War, the Seven Years War, and the Napoleonic wars were all considerably longer. The duration of the American Civil War was comparable.

The First World War was not really a long war, any more than it was a short war. It was, however, a war of extraordinary intensity. Neither weather nor seasons dictated pauses in the fighting; for the first time battlefield injuries, not diseases, at least on the western front, were the major killer. Many individuals, not least because of wounds, had comparatively brief sojourns at the front. Their experience of the war could embrace different theatres, the elation of victory, the despondency of defeat. But for all the variation in extent, in place, and in degree of each participant's experience of the war, cumulatively that experience assumed a collective identity quite unlike that of any other 'total', 'modern', or 'global' war. Its conditioning factor was of course the trenches. And it was they which gave an inner unity to the war, and above all to the memory of the war, in what was in reality—as the subsequent chapters will show—an extraordinarily diverse and multifaceted conflict.

CHAPTER 1

The Origins of the War

SAMUEL R. WILLIAMSON, JR.

K ošutnjak Park, Belgrade, mid-May 1914: Gavrilo Princip fires his
revolver at an oak tree, training for his part in the plot. Those practice
rounds were the first shots of what would become the First World
War. Princip, a Bosnian Serb student, wanted to murder Archduke Franz
Ferdinand, heir to the Habsburg throne, when the latter visited the Bosnian
capital of Sarajevo. Princip had become involved with a Serbian terrorist
group—the Black Hand. Directed by the head of Serbian military intelligence, Colonel Dragutin Dimitrijević (nicknamed Apis, 'the Bull'), the Black
Hand advocated violence in the creation of a Greater Serbia. For Princip and
Apis, this meant ending Austria-Hungary's rule over Bosnia-Hercegovina
through any means possible.

Princip proved an apt pupil. If his co-conspirators flinched or failed on
Sunday, 28 June 1914, he did not. Thanks to confusion in the archduke's
entourage after an initial bomb attack, the young Bosnian Serb discovered
the official touring car stopped within 6 feet of his location. Princip fired two
quick shots. Within minutes the archduke and his wife Sophie were dead in
Sarajevo.

Exactly one month later, on 28 July, Austria-Hungary declared war on Serbia. What began as the third Balkan war would, within a week, become the
First World War. Why did the murders unleash first a local and then a wider
war? What were the longer-term, the mid-range, and the tactical issues that

Sarajevo

Assisted by the Serbian secret society—the Black Hand—with its ties to Serbian military intelligence, the conspirators made two attempts on Archduke Franz Ferdinand and his wife during their visit to Sarajevo. The nineteen-year-old Princip, seated on the right, fired the two shots that killed the royal couple. After his conviction, Princip died in prison in April 1918.

brought Europe into conflict? What follows is a summary of current historical thinking about the July crisis, while also suggesting some different perspectives on the much studied origins of the First World War.

Long-term tensions

After 1905, Europe's diplomats, strategic planners, and political leaders confronted a series of interlocking issues: some had long troubled the continent, others were by-products of still older problems that had either been resolved or evaded. A major issue centred on the perennial Eastern Question. Since 1878 the European powers had helped themselves to large portions of the Ottoman empire, the so-called 'Sick Man of Europe': Egypt and Cyprus had gone to Britain, Morocco and Tunisia to France, Tripoli (Libya) to Italy, and Bosnia-Hercegovina to Austria-Hungary. The Balkan wars of 1912–13 had seen Turkish holdings in the Balkans disappear. But struggle over the Balkans had not ended, as Russia, Serbia, and the Habsburgs still contended for ascendancy. Russia wanted a dominant voice in the name of Slavic brotherhood; Austria-Hungary wanted to continue its historic mission as a bridge to the east through the Balkans; and the Serbs wanted access to the sea.

A second major issue focused upon the Habsburg monarchy, also considered 'sick'. The question for many was whether Europe's third largest state with 50 million citizens could survive as a multinational, dynastic state in an age of increasing nationalism and democracy. While most of its neighbours looked covetously at Austria-Hungary, one desperately wanted it to survive: its northern neighbour and ally since 1879, the German Reich.

Unified by Otto von Bismarck in the 1860s and the Franco-Prussian War of 1870, Germany occupied a pivotal geographic and political position in Europe. A growing economic power and already a formidable military power, Berlin's aggressive policy of *Weltpolitik* and unrestrained navalism after 1900 had alarmed most of Europe. For many, German ambitions constituted a third major European problem. To complicate matters, no German government could easily accept the possibility that Russia might gain from the collapse of the Habsburg monarchy and thus become a still greater threat to Germany's eastern frontier. Germany's very strength would prompt the British and French, for balance of power reasons, to seek Russian help as a way to deter and threaten Berlin.

There were additional contextual issues that shaped the framework of international politics in the last years before 1914. These included alliance alignments, the arms race, imperialism's legacies, economic rivalries, and virulent nationalism. By 1914 Europe had become divided into two diplomatic groupings, loose to be sure but distinct. One, the Triple Alliance, was centred on Berlin and included Austria-Hungary, Italy, and, by secret protocol, Romania. Yet by the summer of 1914 few statesmen believed that Italy and Romania were reliable allies or likely ever to help Vienna. On the other side was the Triple Entente, centred on the Franco-Russian alliance and with Britain as *entente* partner of both. The British had detailed military arrangements, furthermore, with the French in the event of a German attack in the west. But the British never had a formal treaty commitment with France or with Russia, only the far more dangerous one of memories and emotions.

Despite the inherently hostile possibilities between the two alliance alignments, the great powers had managed to maintain the peace through three major international confrontations (two Morocco crises and repeated Bosnian tensions). In 1914, when the three central players—Austria-Hungary, Russia, and Germany—moved to mobilize, the earlier restraints fell away. If the alliance/*entente* structure *per se* did not cause the war, its very existence ensured that the conflict would become a wider war the moment the rigid military mobilization schedules became the ruling logic.

Closely linked to the alliance/*entente* diplomatic arrangements were their strategic and military-naval aspects. The years before 1914 had seen unprecedented arms races, most conspicuously the Anglo-German naval race after 1898. Every member of the alliance/*entente* system participated in the naval competition, but its most dramatic impact had been upon Anglo-German relations. No other issue had such a negative impact upon bilateral ties; no other issue proved such a stumbling block to efforts for restraint. Britain matched the German build-up which Admiral Alfred von Tirpitz had hoped would influence British foreign policy to give more respect to Germany. More radically, London introduced the all-big-gun dreadnought class of battleships and thus revolutionized the entire race.

The very fact of the German threat also forced Britain to move its principal naval forces northward. This in turn gave France the ability to argue that its naval forces were protecting British interests in the Mediterranean. This issue decisively influenced Britain's sense of obligation to its principal *entente* partner, France.

Other powers also spent extravagant sums on battleships, as each sought to match its local neighbour. Ironically, as subsequent chapters in this volume will show, the large capital ships were almost irrelevant to the actual conduct of the naval war, while the submarine and the protected convoy would play a far more decisive role.

The more important arms race has often been overlooked: the sharp increases in continental military manpower after 1911. Except for Britain, every country already had male conscription. Even if not all males actually served, conscription provided a sizeable manpower pool. Each of the great powers counted their standing armies in the hundreds of thousands. For instance, in 1912 the German forces numbered 646,000, the French 611,000, and the Russian 1,332,000. Yet there could never be too many men, or so the Prussian general staff concluded after the second Moroccan crisis of 1911. In late 1912 the Germans would increase their standing army by more than 130,000 and the French would raise theirs by nearly 90,000. Austria-Hungary would increase its forces as well and Russia began plans for still more troops. By July 1914 there were, even before the mobilizations began, approximately 3.6 million men on active duty among the allied/*entente* states.

Buttressing the military and naval preparations was the legacy of decades of imperial rivalry. The scramble for colonies and imperial influence had shaped the agenda of late nineteenth-century international politics. Tensions did not ease in the early twentieth century. The two Moroccan crises and the Bosnian annexation tension of 1908 brought the dangers closer to the continent; the Eastern Question remained as dangerous as ever. The Italian invasion of Tripoli in September 1911 had reinforced this point. The imperial rivalries had, moreover, exacerbated relations between Britain and Germany, Britain and France, Britain and Russia, and between Austria-Hungary and Serbia and Italy and Russia.

For Britain the Boer War (1899–1902) against the Dutch South Africans had exposed the risks of a policy of 'splendid isolation'. Hence, the British government began to search for partners. Its first success came in 1902 with the Japanese alliance to protect Britain's Far Eastern holdings against Russia. Then in 1904 and 1907 there were the *entente* arrangements with France and Russia, each agreement seeking to contain or end imperial rivalries. With these treaties, Britain's imperial and continental politics became fatefully entangled even if technically London retained a free hand.

Imperial frictions were both reinforced and transcended by the economic rivalry among the great powers. Generally, trade flowed easily among the group save for tariff issues. The Austrians would order weapons from the Russians, the British would build ships on demand, the Germans would sell to the Russians, and the French sold weapons wherever possible. Yet the governments became progressively less flexible about their lending policies, as the French gradually moved to exclude the Habsburgs from the Paris money markets in an effort to appease the Russians. Even the usually generous British were less forthcoming with Vienna. Still Vienna found funds in Berlin and New York City without much trouble. The international trading and banking fraternity, Marxist rhetoric notwithstanding, remained international in outlook and was always alarmed at the prospect of war. For the financial community, peace appeared the only rational policy.

Among the tectonic plates shaping the context of international politics, none loomed as dangerous and irrational as rampant, virulent, passion-filled nationalism. Spurred by the French Revolution, the spread of literacy, and the growth of historical mythologies, by 1914 nationalism had become the plaything of politicians and the intelligentsia. After 1900 each country had its own shrill nationalism, but it reached new heights after 1911 and the second Moroccan crisis. Under the leadership of Raymond Poincaré, first as foreign minister and then as president, France had a veritable nationalistic revival. In Britain the Irish Question flamed to new peaks, as the Ulster Protestants refused to accept the prospect of Irish home rule. The German variety was no less strident, often blended with the myopia of Prussian militarism. In Italy, rabid nationalists fixated on Austria-Hungary's possession of the Tyrol and the Dalmatian coast. For Russia, every Balkan issue became a test of Slavic fraternalism and aggressive Russian nationalism. Nationalism had turned much of Europe into a veritable box of inflammable tinder.

But no place matched the Habsburg monarchy, where eleven nationalities competed, struggled, and yet finally managed to live together. Thanks to the Dual Monarchy's constitutional arrangements of 1867, the German-Austrians and the Hungarians controlled the political apparatus in the two states. Yet they had to accommodate the various nationalities and to adjust their internal and external policies accordingly. In fact, the Habsburg leadership struggled to make concessions to the Czechs and Poles and others inside the monarchy. Some leaders, including the Archduke Franz Ferdinand, were prepared to go even further, only to face the intransigent Magyar élites who refused to diminish their political power for other groups. The Habsburg neighbours were less benign. The Romanians wanted Transylvania, the Italians at least the Tyrol, the Russians the breakup of the entire monarchy, and the Serbs in Belgrade a Greater Serbia at Habsburg expense. Others, sparked by the Croatians and the Slovenians, talked of a new south Slav, Yugoslav state.

After the 1903 palace coup brought the Obrenović dynasty to power in Belgrade, Serbia gradually became Vienna's most implacable foe, anxious to accelerate the demise of the Habsburgs. The Bosnian crisis of 1908, the

Vienna's cosmopolitan atmosphere created a misleading impression. Culture, art, opera, music, and the decorative arts flourished in pre-1914 Vienna, indeed represented some of Europe's most enduring cultural legacies. But within the monarchy internal tensions seethed among the eleven nationalities, threatening to tear the monarchy apart. And no group appeared more dangerous than the Serbian-influenced south Slav movement that had its inspiration from Belgrade and St Petersburg.

Balkan wars, and the increase of Serbian territory and population poisoned the relationship still more. And the Serbian government tolerated or encouraged groups who wanted to end Habsburg rule in all of the Balkans. The most dangerous of these societies was Apis's Black Hand. After 1908 Habsburg policy-makers would view Serbia as the major threat to the monarchy's survival in a democratic age. Vienna saw the Serbs, as the west would in the 1990s, as leaders for whom duplicity and evasion were staples of political and diplomatic behaviour. By June 1914 the Habsburg leadership had come to believe that a final reckoning with the Serb menace could not be postponed much longer.

Still, in the spring of 1914 the European scene appeared less volatile than at any point in the last four years. To be sure, the Germans and Russians had quarrelled over a German military mission to Turkey, and the military press in both countries had taunted each other. Rome and Vienna, two erstwhile allies, exchanged acrimonious notes over the future of Albania, which both wanted to control. And Vienna also had to face the fact that Romania was apparently drifting away from the Triple Alliance. By contrast, however, Belgrade and Vienna were involved in a set of economic negotiations that appeared promising. More surprisingly, Anglo-German relations appeared almost serene, with the British navy in late June paying a call on the German fleet at Kiel.

The major issues in each country were domestic. In France the prospect of Madame Henriette Caillaux's trial for the murder of the editor of *Le Figaro* over his slanderous attacks on her husband dominated the public agenda. In Britain the perennial Irish Question had prompted a near mutiny of senior British army officers over the prospect of enforcing a policy of home rule. In Russia the greatest strikes of the pre-war years threatened to paralyse the major cities. In Germany fears mounted about the surging power of the socialists. In Austria the parliament had been adjourned in March because of Czech–German clashes. In Hungary tensions were increasing between the Magyars and the Romanians in Transylvania.

But possibly the most dangerous situation existed in Serbia, where the civilian government (backed by Russia) found itself under assault from the Serbian military who wanted to become a virtual state within a state. The situation worsened when the military pushed Prime Minister Nikolai Pašić from office in early June, only to have the Russians insist on and achieve his restoration. Throughout Europe, these domestic, internal issues were troubling but not inherently dangerous to the international peace. Indeed, Arthur Nicolson, the long-time British under-secretary of state for foreign affairs, asserted in early May 1914 that he had not seen the international scene so calm in years.

Two shots in Sarajevo on Sunday 28 June shattered that illusion. Those shots had the ineluctable effect of converging all of the danger points of European foreign and domestic policies. The First World War would be the result.

The Serbian terrorist plot had succeeded. But that very success also threatened Pašić's civilian government. Already at odds with Apis and his Black Hand associates, Pašić now found himself compromised by his own earlier failure to investigate allegations about the secret society. In early June 1914, the minister had heard vague rumours of an assassination plot. He even sought to make inquiries, only to have Apis stonewall him about details. Whether Belgrade actually sought to alert Vienna about the plot remains uncertain. In any event, once the murders occurred, the premier could not admit his prior knowledge nor allow any Austro-Hungarian action that might unravel the details of the conspiracy. Not only would any compromise threaten his political position, it could lead Apis and his army associates to attempt a coup or worse.

Vienna's response to the assassination

After 28 June Pašić tried, without much success, to moderate the Serbian press's glee over the archduke's death. He also sought to appear conciliatory and gracious towards Vienna. But he knew that the Habsburg authorities believed that Princip had ties to Belgrade. He only hoped that the Habsburg investigators could not make a direct, incontrovertible connection to Apis and others.

Pašić resolved early, moreover, that he would not allow any Habsburg infringement of Serbian sovereignty or any commission that would implicate him or the military authorities. If he made any concession, his political opponents would attack and he might expose himself and the other civilian ministers to unacceptable personal risks. Thus Serbia's policy throughout the July crisis would be apparently conciliatory, deftly evasive, and ultimately intractable. It did not require, as the inter-war historians believed, the Russian government to stiffen the Serbian position. Once confronted with the fact of Sarajevo, the Serbian leadership charted its own course, one which guaranteed a definitive confrontation with Vienna.

The deaths of Franz Ferdinand and Sophie stunned the Habsburg leadership. While there were only modest public shows of sympathy, limited by the court's calculation to play down the funeral, all of the senior leaders wanted some action against Belgrade. None doubted that Serbia bore responsibility for the attacks. The 84-year-old emperor, Franz Joseph, returned hurriedly to Vienna from his hunting lodge at Bad Ischl. Over the next six days to 4 July 1914, all of the Habsburg leaders met in pairs and threes to discuss the monarchy's reaction to the deaths and to assess the extensive political unrest in Bosnia-Hercegovina in the wake of the assassinations. Nor could the discussions ignore the earlier tensions of 1912 and 1913 when the monarchy had three times nearly gone to war with Serbia and/or Montenegro. Each time militant diplomacy had prevailed and each time Russia had accepted the outcome.

The most aggressive of the Habsburg leaders, indeed the single individual probably most responsible for the war in 1914, was General Franz Conrad von Hötzendorf, chief of the Austro-Hungarian general staff. In the previous crises he had called for war against Serbia more than fifty times. He constantly lamented that the monarchy had not attacked Serbia in 1908 when the odds would have been far better. In the July crisis Conrad would argue vehemently and repeatedly that the time for a final reckoning had come. His cries for war in 1912 and 1913 had been checked by Archduke Franz Ferdinand and the foreign minister, Leopold Berchtold. Now, with the archduke gone and Berchtold converted to a policy of action, all of the civilian leaders, except the Hungarian prime minister István Tisza, wanted to resolve the Serbian issue. To retain international credibility the monarchy had to show that there were limits beyond which the south Slav movement could not go without repercussions.

The Habsburg resolve intensified with reports from Sarajevo that indicated that the trail of conspiracy did indeed lead back to at least one minor Serbian official in Belgrade. While the evidence in 1914 never constituted a 'smoking gun', the officials correctly surmised that the Serbian government must have tolerated and possibly assisted in the planning of the deed. Given this evidence, the Habsburg leaders soon focused on three options: a severe diplomatic humiliation of Serbia; quick, decisive military action against Serbia; or a diplomatic ultimatum that, if rejected, would be followed by military action. Pressed by Conrad and the military leadership, by 3 July even Franz Joseph had agreed on the need for stern action, including the possibility of

16

war. Only one leader resisted a military solution: István Tisza. Yet his consent was absolutely required for any military action. Tisza preferred the diplomatic option and wanted assurances of German support before the government made a final decision. His resistance to any quick military action effectively foreclosed that option, leaving either the diplomatic one or the diplomatic/military combination. Not surprisingly, those anxious for military action shifted to the latter alternative.

The Austro-Hungarian foreign minister, Berchtold, made the next move on 4 July, sending his belligerent subordinate Alexander Hoyos to Berlin to seek a pledge of German support. Armed with a personal letter from Franz Joseph to Wilhelm II and a long memorandum on the need for resolute action against Serbia, Hoyos got a cordial reception. The Germans fully understood Vienna's intentions: the Habsburg leadership wanted a military reckoning with Belgrade. The German leadership (for reasons to be explored later) agreed to the Habsburg request, fully realizing that it might mean a general war with Russia as Serbia's protector.

With assurances of German support, the leaders in Vienna met on 7 July to formulate their plan. General Conrad gave confident assessments of military success and the civilian ministers attempted to persuade Tisza to accept a

After their deaths in Sarajevo, the bodies of the dead archduke and his wife were taken to Vienna for funeral ceremonies. Although this picture shows the movement of the funeral procession through Vienna's streets, many believed the Emperor Franz Joseph had slighted his nephew with only modest signs of mourning. Some foreign observers, noting the low-key display, would seriously misjudge the anger of Habsburg officials over the murders.

17

belligerent approach. At the same time the preliminary diplomatic manœuvres were planned. Finally, on 13–14 July Hungarian Prime Minister Tisza accepted strong action and possible war with Serbia. He did so largely because of new fears that a possible Serbian–Romanian alignment would

threaten Magyar overlordship of the 3 million Romanians living in Transylvania. Drafts of the ultimatum, meanwhile, were prepared in Vienna. Deception tactics to lull the rest of Europe were arranged and some military leaves were cancelled.

But there remained a major problem: when to deliver the ultimatum? The long-scheduled French state visit to Russia of President Raymond Poincaré and Premier René Viviani from 20 July to 23 July thoroughly complicated the delivery of the ultimatum. Berchtold, understandably, did not want to hand over the demands while the French leaders were still in St Petersburg. Yet to avoid that possibility meant a further delay until late afternoon, 23 July. At that point the forty-eight-hour ultimatum, with its demands that clearly could not be met, would be delivered in Belgrade.

Germany's decision of 5–6 July to assure full support to Vienna ranks among the most discussed issues in modern European history. A strong, belligerent German response came as no surprise. After all, Wilhelm II and Franz Ferdinand had just visited each other, were close ideologically, and had since 1900 developed a strong personal friendship. Chancellor Theobald von Bethmann Hollweg, moreover, believed that Berlin must show Vienna that Germany supported its most loyal ally. Far more controversial is whether the civilian leaders in Berlin, pressured by the German military, viewed the Sarajevo murders as a 'heaven-sent' opportunity to launch a preventive war against Russia. This interpretation points to increasing German apprehension about a Russian military colossus, allegedly to achieve peak strength in 1917. And Russo-German military relations were in early 1914 certainly at their worst in decades. Nor did Kaiser Wilhelm II's military advisers urge any modicum of restraint on Vienna, unlike previous Balkans episodes. An increasingly competitive European military environment now spilled over into the July crisis.

However explained, the German leadership reached a rare degree of consensus: it would support Vienna in a showdown with Serbia. Thus the German kaiser and chancellor gave formal assurances (the so-called 'blank cheque') to Vienna. From that moment, Austria-Hungary proceeded to exploit this decision and to march toward war with Serbia. Berlin would find itself—for better or worse—at the mercy of its reliable ally as the next stages of the crisis unfolded.

For two weeks and more Berlin waited, first for the Habsburg leadership to make its final decisions and then for their implementation. During this time the German kaiser sailed in the North Sea and the German military and naval high command, confident of their own arrangements, took leaves at various German spas. Bethmann Hollweg, meanwhile, fretted over the lengthy delays in Vienna. He also began to fear the consequences of the 'calculated risk' and his 'leap into the dark' for German foreign policy. But his moody retrospection brought no changes in his determination to back Vienna; he only wished the Habsburg monarchy would act soon and decisively.

The Austrian ultimatum to Serbia

By Monday 20 July, Europe buzzed with rumours of a pending Habsburg *démarche* in Belgrade. While the Irish Question continued to dominate British political concerns and the French public focused on the Caillaux murder trial, Vienna moved to act against Belgrade. Remarkably, no Triple Entente power directly challenged Berchtold before 23 July, and the foreign minister for his part remained inconspicuous. Then, as instructed, at 6 p.m. on 23 July Wladimir Giesl, the Habsburg minister in Belgrade, delivered the ultimatum to the Serbian foreign ministry. Sir Edward Grey, the British foreign secretary, would immediately brand it as 'the most formidable document ever addressed by one State to another that was independent'.

With its forty-eight-hour deadline, the ultimatum demanded a series of Serbian concessions and a commission to investigate the plot. Pašić, away from Belgrade on an election campaign tour, returned to draft the response. This reply conceded some points but was wholly unyielding on Vienna's key demand, which would have allowed the Austrians to discover Pašić's and his government's general complicity in the murders.

News of the Habsburg ultimatum struck Europe with as much force as the Sarajevo murders. If the public did not immediately recognize the dangers to the peace, the European diplomats (and their military and naval associates) did. The most significant, immediate, and dangerous response came not from the Germans, but from the Russians. Upon learning of the ultimatum, Foreign Minister Serge Sazonov declared war inevitable. His actions thereafter did much to ensure a general European war.

At a meeting of the Council of State on 24 July, even before the Serbians responded, Sazonov and others pressed for strong Russian support for Serbia. Fearful of losing Russian leadership of the pan-Slavic movement, he urged resolute behaviour. His senior military leaders backed this view, even though Russia's military reforms were still incomplete. The recently concluded French state visit had given the Russians new confidence that Paris would support Russia if war came.

Facing: Inheriting the Hohenzollern throne in 1888 at the age of 29, the young kaiser soon dismissed Chancellor Otto von Bismarck and embarked on an aggressive policy of *Weltpolitik*. His bombastic statements, his assertive naval plans, and his government's talent for creating diplomatic crises eventually divided Europe into two opposing Alliance/ Entente groupings. His early July 1914 decision to support Vienna guaranteed the start of the First World War.

At Sazonov's urgings, the Council agreed, with the tsar approving the next day, to initiate various military measures preparing for partial or full mobilization. The Council agreed further to partial mobilization as a possible deterrent to stop Austria-Hungary from attacking the Serbs. These Russian military measures were among the very first of the entire July crisis; their impact would be profound. The measures were not only extensive, they abutted German as well as Austrian territory. Not surprisingly, the Russian actions would be interpreted by German military intelligence as tantamount to some form of mobilization. No other actions in the crisis, beyond Vienna's resolute determination for war, were so provocative or disturbing as Russia's preliminary steps of enhanced border security and the recall of certain troops.

Elsewhere, Sir Edward Grey sought desperately to repeat his 1912 role as peacemaker in the Balkans. He failed. He could not get Vienna to extend the forty-eight-hour deadline. Thus at 6 p.m. on 25 July, Giesl glanced at the Serbian reply, deemed it insufficient, broke diplomatic relations, and left immediately for nearby Habsburg territory. The crisis had escalated to a new, more dangerous level.

Grey did not, however, desist in his efforts for peace. He now tried to initiate a set of four-power discussions to ease the mounting crisis. Yet he could never get St Petersburg or Berlin to accept the same proposal for some type of mediation or diplomatic discussions. A partial reason for his failure came from Berlin's two continuing assumptions: that Britain might ultimately stand aside and that Russia would eventually be deterred by Germany's strong, unequivocal support of Vienna.

Each of Grey's international efforts, ironically, alarmed Berchtold. He now became determined to press for a declaration of war, thus thwarting any intervention in the local conflict. In fact, the Habsburg foreign minister had trouble getting General Conrad's reluctant agreement to a declaration of war on Tuesday 28 July. This declaration, followed by some desultory gunfire between Serbian and Austro-Hungarian troops that night, would thoroughly inflame the situation. The Serbs naturally magnified the gunfire incident into a larger Austrian attack. This is turn meant that the Russians would use the casual shooting to justify still stronger support for Serbia and to initiate still more far-reaching military measures of their own.

By 28 July every European state had taken some military and/or naval precautions. The French recalled some frontier troops, the Germans did the same, and the Austro-Hungarians began their mobilization against the Serbs. In Britain, Winston Churchill, First Lord of the Admiralty, secured cabinet approval to keep the British fleet intact after it had completed manœuvres. Then on the night of 29 July he ordered the naval vessels to proceed through the English Channel to their North Sea battle stations. It could be argued that thanks to Churchill Britain became the first power prepared to protect its vital interests in a European war.

Grey still searched for a solution. But his efforts were severely hampered

The first Moroccan crisis was resolved at Algeciras in 1906. In the following year 'Douanier' Rousseau symbolically depicted the European rulers within the larger world context. Imperial legacies, symbols of power, and the flaming urns with the words 'work', 'liberty', and 'fraternity' represent for Rousseau the interlocking connection between Europe and the rest of the world. Prophetically, an American flag flying on the pavilion represents the power whose intervention into the First World War would also ensure its termination.

The Art of War: F. Vallotton's rendering of
the horror of fighting at Verdun, where the
Germans sought to 'bleed France white'
and force it to conclude peace.

by the continuing impact of the Irish Question and the deep divisions within the cabinet over any policy that appeared to align Britain too closely with France. Throughout the last week of July, Grey tried repeatedly to gain cabinet consent to threaten Germany with British intervention. The radicals in the cabinet refused. They wanted no British participation in a continental war.

Grey now turned his attention to the possible fate of Belgium and Britain's venerable treaty commitments to protect Belgian neutrality. As he did so, the German diplomats committed a massive blunder by attempting to win British neutrality with an assurance that Belgium and France would revert to the status quo ante after a war. Not only did Grey brusquely reject this crude bribery, he turned it back against Berlin. On 31 July, with cabinet approval, Grey asked Paris and Berlin to guarantee Belgium's status. France did so at once; the Germans did not. Grey had scored an important moral and tactical victory.

In St Petersburg, meanwhile, decisions were taken, rescinded, then taken again that assured that the peace would not be kept. By 28 July Sazonov had concluded that a partial mobilization against Austria-Hungary would never deter Vienna. Indeed his own generals argued that a partial step would complicate a general mobilization. Sazonov therefore got the generals' support for full mobilization. He then won the tsar's approval only to see Nicholas II hesitate after receiving a message from his cousin, Kaiser Wilhelm II. The so-called 'Willy–Nicky' telegrams came to nothing, however. On 30 July the tsar ordered general mobilization, with a clear recognition that Germany would probably respond and that a German attack would be aimed at Russia's French ally.

The Russian general mobilization resolved a number of problems for the German high command. First, it meant that no negotiations, including the proposal for an Austrian 'Halt in Belgrade', would come to anything. Second, it allowed Berlin to declare a 'defensive war' of protection against an aggressive Russia, a tactic that immeasurably aided Bethmann Hollweg's efforts to achieve domestic consensus. And, third, it meant that the chancellor could no longer resist General Helmuth von Moltke's demands for German mobilization and the implementation of German war plans. Alone of the great powers, mobilization for Germany equalled war; Bethmann Hollweg realized this. Yet once the German mobilization began, the chancellor lost effective control of the situation.

At 7 p.m. on Saturday, 1 August 1914, Germany declared war on Russia. The next day German forces invaded Luxembourg. Later that night Germany demanded that Belgium allow German troops to march through the neutral state on their way to France. The Belgian cabinet met and concluded that it would resist the German attack.

In France general mobilization began. But the French government, ever anxious to secure British intervention, kept French forces 6 miles away from the French border. In London Paul Cambon, the French ambassador,

In each of the belligerent powers, the urban populace greeted the news of war with enthusiasm and aggressive outbursts of national fervour. For many men the war promised adventure, change, even escape from pedestrian jobs. All soon exchanged their straw hats for metal helmets. In the countryside, it should be added, the enthusiasm for war was far more restrained.

importuned the British government to uphold the unwritten moral and military obligations of the Anglo-French *entente*. Still, even on Saturday 1 August, the British cabinet refused to agree to any commitment to France. Then on Sunday 2 August, Grey finally won cabinet approval for two significant steps: Britain would protect France's northern coasts against any German naval attack and London would demand that Germany renounce any intention of attacking Belgium. Britain had edged closer to war.

On Monday 3 August, the British cabinet reviewed the outline of Grey's speech to parliament that afternoon. His peroration, remarkable for its candour and its disingenuousness about the secret Anglo-French military and naval arrangements, left no doubt that London would intervene to preserve the balance of power against Germany; that it would defend Belgium and France; and that it would go to war if Germany failed to stop the offensive in the west. This last demand, sent from London to Berlin on 4 August, would be rejected. At 11 p.m. (GMT) on 4 August 1914 Britain and Germany were at war.

With the declarations of war the focus shifted to the elaborate pre-arranged mobilization plans of the great powers. For the naval forces the issues were relatively straightforward: prepare for the great naval battle, impose or thwart a policy of naval blockade, protect your coast lines, and keep the shipping lanes open. For the continental armies, the stakes were far greater. If an army were defeated, the war might well be over. Committed to offensive strategies, dependent on the hope that any war would be short, and reliant on the implementation of their carefully developed plans, the general staffs believed they had prepared for almost every possible contingency.

In each country the war plans contained elaborate mobilization schedules which the generals wanted to put into action at the earliest possible moment. While mobilization raised the risks of war, in only two cases did it absolutely guarantee a generalized engagement: (1) if Russia mobilized, Germany would do so and move at once to attack Belgium and France; (2) if Germany mobilized without Russian provocation, the results were the same. Any full Russian mobilization would trigger a complete German response and, for Germany, mobilization meant war. Very few, if any, civilian leaders fully comprehended these fateful interconnections and even the military planners were uncertain about them.

The German war plans in 1914 were simple, dangerous, and exceptionally mechanical. To overcome the threat of being trapped in a two-front war between France and Russia, Germany would attack first in the west, violating Belgian neutrality in a massive sweeping movement that would envelop

War by timetable

Confident of their success, German soldiers wrote boastful slogans on their troop transport: 'On to Paris' and 'See you again on the Boulevard'. No German troops got closer than twenty miles to the French capital. Many of these particular soldiers doubtless never returned to Germany, dying on the way to Paris or in the pivotal battle of the Marne in early September 1914.

and then crush the French forces. Once the French were defeated, the Germans would redeploy their main forces against Russia and with Austro-Hungarian help conclude the war. The Russian war plans sought to provide immediate assistance to France and thereby disrupt the expected German attack in the west. The Russians would attack German troops in East Prussia, while other Russian forces moved southward into Galicia against the Habsburg armies. But to achieve their goals the Russians had to mobilize immediately, hence their escalatory decisions early in the crisis, with fateful consequences for the peace of Europe.

The Italians, it should be noted, took some preliminary measures in August 1914 but deferred general mobilization until later. Otherwise Rome took no further action to intervene. Rather the Italian government soon became involved in an elaborate bargaining game over its entry into the fray. Not until April 1915 would this last of the major pre-war allies enter into the fighting, not on the side of their former allies but in opposition with the Triple Entente.

| The process of escalation | By 10 August 1914 Europe was at war. What had started as the third Balkan war had rapidly become the First World War. How can one assess responsibility for these events? Who caused it? What could have been done differently to have prevented it? Such questions have troubled generations of historians since 1914. There are no clear answers. But the following observations may put the questions into context. The alliance/*entente* system created linking mechanisms that allowed the control of a state's strategic destiny to pass into a broader arena, one which the individual government could manage but not always totally control. Most specifically, this meant that any Russo-German quarrel would see France involved because of the very nature of Germany's offensive war plans. Until 1914 the alliance/*entente* partners had disagreed just enough among themselves to conceal the true impact of the alliance arrangements. |

The legacy of Germany's bombastic behaviour, so characteristic of much of German *Weltpolitik* and *Europolitik* after 1898, also meant that Berlin was thoroughly mistrusted. Its behaviour created a tone, indeed an edginess, that introduced fear into the international system, since only for Germany did mobilization equal war. Ironically, and not all historians agree, the German policy in 1914 may have been less provocative than earlier. But that summer Berlin paid the price for its earlier aggressiveness.

Serbia allowed a terrorist act to proceed, then sought to evade the consequences of its action. It would gain, after 1918, the most from the war with the creation of the Yugoslav state. Paradoxically, however, the very ethnic rivalries that brought Austria-Hungary to collapse would also plague the new state and its post-1945 successor.

Austria-Hungary feared the threat posed by the emergence of the south Slavs as a political force. But the Dual Monarchy could not reform itself sufficiently to blunt the challenge. With the death of the Archduke Franz Ferdinand, who had always favoured peace, the monarchy lost the one person who could check the ambitions of General Conrad and mute the fears of the civilians. While harsh, Ottokar Czernin's epitaph has a certain truth to it: 'We were compelled to die; we could only choose the manner of our death and we have chosen the most terrible.'

Germany believed that it must support its Danubian ally. This in turn influenced Berlin's position towards Russia and France. Without German backing, Vienna would probably have hesitated or been more conciliatory toward Belgrade. But, anxious to support Vienna and possibly to detach Russia from the Triple Entente, Berlin would risk a continental war to achieve its short- and long-term objectives. Berlin and Vienna bear more responsibility for starting the crisis and then making it very hard to control.

Nevertheless, the Russians must also share some significant responsibility for the final outcome. St Petersburg's unwavering support of Serbia, its unwillingness to negotiate with Berlin and Vienna, and then its precipitate preparatory military measures escalated the crisis beyond control. Russia's general mobilization on 30 July guaranteed disaster.

Those Russian decisions would in turn confront the French with the full ramifications of their alliance with Russia. Despite French expectations, the alliance with Russia had in fact become less salvation for Paris and more assuredly doom. France became the victim in the Russo-German fight. Throughout the crisis French leaders could only hope to convince Russia to be careful and simultaneously work to ensure that Britain came to their assistance. Paris failed in the first requirement and succeeded in the second.

The decisions of August 1914 did not come easily for the British government. Grey could not rush the sharply divided cabinet. The decade-old *entente* ties to the French were vague and unwritten and had a history of deception and deviousness. Nor did the vicious political atmosphere created by Ireland help. Grey desperately hoped that the threat of British intervention would deter Germany; it did not. Could Grey have done more? Probably not, given the British political system and the precarious hold the Liberal Party had on power. Only a large standing British army would have deterred Germany, and that prospect, despite some recent assertions, simply did not exist.

In July 1914 one or two key decisions taken differently might well have seen the war averted. As it was, the July crisis became a model of escalation and inadvertent consequences. The expectation of a short war, the ideology of offensive warfare, and continuing faith in war as an instrument of policy: all would soon prove illusory and wishful. The cold, hard, unyielding reality of modern warfare soon replaced the romantic, dashing legends of the popular press. The élite decision-makers (monarchs, civilian ministers, admirals, and generals) had started the war; the larger public would die in it and, ultimately, finish it.

CHAPTER 2

The Strategy of the Central Powers, 1914–1917

L. L. FARRAR, JR.

The failure to achieve a quick victory

The First World War was a coalition conflict. Pre-war European relations had been shaped by alliance politics and the July crisis of 1914 had tested these bonds: Russia's support of Serbia, Germany's of Austria-Hungary, France's of Russia, and Britain's of France. Had a single link in this chain broken, the crisis would probably not have culminated in war. The leaders of the Central Powers, Germany and Austria-Hungary, calculated that the crisis would either split the Entente or would prove war necessary because the Entente had held. Just as alliance politics had determined the outcome of the crisis, so the war would be alliance politics by other means.

The conflict began with widespread faith that it would be short and victorious. Popular cries of 'Nach Paris' and 'À Berlin' were echoed by leaders like the kaiser, who told departing troops in early August with characteristic bravado: 'You will be home before the leaves have fallen.' There were attractive reasons for believing these assertions. Most obviously, a war won quickly would produce high rewards at relatively low cost, in effect, the diplomatic success which had eluded both sides in the July crisis. Furthermore, a short war required minimal mobilization, which meant limited concessions to the masses, thereby buttressing the ruling class which had won it. There existed,

26

however, a fundamental contradiction between the conflict's causes and the preconditions for its remaining brief. Begun because the coalitions had held firm, the war could be short only if one alliance dissolved. The assumption of a short war none the less dominated the early months of the conflict and would become one of the Great War's great illusions.

This is nowhere more evident than in the strategy of the Central Powers. Throughout the whole war, strategy and statecraft were inextricably bound together, each depending on and determining the other. The Schlieffen Plan, blueprint for German military success, had been devised in response to a potential two-front war as a result of the Franco-Russian alliance of the 1890s. Alfred von Schlieffen, then chief of the German general staff, argued that the Russians could avoid a rapid defeat by withdrawal, whereas the French could be defeated quickly by a vast, counter-clockwise movement through Belgium to encircle their army east of Paris. The plan's success depended first on a French attack at the German middle, then on the encirclement of the French by the German army, and finally on prompt surrender. In retrospect, however, this was unlikely. France had not surrendered in 1871 immediately after defeat by Prussia but only when it could find no ally and the country was collapsing internally; it would surrender in 1940 because it lacked a Russian ally and feared internal problems. With both Britain and Russia as allies in 1914, however, France was unlikely to surrender even after a severe military setback.

The strategies of Austria-Hungary and Russia likewise rendered a short

The uniform transformed civilians into soldiers: German troops being mobilized for what they were told would be victory in a short war.

war unlikely. Although the Austro-Hungarian chief of the general staff, Franz Conrad von Hötzendorf, projected a large pincer attack on Russian Poland, he was aware that significant German aid would have to await France's defeat. Furthermore, like Germany, Austria-Hungary faced a two-front war and divided its forces against both Russia and Serbia. Similarly, rather than seeking a knock-out blow against one, the Russians separated their forces against Germany and Austria-Hungary, their object being less military than diplomatic, i.e. to reassure France of support even in the event of a French military débâcle.

Only France could ensure a short war by conspiring in its own defeat. Like the Schlieffen Plan, French Plan XVII assumed that quick victory necessitated a rapid offensive. German and French strategies were complementary and provided the preconditions for each other's success: the Schlieffen Plan envisaged a great encirclement which required a French attack at the centre and a weak western flank, while simultaneously Plan XVII presumed a western diversion of the main German forces and sought a breakthrough which would combine with Russian pressure to force Germany to surrender rather than fight a long war. Like the Schlieffen Plan, however, Plan XVII was based on a fallacy. Germany might indeed have surrendered if it had not been able to count on Austria-Hungary—but then it would probably not have gone to war. Yet flawed French strategy proved good statecraft: only by a rapid attack could France ensure Russian support which would allow France to fight on even after a military setback. However, immediate French surrender after defeat was the precondition for the Schlieffen Plan's success. Ostensibly strategy for a short war, Plan XVII effectively ensured a long one.

The Schlieffen Plan also influenced British decisions. Essential to a rapid defeat of France, German violation of Belgian neutrality virtually guaranteed British entry into the war. Although small and unlikely to play a critical role in early battles, the British army was, like the Russian army, most important for the future. By demonstrating British support, it would allow France to persevere even after initial military reverses and thereby made a short war unlikely.

Events soon confirmed these obstacles to a short war. Since a quick victory necessitated taking the initiative, the operative military question during the first weeks was whether Franco-Russian forces would plunge into central Europe or Central Power armies would break out. The French were the first to win and then lose the strategic initiative by seeking to break through the German centre in the hope of isolating the German forces advancing though Belgium. When this failed and the French commander, Joseph Joffre, redeployed to meet the German attack in the west, he effectively precluded German encirclement of the French army. This outcome was confirmed at the battle of the Marne (5–9 September 1914) in which Anglo-French forces halted and then reversed the German advance. Far from being the miracle it is often presented as, the battle was the logical outcome of Joffre's decision: by sacrificing Plan XVII, he scuttled the Schlieffen Plan.

In fact, even before the battle of the Marne, a short war was rendered unlikely by other diplomatic and military events. By declaring war and sending troops quickly, the British demonstrated their commitment to France. At Tannenberg on the eastern front ten days before the Marne (25–30 August), the Germans won a stunning military victory which, however, constituted a profound diplomatic setback for the Central Powers by confirming Russian support of France. Meanwhile the British, French, and Russians agreed in the Pact of London (5 September) not to conclude a separate peace with their enemies. Unable to win quickly themselves, the Entente prevented the Central Powers from doing so.

At the beginning of September, however, this was not yet evident. On the contrary, the apparent imminence of French defeat and surrender prompted German leaders to prepare peace conditions 'for the eventuality of sudden negotiations which should not be protracted'. With the approval of Chancellor Theobald von Bethmann Hollweg, a lengthy memorandum (of 9 September) stipulated that 'France must be so weakened that it cannot revive again as a great power [while] Russia must be pushed back as far as possible from the German eastern border and its dominion over the non-Russian vassal peoples broken.' Although probably designed for the anticipated separate peace with France, the memorandum none the less represented the basic goals of most German leaders, who would adjust them according to military circumstances. As one of them commented, 'so long as the size of our victories is uncertain, no decision can be made on the size of our peace conditions'. Military strategy and diplomatic policy would remain inextricable.

The immediate task for German diplomats was to prevent whatever might complicate a separate peace with France, most notably neutral mediation. With the concurrence of Bethmann and army headquarters, Under-Secretary for Foreign Affairs Arthur Zimmermann finessed an American offer: while claiming openness to Entente suggestions via Washington, Germany sought a 'lasting peace' which 'required a reckoning with not only France but also Russia and England. Otherwise [Germany] would have to expect a new war with the Entente powers in a few years.' In fact, the Entente wanted mediation no more than the Central Powers.

The possibility of a short war evaporated during the autumn. Although the combatants had been too weak to win, they had been strong enough to avoid losing. Entrenched lines from Switzerland to the Channel coast were the logical consequence of roughly equal forces pursuing complementary strategies. Analogous events occurred in the east where first an Austro-German double encirclement and then Russian counter-attack produced a stalemate. Without a disastrous blunder neither side could inflict defeat on the other and a general impasse was the unavoidable result.

This unforeseen and undesired scenario reinforced and was reinforced by the war's coalition character. Most importantly, it obliged allies to shore up

Diplomatic alternatives

The search for allies

L. L. FARRAR, Jr.

their own alliances. The military frustrations of the summer and autumn produced considerable friction between the German and Austro-Hungarian commands. Their initial campaigns had been poorly co-ordinated and Conrad complained that Germany was sacrificing Austro-Hungarian lives merely to protect German interests. It was undeniable that Austro-Hungarian diversion of Russian forces was essential to Germany's defeating France and indeed its diplomatic policy in general. The Austro-Hungarian government threatened to play its trump card by hinting to the Germans that it might conclude a separate peace 'to end a war in which we bleed ourselves uselessly'. Central Power relations worsened after Helmuth von Moltke was replaced by Erich von Falkenhayn as German chief of staff. Although frictions continued, the Germans managed to pacify their ally which, after all, had no better alternative.

At the same time all the combatants sought to win new allies or at least to avoid making new enemies. Although these efforts began with the outbreak of war, they had remained peripheral as long as the possibility of a short war remained. The military stalemate, however, rendered new belligerents more significant and transformed the great powers—above all Germany—in the eyes of the smaller states. Italian Prime Minister Salandra put it bluntly: 'the German was not invincible after all, as had been accepted from 1870 onwards as a matter of course. The charm was broken.' A Turkish general echoed this sentiment: the Marne had produced a 'gigantic impression' and 'doubt whether Germany will win'. None the less alliance politics might yet succeed where military strategy had failed. The Germans tended to be more ruthless in subordinating other concerns to victory: as Moltke commented, 'at such times as these, one must not be doctrinaire'. The Austro-Hungarians may, however, have been correct in construing battlefield events as more critical than diplomatic bribes. As a Turkish general observed, Germany could not expect Turkey to make a 'suicidal offering' by joining the losing side; but, if Germany could 'win somewhere, so that we can believe in final German victory, then Bulgaria and we will enter'. Here, however, was precisely the dilemma: the Central Powers needed victories to win new allies but required new allies to win victories.

In the event, German bribes and military successes against Russia combined with Turkish ambitions and a joint Turkish-German attack against the Russian Black Sea fleet to win over the Ottoman empire at the end of November 1914. Ineffective in producing the desired rapid victory, Turkey's entry fostered a long war by drawing off Entente forces and imposing a blockade on Russia which contributed to its eventual collapse. Pursuing a policy which Salandra felicitously designated as 'sacred egotism', the other neutrals awaited that ephemeral moment when their entry might seem critical.

East versus West   The stalemate's implications became clear to German leaders in November 1914. Falkenhayn asserted to Bethmann that Germany could not prevail as

30

The Austro-German-Ottoman diplomatic alliance in concrete terms: Turkish general Jemal Pasha reviewing Austrian, German, and Turkish troops in Jerusalem.

long as the Entente remained united. But, if the enemy alliance were split by the conclusion of a separate peace with Russia or France, Germany could concentrate all its forces against the remaining enemies, win a decisive victory, and dictate peace terms. Falkenhayn argued that Russia was the most likely prospect and should therefore be let off lightly with payment of an indemnity and border rectifications. Germany should not, however, reject a French request for a separate understanding and should grant 'an honourable peace' to foster good relations after the war. Britain, the main enemy, would be starved out by a submarine blockade based in Belgium. Bethmann reluctantly accepted Falkenhayn's verdict: only a peace with Russia would allow the decisive defeat of France and Britain and 'the Triple Entente thus to be destroyed'. The dilemma which had been implicit in the Schlieffen Plan was thereby rendered explicit: the Central Powers could win a military victory only if the Entente were shattered but could shatter the Entente only if they could win a military victory. They would struggle unsuccessfully to escape this vicious cycle during the next two years.

As their opponents were doing, the leaders of the Central Powers debated whether the key to victory lay on the eastern or western front. There was general consensus among German leaders on the desirability of a separate peace with Russia but not on the means. Falkenhayn and the kaiser believed Russia could be won over by easy terms without augmented military pressure, whereas Bethmann, State Secretary for Foreign Affairs Gottlieb von Jagow, Conrad, German commanders in the east Paul von Hindenburg and Erich

Ludendorff, and many German diplomats contended that Russian military setbacks were required. Thus began a debate over carrot versus stick which would continue until the stick won in March 1918 with the punitive Treaty of Brest-Litovsk. In the spring of 1915 Falkenhayn secured the western front while the Turks successfully defended the Dardanelles against British attack, thereby preventing Anglo-French supplies from reaching Russia and frustrating Russian aspirations for the Straits. Prompted by Conrad's cries for help, German forces were shifted east and unexpectedly produced a major breakthrough against the Russians in the spring of 1915. Strategy seemed to have created the preconditions of diplomatic success.

The Central Powers accordingly launched an extensive diplomatic campaign for a separate peace with the Russians. Through the Danish court, former Russian ministers, German princely families, and other channels, Central Power diplomats sought contacts with those Russian elements which supposedly desired peace out of fear, or animosity towards Russia's allies, or lack of antipathy towards the Central Powers. Although Conrad's plea for 'golden bridges' to the Russians was accepted in principle, war aims at Russian expense none the less remained extensive. At the same time, the Germans had sought since the beginning of the war to prod the Russians into making peace by fostering revolution. Moltke had asserted in August 1914 that 'the seriousness of the situation in which the Fatherland finds itself requires the application of all means which are likely to hurt the enemy'. One approach was to encourage rebellion among the 'non-Russian vassal peoples' living under the Russian 'yoke'. At the same time the Germans sought to promote political and social revolution, most notably but not exclusively through the Bolsheviks. All these soundings, however, failed to evoke a Russian response.

Meanwhile during 1915 the Central Powers pursued new allies with mixed results. German civilian and military leaders joined Conrad in warning the Austro-Hungarian foreign minister, Stephan von Burian, that, 'if the war is to end victoriously for us, war with Italy must be unconditionally avoided'. These pressures, however, produced only bad blood in Vienna, which could never match Entente promises of Austro-Hungarian territory to Italy. In the event, far from tipping the balance, Italian entry in May 1915 provided only marginal aid to the Entente. On the contrary, like other small states which entered the war, Italy would prove to be less of a benefit than a burden to its great power allies.

The Central Powers had more success in the Balkan sweepstakes. Falkenhayn, Bethmann, and Conrad feared that 'the war is lost for us' if the Entente were joined by Romania, which in fact remained neutral in 1915 because of Russian military setbacks. The leaders of the Central Powers were similarly alarmed by the possibility that Bulgaria might join the Entente. But Central Power military success against Russia as well as offers of enemy territory and financial bribes persuaded Bulgaria in October 1915 to join the Central Powers in defeating Serbia. On the assumption that Russia would be discouraged by its own military setbacks, by the defeat of its ally Serbia, and by the British failure to take the Dardanelles, the Germans renewed their soundings for a separate peace with Russia but again without success.

The balance sheet at the end of 1915 was mixed. The Entente had failed to defeat the Central Powers by turning their flanks in Italy and the Dardanelles or by frontal attacks on the western front. The Central Powers had meantime dealt a serious military blow to Russia, won over Bulgaria, and conquered Serbia. They had established dominion from Antwerp to Baghdad and German leaders shared Burian's determination 'to win the greatest possible growth in power and security'. Their war aims admittedly fluctuated with the military and diplomatic prospects but remained extensive. Co-operation between the Central Powers was considerable although marred by disputes over aims and Austro-Hungarian resistance to German pressure for greater economic integration. Conrad acknowledged the fundamental dilemma: 'in spite of the military successes of 1915, we are not in a position entirely to force our will upon the enemy powers and make peace necessary for them.' Victory still required shattering the Entente.

Strategy for 1916

Conrad himself wanted to further Austro-Hungarian ambitions in the Balkans and the Adriatic. In January 1916 and again in May he launched independent offensives without fully consulting his German ally. The first overran Albania. The second, in the Trentino, had lost its impetus by June. In 1915 the Central Powers had agreed to remain on the defensive in Italy, and the Austrians' rejection of this arrangement left them dangerously exposed on the eastern front. The Russians exploited this vulnerability in June when Brusilov launched his offensive in Galicia.

The Germans on the other hand looked to France. Although apparently less likely than with Russia during 1915, a separate peace with France had not been renounced after the Marne. In their discussion of November 1914 Falkenhayn and Bethmann had acknowledged its desirability and two months later Bethmann affirmed German willingness to offer France 'an honourable peace' thereby 'separating France [from its allies] which would enable us to finish the war against Russia and England with the certainty of victory. We would thereby produce a relatively weak France, a dam against the Slavic danger, and a shock to English world hegemony.' Accordingly during 1915 the Germans pursued purported contacts with French left-wing politicians and press through Italian, Turkish, Egyptian, and other channels. The possibility of such a separate understanding with France had implications for German war aims, as a banker close to the German government observed: 'the eventual shape of peace conditions depends on whether the goal of [German] policy is to bleed France into exhaustion or to win it for reconciliation.' Assuming that the French would be discouraged by the failures on the western front, in Russia, Serbia, Italy, and at the Dardanelles, the Germans intensified their peace feelers at the end of 1915 but without success.

Confronted with this failure and concerned about the Central Powers'

Conrad von Hötzen-
dorf, the Austro-
Hungarian chief of
staff: more realistic
regarding Russia, his
aims against Italy and
Serbia exceeded
Austro-Hungarian
means.

ability to survive another year, Falkenhayn proposed in December 1915 to focus German strategy on a separate peace with France. He began from the premise that Britain was Germany's 'arch-enemy' and would stop fighting only when it lost its continental 'tools', France, Russia, and Italy. A separate peace with France seemed most desirable because it was at once Britain's 'best sword' yet most vulnerable enemy; it need not be defeated but only 'bled white' by being forced to defend the exposed fortress of Verdun. Accordingly, at the end of February 1916 the Germans attacked Verdun and simultaneously pursued negotiations which would 'seek the goal above all of shattering the [enemy] coalition through a separate peace and lasting under-standing with France'. Meanwhile, they sought a separate peace with Russia during the spring of 1916 through contacts in Stockholm. Despite horrific casualties, the French did not sue for peace because co-ordinated British and Russian offensives not only diverted German forces but also demonstrated that the Entente remained firm. When Falkenhayn finally discontinued his attacks on Verdun in August 1916, Bethmann asserted that 'the decision lies more than ever in the east'. To the minimal degree that they influenced French decisions, German war aims may have discouraged a separate understanding. Germany was, however, too successful militarily to make extensive concessions seem appropriate but unsuccessful enough to make them advisable.

The continued great power stalemate during 1916 again exaggerated the apparent importance of new allies. Like the other small states, Romania sought the critical moment. Still obsessed by the coalition logic, German leaders and Conrad pressed for concessions to keep Romania neutral but were largely refused by Burian, who probably correctly regarded them as less important than military prospects. Indeed anxiety that Russia might succeed without it and Franco-British offers of Austro-Hungarian territory persuaded Romania to join the Entente in August 1916. Notwithstanding the kaiser's fear that the war was now lost, Romania was in fact conquered by the end of 1916 and the Central Powers had greater access to Romanian oil and grain than they would have if Romania had remained neutral. In fact, Romanian entry marked the end of great power competition for European allies and the conflict reverted more clearly to the great power contest it had been all along.

The Central Powers' objective of splitting the Entente had been pursued on land with France in 1914, Russia in 1915, then France again in 1916. But, since both were viewed as British 'tools' and Britain as their arch-enemy, the Germans assumed that Britain would have to be forced to accept German continental domination even after peace had been concluded with its allies. In his discussion of late November 1914 with Bethmann, Falkenhayn urged that, once separate understandings with Russia and France had been achieved, Britain be starved into submission by a blockade based in Belgium as 'the only lasting insurance against another war'. An alternative was a great naval battle between the British and German high seas fleets in which a decisive German success would threaten British maritime dominion and thus force acceptance of German continental hegemony. But at the beginning of January 1915 German naval commander Hugo von Pohl told Falkenhayn that such an eventuality was unlikely and urged unrestricted submarine warfare instead. When in 1915 the British urged merchant ships to fly neutral flags and the Germans retaliated by declaring the waters around the British Isles a war zone, the British responded by intensifying their blockade of the Central Powers. These decisions were constrained by their effects on the neutrals, above all the United States, which protested against violation of freedom of the seas and the loss of American lives. In late December 1915 Falkenhayn joined the navy in urging unrestricted submarine warfare which might not only defeat Britain but also reinforce his Verdun strategy: just as Britain would be discouraged by a French surrender, so France would be disheartened by the submarine's starvation of its ally. But, contending that unrestricted submarine warfare would not only foster British tenacity but also provoke American entry, Bethmann persuaded the kaiser in March 1916 to allow only limited submarine warfare. The alternative of a battle between the high seas fleets briefly occurred at Jutland in May 1916 but ended in a draw because of the two commanders' cautious tactics. The submarine thus remained the sole recourse against Britain and would become an even more tempting weapon when efforts to split the Entente failed during 1916.

Hindenburg and Ludendorff take over

At the end of 1916 power shifted both within and between the Central Powers. Failure to produce victory weakened those leaders who had theretofore formulated policy. The civil–military balance between Bethmann and Falkenhayn was tipped towards the military when Falkenhayn was replaced in August 1916 by Hindenburg and Ludendorff, who increasingly dominated Bethmann and the kaiser. Meanwhile the Austro-Hungarian civilian leaders imposed greater control over Conrad after the setbacks of summer 1916; the trend was reinforced when the ambitious policies of Emperor Franz Joseph and Burian were succeeded at the end of 1916 by the defensiveness of new Emperor Karl and his foreign minister Ottokar Czernin, who immediately began to seek an escape from the war and even to doubt the desirability of a German victory. At the same time relations shifted between the Central Powers. The alliance was increasingly unbalanced by German military success and Austro-Hungarian failure, German pre-eminence in negotiations with the neutrals, and growing Austro-Hungarian economic dependence on Germany. Tensions intensified over war aims, especially in Poland, where Germany exerted increasing control over a puppet state. Most important, Falkenhayn's idea of a unified command under German control was forced through at the beginning of September 1916 by Hindenburg and Ludendorff. Thus power gravitated into the grasp of the German military.

Under these pressures, Bethmann launched an intensive diplomatic campaign at the end of 1916. After the failure of the Verdun attack in August 1916 to produce peace with France, he advocated renewed military pressure for an understanding with Russia which would 'blow up the Entente' and produce 'a final decision in this war of the peoples'. As a result, during the autumn of 1916 the Germans once more explored purported contacts with both Russian and French politicians but again to no avail. Potentially more promising was the possibility of American mediation which might allow the Central Powers either to preserve their conquests or to conduct submarine warfare without provoking American entry should the Entente appear responsible for the failure of mediation. When American mediation was postponed, Bethmann proposed a Central Power peace offer which would at least pacify Austro-Hungarian concerns and ideally encourage French and Russian pacifists either to force their governments' acceptance of German dominance or shatter the Entente. Bethmann was not so fortunate with Hindenburg and Ludendorff, who approved the plan only after they had first defeated Romania, stipulated extreme aims, and demanded that the offer include an assertion of German power. At the beginning of December 1916 the Central Powers announced their willingness to negotiate without prior terms but were summarily rejected by the Entente.

When American President Woodrow Wilson finally invited the belligerents to state their peace conditions, the Central Powers refused to announce theirs but offered to negotiate in the hope that they would either win Entente approval of their conquests or split their opponents. For their part, the Entente stipulated aims which jeopardized the existence of the Habsburg and Ottoman empires. In fact any negotiated peace was probably pre-ordained to fail: what seemed compromise to one side constituted defeat for the other.

Meanwhile Hindenburg and Ludendorff reoriented German strategy, diplomacy, and domestic policy. On the western front they built the so-called Hindenburg line, elaborate defensive positions to repel anticipated Anglo-French attacks. On the home front they instituted the Hindenburg programme, which envisaged a total war by drafting the entire German civilian population and resources. Finally they pressed ever harder for unrestricted submarine warfare, which Bethmann had sought to avoid with his peace offer. With its failure, he acceded at the beginning of January 1917 to these pressures, which were reinforced by a Reichstag resolution that, 'in making his decisions, the Imperial Chancellor must rely upon the views of the German High Command'. Bethmann none the less grasped at a final straw: to his announcement of unrestricted submarine warfare at the end of January 1917 he attached a personal letter to Wilson indicating watered-down peace terms. After American ships were sunk, Wilson declared war on Germany in April 1917.

In retrospect it is difficult not to condemn the submarine decision as the height of German folly since it virtually guaranteed American entry and eventual German defeat. Indeed it constitutes one of the war's tantalizing might-have-beens: had the Germans postponed submarine warfare for another month until the Russian Revolution and then renounced it permanently, they might have avoided American entry and defeat. The decision was, however, founded on acceptance by Hindenburg and Ludendorff of a probably accurate German assumption which pre-dated even Schlieffen: Germany could not win a long war on two fronts. But winning quickly by splitting the Entente through a separate peace with either France or Russia had proven unfeasible. Furthermore, like Falkenhayn, Hindenburg and Ludendorff regarded Britain as the main enemy and submarine warfare as the only means of forcing acceptance of German continental hegemony. They also worried that their population could not long survive the increasingly effective British blockade. They rejected criticism that unrestricted submarine warfare would bring America into the war on the grounds that the United States was effectively an Entente ally already and that Britain could in any case be starved into submission before American aid arrived. Like the Schlieffen Plan, which promised French surrender in six weeks, the submarine would force British submission in five or six months but likewise at the cost of a new enemy—in 1914 Britain, in 1917 the United States. German strategy was trapped in a vicious circle: the submarine might have forced Britain to surrender if it had not been able to count on America, just as the Schlieffen Plan might have made France surrender if it had not had the prospect of Russian aid. Both were tried when they could not succeed.

Thus German policy in early 1917 remained as it had been in 1914, a desperate effort to escape what Bismarck had called 'the nightmare of coalitions'. With American entry and the Russian Revolution, coalition war was recast and European history profoundly altered.

CHAPTER 3

Manœuvre Warfare: The Eastern and Western Fronts, 1914–1915

D. E. SHOWALTER

A ll of the continental powers' war plans depended on precision and speed. All were predicated on manœuvre: constant offensives at strategic, operational, and tactical levels. But only Germany's involved the deliberate violation of the neutrality of neighbouring states. To avoid a headlong rush against French fortifications designed to channel such attacks into killing zones, the German army had developed in the Schlieffen Plan the concept of a heavily weighted 'right hook' through the Low Countries. The subsequent decision that the Netherlands were more useful as a window to the world than a highway to France made rapid passage through Belgium even more important.

The key to Belgium was the fortress of Liège, regarded as one of the strongest defence systems in Europe. German plans called for storming the works within forty-eight hours. Instead, the overconfident and inexperienced Germans required ten days and a dozen heavy siege howitzers, Austrian 30.5-cm. pieces, and Krupp-designed 42-cm. 'Big Berthas' to complete their victory and clear the way for the main advance.

The battles of the frontiers

39

The war's outbreak generated a broad spectrum of emotions, not all of them exalted and not all of them acknowledged. 'The Evening before War' captures the mix of enthusiasm and anxiety in the context of a near-lustful anticipation of indulgence in behaviour and feelings otherwise forbidden in turn-of-the-century society.

Three armies, no fewer than sixteen corps, swept across Belgium. They met scattered resistance from rearguards and local forces. They responded by vigorous use of threats and reprisals. The Franco-Prussian War of 1870–1 had demonstrated the effectiveness of partisan warfare and convinced the German army that the best countermeasures were stern ones. The advance left in its wake a trail of burned villages and executed civilians. The destruction on 26 August of much of the city of Louvain in response to alleged partisan activity did much to brand the Germans as 'Huns' in the eyes of their enemies—and of neutral states as well. In Talleyrand's words it was worse than a crime. It was a mistake.

As the German right hook swung through Belgium, France thrust towards its enemy's armpit. Plan XVII, developed in its final pre-war form by Joseph

Joffre, assumed the Germans would invade Belgium but would overextend themselves in the process. Plan XVII determined France's concentration, and not its strategy. Joffre proposed to deploy virtually France's entire mobilized strength, organized in five armies, along the eastern French frontier. If the Germans violated Belgian neutrality, as expected, three armies would swing north-east and meet them there. Should Germany come straight ahead, the primary French axis of advance would instead be on either side of the Metz–Thionville fortifications.

The plan's most serious weakness was its positioning of almost three-quarters of the army south of Verdun. Given the offensive emphasis of French doctrine, that deployment set the stage for an early invasion of Alsace-Lorraine. Whatever the symbolic importance of these provinces detached from France in 1871, they were a strategic blind alley. Nevertheless, when on 4 August the French received definite information that Belgium was under attack, Joffre ordered a full-scale offensive into Lorraine. His intention was for this initiative to fix the German left and draw their strategic reserves south while his three northern armies drove into Belgium and Luxembourg, across the presumed axis of a German advance now stripped of support.

French movements were initially characterized by tactical dash and operational caution. 'To encourage the rest' Joffre began a policy of ruthlessly relieving brigade, division, and corps commanders who lacked aggressiveness. By the first week in September, no fewer than fifty French general officers were on their way to rear areas. This 'hecatomb' was in good part a product of an exponential increase in the pace and stress of operations. From battalions upward, commanders and their staffs were kept often literally at ten minutes' notice on a twenty-four-hour basis. Physical and emotional exhaustion was a common result in all armies. The British Expeditionary Force would lose one of its corps commanders to a heart attack on 17 August—another example of a phenomenon that may have contributed as much as more measurable material factors to the general failure to translate peacetime plans into battlefield victories.

Despite a spectrum of expected and unexpected difficulties, the French 1st and 2nd Armies continued to advance into Lorraine against light resistance. The two German armies confronting them were outnumbered. Their assigned role in the Schlieffen Plan was to draw French troops and French attention from the main advance. The German chief of staff, Helmuth von Moltke, was no longer sure this applied. By mid-August there were no clear signs of major French movements to confront the thrust through Belgium. Might it be possible that Joffre was in fact planning his main offensive through the Vosges mountains and directly towards the Rhine?

As important as Moltke's own doubts was the confidence of the 6th Army's commander, Crown Prince Rupprecht of Bavaria, that he could attack successfully in his sector with the troops at his disposal. Moltke was dubious until on 20 August the French came up against the main German positions around

Morhange and Sarrebourg. Their infantry went in with the bayonet, and were chopped down in ranks by rifle, machine gun, and artillery fire. Within two days the Germans drove them back more than 15 miles.

As the 1st and 2nd Armies fell back from Morhange, the French 3rd and 4th Armies drove into the Ardennes with the mission of breaking through the German centre. On 21 August French advance guards entered some of the most difficult terrain in western Europe. Columns lost touch with each other. Neither cavalry nor aircraft could supply systematic intelligence of German strength and movements. Opposite the French, the German 4th and 5th Armies were slightly better off. They expected a fight. Their cavalry was stronger and more aggressive than its French opposition. Nevertheless there was little to choose in terms of surprise when the armies began stumbling into each other on 22 August. In a series of encounter battles whose ferocity was exacerbated by the close terrain, German tactical superiority gave them a general advantage just sufficient to overcome French *élan*. French artillery found it difficult to deploy from the narrow roads, with the result that too many infantry attacks were unsupported. Heavy losses, especially in field and company officers, demoralized the survivors, in some cases to the point of panic.

The 'miracle' of the Marne

Joffre responded by trading space for time, ordering a retreat from the Ardennes for the purpose of stopping a German right wing that by 25 August was posing a threat to Paris itself. The French 5th Army had deployed along Belgium's southern border, with the British Expeditionary Force, at first only four divisions strong, coming up on its left. The 5th's commander, General Charles Lanrezac, was arguably the best of France's peacetime generals, widely respected for his operational insight and widely feared for his acid tongue. In the first two weeks of August his intelligence service developed an accurate and alarming picture of German strengths and movements in the 5th Army's zone of responsibility. Not until 18 August, however, did Joffre order an advance into Belgium. Even then he continued to underestimate the extent of the German advance. Lanrezac was correspondingly worried about his increasingly exposed left flank. His anxieties were not alleviated by the apparent cluelessness of BEF commander Sir John French, who in Lanrezac's mind appeared to have no idea what he and his men were supposed to do.

Meanwhile the German 1st, 2nd, and 3rd Armies scythed through a Belgium whose surviving forces had got out of harm's way by withdrawing to the coastal fortress of Antwerp. On 21 August the French 5th and German 2nd Armies met along the line of the Sambre river. The Germans forced a passage on a 6-mile front; the French commanders on the spot mounted counter-attacks, against Lanrezac's original intention not to fight the kind of forward battle that proved so costly in the Argonne. Once again lack of control above battalion level combined with poor infantry–artillery co-ordination to stop the French in their tracks. The Germans, however, were unable to do more than push the 5th Army backward. Further north around Mons, on 24 August the BEF conducted a seminar on firepower for Alexander von Kluck's 1st Army. British riflemen able to deliver fifteen aimed rounds a minute from improvised defences staggered the Germans and held the field at day's end. They could not keep it. Threatened on both flanks the British joined their allies in what came to be known as the Great Retreat.

By 25 August, both Joffre and Moltke were in the process of agonizing reappraisals. The fog of war did not prevent Joffre from realizing three things. French offensives had been checked all along the line. German forces were stronger by far than anticipated. And they were extended much further to the north than Joffre had expected. On the other hand the French had suffered unheard-of casualties, over 300,000 in less than two weeks, without breaking. This came as something of a surprise to professionals who had openly doubted the ability of hastily mobilized civilians to endure such a hammering. French armies might be retreating, but they were falling back on their own depots and lines of communications. Joffre took advantage of these situations to begin shifting troops to his left flank, eventually creating an entire new army, the 6th, to extend the allied line west of the BEF. No less important, Joffre maintained and exaggerated his normal imperturbability.

This photo of an early trench, manned by the 2nd Scots Guards at Zandvoorde in Flanders, resembles the front line of World War II more than the elaborate defensive systems whose construction began in 1915. Three months after the Great War's outbreak its generals believed a war of movement would recur in the spring. Therefore there was no need to waste thought or energy improving temporary positions.

Perhaps better than any of his counterparts in high command, he recognized that modern armies were bludgeons, not rapiers. They could not respond promptly even to such threats as the German drive through Belgium. In that context arguably the worst thing someone in Joffre's position could do was manifest anxiety and risk its downward spread.

An opposite mood prevailed in the German supreme headquarters. Established at Koblenz for the sake of communications, it was instead losing touch with its increasingly far-flung armies. Apart from the fragmentary nature of the information provided by telephone and courier, the German command system encouraged subordinates on the spot to take the initiative. The initial success of Rupprecht's counter-attacks in Lorraine led the Bavarian prince to seek permission to expand them into a general offensive. On 22 August Moltke agreed.

His decision has been generally excoriated as a product of vanity and indecision. By seeking victory all along the front, critics argued, Moltke diffused German forces that to begin with had no great margin of superiority. On the other hand it was part of the German approach to war to reinforce success, taking advantage of developing opportunities and expanding tactical victories into operational ones. Breakthrough in Lorraine might set the stage for a true Cannae, a double envelopment of the French army—something beyond the dreams of Schlieffen himself. More serious in the long run would prove Moltke's pattern of detaching forces from his right wing for mopping-up operations. His army commanders, however, did not seem to need more men. Even the detaching of two full corps for the eastern front on 26 August, against the advice of the chief of staff for that theatre, met no protests or questions.

None seemed necessary. A corps of the BEF, pressed hard by Kluck, stood at bay on 26 August and bloodied German noses at Le Cateau, but this was no more than a rearguard fight. To relieve pressure on the British Joffre ordered Lanrezac to mount a counter-attack, but the battle of Guise on 29 August was no more than a riposte. With the roads to Paris apparently wide open, on 30 August German supreme headquarters moved forward to Luxembourg. This relocation disrupted already-shaky communications in an increasingly fluid situation. Rupprecht's offensive had been checked within days by desperate French counter-attacks. On the Germans' other wing Kluck altered his line of advance. Instead of moving to envelop Paris, the 1st Army turned south-east in direct pursuit of the French 5th Army and the British. Moltke approved this as fully in accord with the Schlieffen Plan's emphasis on destroying the enemy's principal field forces. On 2 September, however, he ordered Kluck also to drop a bit behind Karl von Bülow's 2nd Army and establish a flank against whatever threat the French might muster from around Paris.

Kluck saw this as a map-driven contradiction. His leading elements were well ahead of Bülow's, and the best way of deciding the campaign seemed to be to press forward. Kluck compromised, sending three of the 1st Army's corps south-east after the allies and leaving two, with most of his cavalry, to face Paris. Meanwhile the French were turning at bay. To lose Paris was to lose the war. Joffre proposed to throw everything he could bring to bear at the tactical centre, Bülow's 2nd Army. The main attack would be supported by a secondary offensive mounted from Paris by the improvised 6th Army. Moltke, increasingly aware of the latter possibility, responded on the evening of 4 September by ordering both 1st and 2nd Armies to halt their southward advance and prepare to face west to meet this new threat.

Kluck felt himself in the position of a man who, stumbling while running down a hill, is told to recover his balance by slowing his pace. Initially he continued his original movement. During 5 September, however, he received a message from the 2nd Army to the effect that the threat from Paris was far more serious than Kluck believed. The 1st Army's commander began by preparing to turn west, as originally ordered. But for the first time in the campaign, the Germans had lost the initiative. On the 5th, forward elements of the 6th French Army struck the 1st Army's flank. By the next day a full-scale encounter battle had developed along the Ourcq river. Kluck marched to the sound of the guns. By 7 September, most of the 1st Army was either engaged in the new sector or on the way towards it. As a result, a 30-mile gap emerged between Kluck and Bülow, whose worn-out men were unable to break through the French on their front despite some significant local successes. Into that gap moved the BEF and the 5th Army, the latter by now under a new commander. Experience had taught lessons. Both allies advanced cautiously into what might prove just another tactical killing ground. But Bülow, himself by now exhausted, believed retreat his best option. Moltke dispatched his chief of intelligence, Lieutenant Colonel Hentsch, as his representative with oral authority to sort out the situation. Hentsch too recommended retreat. On 9 September the 2nd Army began withdrawing to the north. Kluck still wanted to fight it out. But his men were worn out, and when cavalry and airmen reported British troops on the 1st Army's open left flank, even Kluck agreed that it was time to regroup and recalculate. The battle of the Marne was over.

Within days voices on both sides of the line highlighted missed opportunities. Victory might have rested with the Reich, German detractors argued, had Moltke possessed a firmer grip or a clearer vision; or had Kluck and Bülow been willing to mount one more attack aimed at ending the stalemate before Paris. From the allied side, as the war turned to stalemate critics bewailed the failure to take advantage of the kind of gap whose opening later required the sacrifice of tens of thousands of lives. Had the British moved a little faster, had French generals been willing to trust *élan* and *cran* one more time, the war might indeed have ended before the leaves fell.

The limits of both perspectives are clear in retrospect. Well before the Marne was fought the German right wing's initial advantages in numbers and position had been steadily declining. Men and officers unaccustomed to the levels of exertion demanded by Schlieffen's grand design suffered from physical fatigue, emotional stress, and dulled wits to degrees making brilliant tactical or operational initiatives unlikely. Even had the 1st and 2nd Armies won their immediate battle, another allied retreat would have been more likely than the dramatic destruction of the French 5th Army and/or the BEF. On the other hand, fighting it out along the Marne carried a significant risk of having to extricate the 1st and 2nd Armies from isolation—without any readily deployable reserve to implement the operation.

The 'race to the sea'

Allied movements were retarded by inertia, doubt, and not least by skilful German rearguards. Exacerbating these factors was the damage done to both French and British infrastructures earlier in the campaign. Casualties and dismissals had disrupted relationships at all levels of command from army corps to companies. The tenuousness of allied movements during September was correspondingly predictable. Nor were the Germans any more enterprising. The so-called 'Race to the Sea' that ended in mid-October was more of a crawl, with both adversaries throwing a series of short jabs by redeploying troops from their now-quiescent southern and central fronts to each other's northern flanks. These initiatives were stifled by numerical weakness, lack of manœuvring room, and not least by modified tactics. Soldiers on both sides were throwing away the book by digging in, replacing manœuvre with fire, and letting the enemy take the risks of attacking. These changes, seldom reported in detail to higher headquarters concerned with winning the war by Christmas, were no less effective for being unofficial.

As the Germans finally reached the Channel, Erich von Falkenhayn, who *de facto* replaced the discredited Moltke as chief of staff on 14 September, decided on one more try. From 20 October to 24 November the Germans mounted a series of frontal attacks in northern Belgium across terrain flooded when it was not featureless. A heroic resistance that virtually destroyed the original BEF stopped the Germans in front of Ypres. Yet even had the offensive succeeded in breaking through the attenuated allied defences, Falkenhayn had no clear sense of what should happen once his armies reached open country. Within four months of the war's outbreak mobile operations in the west had been transformed from means to strategic ends to ends in themselves.

War plans in the East

The Great War's opening rounds on the eastern front reflected the insecurities of the principal combatants. Germany and Austria had long considered a joint offensive against the Russians. Well before 1914, however, it was clear at least in Berlin that Germany lacked the disposable resources to pursue offensive operations on two fronts. Given the necessity of choice France was more vulnerable to a paralysing first strike than a Russian empire protected as much by its disorganization as by its distances. German war plans correspondingly called for a holding operation by minimum forces—a dozen or so divisions, most of them in the exposed province of East Prussia—until victory against France made possible the settling of accounts with Russia.

Austro-Hungarian strategy was shaped by Chief of Staff Conrad von Hötzendorf's desire to provide for a two-front war involving Russia in the east and Italy or the Slavic states of the Balkans in the south. The Dual Monarchy's final mobilization plan divided the army into three parts. Eight divisions were to deploy against Serbia, twenty-eight against Russia. The remaining twelve might be considered either a swing force or a strategic reserve, to be deployed where the need was greatest. They would spend the war's crucial first weeks shuttling from one theatre to the other, and being nowhere at the right time.

Austrian apologists have made much of Germany's initial refusal to attack eastward in support of Austria. In fact the weakness of Austria's forces made offensive operations imperative no matter what the Germans did. Failing to maintain the initiative, so allowing the Russians to complete their concentration and choose their lines of advance, meant a risk approaching certainty of being overrun in the field or trapped in the fortress systems of Lvov and Przemyśl. In the aftermath of a humiliating and unexpected defeat at the hands of the Serbs, four Habsburg armies began their march into Russian Poland on 18 August.

Russia for its part has preferred to present itself as a victim of its French ally's demands for an offensive as soon as possible. In fact Russia's grand-strategic situation objectively favoured such an operation. Since under no circumstances could Russia fight Germany and Austria alone, its most pru-

Where armies marched, civilians fled. These particular refugees happen to be German; the scene was replicated over and over on all the fighting fronts of 1914—an ugly harbinger of total war.

47

dent course was to take risks at the war's beginning to make sure that France would be neither overrun nor crippled. The only pre-war question was whether that offensive should be mounted against Germany or Austria. In the event there seemed ample strength available to pursue both options—particularly since the forces designated for deployment against Germany ultimately comprised thirty divisions. If almost 500 battalions could not be risked against the kaiser's military leftovers, then the Russian empire was as good as doomed in any case.

Tannenberg

Russia's war plan against Germany involved sending two armies into the East Prussian salient, one advancing west across the Niemen river and the other south-west from Russian Poland. Their missions were to destroy the German forces in the field, pinch East Prussia off from the body of Germany, and thereby create conditions for a direct thrust into the Second Empire. The plan seemed well on its way to success when German senior officers panicked after a local defeat on 20 August. The commanders of the Russian 1st and 2nd Armies, however, failed either to co-ordinate their movements or to press their advantage. Moltke replaced the 8th Army's commander with a retired general, Paul von Hindenburg, and assigned Erich Ludendorff, one of the general staff's best brains, as his chief of staff. Arriving in the theatre on 23 August, they implemented plans already drafted by their new subordinates for concentrating against the 2nd Army to the south. After five days' hard fighting 50,000 Russians were dead or wounded, 90,000 more were prisoners, and Germany had its first heroes of the Great War.

Hindenburg and Ludendorff followed up their triumph by routing the Russian 1st Army in the battle of the Masurian Lakes with the aid of the reinforcements provided by Moltke. But both operations, despite their scale, were no more than local victories. Any chance for exploiting them vanished when the Germans were instead constrained to support an ally that had marched into catastrophe.

Austrian defeats in Galicia

The Russian high command had anticipated Austrian intentions and proposed to counter by deploying two armies north of Galicia and two more on the south-eastern Russo-Austrian frontier, then drive forward, envelop both Habsburg flanks, and cut off their lines of retreat. Cavalry and air reconnaissance provided little useful information to either side. Local successes on his left encouraged Conrad to press forward there while neglecting the threat to his right. Taken by surprise, his 3rd Army was routed south-east of Lvov on 26–7 August. The 2nd Army, still detraining and deploying, could provide little direct support. The offensive in the north was halted when on 4 September the Russians in that sector mounted a counter-attack.

Conrad nevertheless, in contrast to German behaviour at the Marne, proposed to take the fight to the Russians by attacking. As the armies grappled, the front became characterized everywhere by mutually exposed rears and mutually vulnerable flanks. Victory, Conrad reasoned, would go to the side first able to impose its will on events. But Conrad's tool broke in his hands. Initially the Austrians, whatever their ethnic identity, fought hard and well. After three weeks of unparalleled exertion the men were exhausted, their officers confused. There were too many Russians in too many places. By 11 September, even Conrad perceived retreat as the only alternative to encirclement and annihilation. A quarter of a million of his men were dead or wounded. Another hundred thousand were prisoners. Winston Churchill's conclusion that Conrad broke his army's heart and used it up in three weeks is an appropriate epitaph for Austria-Hungary's end as a great power.

Hindenburg and Ludendorff responded by using the German railway network to redeploy four corps from Prussia into Poznań, then attack into the Russian rear towards Warsaw. This time, however, the Russians fell back, reconcentrated, counter-attacked, and cut off an entire corps. The Germans fought their way out, but were satisfied enough, as winter put an end to large-scale operations, to have eased the immediate pressure on Austria.

Germany swings to the east, 1914–1915

The victors of Tannenberg still accepted the premise that the war would be decided in the west. Yet they could hardly avoid speculating what might be achieved in the east with just slightly stronger forces. When Conrad proposed a major Austrian offensive north-east from the Carpathians, Ludendorff supported this idea less for its intrinsic merits than as a means to secure German reinforcements for the eastern front.

Falkenhayn was less sanguine. He regarded Britain as Germany's most dangerous enemy and believed France could be held in check only as long as Germany maintained its forward position on the western front. As early as mid-November of 1914 he concluded that Germany could no longer defeat the Entente by military means. German conquests in the west had been too small to convince the losers that there was no alternative to making peace, and too large for France or Britain to risk negotiations without an effort to redress the situation by force. The probable result was the kind of attritional war that two generations of planners had insisted Germany could not win. Russia, however, might be susceptible to peace offers—particularly if given a bloody nose as a preliminary.

In the event the joint German-Austrian offensive of January 1915 achieved no more than initial local successes. Newly raised German units suffered heavy losses in the broken terrain of Masuria. In the Austrian sector three-quarters of a million men became casualties or disappeared in the Carpathian Mountains. By the end of March massive Russian counter-attacks were encouraging allied hopes of a victory parade through Budapest.

This was manœuvre warfare from the wrong side of the line. Its successes led Falkenhayn to decide in late March that Germany's least worst option involved mounting another offensive in the east. Austria could not be allowed to collapse. German efforts to preserve Italian neutrality were being checked and mated by allied promises. The appeal of those promises was in turn enhanced by Austria's refusal of concessions in either the Mediterranean or the Balkans—concessions the Dual Monarchy was at present too weak to consider making. There was no time for grand combinations. Nor was Falkenhayn comfortable weakening a western front he still regarded as the vital theatre. Were German aid too generous, moreover, Austria might well continue its policy of intransigence through weakness, blackmailing Germany by implying a threat to collapse. Falkenhayn sent eight divisions east to provide the nucleus for a limited breakthrough operation in central Poland. On 2 May the newly formed 11th German Army, nominally under Austrian command, tore open the front on a 40-mile sector between the Galician towns of Gorlice and Tarnow. Unexpectedly the Russians snapped. Local retreats interfaced and multiplied. By the third week of June a quarter of a million Russians had surrendered. Hundreds of thousands more were dead or wounded. The army's peacetime cadres of officers and NCOs had been virtually destroyed; its deployable reserves of *matériel* virtually exhausted. Nevertheless the east was still giving nothing back—at least in the short term.

The spring 1915 offensives in the west

In the aftermath of first Ypres the western front was stalemated but not stagnant. Despite over 800,000 casualties in the war's first four months, the French army and the French government were viscerally committed to recovering their occupied territory as quickly as possible. Britain's initial hope of limiting its continental involvement gave way to a decision to raise the first mass army in its history and make its primary effort across the Channel. The often-sentimentalized Christmas truce of 1914 was no more than a pause in a counter-attack that began on 20 December with a major French offensive in Champagne. The operation continued on and off for three

The famous 'Christmas truce' of 1914 was in fact a series of local armistices, usually initiated by the Germans and more often involving the British than the French. Terms ranged from a temporary cease-fire to battalion-scale fraternization in No Man's Land. By 1915 the respective high commands put a damper on the practice; nevertheless informal halts or limitations to hostilities remained part of the trench-warfare experience. It requires a sharp eye to distinguish British from German in this snapshot.

months with prototypical results: local gains at high costs. A BEF reconstituted from old reservists, young recruits, and units redeployed from the empire replicated the French experience on 10 March at Neuve Chapelle.

When evaluating their respective achievements, however, both allied armies concluded that, with incremental improvements in tactics and techniques, a few more men, and a little more artillery, it would be possible to break through the German positions as well as break into them. Joffre planned a full-scale attack with British support for May in the Artois sector. The Germans were sufficiently concerned at that prospect to mount a preemptive strike in Flanders.

The second battle of Ypres was not a product of vaulting strategic ambition. Falkenhayn sought to throw the allies off balance and camouflage the withdrawal of troops for the Russian theatre. The fighting of 1914 had created a salient around Ypres whose elimination would tidy the German lines and whose retention would draw allied troops into a convenient killing ground. As part of the operation Falkenhayn authorized the use of a new weapon, chlorine gas. He was not, however, particularly optimistic regarding its prospects. And in fact the gas clouds did not prove harbingers of a breakthrough. The suicidal resistance of the green 1st Canadian Division blocked the German advance just long enough for reserves to reach the front. They in turn were expended in a series of improvised counter-attacks that bled the 'second BEF' almost white.

The development of the trench system since the autumn of 1914 is clearly evident in this photo of a portion of the British line in the Ypres sector, almost on top of the forward German positions.

The allies achieved nothing of significance in a fresh series of attacks in May and June, this time against increasingly sophisticated German defences on Vimy Ridge and around Festubert. Instead they exhausted their ready reserves of ammunition and their available pool of replacements. Until the factories could keep the guns supplied and the training camps and hospitals furnish more 'bayonets', offensive operations in the west were suspended.

World War I saw the final appearance of the 'realistic' sketch art that had been the feature of war reporting since the Crimea. This depiction of an early 'cloud gas' attack in 1915 nevertheless conveys to readers of *The Sphere* something of what it was like to drown as seared lungs filled with fluid. An early countermeasure involved urinating on a handkerchief, then breathing through the cloth until the gas dispersed.

Facing: This Russian poster features a heroic St George slaying the multi-headed dragon of the Central Powers against a background of ruined churches in a devastated landscape. It highlights the strong religious element of the mythic motifs employed by all combatants in their early propaganda posters.

THE SPHERE

AN ILLUSTRATED NEWSPAPER FOR THE HOME

With which is incorporated "BLACK & WHITE"

Volume LXI. No. 801. | REGISTERED AT THE GENERAL POST OFFICE AS A NEWSPAPER | London, May 29, 1915 | Price Sixpence.

Between late September and early November, Joffre mounted another series of frontal attacks in Champagne. Further north the BEF, now freshened by the arrival of the first divisions of the 'new army' created by Earl Kitchener, struck the Germans at Loos with the aid of poison gas. The results in both sectors were heavy losses with no commensurate gains. The Germans suffered as well, but were by this time beginning to revamp their tactics, moving towards the combination of strong forward positions and prompt counter-attacks that would dominate later western battlefields. The allies for their part were victimized by a constantly interrupted learning curve. Even their ostensibly experienced formations were increasingly manned and led by men unprepared at their levels of responsibility for the conditions they faced. And so many died in the process of gaining relevant experience that the process of transmitting lessons to the next battlefield generation remained haphazard.

The final effort to break the Great War's stalemate came from the Germans. Hopes that Gorlice–Tarnow might be the first step to a negotiated separate peace foundered on Russian dreams and Franco-British promises. Austro-German armies continued their advance into Russia, reaching a line from Riga in the north to Czernowitz in the south by late September. But the tsarist empire, more even than the other combatants, had invested too much of its domestic legitimacy to risk considering anything like the status quo ante bellum. Bulgaria's joining the Central Powers on 6 October generated a brilliantly executed operation that overran Serbia in six weeks. It also left a remnant of the Serbian army still in existence, and in due course helped bring Bulgaria's regional rival Romania on to the allied side. Austria-Hungary was strained to its limits. The improvised and inefficient mobilization of German resources begun in the war's early months had to date done no more than sustain a status quo untenable in the long run. As the year turned the Central Powers seemed well into the process of conquering themselves to death—or at least exhaustion.

Facing: War in 1914 still had a lighter side. This advertisement issued by a Hungarian brewery has the Entente's fighting men abandoning their rifles for the sake of a cold beer.

CHAPTER 4

The Strategy of the Entente Powers, 1914–1917

DAVID FRENCH

The Entente lacks a strategy

The opening weeks of the First World War demonstrated that the Triple Entente of France, Russia, and Britain suffered from a fundamental weakness. It did not have a co-ordinated strategic policy. This was partly because none of its members had any recent experience of fighting a coalition war. The last occasion on which France and Britain had fought as allies was in the Crimea between 1854 and 1856. It was also a reflection of the fact that, although the Entente had developed because France, Russia, and Britain shared some common interests, there still remained many issues which divided them before 1914 and were to continue to do so during the war.

Between 1905 and 1914 most members of the policy-making élites of Britain, France, and Russia saw Germany's growing assertiveness as the main threat to their national security and interests. But even after the formation of the Anglo-French Entente in 1904 and the signing of the Anglo-Russian agreement in 1907, three sources of tension divided the three partners. First, there were vocal critics of the Entente in each country. In Britain Conservative politicians remained suspicious of Russian ambitions, whilst Liberals deplored the domestic repression of the tsarist regime. Secondly, the agreements did not eliminate all colonial rivalries. The British and French contin-

54

ued to bicker over Egypt, the arms trade in the Persian Gulf, and the future of Morocco. However, these disputes were small compared with continued tensions between Russia and Britain. The two partners remained deeply suspicious of each other's ambitions in the Middle East and around the frontiers of India. The result was a paradox, for while during the war each member of the Entente attempted to adjust its strategy to placate its partners, it simultaneously kept a wary eye on its allies' post-war ambitions.

Thirdly, although in 1913 the Russians and French had reached agreement on a concerted strategic policy, they never achieved the same level of co-ordination with the British. Indeed, some French and Russian politicians and generals doubted whether Britain was a worthwhile ally in a continental war, for it did not have a large conscript army to throw into the military balance against Germany and its navy could have little immediate impact on the outcome of the land war. Furthermore, both the Russians and the French were annoyed by Britain's refusal before 1914 to give an unequivocal promise that it would stand by its partners in the event of war. A few took their doubts even further and believed that a better option would be to bring about a *rapprochement* with Germany.

France and Russia turn to Britain

The French and Russians had agreed that in the event of war they would try to attack Germany simultaneously from the east and the west. But by late August the Germans had repulsed the French, whilst in East Prussia a whole Russian army was annihilated by the Germans at Tannenberg. With the Germans advancing towards Paris, the Russian foreign minister, Sazonov, was afraid that his partners might be about to desert him. He therefore suggested that each member of the Entente should sign an agreement promising not to make a separate peace. The Pact of London was concluded on 5 September 1914 and the ambiguities of the pre-war Entente were replaced by a formal alliance. The pact ensured that the war would not come to a quick end, because if one ally faltered it could look to its friends for support, but it did not impose a coherent strategy on the Entente and so the terms upon which that support were given remained to be decided.

Fortunately the French commander-in-chief, General Joffre, with minimal British assistance, was able to effect France's salvation on the Marne and the Germans were forced to retreat before they could occupy Paris. But Joffre could not drive the Germans back into Germany and by late November the entire line, from Switzerland to the North Sea coast, had stabilized. Paris was safe, but the French army had suffered nearly 200,000 casualties in August alone, a rate of loss probably never again reached by any other army throughout the war. The Germans were in occupation of most of Belgium and some of the most valuable industrial departments of north-eastern France. There seemed little prospect that the Russians would be able to break the stalemate, for although they had won victories over the Austrians, they had proved to be no match for the Germans and were in no position to march on Berlin.

DAVID FRENCH

Facing: On 10 August 1914 the German cruisers *Goeben* and *Breslau*, having evaded the Royal Navy, successfully sought sanctuary at Constantinople. Shortly afterwards the Turks purchased them, although both ships retained their German crews. At the end of October they bombarded the Russian port of Sebastapol and hastened the spreading of the war to the Middle East.

In such circumstances it was hardly surprising that the continental allies looked to Britain for more support and complained that the British were not bearing their fair share of the burden when they did not receive it. But the British army was tiny compared with those of its partners and would remain so until the vast new armies of volunteers which Lord Kitchener had begun to raise in August 1914 were trained and equipped. However, they could not ignore the pleas of their allies. By the end of 1914 they were aware that the Germans were determined to disrupt the Entente alliance by playing on their mutual suspicions so as to secure a separate peace with either France or Russia. The British therefore began to lend their allies money and to seek a theatre of operations where they could make full use of their main strategic asset, the Royal Navy.

In 1914 the British hoped to avoid war with Turkey because the Ottoman empire acted as a bulwark to defend their possessions in India and Egypt from Russian incursions. But they had little option in the matter. In August two German cruisers, the *Goeben* and the *Breslau*, had evaded the Royal Navy in the Mediterranean and successfully sought sanctuary at Constantinople. The Committee of Union and Progress, which ruled Turkey, then signed a secret treaty with Germany and at the end of October allowed the two ships to attack Russia's Black Sea coast. Britain and France had to support their ally and declare war on Turkey at the beginning of November. This not only compelled the British to open two new fronts, in Mesopotamia and Egypt, but it also raised a major bone of contention between the Entente partners, because each of them had their own interests to pursue in the Ottoman empire.

However, Turkey's entry into the war also gave the British the opportunity to give a tangible demonstration of their support for Russia. In January 1915, with their own troops hard pressed by the Turks in the Caucasus, the Russians asked for action by the British to distract the Ottoman forces. The British responded in February and March by mounting a naval attack in conjunction with the French through the Straits with the object of taking Constantinople. The operation failed and, even when it was transformed into a major amphibious expedition by the addition of British, Australian, New Zealand, and French troops, stubborn Turkish resistance continued to block the Straits. By the time the last allied troops were evacuated from the Gallipoli peninsula in January 1916, the operation had cost them over a quarter of a million men.

The Gallipoli campaign also highlighted the fact that, beneath the public rhetoric of unity, each member of the Entente was pursuing a different agenda for the post-war world. Each of them wished to curb Germany's power, but each also sought to enhance its own power. In March 1915, the Russians, fearful that the British were about to invite the Greeks to join them in taking Constantinople, insisted that before they would allow any other country to join the Entente their existing allies had to promise that Constantinople would become a Russian city at the end of the war. To give force

to their request, Sazonov hinted that if it was not met Russia might seek better terms from the Germans. The British and French had no option other
than to agree, even though Sazonov's demands made a negotiated peace with
Turkey impossible, and even though it would make Russia a major power in
the eastern Mediterranean after the war and so menace their own interests in
the region. They in turn could only respond by jockeying for advantage when
they considered their own desiderata in the Ottoman empire, discussions
which culminated in February 1916 in the Sykes–Picot agreement which
threatened to divide Turkey-in-Asia into spheres of interest dominated by
Britain, France, and Russia.

Faced by the prospect of a long war, the Entente began to cast around for
new allies, but it could point to few other successes in 1915 to counterbalance
its failure at Gallipoli. The prospect of territorial spoils gained at the expense
of Austria-Hungary and Turkey did not persuade the Balkan neutrals, Bulgaria, Romania, and Greece, to sink their differences and form a pro-Entente
confederation. In reality the belief that they might do so, entertained most
passionately by British politicians like David Lloyd George, rested on the
mistaken assumption that the national rivalries which divided the Balkan
states could be overcome by a series of pragmatic compromises. They could
not, for the suspicions generated by the Balkan wars of 1912–13 ran too deep.
In October 1915, when the British and French finally did send troops to the

**The search for
allies**

Balkans to support their diplomacy, it was not to find new allies, but to rescue an old one. Serbia had repulsed two Austro-Hungarian invasions in 1914, but when the Austrians, acting in concert with Germany and Bulgaria, invaded Serbia for a third time in September, Serb resistance was overwhelmed. Initially the British and French landed troops at Salonika in northern Greece to open an escape route for the Serb army. When that plan failed the British wanted to withdraw the force, but encountered fierce French resistance. General Sarrail, the commander of the operation, was the darling of the left in the French Chamber of Deputies. He had been dismissed from his command on the western front, but the government of Aristide Briand knew that it had to find an important command for him or risk seeing its support in the Chamber collapse. The Anglo-French force therefore remained at Salonika for the remainder of the war.

The Salonika operation soon became a source of deep disquiet for many British policy-makers. They came to believe that France's commitment to the campaign had little to do with defeating the Central Powers and more to do with establishing French predominance in the Balkans after the war. They were correct. Briand had long been a supporter of opening a Balkan front. He saw the expansion of French influence in the region as desirable in its

Public displays of Anglo-French amity, such as this meeting between the French C-in-C, Marshal Joffre, the commander of the BEF, Field Marshal Sir John French, and his subordinate General Sir Douglas Haig, disguised the fact that by mid-1915 the two powers were pursuing radically different military agendas.

own right as it would safeguard France's interests against both the Italians and the Russians and because it might assist France's post-war economic recovery. Sarrail could not win the war for France, but he might ensure that France won the peace.

The Entente had more success in winning Italy to its side, but the latter's entry into the war was not enough to break the military stalemate. When the war began most members of the Italian ruling class had accepted that immediate Italian intervention was impossible because the Italian army and Italian public opinion were unprepared for it. But they also knew that if Italy wished to remain a great power it would have to participate in the war on the winning side. Their problem was to decide which side would win. It was not until May 1915 that Italy finally opted for the Entente, but only after driving a hard bargain in terms of territory to be ceded to them at Austria-Hungary's expense at the end of the war. But with their army poorly prepared, and their society divided, the Italians were unable to make much headway against the Austro-Hungarians and the new front was soon stalemated. Furthermore, their commitment to the common cause remained doubtful in the eyes of their allies for it was not until 1916 that Italy declared war on Germany.

On the main fronts the Russian, British, and French armies suffered nothing but defeat in 1915. The Germans broke through the Russian line at Gorlice–Tarnow in May and drove the Russians steadily eastward, capturing Warsaw on 5 August. The French were repulsed when they tried to break the German line in Champagne and Artois. The British also attacked, although on a much smaller scale, and after two defeats, at Neuve Chapelle in March and Aubers Ridge in May, they wanted to remain on the defensive in France until they had amassed sufficient troops and shells to guarantee success. But time was a luxury they were not allowed. The French were becoming increasingly impatient that the Germans remained in occupation of so much of their territory and suspicious that the Gallipoli expedition was no more than a selfish attempt by the British to expand their empire in the Middle East. Eventually, after the failure of a second major effort to break the stalemate at Gallipoli in August, the British succumbed to the demands of their allies. 'We had to make war as we must', admitted Lord Kitchener, the British secretary of state for war, 'and not as we should like to.' In September, when the French and British armies mounted a major offensive, the British acted in concert with their ally not because they expected to gain a major military victory, but because they feared that, if they did not demonstrate their willingness to assist them, either France or Russia might make a separate peace.

By the end of 1915 it was apparent that the Entente's strategy had been undermined at every turn by an almost complete lack of co-ordination. Between 6 and 8 December military representatives of the alliance therefore met at Chantilly, General Joffre's headquarters, to remedy that defect by producing a common plan for 1916. Convinced that one of the keys to the Central Powers' success in 1915 lay in the fact that they enjoyed interior lines of

1916: the Entente's plans frustrated

communication which enabled them to rush reinforcements from one threatened battlefront to another, the Entente's generals decided that in 1916 they would nullify this advantage by mounting a series of concerted offensives on the Russian, French, and Italian fronts. They hoped that this would negate the Central Powers' geographical advantage and that if they acted in concert they might be able to exhaust their manpower reserves and force them to sue for peace by the end of 1916.

But on 21 February 1916, before they could begin to put this plan into operation, the Germans began their offensive at Verdun, intended to persuade France to make peace. French diplomats curtly rejected German overtures, but, as their casualties mounted, rising to 350,000 by August when the Germans ceased offensive operations, the French turned to their allies with increasingly urgent pleas for assistance. The Italians could do little, for in May the Italian army was itself attacked by the Austrians, who for a time threatened to break through into the Lombard plain. Russian assistance was more substantial, for although what had been planned to be the main Russian summer offensive, north of the Pripyat marshes, was a failure, a subsidiary operation, executed by General Brusilov and mounted against the Austrians, was a resounding success. In three weeks in June 1916 Brusilov killed or captured between a third and a half of the Austro-Hungarian army. He thus won the first substantial victory gained by the Entente's armies since the battle of the Marne in September 1914.

The Anglo-French forces on the western front failed to achieve a similar success. Between December 1915 and April 1916 the British government was divided by a bitter debate over whether or not to approve the Chantilly plan. All ministers recognized that if they did their army was bound to suffer heavily and, with the pool of voluntary recruits fast drying up, the only way to make good its losses was to introduce conscription. Some ministers, led by the chancellor of the exchequer, Reginald McKenna, deprecated this on the grounds that, if more men were taken from industry and agriculture, Britain's deteriorating balance of payments situation would collapse and Britain would be bankrupt before the war was won. Others, like Lloyd George, insisted that it had no option. It had to gamble on winning the war before the onset of bankruptcy, for, if it did not take part in the summer offensive, the Entente alliance would collapse. The conscriptionists won the argument. Sir Douglas Haig began the battle of the Somme on 1 July hoping that he could quickly break through the German line. When he failed to do so the campaign degenerated into a grim battle of attrition. The final casualty figures are much disputed, but they probably amounted to nearly 420,000 British troops, 195,000 Frenchmen, and about 400,000 Germans.

The British and French continued doggedly with the Somme offensive even after the Germans had closed their offensive at Verdun partly because of their obligations to Russia, partly because of a persistent and probably mistaken belief that they were killing Germans more rapidly than the Germans were killing British and French soldiers, and partly to assist Romania.

Encouraged by the success of the Brusilov offensive and by the prospect of territorial gains at the expense of Austria-Hungary, Romania had joined the Entente in August. In the short term this had a demoralizing effect in Berlin and Vienna, for the Austrians had only 30,000 troops in Hungary, facing a Romanian army ten times as numerous. But Romania's entry into the war coincided with the end of the Brusilov offensive and the Central Powers were thus able to concentrate their reserves against the newest member of the Entente and crush it. By Christmas 1916 the Central Powers had occupied Bucharest, and the Chantilly plan was in ruins.

In December 1916 the Entente powers received two peace notes. The first **Peace rejected** was from Germany and was designed to sow dissension amongst its enemies. The second, from the American President Woodrow Wilson, was intended to discover if there was sufficient common ground among the warring nations to open the way for a negotiated peace. The Entente refused to be divided or to be conciliatory. It rejected the German offer as a sham because it did not include specific proposals. The reply to Wilson, drafted at an Anglo-French conference in London in late December, was superficially more conciliatory but did not seek to conceal the allies' determination to continue fighting. The Entente denied it was seeking the total overthrow of Germany but insisted that it would not make peace until the Central Powers had evacuated all occupied allied territory and provided indemnities for the damage they had done. In Europe it put forward a deliberately vaguely worded claim that it sought a peace based upon national self-determination. The reality, however, was that the original three members of the Entente had already made promises to Italy which broke that principle and the British and French still wanted to preserve the multinational Habsburg empire in some form to act as a counterbalance to Germany in eastern Europe in the post-war world. In the Middle East, in an effort to hide the reality of its imperial objectives, it disguised its ambitions beneath a rhetorical commitment to free the oppressed Jewish, Arab, and Armenian inhabitants of the Ottoman empire from the tyranny of Turkish rule. And it publicly associated itself with Wilson's vaguely formulated desire for a League of Nations, although it was careful to insist that such an organization could only follow a satisfactory peace settlement and could not be a substitute for one. The Entente's reply showed that, even after more than two years of hideously costly fighting, the idea of a compromise peace which fell short of the overthrow of its enemies was not acceptable to any of the Entente governments.

Since August 1914 the Entente's strategic policy had rested on four pillars. **The Entente's** The Royal Navy was to keep open the Entente's maritime communications. **strategy collapses** Britain was sufficiently rich to act as paymaster to the Entente. And the French and Russian armies would fight to contain the armies of the Central Powers on the continent of Europe with only minimal direct British assistance until, Kitchener predicted, a point was reached in early 1917 when the

61

armies of all of the belligerents were exhausted. Britain's New Armies could then intervene decisively in the land war, inflict a final defeat on the Central Powers, and, he secretly hoped, enable the British government to dictate the peace settlement.

But between November 1916 and May 1917 each of these pillars began to crumble. At the end of November the US government advised American bankers to stop lending money to the belligerents. This was a serious threat to Britain's economic predominance within the Entente, for by 1916 it was borrowing in America much of the money it was lending to its allies. The French refused to assist the British by shipping part of their own gold reserve to New York and so the British found themselves desperately short of the money they needed to fund their own and their allies' purchases in the USA. Britain's continued ability to act as paymaster to the Entente was fast disappearing.

At sea the Royal Navy was taken for granted by Britain's allies, who easily overlooked the part it was playing in weakening the Central Powers by blockading them. When the French politician and future wartime premier Georges Clemenceau was told that the Royal Navy would sink the German fleet if it ventured into the North Sea, he replied that 'that would make a nice hole in the water' but it would not win the war. His dismissive attitude was

In September 1915, following the collapse of the Russian position in Poland, Tsar Nicholas dismissed his uncle, the Grand Duke Nicholas, from his post as C-in-C of the Russian army, and assumed nominal command himself. It was a disastrous mistake for henceforth he had to shoulder the responsibility for Russia's defeats.

understandable in view of the fact that Britain's Grand Fleet could not inflict a decisive defeat on its German counterpart. Before 1914 the British had believed that if war came they would sink the German navy in a second Trafalgar. They were disappointed, for the numerically inferior German High Seas Fleet had no intention of encountering the Grand Fleet until, through a combination of submarines, mines, and ambushes, it had reduced the latter's superiority. British command of the surface of the sea remained secure. Frustration finally convinced the German admirals that their only hope of decisively influencing the outcome of the war was by a full-scale submarine offensive, and on 1 February 1917 Germany declared unrestricted U-boat warfare against the Entente. In April the British alone lost over half a million tons of merchant shipping and the Royal Navy's ability to protect the Entente's maritime communications was called into question.

In Russia during the autumn and winter of 1916–17 the morale of the Russian army and Russian people collapsed under the weight of a combination of appalling casualties, inflation, and food shortages. Reports prepared by the Russian police and secret service showed that most ordinary Russians thought that the war could not be won and that Russia should make peace. The result was a revolution in March 1917 and the downfall of the tsarist regime. Its successor, the Provisional Government, quickly reassured its allies that Russia would continue the struggle, but the emergence of a rival centre of power in the shape of the Petrograd Soviet soon made this seem to be a hollow promise, especially when the new Russian commander-in-chief, General Alexiev, informed Russia's allies that the morale and discipline of his army had collapsed so badly that it would not be able to mount any offensive before the summer.

That was significant because, in November 1916, undaunted by their previous failures, the British and French generals, meeting again at Chantilly, persuaded their political masters that their policy in 1917 should be much the same as it had been in 1916. Each ally would again try to mount an offensive on its own front timed to coincide with the operations of its allies. In February 1917 they held another conference, at Petrograd, designed to concert Russian strategy in 1917 with that of its western partners. It was a failure. Despite French pressure, the Russians refused to attack in concert with the planned Anglo-French offensive in the spring, and, despite Russian pressure, the British and French insisted that their forces at Salonika would remain on the defensive.

Not everyone was happy with the idea of repeating the same plan as in 1916. In Britain Lloyd George replaced H. H. Asquith as prime minister in December 1916. He came to power promising to deliver the 'knock-out blow' against Germany, but he was also determined to minimize British casualties. At the beginning of January 1917, therefore, he attended an inter-allied conference at Rome in the hope of persuading the French and Italians to launch a powerful offensive against Austria-Hungary on the Isonzo front with the objective of gaining Trieste and the Istrian peninsula. He hoped that the Italians would agree to it because it promised them territory they coveted, and that the French would do so because it would relieve pressure on Russia and because he was not asking the western front generals to cancel their offensive, merely postpone it. But he was disappointed. By November 1916 the Italian army had suffered over 600,000 casualties and had tried and failed nine times to break through on the Isonzo front in a series of vain attempts to reach the Ljubljana plain and to march on Vienna. General Luigi Cadorna, the chief of staff of the Italian army, rejected Lloyd George's idea, because he knew that if the other allies remained inactive the Central Powers would be able to concentrate their reserves against him and the Italian casualty list would only grow longer.

Stymied in his Italian plan, Lloyd George was therefore delighted when Joffre's successor as commander-in-chief of the French army, General Nivelle, offered the allies another option. He claimed that he had discovered the secret of breaching the German line within one or two days by using massive artillery bombardments. He proposed that in the spring the British and French armies should mount two concerted offensives. The British were to attack Vimy Ridge in an operation designed to absorb the German reserves, while the French mounted a larger offensive to the south intended to break the German line on the Aisne front. Lloyd George gave the plan his enthusiastic support. Haig and Sir William Robertson, the chief of the imperial general staff, did not, fearing that Nivelle was a charlatan and disappointed that his plan stood in the way of their preferred policy of attacking in Flanders in order to liberate the Belgian coast. But after an acrimonious confrontation at the Calais Conference in February 1917 they were compelled to agree and the BEF was temporarily placed under Nivelle's command.

The British generals were right to harbour doubts about Nivelle's plan. Within a few days the French lost about 100,000 men. The resulting disappointment, coming on top of so many earlier disappointments, caused the morale of a large part of the French army to collapse. Nivelle's successor, General Pétain, immediately ended his predecessor's offensive policy and determined to build up his army's reserves of munitions and tanks and to await the arrival of the Entente's newest member, the United States, before mounting another major offensive.

The entry of the USA into the war on 6 April was almost the only encouraging development for the Entente in the spring of 1917, but even it was a mixed blessing. Woodrow Wilson was almost as suspicious of allied imperialism and British 'navalism' as he was of 'Prussian militarism', and therefore deliberately refrained from signing the Pact of London. The USA became an associated power, not an ally of the Entente. It also soon became apparent that the Americans were so unprepared for war that they would not be able to give their new partners significant military assistance until 1918. For the remainder of the war, therefore, the Entente governments embarked upon the delicate task of extracting the greatest possible quantity of manpower and resources as quickly as possible from the USA while making the fewest pos-

sible concessions to those parts of Wilson's programme which ran contrary to their own national interests.

The entry of the United States into the war did not, therefore, change the essential nature of the Entente alliance. Each partner had its own selfish national interests which it was intent on pursuing. The only force keeping it together was fear; the fear its members shared of their common enemies. The consequences of this were apparent in both the extreme difficulty the members of the alliance had in agreeing a common strategic plan and the deep mutual suspicions each entertained of the others on every occasion when they discussed their ideas for the post-war settlement. The alliance was a marriage of convenience. It never became a love match.

When the Italians joined the Entente in May 1915 they drove a hard bargain for their support and the British, French, and Russians expected them to fight equally hard to achieve it. Between 1915 and 1917 General Cadorna, the Italian C-in-C, shown here with the king of Italy and Lord Kitchener, tried and failed no fewer than eleven times to break through the Austrian line on the Isonzo.

CHAPTER 5
The Balkans, 1914–1918

R. J. CRAMPTON

The third Balkan war

The First World War in the Balkans differed from the conflict elsewhere in three respects. First, the campaigns were sporadic, relatively short, and usually decisive. Second, the Balkans was the only theatre of war which involved a number of independent states. Each state had its territorial aspirations and so would sell itself to the highest bidder: diplomacy, therefore, could be as decisive as military campaigning. Third, the Balkans was the only area in which there had been recent military action. In 1912–13 Bulgaria, Serbia, Greece, and Montenegro had driven the Ottoman armies from Europe, and in a short, savage war in 1913 Greece, Serbia, and Turkey had deprived Bulgaria of much of its recent gains whilst Romania had sliced off a valuable chunk of Bulgaria's north-eastern lands. Much of official and public opinion was wary of renewed conflict, and this made any Balkan state which had the choice even more determined to align itself with the presumed eventual victors and, in doing so, to extract the highest price for its favours. The Balkans was similar to other areas in that internal economic and social problems were a vital factor in the Central Powers' defeat.

Austria-Hungary declared war on Serbia at 1.20 p.m. on 28 July 1914; it was the first time war had been declared by telegraph. That evening the Serbian capital came under bombardment from the Austrian fort at Zemun and from Habsburg gunboats on the Sava and the Danube. On 12 August three Austro-Hungarian armies crossed the Sava and the Danube into Serbia; the

Serbs had been expecting the attack further east at Belgrade and were caught off guard; they abandoned their capital, the government withdrawing to Nish. But if they had been caught off guard the Serbs were far from daunted. General Putnik rushed reinforcements westwards, some men marching 60 miles in twenty-four hours before going straight into battle. The main encounter took place from 15 to 18 August on Mount Tser in the north-west of Serbia. The invaders were checked and by 24 August had been pushed back across their borders. The Serbs, bowing to allied, and in particular to Russian, pressure, followed them. The Serbs, however, were not equipped for offensive operations and a lack of supplies soon forced them to withdraw. The Austrians, led by General Potiorek, who had been at Franz Ferdinand's side in Sarajevo a few weeks before, resumed their invasion on 8 September and took Belgrade on 2 December. Discontent grew amongst younger Ser-

General, later Marshal, Radomir Putnik, minister of war in 1914 and chief of the general staff since 1903. He masterminded the successful Serbian campaign against the Habsburg armies in 1914. Born in Kragujevac in 1847, he died in Nice in May 1917.

bian officers who in the Balkan wars had known only conspicuous success, but Putnik was in no position to contemplate a counter-offensive until western supplies, shipped via Salonika, began to reach his army.

On the day Belgrade fell Putnik at last felt able to make his riposte. He launched an attack as the Austrians were struggling to move their heavy guns and baggage trains through narrow defiles along the Kolubara river. The Serbs did not have enough ammunition for a preliminary artillery bombardment but they attacked with their customary savage valour and General Mičić's 1st Serbian Army soon broke through the centre of the enemy's line. On 15 December Belgrade was back in Serbian hands; General Putnik informed his masters of his victory with a laconic telegram to the effect that no Austrian soldiers remained on Serbian soil except as prisoners.

The Austrians had been weakened by the need to divert troops to Galicia to meet the Russian attack, but the Serbian victory on the Kolubara had been gained at great cost. The campaign had taken the lives of 100,000 Serbs, many of them battle-hardened veterans of the Balkan wars. Even more seriously, amongst the sick and wounded left behind by the Austrians were many suffering from typhus. The disease spread with devastating speed. Not only did it claim the lives of another 135,000 Serbs, civilians and soldiers, but it forced the allies to suspend rail traffic into Serbia for over a month. The Serbs, already desperately short of ammunition, were further weakened for the decisive struggle which was to come in the following year.

The only other military events in the Balkans in 1914 centred upon Albania. Created in 1913, the new state, with its strong local and tribal forces, had little chance of evolving any effective central government. By the autumn of 1914 it was dissolving into chaos as local warlords entrenched their already considerable powers. In October Greek forces moved into the areas of southern Albania claimed by Greece and the Italians occupied the strategically important island of Saseno; in December they moved into the nearby port of Valona.

The pursuit of Bulgaria

During the autumn of 1914 and the spring of 1915 there were important developments in the diplomatic arena. When war broke out Montenegro joined Serbia, but Turkey, Bulgaria, Greece, and Romania remained neutral. The Greek prime minister, Venizelos, was keen to join the allies. His king, Constantine, who had undergone military training in Germany and who had married a sister of the kaiser, was not so keen. Nor were all allied statesmen. The Russians feared the Greeks might mount competing claims to Constantinople, whilst Sir Edward Grey believed that if the Greeks joined the allies this would precipitate Turkey and Bulgaria into aligning with the other side. The Greek offer was declined but it made little difference to Turkey, which threw in its lot with the Germans and Austrians in November.

This made Bulgaria a pivotal factor. If it joined the Central Powers the supply lines between Germany and Turkey would be secured, whilst those between the western allies and Russia would be severed; and Serbia would have opponents on three sides. Bulgaria's price was as much of Macedonia as possible. The allies could offer little in this regard without the Serbs making concessions. And this they were not willing to do. In the spring of 1915 the Treaty of London between the allies and Italy made the Serbs even less willing to concede. Rightly fearing that the treaty involved granting Italy territory on the eastern seaboard of the Adriatic, the Serbs were the more determined to hold on to all of their Macedonian possessions.

The Central Powers, meanwhile, enjoyed two enormous diplomatic advantages. As the allies of Turkey they were in a position to put pressure on Constantinople to make concessions to Bulgaria; this the Porte eventually did when it agreed that the Maritsa valley, and with it the railway to Dedeagatch, should be ceded to Bulgaria. Secondly, as the enemies of Serbia they could promise to Bulgaria all Serbian territory it might capture.

The allies did not help their own cause by inept diplomacy in Sofia. Bulgarian foreign policy was determined by King Ferdinand and, to a lesser degree, by his prime minister, the pro-German Radoslavov. Rather than attempting to win over or suborn these two figures, the allies tended to court pro-allied opposition politicians who in reality had no access to the levers of power. In the final event, the most decisive factor was the shift in military fortunes. Ferdinand and Radoslavov would only commit themselves to the Central Powers if the latter appeared likely to win the war. And in the midsummer of 1915 this they seemed about to do. The entry of Italy into the war on the allied side in May had made little impact; the Russians were retreating pell-mell from Poland and, nearer to home, the allies were bogged down in a hopeless struggle on the Gallipoli beaches. When the Central Powers offered Bulgaria the lion's share of Macedonia plus the Maritsa valley Ferdinand could not refuse.

On 23 September 1915 the Bulgarian government mobilized and on 14 October King Ferdinand declared war on Serbia. In retaliation Britain and France declared war on Bulgaria on 16 October, Russian following suit a few days later.

The Bulgarians had declared war in order to join the massive Central Powers assault on Serbia. Recognizing that the German drives against the Russians were losing their impetus, and anxious to open direct communications with Turkey, Falkenhayn had begun planning the elimination of Serbia in early September. The German general August von Mackensen, fresh from his successes in Poland, was given the command—much to the chagrin of Conrad, who saw the Balkans as Austria's sphere of interest. On 6 October, Serbia was assailed from the north by three Austrian and two German armies; from the east came two Bulgarian armies, in all a total invading force of 600,000 troops. The Serbs and the Montenegrins could hardly muster half that number. By 9 October, even before the Bulgarian declaration of war, Belgrade was in enemy hands. While the Germans and Austrians pressed down from the north the Bulgarian 1st Army under General Boyadzhiev and the 2nd Army under General Todorov pressed into south-eastern Serbia and Macedonia. Within two weeks the Bulgarian 1st Army had taken Pirot and Nish, where they joined up with Mackensen's men; to the south Todorov's 2nd Army took Shtip, Veles, Kumanovo, Skopje, and Vranja. In December the Bulgarians were in Bitola, whither the Serbian government had moved when Nish was threatened. There was no major town left in Serbian hands. The Serbs, their supply lines from and their escape route to the Aegean cut, retreated to the west of the Vardar and into Kosovo Polje, where they hoped to join with the Montenegrin army. In this, as in much else, they were disappointed. Faced with the choice between surrender and a retreat across the Albanian mountains, they chose the latter. Late in 1915, harried by hostile local tribes and enemy aeroplanes, savaged by typhus, and at the mercy of the pitiless terrain and climate, the Serbian army trudged to the Adriatic coast whence the French took them to haven in Corfu. For sheer heroism and endurance the Serbian retreat has few equals.

The eventual destination of the Serbian army was Salonika. The Bulgarian mobilization had complicated yet further the political situation in Greece. A treaty of 1913 obliged Greece to go to the aid of Serbia if the latter were

Serbia overrun

Salonika

69

Personifying his army's extraordinary endurance, a Serbian soldier on guard duty during the retreat across the Albanian mountains in 1915. The convoy has reached Ljuma, the end of the carriage road. From here supplies will have to be carried by pack animal and by men.

attacked by Bulgaria. Venizelos seized this opportunity to bring Greece closer to the allies and invited them to land troops in northern Greece, promising to join the war if 150,000 allied troops were committed to the Balkan front. The allies, particularly the French, responded enthusiastically, but in Greece the anti-Venizelists, with the king at their head, though agreeing to general mobilization, refused to accept the need for Greece to join the war: the 1913 treaty, they argued, did not apply if a great power fought alongside Bulgaria against Serbia, and the king, having initially agreed to the allied landings in Salonika, now opposed them. Venizelos was forced to resign, but this could not stop the landings in Salonika, which began on 3 October.

The landings made political sense, in that it was hoped, vainly, that they would strengthen Venizelos's hand against the king and make Greek intervention in the war more likely. But once that stratagem had failed the allied presence in northern Greece served no useful military purpose. The allies could do little, if anything, to help the Serbs and the troops sent to Salonika could have been used to better effect in Gallipoli. Indeed, the landings defeated even their own political purpose. King Constantine interpreted them as a sign that the Gallipoli adventure had failed, the more so when four fresh French divisions under General Sarrail were diverted from the Dardanelles to Salonika. If the Gallipoli campaign had been abandoned, King Constantine not unreasonably calculated, he had even more cause to remain neutral because to commit himself to the allies would expose Greece to conflict with a Bulgaria victorious over Serbia and a Turkey elated by its defeat of the allies at Gallipoli.

Facing: Though the major component of the allied forces in the Balkans were British and French, the landings at Salonika were an international affair and the allies imposed joint control in the city. This photograph shows a medley of policemen: from left to right: Greek, British, French, Serbian, Russian, and Italian.

Whilst the Greeks were plunged into division and indecisiveness the fighting continued in Macedonia. Allied troops advanced up the Vardar from Salonika and at Krivolak in Macedonia confronted the Bulgarian 2nd Army.

After a sharp encounter the allies withdrew into Greek territory. The Bulgarians were keen to pursue their foe across the border and into Salonika, a prize which had narrowly eluded them in the first Balkan war three years before. This the Germans forbade. It was feared that if Bulgarian or Central Powers troops entered Greece, King Constantine would no longer be able to preserve Greek neutrality; furthermore, if the allied armies were driven out of northern Greece the survivors would be sent to strengthen British and French forces on the western front. By the end of 1915, therefore, the Bulgarians had dug in along a 300-mile front from the river Shkumbi in the Albanian mountains to the mouth of the Maritsa in eastern Thrace. It was a strong defensive position but, as subsequent events were to show, it was one which was extremely difficult to supply.

In June 1915, before their retreat across the mountains, the Serbs had occupied areas in central Albania. The Montenegrins, at the same time, had moved into the north of the country, occupying the area down to the river Drin, including Scutari. The Serbs abandoned their occupied areas when

The partition of Albania, 1916

they evacuated their troops at the end of 1915. They were replaced partly by the Bulgarians who pushed from Macedonia into south central Albania, occupying Elbasan. At the same time the Italians moved out from their bridgehead in Valona into areas previously in Greek hands, the Greek forces withdrawing without contesting the Italian expansion. The local Albanians rejoiced at least at the departure of the Greeks, whose Albanian holdings were soon reduced to a pocket around the southern town of Korca, and after the allied landings in Salonika even this was placed under French control. In January 1916 the Austrians moved into northern Albania, driving out the Montenegrins and occupying the country to a line from Vjosa to Lake Ohrid. There was subsequently little serious fighting in Albania where the First World War proved to be a period more of construction than destruction with the occupying troops of all sides building roads, bridges, and narrow-gauge railways.

Despite the Austrian move into Albania, there was little action on the Macedonian front in the first half of 1916. The allies had wished to occupy the Greek Fort Rupel which commanded the entry into the Struma valley and thence into the heart of Bulgaria, but in May they were thwarted when the Bulgarian 7th Rila Division seized the fortress.

| The Central Powers conquer Romania | In the summer of 1916 the focus of attention in the Balkans shifted northwards to Romania. An ally of Austria-Hungary and Germany before the war, Romania had nevertheless refused to enter the conflict. As with Greece and Bulgaria, both the Entente and the Central Powers courted the uncommitted state, but whereas Germany and Austria were in a strong position *vis-à-vis* Bulgaria because they could offer it unlimited amounts of enemy (Serbian) territory, in the case of Romania it was the allies who could offer unlimited amounts of enemy territory in Transylvania and the Bukovina; Bessarabia, however, was a possible complication because here Romania's aspirations could conflict with the interests of an allied power: Russia. |

By the early summer of 1916 the allies could wait no longer. With the forthcoming offensives on the Somme and in Galicia in mind, they put extreme diplomatic pressure on Bucharest, finally insisting that the Romanian prime minister, Brâtianu, make up his mind. The early successes of the Brusilov offensive were a decisive factor and Romania joined the allies. It had been agreed that Romania was to take the Bukovina and Transylvania together with a further huge slice of Hungarian territory; the French urged their allies to agree to any terms Bucharest dictated and to renege on those whose fulfilment proved difficult or disadvantageous.

The Romanian army had by August 1916 an effective strength of 19,900 officers and 813,800 men. Its main problem lay in supplies. It had little in the way of modern weaponry such as trench mortars, aeroplanes, or field telephones. Nor were armaments plentiful; internal sources were meagre, with Romanian industry being able to provide no more than two shells per gun and one round per rifle per day, and with the Straits closed imports from the

In the allies' original grand strategy for the 1916 campaign the Romanians were to be aided by a thrust northwards from Salonika. In August British and French forces moved towards Lake Doiran but they made little progress. The Bulgarians had better fortune. Their 1st Army took Lerin and advanced south-westward until checked near Ostrovo by allied troops whose main advantage was their superiority in artillery. The Bulgarian 2nd Army enjoyed more success, pushing into south-western Thrace and taking possession of the area between the lower Struma and the lower Mesta, including the port of Kavalla. This was balanced towards the end of the year by Serbian successes on the far west of the Macedonian front. A huge and immensely costly battle was fought for Mount Kaimakchalan, which the Serbs eventually took, whilst an equally bloody two-month slogging match between the allies and the Bulgarian 2nd Army on a bend in the river Cherna also ended in an allied victory. In December the Serbs entered Bitola.

The allies were also active in Greece. In August 1916 a group of Venizelist officers had launched a coup in Salonika, after which Venizelos himself left Athens, eventually joining his supporters in Salonika in October. The allies delayed recognizing the Venizelos government for fear of provoking a Greek civil war but in return they demanded more favourable treatment from the official government in Athens. To emphasize this demand and to secure control of the Athens–Salonika railway, allied troops were landed in December near the Greek capital. They were repulsed with severe losses, after which the allies recognized the Venizelos administration in Salonika.

A more salutary political solution was reached in the Korca pocket in Albania. After the Venizelist coup its French administrators handed the area over to the Salonika authorities, but this caused the indigenous Albanians to form resistance groups. In December 1916 Sarrail bowed to local pressure and granted the area autonomy under an administrative council of seven Muslim and seven Orthodox Christian Albanians. The council functioned until June 1917 when Korca returned to French military rule after Greece had formally joined the allies.

In 1917 there was relatively little action on the Macedonian front. The Bulgarian and German lines, being for the most part along the foothills of mountains, were ideal for defence; one British officer believed that well-supplied troops could hold such positions for ever. How important that qualification was did not become apparent until 1918.

In Greece the allies were able to record a diplomatic victory. After recognizing the Venizelist government in Salonika an allied blockade had been mounted against those areas in Greece which remained loyal to King Constantine, the excuse being that the allies should be paid compensation for the losses suffered in the landing of December 1916. In June 1917 Constantine bowed to allied pressure and went into exile. Venizelos returned to Athens and a parliament boycotted by the opposition agreed to commit Greece to the allied cause. Nine divisions were placed at the disposal of the allied commander in Salonika, as was the far from inconsiderable Greek navy.

The Entente and Greece, 1916–1917

Romania seeks an armistice

These Greek forces were in no position to contribute to the main fighting in the Balkans in 1917 because this took place on the Romanian front. The Romanian army had been reorganized by a French military mission and by the summer of 1917 had almost half a million men in regular units with a further quarter of a million in reserve and in training groups. As part of the grand allied strategy to finish the war in 1917 the Romanians were to attack across the Seret. On 22 July the 2nd Army under General Averescu took the offensive near Mârâşti. Despite initial gains the advance could not continue. The Russians' reverses to the north forced them to withdraw some units from Romania, whilst political disaffection spread among those which remained. The Romanian commanders opted for caution. Even if it had little impact on the Austro-German forces ranged against it, Averescu's advance did, however, affect Mackensen, who was attacking from the south. He was forced to divert his 9th Army into less favourable territory. Between 9 and 16 August he met the Romanians near Mârâşeşti on the Seret. It was the largest encounter in which the Romanian forces took part; after huge losses Mackensen's advance was halted.

Mârâşeşti could be accounted a Romanian victory but it was one which greatly depleted Romanian reserves. As Russia's commitment to the war faltered Romania's position became even more dangerous. Should Russia conclude a peace allied supplies would be unobtainable, and, with much of the armaments industry and the Ploeşti oilfields in occupied areas, Romania

The spoils of war in the Balkans: undamaged grain warehouses in Constanţa, Romania. Each of the warehouses held 750,000 tons of precious grain; they are shown here in 1917 guarded by German soldiers.

could not sustain modern warfare. With the Bolshevik seizure of power in Petrograd the position became much worse, and, when they learned that the Russians were to ask Mackensen for discussions on an armistice, the Romanians joined them.

A ceasefire between the Romanians and the Central Powers was negotiated at Focşani early in December 1917 but the political establishment was in no hurry to sign it. The Germans had no more patience than the British and the French had shown in 1916 and in February 1918 Mackensen gave Brătianu four days to sign a peace or face renewed war. Brătianu resigned and on 5 March a government under General Averescu signed a preliminary peace at Buftea. Two days earlier the Treaty of Brest-Litovsk had removed Russia from the war, leaving Romania totally isolated.

Averescu soon resigned and made way for Marghiloman, a noted Germanophile who had remained in Bucharest after the defeats of 1916. It was hoped that his pro-German credentials would soften the harsh terms of Buftea. They did not. The Treaty of Bucharest, signed on 7 May, was every bit as rigorous. Romania was to demobilize most of its army and hand its equipment to the Germans; it had to relinquish the Carpathian passes and the Dobrudja; and the Romanian economy was virtually bound over to the Germans who were to take control of the country's ports and of navigation on the Danube, and to enjoy a ninety-year monopoly over the Romanian oil industry. A parliament elected on a narrow franchise ratified the treaty but King Ferdinand refused to sign it.

The king's refusal to sign the Treaty of Bucharest was symptomatic of the general truth that the Central Powers' victory and dominance in the Balkans were more apparent than real. In all areas of central and eastern Europe populations facing ever intensifying shortages of food and fuel, as well as the seemingly endless waste of human life, were easy prey for Bolshevik and socialist agitators. In the military sector condign punishment of agitators could contain the dangers but such measures could do little to restore military morale. It was in Bulgaria, the Central Powers' chief ally in the Balkans, that the corrosion was at its greatest.

Entente victory in Macedonia

In the first place supplying the army in Macedonia was an extremely difficult task. There was only one railway in the area and it ran north–south, whereas to bring *matériel* from Bulgaria a north-east to south-west axis was needed. Supplies had to be brought along the roads, but even these were few in number and so inadequate in quality that they were mostly inoperable as far as Bulgaria's limited number of motorized vehicles were concerned. Draught animals alone could negotiate most of the mountain tracks, but so long and so slow were the journeys involved that a high proportion of the goods carried had to be fodder for the animals themselves.

To maintain the supply columns a huge number of draught animals were requisitioned for the army with an inevitably deleterious effect on an agricultural productivity already affected by massive mobilization of manpower,

Winter always made transport difficult in the Balkans where roads were seldom more than unpaved tracks. Here a German army supply wagon drawn by oxen makes slow progress through the Romanian mud, 1917.

Bulgaria having called up a greater proportion of its population than any other state engaged in the First World War. The supply of food to both the army and the civilian population was further impeded by the activity of the Germans. Official procurement agencies cornered part of Bulgaria's output but unofficial purchasing by German troops took at least as much. The Germans criss-crossed the country in lorries setting up telephone lines and the soldiers bought what they could where they could, paying high prices in German marks, which had become legal tender in Bulgaria in December 1915. The Bulgarian peasants frequently withheld food from the official German and Bulgarian purchasing authorities in order to sell at higher prices to German soldiers; in 1917 the Germans even established a separate railway station near Sofia to entrain their food; the station was off limits to Bulgarian personnel.

By the beginning of 1918 food shortages in Bulgarian cities were becoming acute. There were a number of disturbances and in the occupied territories the threat of widespread civil disorder posed a danger to the supply lines to the Macedonian front, whilst an attempt to conscript young men in some parts of occupied Serbia provoked outright rebellion. The situation became more acute as the year progressed. An expected improvement following the conquest of the grain-rich Dobrudja failed to materialize. The Bulgarians had expected that the area would be ceded to them but the Treaty of Bucharest placed it under joint Austro-German-Bulgarian control. Radoslavov resigned, complaining that Bulgaria had been treated more like a conquered enemy than a victorious ally. Nor were the Bulgarians allowed to purchase sizeable quantities of grain in Ukraine. A Bulgarian officer sent to the area in 1918 was deliberately delayed in Budapest and Lvov so that he could not arrive before Austrian officials, and when the port of Odessa did come into use another Bulgarian officer had to resort to the threat of force to prevent Austrian soldiers unloading a cargo of food destined for Bulgaria. By the summer of 1918 the food shortages in Bulgaria were critical and were affecting front-line troops as well as civilians.

By September 1918 the Bulgarian army was thoroughly demoralized. Ill-fed, ill-supplied with ammunition, resentful at the privations of its families and at the comparative well-being of Germans in nearby trenches, the Bulgarian soldier was in no state to meet the onslaught which well-equipped troops under Sarrail's successor, General Franchet d'Esperey, launched from Salonika in August. By the middle of September the Bulgarian army was retreating into the narrow defiles of the Struma valley where it was a juicy target for allied pilots. By the end of the month discontent was manifest both amongst troops and civilians. On 27 September a Bulgarian delegation arrived in Salonika to sue for peace. An armistice was signed on 29 September. Bulgaria, the last state to join the German-dominated coalition, had become the first to leave it. In doing so it precipitated the final collapse of the Central Powers.

Military action in the Balkans did not cease with the Bulgarian armistice. On 10 November, after Austria-Hungary had accepted allied peace terms, the Romanians re-entered the fray, desperate to establish some claim to the spoils which would now be available.

Surprisingly, perhaps, the final collapse of the Central Powers in the Balkans had come about through social deprivation rather than national tensions. In 1914 5,000 Bosnian Serbs had joined the Serbian army's 1st Serbian Volunteer Division and there were three battalions of Hercegovenians in the Montenegrin army, but most of the Habsburg monarchy's south Slav subjects remained loyal to their emperor and his army. This the Serbs did not forget.

CHAPTER 6
Turkey's War

ULRICH TRUMPENER

Turkey enters the war

When the Ottoman government entered into a secret alliance with Germany on 2 August 1914 it did so because of its concern for the balance of power in the Near East. Germany, in turn, saw the opportunity to add to its military strength and to launch a holy war, which might foment rebellion across Asia and Africa among the Muslim peoples of the Entente empires. With its cabinet divided, Turkey's foreign policy was dominated by an inner group who saw involvement in Great Power politics as a means to avoid the further fragmentation of the Ottoman empire, but who were themselves split as to whether the Central Powers or the Entente presented the best option. In one sense Turkey's decision was made for it by Entente indifference: Ottoman neutrality, which the British favoured, would not enable the Young Turks to escape the spiral of territorial decline and financial indebtedness. In another it was eased by German ships and German gold. By late October 1914 the men who dominated the central committee of the ruling Ittihat ve Terakki (Union and Progress) party were briefly but sufficiently agreed to release the Turkish fleet into the Black Sea to attack Russia's naval bases. War was declared at the beginning of November, and holy war proclaimed two weeks later.

The leading figures of the Ottoman government were inspired by the hope of regaining at least some of the former possessions the empire had lost in previous decades, both in Europe and elsewhere. Moreover, some of the most influential ministers, and their supporters in the party, were determined to expand eastward into the Caspian region and beyond. This 'pan-Turanian' dream was accompanied by the firm determination of practically everyone to restore the Ottoman empire to the status of a fully sovereign

80

state, that is, to abolish the capitulatory system and various other special privileges which certain foreign governments had been granted by the Ottoman sultan in the past.

The empire was in no particular position to fight against some of the major powers of the world, but with brave soldiers and with growing technical assistance from its central European allies, it kept going for four long years. Apart from having a chronically empty treasury, limited industrial facilities, and a woefully underdeveloped transportation system, the sprawling empire of the Turks was also severely handicapped in its war effort by the existence of several large ethnic-religious population groups whose loyalty to the sultan's government was, at best, uncertain. Some Kurdish tribes were reluctant to abide by the rules and regulations issued by the authorities, while a good many Arabs, Armenians, and Greeks dreamt of greater autonomy for the regions they lived in or even of outright separation from the Ottoman empire.

With a total population of well over 20 million, the Ottoman empire was able to recruit approximately 3 million soldiers during the Great War, but due to high rates of casualties, and even higher rates of disease and desertion, the sultan's army at any one time rarely had more than 500,000 men under arms. At the beginning of the war, roughly seventeen Ottoman divisions were deployed in the region around Istanbul (Constantinople), ten divisions in eastern Anatolia, seven divisions in Syria/Palestine, four divisions in the Arabian peninsula (Hijaz and Yemen), and two divisions in Mesopotamia (Iraq). During the next three years, several additional divisions were formed, and many of the existing ones redeployed. In 1916, for example, seven divisions were transferred to various European theatres of war, namely two to Galicia, three to Romania, and two to Macedonia. The two divisions dispatched to Galicia made a valiant contribution to the consolidation of the eastern front after the Brusilov offensive and suffered heavy casualties.

As the war dragged on, most Ottoman divisions became woefully understaffed and suffered from growing shortages of draft animals, equipment, and weaponry. Indeed, in some theatres of war, many Turkish soldiers were dressed in rags and had totally inadequate footwear. Beginning in the autumn of 1914, and much more so from mid-1915 on, Germany and (on a much smaller scale) the Austro-Hungarian monarchy transferred military, naval, and aviation specialists, as well as small units of service and combat troops, to Turkey. They also sent numerous trainloads of coal and equipment to Istanbul. In 1917, Germany's contribution to Ottoman combat strength was further raised, when around six battalions of infantry and machine gunners were transferred to Syria. Called the *Asienkorps*, these units, plus small groups of gunners and combat engineers, would provide much needed support to the Ottoman divisions in Palestine.

While, under peacetime laws, Christian and Jewish citizens of the Ottoman empire were eligible for military service, most of those soldiers were transferred into (unarmed) labour battalions in 1915. Among the exceptions was Moshe Shertok, who served as a warrant officer on the Macedonian front and later, thanks to his knowledge of languages, as an interpreter for a German unit commander in Palestine. Under his new name, Sharett, he would become the prime minister of Israel in 1953.

Serving as minister of the interior from 1909 to 1911, and again from 1913 onwards, Mehmet Talât Bey (later Pasha) was probably the most influential member of the Ittihat ve Terakki regime. In February 1917, he formally became head of the Ottoman cabinet as grand vizier. After the war he lived in Berlin, where he was assassinated by an Armenian student in 1921. Called by Russian foreign minister Sazonov 'the most infamous figure of our time.' Talât's mortal remains were solemnly transferred to Istanbul in 1944.

Following the ascent of the Young Turks to power, the Ottoman officer corps had been drastically rejuvenated. As a result, supreme command during the war years was exercised by a general barely 32 years old in 1914, Enver Pasha, who held both the post of war minister and that of vice-generalissimo (acting on behalf of the powerless Sultan Mehmet V). Though he was assisted and advised by several well-trained German staff officers, including Major General Friedrich Bronsart von Schellendorff (1914–17) and Major General Hans von Seeckt (1918), Enver's conduct of the war at all times was governed by what he (and his associates in the cabinet and in the Ittihat ve Terakki party) perceived to be in his country's best interest. Among those associates, Mehmet Talât was undoubtedly the most important, serving first as minister of the interior (1913 to July 1918) and then also as grand vizier (February 1917–October 1918). The radical and nationalistic policies of Talât and his supporters were at least occasionally curbed by a more moderate (and less Germanophile) group headed by Mehmet Cavit Bey, who ran the Ministry of Finance in 1914 and again from February 1917 on.

Like Enver, almost all Ottoman army and corps commanders were in their thirties, usually holding the rank of brigadier or colonel. Moreover, most Ottoman divisions were headed by mere lieutenant colonels who were sometimes even younger than that. Many of these young warriors would play a major role in Turkish national life during the next five decades. The most famous of them were Mustafa Kemal Pasha (later Atatürk), president of Turkey 1923–38; and Mustafa Ismet Pasha (Inönü), who followed Atatürk as president (1938–50) and served as prime minister of Turkey on three different occasions, with his last tenure in office extending from 1961 to 1965. But there were many other war veterans with similar longevity, such as Ahmet Fevzi (Çakmak), chief of the general staff until 1944; and Kâzim (Karabekir) and Ali Ihsan (Sâbis), who both sat in the Turkish National Assembly until their deaths in 1948 and 1957 respectively.

While most of the youthful Ottoman army leaders brought energy and *élan* to their tasks, they often lacked experience in the finer points of staff work, especially in logistics, and thereby taxed the patience of many German officers who served with or under them. As for the most senior German military figures in Ottoman service—General Otto Liman von Sanders (1913–18), Admiral Guido von Usedom (1914–18), Field Marshal Colmar Baron von der Goltz (1914–16), and General Erich von Falkenhayn (1917–18)—they suffered numerous bouts of frustration over the conduct of some of their Turkish colleagues, but all of them remained great admirers of the stamina and tenacity of the ordinary Anatolian soldier.

The general underdevelopment of the Ottoman empire was most strikingly reflected in its transportation system. The railway network in 1914 had 3,580 miles of track serving an area of 679,360 square miles. The so-called Baghdad line, with a total length of 580 miles, had three big gaps in it, necessitating multiple loadings and reloadings for all personnel or supplies moving between Istanbul and the eastern and south-eastern regions of the empire— Mesopotamia, Syria, Palestine, Arabia, etc. During the latter part of the war, tunnels through both the Taurus and Amanus ranges were completed, but the large gap existing in the region east of the Euphrates river was only partly closed before the end of hostilities. The Ottoman regions adjacent to Russia had no train service at all, requiring transportation by oxcart and foot marches over primitive roads from the nearest railheads of 370 miles or more. As for the Ottoman garrisons in the Hijaz, they depended on a rickety pilgrim railway extending from Syria to Medina, while the Ottoman VII Corps in Yemen was completely cut off from the rest of the empire by impassable deserts and mountains.

With only a few roads in passable shape, maritime transport would have been of great value to the Turks, especially in the Black Sea, the eastern Mediterranean, and the Red Sea, but massive allied naval superiority in all of

Narrow gauge tracks leading to a partially finished tunnel on the Baghdad line. On 9 October 1918, just three weeks before the Armistice of Mudros took the Ottoman empire out of the war, a standard-gauge track through the Taurus Mountains was completed, thus allowing for the first time uninterrupted train service between the Bosporus and Syria.

these waters (except parts of the Black Sea) made it all but impossible for the Turks to use these sea lanes during the war. If one considers that coal and other fuels were in short supply or located in inaccessible places, it is amazing that the Ottoman war effort did not collapse any sooner than it did.

Anatolia and Transcaucasia

The first major Turkish clashes with the enemy occurred in eastern Anatolia, where units of the Russian Caucasus Army advanced to Köprü-Köi and inflicted heavy losses on the Ottoman 3rd Army. In mid-December 1914 the Turks launched an ambitious counter-offensive. Personally directed by Enver Pasha, the operation involved a hazardous flanking movement by several Ottoman divisions through snow-covered mountains and high plateaux. The operation soon got bogged down around the Russian railhead of Sarikamish, and large numbers of Ottoman soldiers were either killed in action or froze to death. Many others were captured, including the commander of IX Corps and three divisional commanders. (Two of them eventually escaped and returned to Turkey.)

Facing, above: The landing of British, Anzac, and French troops on the Gallipoli Peninsula in April 1915 was intended to open the Straits to Entente warships, bring about the rapid collapse of Turkey, and enable the western allies to give Russia direct assistance. Instead, it marked the start of a nine-month-long battle of attrition which weakened the Turks but which also cost the Entente at least 250,000 soldiers.

This catastrophe in the Armenian highlands cost the Turks well over 60,000 men and over 60 guns, but just as in the spectacular defeat of General Samzonov's army in the battle of Tannenberg four months earlier, it did not mean the end for the losing side. With their ranks gradually being replenished and placed under a new commander, Mahmut Kâmil Pasha, the seventeen divisions of the Ottoman 3rd Army engaged in a war of movement around Lake Van and elsewhere for the remainder of the year.

It was during this campaign that the infamous Armenian deportations began. Citing Armenian rebelliousness and collaboration with the Russians (which in a few localities was certainly true), the Ottoman authorities in April 1915 launched a brutal programme of deportations and massacres in the eastern provinces which would continue into 1916 and cost hundreds of thousands of men, women, and children their lives. According to official Turkish pronouncements, the total toll was less than half a million and was a regrettable by-product of a legitimate national security programme. Most Armenians and many western historians regard the 'deportations' as a deliberate attempt at genocide which victimized at least a million people and probably more.

Facing, below: Fighting on the barricades in Belgrade in the early morning of 9 October 1915, when the Habsburg army launched its successful assault on the city. The fighting is taking placed beneath the Kalemegdan, the ancient fortress at the confluence of the Danube and the Sava. Old Belgrade, with its mosques as well as churches, is clearly visible.

The year 1916 brought fresh defeats to the Turks. Under its new commander, Grand Duke Nikolai Nikolaevich, the Russian Caucasus Army launched a surprise winter offensive along the whole front. On 16 February Russian units seized the obsolete fortress of Erzurum, capturing over 13,000 Turks in the process. Other Russian units, supported by strong naval forces, occupied the principal Black Sea port city of Trabzon on 18 April, thereby further dislocating the supply services of the Ottoman 3rd Army. The latter was now led by the fiery Ferit Vehip Pasha (who would end his career in 1935/6 advising the emperor of Abyssinia during the Italian invasion of that country). Despite great effort, the Turks suffered further setbacks during the following weeks, losing Bayburt on 16 July and Erzincan and 17,000 prisoners nine days later.

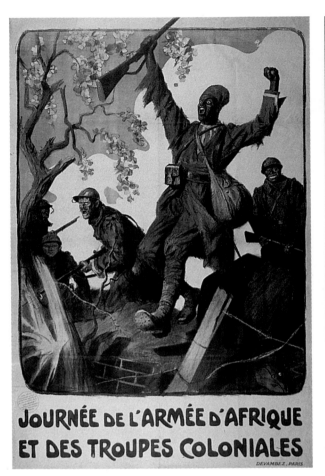

JOURNÉE DE L'ARMÉE D'AFRIQUE
ET DES TROUPES COLONIALES

DEVAMBEZ, PARIS

LE BLÉ
CANADIEN

Pour Vendre Nos
Blés, il Faut
Souscrire à
L'EMPRUNT
de la
VICTOIRE

Soldiers from all parts of the French colonial empire fought on the western front against the Germans. The men of the *Tirailleurs Sénégalais* came from French West Africa. French African troops were used in the post-war occupation of the Rhineland to the anger of many Germans.

North American wheat was the most efficient wartime food import in relation both to shipping space and calorific content. The transatlantic journey was shorter than that from elsewhere in the world, and the bulk-to-weight ratio of cereals was much more favourable than that of livestock. The effect on working-class diets in Britain, particularly when combined with a guaranteed minimum food intake through rationing, was highly beneficial to health.

Because of the existing bottlenecks in the Baghdad line, the transfer of 'fresh' Ottoman divisions from Gallipoli and Thrace to eastern Anatolia took six months to complete, and it was only in August that the Ottoman 2nd Army, under Ahmet Izzet Pasha (Furgaç), was ready to strike into the left flank of the Russian Caucasus Army from the region around Diyarbakir. Though Izzet's troops recaptured some lost ground, including the towns of Bitlis and (temporarily) Muş (west of Lake Van), no decisive blows were delivered, and the east Anatolian front eventually froze in place. By the end of 1916, nearly half of all Ottoman troops had been deployed against the Russian adversary, a point often overlooked in western accounts of the war.

The year 1917, the year of the Russian revolutions, would increasingly bring relief to the Turks in eastern Anatolia; indeed, during the summer hostilities died down almost everywhere in that theatre. Once the Bolsheviks took power in Petrograd, formal armistices were concluded both at Brest-Litovsk (affecting the eastern front in Europe) and at Erzincan (governing the ceasefire in eastern Anatolia). With the Russian Caucasus Army rapidly disintegrating and the peoples of Transcaucasia asserting their independence from Lenin's regime, the Ottoman government saw a welcome opportunity to regain its lost territories and, indeed, to establish control over most of Transcaucasia. As a result, on 12 February 1918 Ottoman troops began crossing the armistice lines against minimal resistance from Armenian and (later) some Georgian units. Advancing steadily eastward, the Ottoman I Caucasus Corps, under Kâzim Karabekir Pasha, took Erzincan on 13 February, Erzurum on 12 March, and then closed up to the border. Simultaneously, the II Caucasus Corps, under Shevket Pasha, moved along the coast toward the pre-war Russo-Turkish border, taking Trabzon on 17 February. Further south, the Ottoman IV Caucasus Corps, under Ali Ihsan (Sâbis), likewise made good progress, recapturing Van and reaching the pre-war borders with Persia and Russia by the second week of April.

Facing, left: Soldiers from all parts of the French colonial empire fought on the Western Front against the Germans. The men of the *Tirailleurs Sénégalais* came from French West Africa. French African troops were used in the post-war occupation of the Rhineland to the anger of many Germans.

A Kurdish cavalry squadron behind the Transcaucasian front. The white horses provided some camouflage in the snow-covered high plateaus of eastern Anatolia.

During the deportation of the Armenian population from the eastern provinces of the Ottoman empire in 1915 and subsequent years, hundreds of thousands were massacred *en route* or died of hunger and disease.

Shortly thereafter the Turks continued their advance, occupying the regions they had lost to Russia in 1878. They took the port city of Batum on 15 April and the great Russian fortress of Kars about ten days later. Despite German protests, they then moved on in the direction of Tbilisi and Baku. While the Germans sent troops to Georgia to keep that newly created republic out of Turkish hands, they were unable to block the 'Army of Islam' from moving towards the Caspian Sea. Composed of over 10,000 Azerbaijani volunteers and about 6,000 Ottoman soldiers, that task force was commanded by Enver Pasha's younger brother, Lieutenant Colonel Nuri Bey (Killigil), and reached Kurdamir, half-way between Elizavetpol and Baku, by mid-July. With help from a small British unit under Major General L. C. Dunsterville, the newly formed 'Centrocaspian Dictatorship', made up of Social Revolutionaries and Armenian nationalists, successfully defended the city against Nuri's troops until 15 September, but then departed under chaotic conditions.

The Turkish conquest of oil-rich Baku was greatly resented both by Lenin's government in Moscow and by the Germans, but neither could do much about the *fait accompli*. The wrath of Berlin was heightened by the fact that the Ottoman armies in the other theatres of war, especially in Iraq and Palestine, were on the brink of collapse and badly needed support from units now squandered on the Turkish drive to the east. Suffice it to note that the Turks stayed in Baku until November, when they slowly withdrew from all Trancaucasian regions of the defunct Russian empire.

Mesopotamia

As soon as Ottoman intervention had become clear, Anglo-Indian troops had landed in the Shat el Arab and, after overcoming weak Turkish resistance, reached Basra on 22 November 1914. By the end of the year, the British had advanced to the confluence of the Tigris and Euphrates rivers. Despite harsh climatic conditions, they gradually moved up both rivers and had reached Selman Pak, *c.*30 miles south of Baghdad, by early October 1915.

The first Ottoman commander in Iraq, Colonel Subhi Bey, had been taken prisoner in December 1914; his successor, Lieutenant Colonel Süleyman Askerî, had committed suicide in April 1915. Appointed in his stead, Colonel Yusef Nur-ed-Din eventually slowed down the British advance. By the time the elderly German field marshal Baron von der Goltz reached Baghdad to take charge of the situation in both Iraq and Persia in early December 1915, Nur-ed-Din's troops had repulsed a major attack by General Charles Town-shend's 6th (Poona) Division at Ctesiphon and subsequently encircled it at Kut al Amara. Four months later, after several British attempts to relieve him had failed, Townshend and his men surrendered to the new leader of what was now known as the Ottoman 6th Army, Brigadier Halil Pasha (Kut). One of Enver's youthful uncles, Halil would continue as senior commander in the Iraq/Persia theatre until June 1918, losing Baghdad (in March 1917), Samara (in April 1917), Tikrit (in November 1917), and Hit (on the Euphrates, in March 1918) to the strongly reinforced Anglo-Indian forces arrayed against him. Under his successor, Ali Ihsan (Sâbis), the Ottoman 6th Army tempor-

A company of Ottoman infantry on the march. Well-clad and properly equipped at the beginning of the war, many Turkish regiments would eventually become groups of emaciated figures in rags and without adequate footwear.

C.7654.

arily rallied against the British but was eventually pushed back towards Mosul.

According to the official British history of *The Campaign in Mesopotamia, 1914–1918*, the Anglo-Indian forces deployed in Iraq during the war numbered close to 890,000 officers and men, of whom over 27,600 died of wounds or disease, while approximately 51,400 were wounded and close to 13,500 went missing or were taken prisoner. The Ottoman forces employed in that theatre were only about half that number, but their casualties were equally heavy, especially as a result of logistic bottlenecks which condemned many Turkish soldiers to go hungry and without shoes for long periods of time.

Persia

Since parts of 'neutral' Persia were garrisoned by both Russian and British troops, the Turks, encouraged by Berlin, invaded northern Persia in late 1914 and had advanced as far as Tabriz by January 1915. Russian troops counterattacked and eventually pushed the Turks back to the border. During the next two years, the Turks, with the support of some Persian irregular forces and a handful of German officers, engaged in intermittent fighting against a Russian expeditionary cavalry corps under General N. N. Baratov, but once the Bolsheviks took over in the autumn of 1917, the task of resisting the Turks in Persia fell more and more on British shoulders.

While 'neutral' Persia found itself turned into a battlefield between the two hostile camps and suffered accordingly, the Germans also launched several small expeditions through Persia to reach Afghanistan and incite its ruler and people to action against the Entente. The Turks, who had aspirations of their own in central Asia, gave little support to these German efforts and frequently blocked them altogether.

Gallipoli

As soon as the Turks had entered the war, on 3 November 1914, an Anglo-French naval squadron had bombarded the outer forts guarding the Dardanelles. Three and a half months later, on 20 February 1915, a more systematic naval attack was launched which culminated in a major battle on 18 March, during which several allied battleships were sunk or crippled in a newly laid Turkish minefield. By the time British empire and French colonial troops, under the overall command of Sir Ian Hamilton, were landed on 25 April on both sides of the Dardanelles, the Ottoman defences had been effectively reorganized and reinforced under the direction of General Liman von Sanders and Admiral von Usedom. Although British and Anzac troops repeatedly came close to seizing the commanding heights of the Gallipoli peninsula, General Liman von Sanders's 5th Army, supported by units of the Ottoman 2nd Army and some German naval gunners, eventually prevailed and the allied divisions, now commanded by Sir Charles Monro, withdrew from their bridgeheads in December 1915 and January 1916.

It was during the Gallipoli campaign that the young commander of the Ottoman 19th Division, Lieutenant Colonel Mustafa Kemal (Atatürk), first

General Otto Liman von Sanders in Haifa. Having successfully defended Gallipoli in 1915, he reluctantly accepted command of the crumbling Turkish front in Palestine in February 1918. The scion of a wealthy bourgeois family (his grandparents were converts from Judaism), Liman was unique among German generals in the Ottoman empire in surrounding himself with capable Turkish staff officers and adjusting his tactics to local circumstances.

made a name for himself by bold and decisive action, and was eventually elevated to a major sector command, taking charge of the 'Anaforta Group'. The successful defence of the Dardanelles not only heightened the pride and self-confidence of the Turks but also contributed to the weakening of the Russian war effort by keeping a vital communications route between Russia and the west closed. This great Ottoman achievement, alas, was bought at a high cost in lives and equipment, and several Turkish divisions had to be rebuilt from scratch in 1916.

Even before entering the war, the Turks had begun preparing for a descent on Egypt. Encouraged by Berlin, an expeditionary corps of about 20,000 men set out in January 1915 on a forced march through the Sinai desert, but its attempt to cross the Suez Canal failed. While overall command in this theatre of war was in the hands of General Ahmet Cemal Pasha (a leading member of the Ittihat ve Terakki party, and simultaneously also navy minister in the cabinet), the front-line action in the Sinai and southern Palestine was directed increasingly by a Bavarian colonel, Friedrich Baron Kress von Kressenstein, who eventually, in 1917, was named commander of the Ottoman 8th Army.

Egypt and Palestine

After numerous smaller raids, a second major advance to the Suez Canal was attempted by the Turks in July 1916, but they were effectively repulsed in the battle of Romani. Thereafter, British empire forces slowly worked their way north through the Sinai desert. Pushed back in the first two battles of Gaza, they broke through the Turkish lines in the third Gaza battle and captured Jerusalem in December 1917. By that time, the former head of the German supreme army command (OHL), General Erich von Falkenhayn, had arrived with a large staff of German officers—initially to plan the recovery of Baghdad but in practice to direct the defence of Palestine. However, his military setbacks as well as growing friction with various Ottoman dignitaries led to his recall in February 1918.

To replace him as commander of 'Army Group Yilderim', Enver Pasha sent General Liman von Sanders to Palestine. With three exhausted and undermanned Ottoman armies under his command, he tried desperately to get reinforcements and supplies for the coming showdown with General Allenby's forces, but his efforts were largely in vain. By September 1918, the thinly held Ottoman front line ran from the Mediterranean coast north of Jaffa roughly east-south-east through the Judaean hills into the high plateaux east of the Jordan river. The opening British attack, launched on 19 September, rapidly smashed the Ottoman 8th Army under General Cevad Pasha (Çobanli), forcing the adjacent 7th Army, under Brigadier Mustafa Kemal Pasha (Atatürk), to pull in its right wing. In the area east of the Jordan river, the 4th Army, under Brigadier Mersinli Cemal Pasha, likewise soon found itself threatened by potential flank attacks, and General Liman von Sanders himself barely escaped capture during a cavalry raid on Nablus. During the next six weeks, the remnants of his army group (Turks, Germans, and a handful of Austro-Hungarians) retreated northward under steady harassment from the air and by roving Arab bands. By late October, Allenby's forces had overrun all of Palestine and Lebanon plus most of Syria, taking 75,000 prisoners in the process.

Faced with the utter rout of its forces in Palestine and threatened by allied troops advancing through the Balkan peninsula, the Ottoman government, now headed by General Izzet Pasha (Furgaç), opened armistice negotiations with the British on 20 October. After prolonged discussions, during which the French vainly tried to secure a seat at the table, on 30 October the Ottoman delegation, headed by Navy Minister Hüseyin Rauf Bey (Orbay), signed the armistice agreement aboard Sir Somerset A. Gough-Calthorpe's flagship, HMS *Agamemnon*, off the island of Lemnos.

While the armistice of Mudros effectively took Turkey out of the war, some Ottoman garrisons held on to their positions for a while longer. In Medina, for instance, the Turks proved reluctant to leave. In Mosul, facing British demands after the armistice for the surrender of the town, the local commander initially refused to comply. The fact that the British only gained possession of Mosul in mid-November 1918 would later cause controversy over the legal status of the area.

Arabia

After bargaining with both the British and his nominal Ottoman overlords, the grand sherif of Mecca, Hussein, threw in his lot with the western allies. In June 1916 he proclaimed the independence of the Hijaz and launched assaults on the Ottoman garrisons in Mecca and Medina. Mecca quickly surrendered, while the Ottoman troops in Medina were able to hold out until the end of the war. During the next two and a half years, Arab insurgents, guided by Colonel T. E. Lawrence and other British officers, would conduct raids against the Hijaz railway and isolated Turkish army posts. Eventually, Hussein's followers would participate in large numbers in General Allenby's last great offensive, harassing the retreating Turkish columns and occupying a number of important towns along the way, including Damascus. Their expectation of huge rewards in the post-war peace settlement would, however, prove largely mistaken.

The intervention of the Ottoman empire on the side that lost the war ultimately led to its disintegration and opened the door to drastic political changes throughout the Middle East. However, before they suffered defeat and the dismemberment of their sprawling empire, the Turks played a remarkably active role in the Great War and contributed to its geographical extension and, at least indirectly, to both its prolongation and its intensification. Both by their military efforts and by launching a potentially dangerous programme of subversion and Islamic propaganda in various regions of Asia and Africa, especially in the Maghreb, the Turks tied down large contingents of British empire and Russian troops (as well as a smaller number of French and Italian divisions) which might otherwise have been used against the Central Powers in Europe. Perhaps even more important, with minimal help from their German and Austro-Hungarian allies, the Turks successfully prevented the use of the Black Sea Straits for communications between Russia and her western allies and thereby contributed significantly to the weakening of the tsarist war effort. The alliance with the Turks cost the Germans a great deal of money—roughly 5 billion marks in loans and credits, part of it paid in gold and silver—but there can be no doubt that the Turks contributed more than their fair share to the common war effort of the Central Powers.

    After 1918, bitter criticism of the Ittihat ve Terakki wartime leaders and of their support of the Central Powers dominated official debate in Turkey for over two decades, but in more recent years Enver Pasha, Talât Pasha, and most of their numerous associates in the government and the party have gradually been rehabilitated in the public mind and in the historical literature of Turkey.

CHAPTER 7
The War in Africa

DAVID KILLINGRAY

Africa became involved in the Great War in 1914 because most of the continent was under European imperial control. Initial attempts to keep the continent neutral failed; Africa's economic resources, its strategic ports, lines of communication, and radio stations inevitably drew the colonies into what became a total war. In a conflict that was not its own, the peoples, resources, and materials of Africa were mobilized for the European war effort. The first British shots of the war were fired by African troops invading the German colony of Togoland, and German African soldiers (*askaris*) led by General von Lettow-Vorbeck in East Africa fought on until the armistice was announced in Europe in November 1918. In a global conflict the campaigns in Africa were minor sideshows. Compared to people in Europe, most Africans hardly felt the direct impact of the war, other than in East and Central Africa where the death toll and devastation were high. Nevertheless, the war touched the lives of millions of Africans who were affected by its economic, social, and political consequences.

The military campaigns

By August 1914 most of Africa had been recently divided between the European powers. In many of those territories colonial administrative control was thinly spread and tenuous. Germany's four colonies of Togoland, Kamerun, South West Africa, and German East Africa were weakly defended, posed little threat to neighbouring French and British territories, and were isolated by allied control of the high seas. In a two-week campaign German Togoland, in West Africa, was quickly overrun by British and French colonial forces. The larger colony of Kamerun required more effort involving naval and military forces against much stiffer German resistance; German troops retreated to the northern plateau, where they eventually surrendered in February 1916. The conquest of South West Africa was undertaken by South African forces, mainly white troops. The military campaign was briefly delayed by a revolt of Afrikaner republicans opposed to South Africa's participation in the war. In September and December 1914 British and South African forces captured the coastal towns of Luderitz and Swakopmund and drove the Germans out of Walvis Bay. Greatly outnumbered, the German forces, composed mainly of Europeans, retreated northwards and finally surrendered at Tsumeb in July 1915. As they advanced into the colony the South Africans built a new railway which provided a supply line for the war and also tied the defeated German territory more closely to the Union.

The campaign in East Africa was the most costly and destructive and lasted until late 1918. The British had the military advantage over the Germans with control of the sea and larger military forces. General von Lettow-Vorbeck, the German commander, never had more than 15,000 soldiers whereas the allies eventually had an army of 100,000 men drawn from India, South Africa, East and West Africa, the Belgian Congo, and Portuguese East Africa. The British rapidly gained naval control of the large lakes of East and Central Africa. However, their ambition to seize German East Africa quickly was dealt a severe blow when an Indian and British force failed to capture the port of Tanga in November 1914. Severe fighting raged in the Kilimanjaro

Soldiers of the Nigerian Brigade, West African Frontier Force, disembarking at Lindi in German East Africa in December 1917. Britain's West African colonies provided soldiers and carriers for the East African campaign. Officially all the men were volunteers but in reality many were sent by chiefs or taken in quotas.

Despite the often harsh German colonial rule in East Africa, General von Lettow-Vorbeck was able to keep the loyalty of his soldiers (*askaris*) throughout the war. This photograph shows the German column marching through Portuguese East Africa in 1918. The force eventually surrendered in Northern Rhodesia after the armistice was signed in Europe.

region and German flying columns struck at the Uganda railway. By early 1916 the Germans had retreated south towards the central railway line. Avoiding attempts to trap his forces, Lettow-Vorbeck staged a tactical guerrilla retreat into southern Tanganyika. The German commander knew that he could not defeat the allies but continued resistance ensured that they would have to commit a large number of troops and vital resources to the pursuit of his forces. Despite harsh conditions many *askari* remained loyal to the Germans. The small and steadily depleting force retreated across the river Ruvumu into Portuguese East Africa, crossed back into Tanganyika, and eventually surrendered in Northern Rhodesia. A large swathe of destruction marked the paths of the rival armies through East and Central Africa.

The entry of the Ottoman empire into the war as an ally of the Central Powers in November 1914 posed a threat to British and French interests in North Africa and the Middle East. Ottoman and German propaganda promoted ideas of a militant, anti-colonial Islam and this helped to encourage existing and also new resistance movements to French expansion in Morocco and the Sahara, Italian control of Libya, and the extension of British rule in the Sudan. The security of Egypt, and of the strategic Suez Canal route to India and east Asia and the newly acquired oil supplies of southern Persia, was vital to Britain's war effort. Egypt, nominally an Ottoman province, but occupied by Britain in 1882, was now annexed in the face of considerable popular local opposition. During the war Egypt became an important depot for operations against the Turks as well as a valuable source of raw cotton for Britain. A defensive line in Sinai guarded the Suez Canal against repeated Ottoman attacks. The Sinai front was held throughout 1915–16 as the British suffered reverses at the Dardanelles and in Mesopotamia. However, as the Ottoman military effort weakened in early 1917 British forces advanced across Sinai and into Palestine.

In 1914 large parts of Africa had either only recently been subjugated or were not yet under formal colonial control. The withdrawal of troops for the war interrupted the conquest of Morocco and Libya, and provided opportunities for Africans in many parts of the continent either to continue to resist European conquest or to rise in revolt. Colonial wartime policies of taxation, conscription, and the commandeering of crops and cattle also led to popular revolts. There were serious risings in West Africa in 1915–16, particularly against French rule in Niger, Upper Volta, and Soudan; colonial rulers feared that subversive Islamic ideas encouraged by Ottoman propaganda might lead to a general anti-European revolt. Small revolts, such as that led by John Chilembwe in Nyasaland in 1915 in opposition to recruitment, were quickly crushed. However, a larger revolt in 1917 among the Makonde in neighbouring Mozambique, mainly sparked off by harsh Portuguese labour conscription policies, was not defeated until 1920. Such revolts threatened colonial rule, disrupted the war effort, diverted troops to deal with them, and resulted in more deaths. By contrast, and with few exceptions, the small educated African élites in the British and French colonies and in South Africa supported the colonial war effort by encouraging recruiting and providing financial gifts. They hoped, for the most part in vain, that their loyalty would be rewarded by the ending of racial restrictions, the extension of citizenship, and new economic and political opportunities once the war was over.

Africa's human and material contribution to the war effort was considerable. The campaigns in tropical Africa were fought with mainly African soldiers but France also drew on colonial manpower in order to compensate for its demographic and thus military weakness against the Germans. General Mangin, in 1910, advocated the recruitment of a large West African army, *la force noire*, to be used as garrison troops in North Africa, thus freeing French regiments for use against the Germans. However, by the autumn of 1914 thousands of West African *tirailleurs* were on the western front confronting the Germans. As the war continued so the French sought to recruit even more troops from their tropical African colonies, using chiefs as recruiting agents. By 1918 manpower needs were desperate and the

Soldiers, labour conscription, and revolt

France conscripted more than 170, 000 black soldiers from Africa for the war effort. The *Tirailleurs Sénégalais*, mainly recruited in West Africa, fought in France, the Balkans, and later in Russia, as well as serving as garrison troops in North Africa. In this photograph men of the 1st Regiment parade with their colours.

conscription campaign in West Africa was entrusted to Blaise Diagne, the African deputy from Senegal, who was given the rank of commissioner. In the face of revolt and strong resistance he raised 63,000 men. To avoid conscription in all colonies men fled to the bush and sometimes whole villages crossed frontiers. Throughout the war the French had a total of 171,000 West African soldiers serving in Europe, with others in the Levant. A slightly smaller number came from the North African colonies, and 45,000 from Madagascar. At the end of the war African regiments served as occupation troops in the Rhineland, to a chorus of German and some allied disapproval, as well as in Hungary, Bulgaria, and Turkey. French African casualties in Europe numbered well over 80,000 men.

Unlike the French, the other European colonial powers in Africa did not raise large armies for service outside the continent. Most colonial armies were small forces of a few thousand locally recruited men, led by white officers, and intended for internal security roles and to safeguard frontiers. They were infantry armed with a few pieces of light artillery and machine guns, certainly not equipped or trained for a modern war. The largest of these gendarmerie forces was the 15,000-strong *Force Publique* in the Belgian Congo. British, German, Italian, and Portuguese colonial armies were considerably smaller; for example, the Nigerian Regiment of the West African Frontier Force numbered barely 5,000 men in 1914. On the outbreak of war the small British garrison in South Africa was withdrawn and the defence of the Union rested with the recently created Defence Force, a small professional corps which in an emergency was supplemented by a volunteer burgher force of 30,000.

From the start of the war all the imperial powers expanded their African colonial armies, enlisting conscripts and some volunteers. African forces were used in the various military campaigns within the continent. For example, troops from British West Africa fought in Togoland and Cameroon, were used to suppress internal unrest, and were then shipped round the Cape to serve in the long drawn-out military operations in East Africa. Because of the harsh climatic conditions in East Africa the British decided by 1916 that the campaign would be fought exclusively with African troops. At the same time, as the imperial manpower situation grew more serious, military and political voices in London demanded that Britain should copy the French and recruit a large black army for service outside Africa. Opponents of this policy argued that African troops were not trained to fight European armies and that they would not be able to withstand a European winter. As it was, French strategy after 1915 was to withdraw their African regiments from the battle line in winter so that they could recover in the warmer conditions of southern France. The climatic argument did not apply to the small number of British West Africans who had been recruited for service on the rivers of Mesopotamia, to the several thousand Egyptian labourers working in France, Cape Coloured soldiers in the Middle East, or to the 20,000 men of the South African Native Labour Contingent, a uniformed but non-

combatant force, that served behind the lines on the western front in the
years 1916–18. In France the Contingent was kept in compounds not unlike
those used for migrant mine labour in South Africa. By 1918 British military
commanders were seriously considering recruiting Africans for combatant
service in Europe, but the war ended before this became necessary. White
South African regiments served in Europe, most notably in the bloody
engagement at Delville Wood in July 1916, the site of the main South African
war memorial. The tragedy remembered by black South Africans was the
sinking of the troopship *Mendi* in February 1917 when 600 men of the Native
Labour Contingent were drowned in the English Channel.

All military operations in tropical Africa were hindered by climatic conditions, disease, and poor communications. Draught animals could not be used
as they died from trypanosomiasis carried by the tsetse fly. Thus, away from
the rivers and the few railways, the main means of moving supplies was by
head carriers, who were the 'hands and feet' of the army. The rival armies
required thousands of porters to carry munitions and food up to the front line
and to evacuate the wounded. Porterage was heavy work and hated by many
Africans even in peacetime. In wartime it was far worse with little reward and
the added risk of death. Tropical military campaigns required a constant and
large supply of labourers and these could only be secured by force. Men,
even women and children, were pressed into service. The forced removal of
men from villages placed a heavy burden of production on those left behind,
principally women, children, and the elderly, resulting in food shortages, in

Thousands of labour-
ers from Egypt, China
and South Africa were
recruited for supply
work on the Western
Front. Men of the South
African Native Labour
Corps, shown here with
their white officers,
served in France from
1916 to 1918.

some cases famine, especially when the rains failed as they did in the East African Protectorate in November 1917.

Even short campaigns, such as that against the Germans in Togoland, required thousands of carriers. The German medical missionary Albert Schweitzer recalled seeing in French Congo in 1914 the emaciated bodies of dead carriers lying beside the road far from the scene of the fighting. The South Africans recruited over 35,000 labourers for the campaign in South West Africa, men needed to build railway lines, cut roads, move stores, unload ships, and carry food and munitions. The long and bitter fighting in East Africa required the largest number of carriers, who suffered the most horrifying casualties. The number of carriers involved in that campaign is unknown, but a reasonable estimate for those recruited by both the Germans and the allies from East and Central Africa throughout the war is about 1 million.

In the East African Protectorate wages failed to attract sufficient volunteer carriers and pressure from chiefs produced too few men; by 1915 extensive impressment began and in the following year carriers were organized into the Military Labour Bureau. Shortages of food and high death rates increased resistance to carrier work. The mass levy of 1917 produced only 120,000 carriers and the authorities suspended conscription, fearful of its consequences. A recent estimate suggests that over 200,000 of the total male population aged 16–40 were enlisted and that the casualty figure reached 50,000, one-eighth of the total male population of the Protectorate. The heaviest demand for carriers was in German East Africa, where labour was conscripted by both sides. Even the small colony of Nyasaland provided more than 200,000 carriers for a conflict that Africans called the war of *thangata*—work without real benefit. Altogether the carrier death rate in

South African troops of all races fought in most of the theatres during the war. By 1917–18 the campaign against the Germans in tropical East Africa was a war mainly between rival African armies. Supply lines were maintained by conscripted carriers. Here a machine gun section of the South African Cape Corps, recruited from coloured men, patrols in Tanganyika.

East Africa probably exceeded 100,000, mainly from disease and starvation brought about by official incompetence and neglect. The British operations in Sinai also required a vast army of Egyptian labourers. These were conscripted from among the peasant *fellahin* to carry, dig, and serve the army. Between March 1917 and June 1918 nearly 300,000 labourers were enlisted on three-month contracts. A senior British officer said recruitment was 'a new form of the corvée', although a recent assessment argues that recruitment was only slightly resisted and that service was tolerable and actively sought by *fellahin* because it paid well. The army also required a large number of camels and huge quantities of foodstuffs, most of which came from the peasant producers of Egypt and the Sudan. Thousands of North Africans were recruited for the vast army of labourers from all over the world that served behind the lines in Europe. The French also conscripted 90,000 Algerians for work in France because of a severe wartime labour shortage.

In 1914 the economies of tropical Africa were weak, largely dominated by foreign companies, and dependent on the export to Europe of cash crops and minerals. Investment in the colonies was meagre; the few railways mainly linked export areas to the coast. In 1914 Europe's volume of trade with tropical Africa was relatively small; for Britain and France, the major colonial powers, this amounted to less than 3 per cent of their total trade. Commercially the most important parts of Africa for Britain and France were South Africa, Egypt, and Algeria. South Africa produced gold and diamonds, and also large volumes of wool and foodstuffs; Egypt was a major source of cotton; Algeria exported tobacco, wine, and wool to France. The war disrupted African economies, arrested the meagre flow of investment to the colonies, reduced government revenues, and interrupted shipping and trade routes. In most colonies the war increased taxation and decreased development expenditure on public works programmes and social welfare. The prices of most African export commodities fell during the war and the colonial terms of trade worsened. Most Africans were economically worse off in 1918 than they had been in 1914. Early in the war German markets were closed to tropical products by an allied trade embargo. French and British merchants and politicians planned to exclude German trading companies permanently from African trade, and to this end various official and unofficial schemes were promoted to protect imperial economic interests once the war was over.

The economic impact of the war

It took time for the allies to organize colonial production for the war effort. The idea of 'total war' was new, and colonial administrations, already understaffed, lost further personnel to the armed forces. By 1916 serious attempts were being made to integrate colonial production into the war economy. The trade in strategic minerals and agricultural products came increasingly under some form of government direction. For example, the British, having expelled Germany from the West African trade, set about ensuring that an increased supply of palm oil products and cocoa reached the British market. South Africa exported larger quanties of foodstuffs, particularly fruit and meat, to Britain. From her mineral-based economy new industries were established to produce once imported goods now in short supply. By the end of the war, South Africa had the basis of a new steel industry and was manufacturing a range of goods for the domestic market. This growth in the economy inevitably led to increased migration of people to towns to work in new factories. In South Africa many Africans and Afrikaners became urban workers; a similar process occurred in Algeria but with many Algerian labourers also leaving to work in France. Throughout Africa the population of towns grew more rapidly as a result of the new demands on men and materials for the war. Rapid urban growth in South Africa eroded the customary and legal lines of racial segregation in housing and employment. By 1918 Africans were doing jobs in mines and on farms once reserved for whites. Elsewhere in the continent Africans also took over positions in administration, commerce, and church that had been vacated by whites.

The wartime disruption of shipping and trade led to shortages of imported goods and price rises. The price inflation touched every part of Africa but was particularly marked in towns, where many Africans had come to rely on imported goods such as food and kerosene. At the same time the real wages of many African workers fell. Prices in South Africa and Algeria doubled in the period 1914–18; in Senegal they trebled, and in Madagascar rose fivefold. This led to widespread discontent and in some colonies the creation of labour unions by clerks, mine, dock, and railway workers, who struck for increased wages. Most of these unions were small and easily dealt with by government and commercial companies. The largest unions were in South Africa, among both black and white workers, and their strikes seriously worried the authorities. Striking black miners were forced at bayonet point back to work, while many white workers fought fiercely to uphold their privileged labour and wage status based on race. At the end of the war the brief post-war economic boom of 1919–20 also touched Africa, further pushing up prices and increasing discontent.

The social impact of the war

The long drawn-out fighting in East Africa severely dislocated the life of communities and families. This was not confined just to the areas where the small military engagements took place; the destructive impact was felt over a vast area from which men were conscripted and cattle and foodstuffs seized for the war effort. The long and depredatory tentacles of the war suppliers reached deep into Kenya, Uganda, the Belgian Congo, Northern Rhodesia, Nyasaland, and Portuguese East Africa. Men forced into the war machine went away, never to be seen again by wives and children. To this heavy, but not exactly known, number of casualties must be added those who died from the disease and famine that came with the war. In East and Central Africa the harshness of the war resulted in acute shortages of food with famine in some areas, a weakening of populations, and epidemic diseases which killed hundreds of thousands of people and also cattle. Wartime destruction and dislocation resulted in serious ecological consequences as populations moved, the tsetse fly spread, and land was devastated. The war years for many parts of East Africa were truly a period of crisis.

In the last year of the war, and in early 1919, the world was hit by the influenza pandemic which in a brief span of six months killed c.30 million people around the globe, more than all the casualties of the war itself. Although the influenza pandemic was not a result of the war, it came at a time when the authorities were distracted by the war and in a form that they were unable to control. The pandemic was spread into Africa from Europe and America along the routes of war and rapidly penetrated the continent, carried along railways, rivers, and trade routes. Sickness and death were often sudden and inexplicable. Death rates ranged from an estimated 2–3 per cent over much of Africa to a possible 5–6 per cent in East Africa. South Africa suffered most heavily. At the crossroads of international shipping and with an extensive railway network the disease spread rapidly throughout the Union. A recent revision of the official mortality figure suggests that c.300,000 people died from influenza with long-lasting demographic consequences for the country. Many people throughout Africa responded to the sudden and disastrous impact of influenza by turning to religion. Revivalism occurred amongst Christians, Muslims, and those who adhered to indigenous beliefs. In Central and East Africa the effects of the war compounded by the influenza pandemic encouraged anti-colonial millenarian beliefs, such as the Watch Tower movement, which preached that European rule was about to end. New religious movements that emphasized the power of prayer or the word of prophets were also spawned in this post-war period in response to the war and its aftermath. The war had loosened the control of Christian missions over large parts of Africa; German missionaries had been excluded and their place taken, at least in the short term, by African clergy and catechists. The activities of mission-run schools and hospitals were curtailed. However, the war appears to have stimulated African interest in western-style education and by 1918 there were more Africans in school than in 1914. Colonial social and welfare expenditure, always small before 1914, was severely reduced during the war years.

In 1914 the only independent states in Africa were Liberia and Abyssinia. The war encouraged nationalist ideas and stimulated ambitions to throw off European colonial rule, most notably in Muslim North Africa where *jihads*, or religious struggles, were fought against the European infidels throughout the war years. These wars of resistance were most prolonged in Morocco where Ma'al-Hayba drove back the French, in Cyrenaica as the Sanusi continued to resist Italian control, in the Darfur region of central Sahara where 'Ali Dinar sought to secure his independence from both the French and the British, and in the long drawn-out struggle for independence by Muhammad 'Abdullah Hassan in Somalia against the British and Italians. Foreign occupation and pan-Islamic ideas helped fuel nationalist sentiment in North Africa. Egyptian nationalism grew in response to British military control and annex-

Politics and the war

ation in 1914. By 1920 the Wafd party led the country in open revolt against British rule. Egypt gained a nominal flag-independence in 1922 but Britain maintained military control over the strategic Suez Canal. A Moroccan nationalist Rif Republic, proclaimed in 1922, was crushed by superior European military firepower; all attempts by Africans to regain or preserve their independence were similarly treated. However, in South Africa the war encouraged ideas among white people of autonomy from London, which were realized in the 1920s as dominion status and membership of the League of Nations were achieved.

Few Africans gained any reward for their wartime loyalty. The modest ambitions of many educated Africans for greater political and social equality within the colonies, stimulated by President Wilson's Fourteen Points and to some extent by pan-Africanism, were frustrated. There were small gains for Algerian Muslims and some French West Africans with the extension of franchise and citizenship rights. However, in sub-Saharan Africa, the lobbying and petitions of small élite-led bodies such as the National Congress of British West Africa and the South African Native National Congress gained little return in colonial capitals or in London. Whites in South Africa and the settler colonies strengthened their political position after the war with African protests at settler alienation of land in Kenya ignored. However, an attempted white mine workers' revolt under a revolutionary and racist banner on the Rand in 1922 was crushed by the South African military.

All the colonial belligerents had ambitions for further territory in Africa. Defeat in Europe ended the German African empire and the plans for a large *Mittelafrika* astride the continent, although Germany continued to demand the return of its 'lost colonies' through the inter-war years. The African spoils of war fell to the allied victors in what has been called the 'second partition of Africa'. This was agreed at the Paris Peace Conference in 1919, and confirmed by the League of Nations, with the British and French dividing the German colonies between themselves. Britain now held continuous territory from Cairo to the Cape. Belgium gained a small but densely populated part of German East Africa; Portugal and Italy received territory as a result of post-war border adjustments. South Africa held on to South West Africa but failed to persuade the white settlers of Southern Rhodesia to join the Union. The former German colonies became mandates of the League of Nations and the colonial powers entrusted with them had to report annually to the world body on how they administered those territories; for the first time colonial rulers were subject to a limited form of international accountability, a concern which the League later extended in efforts to end slavery and forced labour and to regulate the supply of alcohol in Africa.

Conclusion

The Great War in Africa was a watershed. The conflict showed all the belligerents the strategic value of imperial resources of men and material in Africa. 'Empire' took on a new meaning; colonies needed planned economic development, by the state if necessary, within an integrated imperial system, while the welfare of colonial peoples also had to be looked after. An uneasy tension existed between these ideas of economic development and trustee-ship which characterized post-war French and British colonial policies, although there was little new investment in colonial Africa. Much less is known about the impact of the war on the hundreds of thousands of Africans who fought or were caught up in the war. European racial superiority was certainly dented, as many feared, by African soldiers fighting and killing white men. Travel overseas, contact with people from other countries and continents, and exposure to different cultural ideas all helped give Africans new perceptions of themselves and their colonial rulers.

CHAPTER 8

The War at Sea

PAUL G. HALPERN

Strategy in the North Sea

On the outbreak of war the Royal Navy still enjoyed a comfortable lead—in dreadnoughts 21:13—over its German rival, but the British also had worldwide trade interests and an empire to defend and their resources were actually stretched to the limit in the first few months of the war. The new weapons of naval war—mines, submarines, torpedoes—forced the British to abandon the traditional strategy of close blockade and the idea that the front line began on the enemy coast. Distant blockade was adopted, and the geographical situation actually favoured this because the British Isles could be compared to a breakwater or the stopper in the bottle. German ships had to pass around them in order to leave the North Sea and reach the rest of the world. The naval leaders of 1914 were also not oblivious to the dangers of the new weapons and Admiral Sir John Jellicoe, commander-in-chief of the Grand Fleet after the outbreak of the war, was constantly preoccupied with avoiding being drawn into a submarine ambush or over a previously laid minefield.

The German navy, despite the great material strides it had made since the introduction of the naval programmes of 1898 and 1900 associated with the state secretary of the Imperial Naval Office, Admiral Alfred von Tirpitz, was actually in search of a strategy. Mindful of the British superiority in numbers, the Germans hoped to whittle down the Grand Fleet's advantage through mines and torpedoes off the German coast until the numerical situation was favourable for a major encounter. This, however, presupposed that the British would follow their traditional policy of close blockade. Tirpitz indeed realized the flaw in this thinking when he asked the German fleet commander: 'But what will you do if they don't come?' There was no satisfactory reply

and the Germans never really found one. What could they do if the British naval leaders were not stupid enough to oblige them by putting their heads into the noose? The basic idea remained to try and catch a portion of the Grand Fleet with the entire High Seas Fleet and by destroying it equalize the numbers. The British objective remained to avoid this and bring the High Seas Fleet to battle with the entire Grand Fleet. In one way or another the major encounters of the war in the northern theatre resulted from these strategies. They were complicated by the fact that the kaiser was reluctant to risk the destruction of his precious fleet. He hoped to preserve it as a bargaining chip in any future peace negotiations. The British, in turn, were conscious of the fact that as an island nation they were dependent on use of the sea for their survival. This was best expressed by Churchill's comment that Jellicoe was 'the only man on either side who could lose the war in an afternoon'. Given these circumstances, it is not surprising that the British and German naval commanders were inherently cautious and that only one major battle would take place during the war.

The naval superiority of the Entente powers over the Central Powers was not necessarily inevitable in other portions of the world, notably the Mediterranean. Here Germany's ally Austria-Hungary had embarked on a significant naval building programme before the war with the objective of turning what had been primarily a coast defence force into a 'blue water' navy with powerful dreadnoughts of its own. The Austrians were of course building as much

Three *Arethusa* class light cruisers, each with a Sopwith Camel on a flying-off platform over A-gun, passing under the Forth bridge. In the background, recognizable by their cage masts, are United States battleships serving with the Grand Fleet as the 6th Battle Squadron.

The Mediterranean

against their erstwhile ally in the Triple Alliance, the Italians, as against any other potential foe. The Austrians, Italians, and Germans concluded a naval convention in 1913 and the possibility of a Triple Alliance naval combination caused the French and British a good deal of worry. The French navy, traditionally second only to the Royal Navy in European waters, had fallen steadily behind the Germans in the decade before the war. Its superiority over the Triple Alliance force would only have been marginal—at least on paper. In the long run the threat proved to be a mirage. The Italian government declared its neutrality at the beginning of the war and the Austrian fleet was fated to remain on the defensive in the Adriatic. There would be no real challenge to the Entente in the Mediterranean *on the surface*.

The Germans had maintained a naval force in the Mediterranean known as the *Mittelmeerdivision* ever since the Balkan wars of 1912–13. In July 1914 this consisted of the battle cruiser *Goeben* and the fast light cruiser *Breslau*. Rear Admiral Wilhelm Souchon, the German commander, opened the war on 3 August by bombarding the French Algerian ports of Bône and Philippeville. Souchon had no desire to be bottled up in the Adriatic with his Austrian allies and made for the Dardanelles. Thanks to both British and French mistakes, he succeeded. To evade neutrality regulations, the *Goeben* and *Breslau* were ostensibly sold to the Turkish navy and henceforth wore the Turkish ensign. They retained their German officers and men and the sale was a fiction. The British and French suspected as much and were now obliged to maintain a blockade off the Dardanelles.

Operations in the North Sea 1914–1915

In the north the first of the British naval objectives was to cover the passage of the BEF to France and it is significant that the German navy was unable to make any attempt to impede this. The British and French established a blockade cutting off German access to the outside world. The blockade was initially carried out by obsolete cruisers which no longer had any role in the major battle squadrons. The Royal Navy also made increasing use of auxiliary cruisers, merchant ships (often passenger liners) armed and used as warships. Probably their best-known employment was in the 10th Cruiser Squadron which carried out the so-called Northern Patrol in the waters north of Scotland where weather conditions soon exposed the old cruisers first employed as unsuitable. The larger liners could withstand the frequent rough seas and could be crammed with large quantities of coal and remain on patrol for long periods.

The working of sea power in the blockade was slow and steady but certainly not dramatic. This contrasted with the heavy fighting and casualties on land and inevitably the unfair question was heard: 'What is the navy doing?' In the opening weeks of the war most expected a major encounter. When it did not occur there was certainly a sense of disappointment in the Grand Fleet. How could one get the Germans to come out? The first significant naval action of the war occurred on 28 August when the light cruisers and destroyers of Commodore Reginald Tyrwhitt's Harwich Force attempted to mop up German patrols in the Heligoland Bight. British submarines would be deployed to attack any German heavy ships that might come out. The action—complicated by fog and haze—nearly turned into a fiasco for the British because of faulty liaison between the Admiralty, the Grand Fleet, the Harwich Force, and British submarines. There was considerable confusion when light cruisers from the Grand Fleet arrived and at one point a British submarine which had not been told they would be present fired on a British light cruiser. The British light forces had a hot time of it as increasing numbers of German cruisers came out in support of the German destroyers. Fortunately for the British the German cruisers were committed piecemeal while low water prevented the heavy ships of the High Seas Fleet from crossing the Jade bar. Rear Admiral Sir David Beatty finally decided to intervene with his Battle Cruiser Squadron despite the poor visibility and the uncertain situation in regard to German heavy ships, mines, and submarines. The arrival of his battle cruisers was decisive. By the end of the action the German cruisers *Mainz*, *Ariadne*, and *Köln* and destroyer *V.187* had been sunk. The British lost no ships although two destroyers and Tyrwhitt's flagship, the cruiser *Arethusa*, eventually had to be towed on the way home. The German defeat just off their coast without the High Seas Fleet being able to intervene in time was certainly a psychological shock and the kaiser was confirmed in his defensive attitude. The precious battle fleet must not suffer the same fate and he ordered the fleet commander to obtain his express consent before engaging in any fleet action.

In September 1914 submarines demonstrated their potential. On the 5th *U.21* torpedoed and sank the scout cruiser *Pathfinder*, the first British warship to be sunk by a submarine. A little over a week later, the British submarine *E.9* sank the old German cruiser *Hela*. Jellicoe was highly conscious of the vulnerability of the fleet anchorage at Scapa Flow to submarines and early in the war shifted the fleet to Loch Ewe on the north-west coast of Scotland until the defences at Scapa could be improved. Unfortunately Jellicoe's respect for the submarine was not always shared by the Admiralty staff. Despite warnings of the potential danger, they maintained a patrol of old armoured cruisers—sardonically dubbed the 'live bait squadron'—in an area off the Dutch coast known as the Broad Fourteens. On 22 September the German submarine *U.9* sank the *Cressy*, *Aboukir*, and *Hogue* with heavy loss of life, demonstrating in a spectacular fashion that the submarine was now the greatest threat to British control of the sea. Jellicoe shifted the fleet's anchorage to Loch na Keal further south on the Scottish coast and then to Lough Swilly on the north coast of Ireland. He admitted he felt safer at sea until the defences of Scapa were finally brought to an acceptable state in early 1915.

Outside European waters German and Austrian shipping was soon driven from the seas and ships were either captured or forced to seek shelter in neutral ports. The German overseas colonies quickly became the target of allied

Cruiser warfare

expeditions and one by one were snapped up, although in some cases only after lengthy campaigns. On the outbreak of war there had been a few scattered German cruisers overseas and some German liners also converted themselves into auxiliary cruisers. The cruiser *Karlsruhe* in the South Atlantic proved troublesome before it sank after an internal explosion. Another, the *Königsberg*, required extensive operations before it was finally located and destroyed in its anchorage in the Rufigi river in East Africa. It accomplished relatively little. The same was true of the German auxiliary cruisers. The big liners were disappointing as raiders. They had prodigious appetites for coal that was hard to come by and harder still to transfer at sea or in improvised anchorages. Although they made some captures, by the end of the year they had either been sunk or interned in neutral ports.

The only significant German force at large at the beginning of the war was the East Asiatic Squadron under the command of Vice Admiral Maximilian Graf von Spee. Spee's two armoured cruisers, the *Scharnhorst* and *Gneisenau*, were crack ships, renowned for their gunnery. He also had the light cruisers *Emden*, *Nürnberg*, and *Leipzig*. The German Squadron had been based on Tsingtau, the German protectorate on the Shantung peninsula of China. Tsingtau was doomed once Japan entered the war against Germany on 23 August. The Japanese sent an expedition to Tsingtau and began a siege which ended with the inevitable surrender of the Germans on 7 November. There had been no way they could be reinforced from home. Spee, however, was long gone by the time the siege began. He detached the *Emden*, the newest and fastest of his cruisers, to raid in the Indian Ocean. The *Emden*'s commander, Fregattenkapitän Karl von Müller, went on a highly successful cruise that became one of the legends of the war, sinking sixteen British steamers, a Russian light cruiser, and a French destroyer. He thoroughly disrupted trade in the Indian Ocean and caused considerable problems for the British and French at a time when they were also occupied with the great so-called 'imperial convoys', substantial movements of troops from Australia and New Zealand and other portions of the empire. Indeed, the Royal Navy would have been hard put to fulfil all its obligations without the assistance of the Japanese. The *Emden* was finally destroyed on 9 November by the Australian light cruiser *Sydney* in the Cocos Islands. The cruises of the German raiders may have captured the public's imagination and caused considerable trouble, but the losses they inflicted represented only a small portion of British and allied tonnage. They were nothing like the threat posed by the submarine later in the war.

Spee worked his way eastward across the enormous Pacific Ocean and eventually reached the west coast of South America where he was joined by the light cruiser *Dresden*, which had been operating off the Chilean coast. Spee therefore had two armoured cruisers and three light cruisers when he encountered a British force under Rear Admiral Christopher Cradock off Coronel on 1 November. Cradock's force, the old cruisers *Good Hope* and *Monmouth*, light cruiser *Glasgow*, and auxiliary cruiser *Otranto*, was inferior but he had declined to wait for the old battleship *Canopus* in the belief that her slow speed would prevent him from ever bringing the Germans to action. Coronel resulted in a sharp defeat for the British, *Good Hope* and *Monmouth* being sunk with no survivors. It was the first defeat suffered by the Royal Navy in a century. Spee, though, had few illusions about his momentary triumph. When his squadron called at Valparaiso to coal an admirer presented him with a bouquet of flowers on his departure. Spee is reported to have said: 'Thank you, they will do very nicely for my grave.'

Spee's intuition was correct. Lord Fisher, the new First Sea Lord, reacted swiftly and taking a calculated risk detached the battle cruisers *Inflexible* and *Invincible* to South American waters and the *Princess Royal* to North America. Naval forces were redeployed throughout much of the world for Spee now represented a potential threat to allied expeditions or trade in Africa, the Caribbean—or the Pacific, should he elect to turn back to the west. Spee decided to round Cape Horn and raid the Falkland Islands. It was a fatal decision. The British force under Vice Admiral Sir Doveton Sturdee had just arrived. The sight of ships with heavy tripod masts in Port Stanley harbour meant doom. Sturdee put to sea with the battle cruisers *Invincible* and *Inflexible*, armoured cruisers *Kent*, *Carnarvon*, and *Cornwall*, and light cruiser *Glasgow*. In the running action that followed on 8 December all German ships were eventually sunk with heavy loss of life (including Spee) except for the cruiser *Dresden*. The latter led a fugitive existence until discovered by British warships at Mas a Tierra, a remote Chilean island in the Pacific. The Germans scuttled *Dresden* themselves. The Falklands had cancelled Coronel and no more German naval squadrons (as opposed to individual raiders) would be overseas for the remainder of the war.

The Baltic

The naval war was not merely a contest between the British and Germans. Other navies, for example the Russians in the Baltic, played roles as well. The Russian Baltic fleet was far inferior to the German High Seas Fleet in 1914, although the Russian pre-war building programme was beginning to bear fruit and Russian dreadnoughts as well as large fast destroyers were beginning to enter service. However, the Germans normally chose to keep the High Seas Fleet in the North Sea and their forces in the Baltic under the command of the kaiser's brother, Prince Heinrich of Prussia, were largely composed of obsolete ships which initially remained on the defensive. This gave the Russians an apparent advantage but one that they could swiftly lose should the Germans decide to send ships through the Kiel Canal into the Baltic. The primary Russian naval objective was to defend the Gulf of Finland and the capital, Petrograd. Acting on the assumption that their fleet would be inferior to the potential enemy, the Russians developed extensive minefields between the Finnish and Estonian coasts—the 'central position'. They planned to cover these minefields with coastal batteries and their fleet would fight and manoeuvre behind this position. The tsar was extremely cautious in his attitude towards naval affairs, determined to avoid a repetition of the disasters of the Russo-Japanese War. The Russian naval commander until his death in May 1915 was Admiral Essen, possibly the ablest Russian admiral of the war, and once it was apparent German naval forces were concentrated in the North Sea Essen began a more active role for his cruisers and destroyers outside the Gulf of Finland, notably raids to lay mines along German lines of communication in the southern Baltic. The Germans replied with periodic sweeps, some submarine activity, and of course their own mining. The Germans were able to maintain their crucial traffic in iron ore from Sweden and could claim they successfully contained the Russians in what for them was only a secondary theatre. The extensive mining on both sides eventually made the Baltic a very unhealthy place. It became even more unhealthy for the Germans with the arrival of British submarines in the autumn of 1914. Fisher's idea of sending a battle fleet into the Baltic to assist the Russians was impracticable, but it was possible for small numbers of submarines to reach the Baltic via the Sound, the narrow passage between Denmark and Sweden. Two British submarines managed to join the Russians before the end of the year and three more in 1915. In 1916 the Germans made the passage of the Sound too dangerous but the British were able to send four small 'C' class boats by way of Archangel and the rivers and canals of northern Russia. The British submarines enjoyed a certain amount of success, but operations were hampered by logistic and climatic difficulties—the eastern Baltic froze solid during the winter—and also by the fact that the Swedish navy began convoying vessels through their own coastal waters to enforce Swedish neutrality. After the major advances of the German armies on land in 1915 brought the Gulf of Riga into prominence, the Germans attempted to force the entrance to the gulf but failed and it would not be until October 1917 that the Germans secured naval control of the gulf. Even then it required an amphibious operation—Operation 'Albion'—against the island of Ösel and fairly arduous fighting to achieve the goal.

Naval intelligence

Baltic naval operations were also responsible for an invaluable British intelligence coup early in the war. On 26 August 1914 the German light cruiser *Magdeburg* ran aground on the Estonian coast while engaged on a sweep against Russian patrols. The ship had to be abandoned when Russian warships approached and the Russians recovered the German code books and passed a copy to the British. This, when joined with other code books captured from a German freighter in the Pacific and recovered from a German torpedo boat sunk in the North Sea, enabled the British to establish an effective decrypting organization commonly known from its location in the Admiralty as 'Room 40'. The British realized the value of this asset and guarded the secret closely, so closely that vital information was not always disseminated to those who could use it and opportunities were missed. It was not until later in the war that the organization, combined with an elaborate system of listening and direction-finding stations, realized its full potential, particularly in the anti-submarine war.

The ability of the British to read German wireless traffic led to another encounter in the North Sea early in 1915. In the autumn of 1914 the Germans had adopted the tactic of sending their fast battle cruisers to bombard British coastal towns, notably Yarmouth, Scarborough, Hartlepool, and Whitby. The objective, aside from doing whatever one could to hurt the British and raise morale, was to lure the Grand Fleet or a portion of it over freshly laid minefields or in range of U-boats. The Germans nearly succeeded inadvertently in achieving their goal of catching a detached portion of the Grand Fleet. Room 40 gave warning of the impending German raid but did not realize the entire High Seas Fleet would be at sea in support. The Admiralty considered one battle squadron from the Grand Fleet in support of Beatty's battle cruisers would be sufficient and prohibited Jellicoe from putting to sea with the whole fleet. The Germans, in turn, did not realize the British had been forewarned. They carried out their bombardments successfully on 16 December but poor weather and poor visibility combined with human errors in signalling and reporting prevented the main portions of the forces at sea from making contact with each other.

The Germans were not so lucky on 24 January 1915 when the German battle cruisers under Admiral Hipper raided the Dogger Bank in the centre of the North Sea in order to mop up British patrols thought to be operating here. Room 40 was able to give warning and Beatty and the battle cruisers attempted to trap the Germans. In the running battle that ensued the German armoured cruiser *Blücher* was sunk, but as a result of damage to Beatty's flagship *Lion*, and errors in signalling and the interpretation of his orders, the remaining Germans escaped. Nevertheless the loss at the Dogger Bank action resulted in Admiral von Pohl replacing Admiral Ingenohl as commander of the High Seas Fleet and made the kaiser more determined than ever that, aside from occasional sorties, the fleet would not seek battle outside of the Heligoland Bight, where it would be supported by light forces and extensive minefields. Jellicoe, in turn, would not oblige the Germans by deliberately putting the Grand Fleet in a vulnerable position. Therefore it is hardly surprising that as far as the major fleets were concerned the prospect of a battle diminished in 1915. Although British and German light forces clashed periodically, one might say that a stalemate existed in the North Sea, but it was a stalemate that operated to the disadvantage of the Germans for it meant that the British blockade was unbroken.

A similar stalemate developed in the Adriatic. Once Italy dropped out of the Triple Alliance the Austrian fleet was left in a position of great inferiority compared with the French and was faced by the prospect that its former Italian ally might soon join its enemies. Admiral Haus, the Austrian commander, rejected German requests at the beginning of the war for the Austrian fleet to proceed to Constantinople and wisely refrained from seeking battle with the superior French on their periodic sweeps into the southern Adriatic. On 16 August the French had overwhelmed the small cruiser *Zenta* off the Mon-

Operations in the Adriatic

British drifters at Taranto. They formed part of the Otranto barrage, an increasingly elaborate and largely futile attempt to block the straits with mine and net barrages. Around the British Isles large numbers of similar trawlers and drifters of the Auxiliary Patrol played an important role in the anti-submarine war.

tenegrin coast but they were hampered by the lack of a suitable base and on 21 December 1914 the French flagship, the dreadnought *Jean Bart*, was torpedoed by the *U.12*, one of the handful of Austrian submarines. The *Jean Bart* was not sunk but the French no longer risked major warships in the Adriatic and established a distant blockade across the Strait of Otranto. When they unwisely shifted the patrol too far to the north in April 1915, they lost the armoured cruiser *Léon Gambetta* to the *U.5*.

The entry of Italy into the war on 23 May did not substantially alter the situation. The Austrian surface warships were now in a position of hopeless inferiority but on the very first day of the war Haus brought the battle fleet across the Adriatic for a surprise bombardment of Italian ports. It was the only fleet action on the part of the Austrians during the war. During the first two months of the war the Italians learned the same lessons as the British in the North Sea and lost the armoured cruisers *Amalfi* and *Garibaldi* to Austrian submarines. They did not risk their dreadnoughts in the Adriatic and the naval war in the Adriatic became one of light forces, scout cruisers, destroyers, and torpedo boats. Nevertheless the existence of a nucleus of powerful Austrian warships acted as an inhibiting factor whenever the Italians thought of amphibious operations on the vulnerable Dalmatian coast. One could not risk operations of this sort without heavy support lest the Austrian battleships intervene, and the use of large Italian warships in the Adriatic was now considered too dangerous because of submarines. The Austrian navy in this case fulfilled the classic role of a 'fleet-in-being'. Hit-and-run raids between the light forces continued throughout the war and when the Central Powers overran Serbia in late 1915 the Austrian navy conceivably missed an opportunity to prevent the evacuation of the remnants of the Serbian army which had retreated to the coast. The Austrians did raid Durazzo on 29 December 1915 but lost two destroyers to mines and had a narrow escape from a superior allied force in the running battle that followed.

The Black Sea also became the scene of naval operations after Turkey entered the war on the side of the Central Powers on 29 October 1914. Souchon connived with the pro-war faction in the Turkish government and precipitated events by leading the Turkish fleet in a surprise attack on Russian ports. The Russians replied by declaring war. Aside from the *Goeben* and *Breslau*, the Ottoman navy possessed only a handful of relatively modern destroyers suitable for operations in company with the German ships. The few Turkish battleships and cruisers were obsolete and slow. The balance of power shifted in favour of the Russians in 1915 as Russian dreadnoughts, large destroyers, and submarines entered service. The Russians established a blockade of the Bosporus and sought to interdict the traffic in coal from the

The German submarine *U.35*, flying victory pennants, approaches the Austrian depot ship *Gäa* at the Austrian naval base in the Gulf of Cattaro. In the summer of 1916 the submarine's commander, Arnauld de la Perière, made the most successful submarine cruise of the war, sinking 54 steamers and sailing craft in the Mediterranean.

Turkish coal ports on the Black Sea to Constantinople. In 1916 the Russians made use of their naval superiority to execute successful amphibious operations in support of the Russian army on the coast of Lazistan in the eastern Black Sea. The campaign ended with the capture of Trabzon by the Russian army. The Russian navy was also largely successful in cutting off the coal trade and there were shortages in Constantinople, but Russian naval successes were curtailed by the revolution of 1917 and the disorder that slowly spread to the Black Sea Fleet.

British and French naval forces failed at the Dardanelles in 1915 in the attempt to silence Turkish batteries, sweep minefields and force a passage through the Narrows, and bring Constantinople under the guns of the allied fleet. The attack on 18 March ran into an unsuspected line of newly laid mines and two British battleships and one French were sunk and others badly damaged. The subsequent landings by the army ended in a stalemate and, while British submarines were able to pass through the Dardanelles under water and operate successfully in the Sea of Marmora and a renewed attack by the reorganized and strengthened naval forces might well have succeeded, the entry of Bulgaria into the war on the side of the Central Powers eventually doomed the campaign.

The Dardanelles campaign also resulted in the arrival of German submarines in the Mediterranean. The Germans responded as a result of the inability of the Austrians to do anything to help the hard-pressed Turks in the spring of 1915. The first to arrive at the Dardanelles, *U.21*, sank the battleships *Triumph* and *Majestic* and forced a revision of British tactics. However, the submarines achieved their greatest success against merchant shipping in the Mediterranean and the Germans eventually had a submarine flotilla at Pola and another in the Gulf of Cattaro.

Submarine warfare

In the course of 1915 the Germans discovered that the most profitable role for the submarine was operating against merchant shipping rather than warships. Because submarines were too small to follow the traditional rules of cruiser warfare concerning the safety of passengers and crew, the Germans were inevitably involved in friction with neutrals. Incidents involving loss of American life had resulted in sharp American protests and orders restricting the activities of German submarine commanders. Renewed restrictions on German submarine commanders following the *Sussex* incident of March 1916 led to a resumption of activity by the High Seas Fleet. The more aggressive Reinhard Scheer succeeded von Pohl in command after the latter was forced to step down as a result of illness. On 31 May 1916 Scheer's sweep against British patrols off the Skagerrak and Room 40's knowledge that the Germans were out led to the battle of Jutland—Skagerrak to the Germans—the greatest naval encounter of the war. The battle has been a subject of debate ever since for it began relatively late in the day and poor visibility and the onset of darkness ended with the battered Germans able to break off, pass behind the British fleet in the dark, and eventually reach the safety of

their bases. The British suffered heavier losses: three battle cruisers, three armoured cruisers, a flotilla leader, and seven destroyers; compared to German losses of one battle cruiser, one pre-dreadnought, four light cruisers, and five destroyers. But the strategic situation had not changed. The Grand Fleet's margin of superiority remained unshaken and the relentless blockade continued. A few weeks later Scheer reported to the kaiser: 'Even the most successful result from a high sea battle will not compel England to make peace.' He urged the resumption of unrestricted submarine warfare.

Scheer made another attempt to draw the Grand Fleet into a submarine ambush on 18 August; the British were forewarned again but unable to intercept the Germans and lost two cruisers to submarines. They then decided not to risk the Grand Fleet in the southern part of the North Sea. The waters south of 55° 30' N and east of 4° E would be left to submarines. The stalemate resumed and by the beginning of 1917 the balance within the German government was tipped in favour of those advocating unrestricted submarine warfare.

The Germans resumed unrestricted submarine warfare on 2 February 1917. They quickly achieved spectacular success which peaked in the month of April. If the Germans had continued to sink ships at this rate they would indeed have won the war. The submarine menace was countered by the adoption of the convoy system. Convoy had been a time-honoured device in the days of sail but the British had been reluctant to adopt it for a multitude of reasons, including fear of congestion in ports or excessive delays, plus a faulty assumption about the number of vessels that would have to be escorted. Convoys and evasive routeing had the advantage of making ships harder for submarines to find and the extra dividend of bringing submarines to a position where they could be engaged and sunk by the escorts, something fruitless submarine hunting had failed to do. Consequently German submarine losses rose while allied merchant shipping losses declined. As convoys proved their value, an elaborate system was developed in the North and South Atlantic and Mediterranean. The Germans tended to shift their attacks to coastal waters and to the vulnerable points between ports and convoy dispersal or assembly points. The British responded with a system of local convoys. In addition aircraft and dirigibles were now able to play an important role close to the shore by keeping submarines from operating on the surface and reaching favourable firing positions. Losses to submarines were never entirely eliminated, but they were eventually brought to acceptable levels and in the second quarter of 1918 for the first time tonnage of new construction exceeded losses. The anti-submarine war required immense effort to organize and route convoys, co-ordinate routeing with wireless interception and intelligence, standardize construction, and produce specialized anti-submarine craft such as sloops. But it worked: submarines would not win the war for Germany.

Allied naval leaders were curiously slow to recognize the convoy as the major antidote to the submarine and wasted considerable energy on alterna-

View from the quarter-deck of the *Queen Elizabeth* class battleship HMS *Barham* on 21 November 1918 as the Grand Fleet prepares to meet the surrendered ships of the High Seas Fleet. A picket-boat is alongside and astern a battle cruiser, probably HMAS *Australia*. In the mist to the right, the aircraft carrier *Furious*, foreshadowing the capital ship of the future.

mand in the Adriatic kept a far larger force masking the Austrians than necessary, the French fleet at Corfu and the bulk of the Italian fleet at Taranto. Nevertheless French battleships reinforced British forces in the Aegean and the threat of the Black Sea Fleet proved to be a mirage. The Germans only got their hands on some of the ships, the Russians scuttled others, and material difficulties and manpower shortages resulted in very few being put into service by the time the war ended.

Until the very end of the war the Grand Fleet always had to be prepared for a naval action at any moment. This required keeping large numbers of destroyers with the fleet that might better have been used in protecting shipping. But nothing is preordained in war and Jellicoe and Beatty, his successor in command of the Grand Fleet, did not enjoy the benefits of hindsight. Indeed, a great battle might well have occurred, for when the German government began the negotiations leading to the armistice Scheer and the naval high command were not willing to accept the verdict and planned a final action. They were frustrated by their own men, for the relative inactivity of the big ships of the High Seas Fleet had been damaging to morale, and the quite human sentiment that few would want to be killed in the final days of the war resulted in a mutiny. When the High Seas Fleet did eventually sail, it was to meet the Grand Fleet off the coast of Scotland to be escorted to Scottish waters and eventual internment at Scapa Flow.

CHAPTER 9

Economic Warfare

B. J. C. MCKERCHER

D uring the First World War, the first total war of the modern period, the economic vitality of the allied and Central Power alliances became as important as their military strength in pursuing victory. Thus, the strategic goal of economic warfare between 1914 and 1918 was to disrupt the enemy's economy and enervate his financial sinews so as to impair his ability to conduct military operations. Drawing on past experience, creating innovative bureaucratic structures to meet new conditions, and using modern weapons like the submarine to starve enemy populations and enfeeble their industrial production and commerce, the allies and the Central Powers worked to disrupt each other's economic life. Thus, reducing supplies that reached enemy armed forces became integral to the grand strategies of each alliance coalition. Material privation had another dimension: it could foster domestic pressures on enemy governments that might deflect their energies away from the battlefield and weaken their internal cohesion. Admittedly, the importance of some elements of the economic side of the struggle might later have been overemphasized—for instance, the impact of Britain's naval blockade on Germany; yet, no doubt exists that economic warfare was indispensable to the Central Powers' defeat and to allied victory.

Not surprisingly, the overall strategies of economic warfare for the two alliances were determined by the leading economic powers on each side: Great Britain, for the allied coalition, and Germany, for the Central Powers. This meant two contrasting approaches to economic warfare based on differing national development, dissimilar geographies, and different armed strength and diplomacy, to constrain the adversary's industrial, financial, and commercial life. For Britain, an island state whose national survival

Strategies of economic warfare

depended on seaborne imports of food and raw materials and the export of industrialized goods, the concept of economic warfare was not new in 1914. During the French wars of 1792–1815, the British had confronted the 'continental system', Napoleon's effort to weaken their economy—and their war effort—by barring British trade with continental Europe. This action forced the British to find alternative markets and supplies of necessary commodities in other places around the globe. Utilizing the strength of the Royal Navy, London also imposed a maritime blockade against France and its continental allies. Though the British blockade created ill-feeling amongst some neutral trading powers—which in the case of the United States led to the Anglo-American War of 1812—it broke the 'continental system' and helped produce Napoleon's defeat.

For the next century, for instance during the Crimean War of 1854–6, the British did not abandon blockade; and whilst the British participated in international conferences to codify the laws of war, especially at Paris in 1856 and London in 1909, domestic opposition to any restrictions on Royal Navy freedom of action led successive governments to avoid formal limitations on British naval power. Free-trade Britain, of course, opposed belligerent interference with trade when it endangered its maritime commerce, an issue when the northern states in the American Civil War blockaded the South. And at the 1909 London Conference, British delegates helped draft a declaration outlining 'absolute contraband'—arms and munitions—that could be seized on the high seas. But difficulty arose over whether to interfere with 'indirect trade', an enemy importing and exporting these and other goods through neutral powers. Whilst the conference finally allowed the interception of absolute contraband destined for neutral ports if it could be proved that these goods were to be sent on to an enemy, parliament refused to ratify the 'Declaration of London'. By 1914, the Admiralty and the Committee of Imperial Defence readied war plans to use Royal Navy surface vessels to disrupt the German economy by intercepting all merchantmen carrying contraband to and from Germany, even via neutral ports. Importantly, however, Admiralty manuals produced after 1909 compelled Royal Navy officers to observe the Declaration of London if their warships intercepted neutral vessels carrying cargoes other than absolute contraband. The other side of these plans was to ensure the maximum ingress and egress of British supplies and trade goods under Royal Navy protection.

For Germany, the concept of economic warfare before 1914 was determined by its central geographical position on the continent, notions of autarky, and threats from hostile powers. Beginning in the early 1880s, German military planners began considering the possibility of fighting a two-front war, a problem that became critical with the conclusion of the Franco-Russian alliance in 1894. Despite assumptions that enemy efforts would be made to blockade the German coast, the general staff reckoned that essential supplies of grain, meat, and industrial raw materials could be met from within Germany for the duration of such a conflict. It then devised

war plans to achieve a quick land victory against France and Russia—within nine months, the period before German supplies would begin being depleted. The ultimate expression of preparing for a short war came with the Schlieffen Plan in 1905. But by this juncture, Anglo-German relations were poisoned by the German decision to challenge the pre-eminence of the Royal Navy.

As the possibility of Britain joining a war against Germany began to pre-occupy Berlin after 1905, a division opened in the German government between the army and naval staffs. Admiral Alfred von Tirpitz, the naval minister, felt it necessary to assess the economic difficulties that Germany might face should quick victory prove an illusion. The chief of the general staff, General Helmuth von Moltke, sanguine about a German victory, judged that the country's expanding economy was a component of national strength that would provide 'a great source of endurance in war'. Whilst the army won the day, concern about supply in wartime began to animate German industrialists. In 1912, because of pressure from these sources and the navy, German ministers established a permanent commission to collect up-to-date statistics on agricultural production, determine raw material requirements for industry, and chart how both food and raw materials should be stored and allocated. The Germans also assumed that a naval blockade could be minimized by both direct and indirect trade with neutrals like Holland, the Scandinavian powers, and the United States. Still, because of the surmise that the next

The heart of the German war economy resided in the Ruhr steel industry. The greatest of the German steel makers was the Krupp industrial conglomerate. It produced steel for weapons, especially artillery, for armour plate of all sorts, for ship-building and more; and, on the economic side of total war, its workers were as integral to success on the battlefield as were the armed forces.

war would be short, the precise means of breaking a probable enemy blockade were not addressed. As one analysis of pre-war German planning points
out: 'very little was suggested on the great question [of] how the siege was to
be broken.'

To be honest, the general staffs of each European great power hoped that
the next major war would see quick, decisive victory. These staffs planned
accordingly: using ships and railways to deploy troops, artillery, and other
supplies; quickly getting the maximum number of units to the front; and
devising operational plans to defeat enemy armies in the field. Agricultural
production and industrial capacity, necessary for an extended struggle,
received little consideration. When the war broke out in Europe in late
July–early August 1914, of course, each coalition moved immediately to disrupt the enemy's economy. The Germans laid mines off the east coast of England on 4 August. The British responded by mining German North Sea
routes; and they warned neutral powers of this operation, especially Holland,
since the port of Rotterdam handled goods travelling to and from western
Germany. In the face of American pressures to have Britain ratify the Declaration of London, and despite initial French and Russian willingness to honour the declaration if Germany and its allies did so, the British refused to
buckle.

The blockade of the Central Powers

A Foreign Office–Admiralty committee was quickly established under Sir
Edward Grey, the foreign secretary. It examined Britain's legal position
respecting blockade. As a result of these deliberations, spurred on by German mine-laying, the British issued an order-in-council on 20 August. It
stated that the Declaration of London would be observed with certain addi-
tions concerning conditional contraband (foodstuffs and industrial commodities like barbed wire and nautical instruments essential for conducting
war); these products would be subject to capture if destined to help the Central Powers' war effort. Following the precedent of the Napoleonic wars, the
British also established prize courts, independent judicial panels to hear the
cases of captured ships and, on the basis of accepted international law about
contraband, to decide whether these vessels and their cargoes should be
expropriated by the British government or set free. Facing the German
onslaught in north-eastern France before the first battle of the Marne, Paris
supported these initiatives.

By December 1914, the war of movement and mobility on both the eastern and western fronts was superseded by trench warfare and mounting
casualties. Total war had begun. With civilian leaders and general staffs having to plan for a lengthy struggle, economic warfare gained increasing importance. Allied efforts to disorganize the Central Powers' economies took
additional forms: restricting mail (including telegraphic messages), licensing
exports, enforcing legal prohibitions on trading with the enemy, and expanding contraband lists.

British blockade methods were conditioned, and even moderated, at least in the early years of the war, by the importance of international commerce—not only for Britain's post-war position but also for its wartime function as the financier of the Entente. French policy, on the other hand, was driven by a determination to prevent the recrudescence of German economic power after the war. France, therefore, persistently tried to establish greater inter-allied co-ordination, both as a means to further the wartime blockade and as the basis for a post-war economic bloc. Despite an inter-allied economic conference in Paris in June 1916, these objectives were never fully met. Instead a *de facto* division of labour resulted, with France controlling the trade of the land-locked and southernmost neutral bordering on the Central Powers, Switzerland. The management of the relationship became much easier when Italy entered the war in May 1915. Italy could not only orchestrate Switzerland's access to the Mediterranean, but was also able to blockade the Adriatic coast of the Balkans.

The British blockade was co-ordinated by the Foreign Office. This allocation of responsibility reflected the fact that much more than naval strength was vital to the blockade's effectiveness. Most importantly, diplomacy was required in the management of the neutrals bordering on Germany, in order to prevent them from becoming conduits for German imports. Secondly, the monitoring of the trade of the border neutrals relied on a mass of commercial intelligence. A Contraband Department was established under the leader-

Given that the struggle on the Western Front was a war of attrition, artillery barrages became essential to its evolution. With hundreds of thousands of shells necessary for both attack and defence, vast allied economic resources were expended to produce this indispensable weapon.

ship of a senior official, Sir Eyre Crowe. Working with the Admiralty, the Board of Trade, and the intelligence services, in tandem with British embassies and consulates in neutral countries, Crowe played a decisive role in establishing mechanisms by which the Central Powers were increasingly denied imports of foodstuffs, crucial industrial raw materials, and machinery of various sorts. The centre of allied blockade policy resided in London, where economic constraints on the Central Powers were enhanced by refining the legal basis of the blockade (additional orders-in-council and broader contraband lists) and ensuring the completeness of interdiction (the operational potency of the Royal Navy). These two elements of economic warfare were conjoined since, under established international law, a blockade was legal only if it was effective.

The smaller European neutral powers sought to balance between the belligerent alliances: to antagonize either one would invite major social and economic disruption and, perhaps, jeopardize their political survival. One of the most innovative responses occurred in neutral Holland. The Dutch government found itself caught between the Germans on one side, who might invade and occupy Holland if Berlin felt that it sided too much with the allies, and the allies on the other, who might impose the most stringent blockade if the Dutch were seen to be tied closely to the Central Powers. In late autumn 1914, when it became clear to The Hague that the war would not end soon, the Dutch government decided to allow the country's leading trading and shipping firms to control trade. The result was the establishment of the Netherlands Overseas Trust. Through the Trust, private companies rather than the government assumed the responsibility of conforming to the fiats of the British blockade concerning absolute contraband and indirect trade; they also endeavoured to maintain as much as possible normal trading links with Germany. By the same token, the Swiss government found its trade with Germany, a trade essential to Swiss economic survival, curtailed by the land blockade imposed by the French and, later, the Italians. Bern followed the Dutch practice and established a metals trust and other devices to allow Switzerland to survive economically.

In February 1916, because of bureaucratic friction over blockade policy between the Foreign Office and Admiralty, Herbert Asquith, the prime minister, created the Ministry of Blockade as an adjunct of the Foreign Office. This act did not only signal Foreign Office primacy in blockade policy-making; it also re-emphasized the vital importance of economic warfare in allied strategy, something of even greater gravity after the bloodletting later that year at Verdun, the Somme, and in eastern Europe. The new minister was Lord Robert Cecil, the Foreign Office under-secretary; Crowe continued as the senior adviser. Over the next three years, as before, the allied economic noose around the Central Powers' neck tightened. A wide range of commodities beyond absolute contraband were slowly prevented from reaching the Central Powers: meat and meat products, metals and ores, animal and vegetable oils, mineral oils, cotton, and wool. As the war progressed and allied battlefield losses multiplied, any products that might strengthen the Central Powers' armed forces, sustain their industries, or nurture their populations became a target of the blockade.

Allied success is undeniable. For instance, before the war, the weekly per capita German urban consumption of meat was 2.3 pounds; by 1917–18, it fell to 0.3 pounds. Additionally, the number of German civilian deaths attributed to the blockade in 1915 was 88,235 (9.5 per cent above the 1913 total); by 1918, this figure had climbed to 293,000 (37 per cent above the 1913 total). There is controversy about whether the German people actually starved during the war, especially in the difficult winter of 1917–18. The argument is made that weight loss results in a demand for less food and that, when the body adjusts, it can be made to work as hard as ever. In all of this, moreover, it must be admitted that between 1914 and 1918, the blockade impaired little the fighting efficiency of the German armed forces. But the blockade had a social and psychological and, therefore, a political impact on Germany. As General Kuhl, a senior staff officer, argued: 'Many things combined to bring down the German people . . . but I consider the blockade the most important of them. It disheartened the nation.' Economic hardship was one factor that saw many Germans become critical of their government after 1915. Disparities existed in the distri-

Käthe Kollwitz, *Germany's children are hungry.* The allied naval blockade of Germany was designed to weaken the enemy economy and blunt the effectiveness of the German armed forces on land and sea. However, its necessary brutality also hit the civilian population. The vision of starving German children during the war has not abated over time.

bution of food and necessary commodities. For instance, rural areas had reasonable supplies of food, whilst urban areas did not. Within cities, disparity also existed between and within classes. Those people with money or political influence could obtain products on the black market. Within the working class, armament workers were better provided for than unskilled workers, white-collar workers, and even minor government officials. Public discomfort grew as a range of ordinary consumer goods like woollen blankets and leather shoes were in short supply and German prices inflated because of scarcities; over fifty food riots occurred in Germany in 1916, a number that increased in 1917–18. Along with food rationing—the harsh winter of 1917–18 compounded German unease—the impact of the blockade played a part in the revolution of November 1918 that led to the abdication of Kaiser Wilhelm II and the advent of the Weimar Republic.

The move to unrestricted U-boat warfare

The Central Powers' approach towards economic warfare was less sophisticated than that of the allies. In the first months of the war, along with mining the North Sea, the Germans and Austro-Hungarians forbade trading with the enemy, proscribed money payments to the British empire, and censored mail and telegrams (the Bulgarians and the Turks later did the same). When it became obvious by January 1915 that the war would not end with quick victory, and that achieving this victory would require substantial amounts of blood and treasure, the Central Powers' conduct of economic warfare developed two strands. The first was to ensure adequate food and raw material supplies. Given the autarkic suppositions of pre-1914 war planning, German resources had to be exploited to the full. The agricultural and raw material wealth of conquered territory could supplement these resources. Here, the western reaches of the Russian empire beckoned as a means to overcome supply problems caused by the allied blockade—and the capture of these territories was a German war aim. In the case of Belgium, German occupation forces so mercilessly expropriated food and fodder that the civilian population faced starvation. Further afield, Berlin endeavoured to maintain its trading links with neutral powers, especially the Scandinavian states, Holland, and the United States. This involved using both German and neutral merchantmen and, often, being less than truthful in issuing cargo manifests so as to outwit allied naval officers who intercepted these vessels.

The second strand of Central Power economic warfare involved efforts to disrupt the enemy economies, especially that of Britain, the allied paymaster. Shipping, trade, and insurance were all vulnerable to operations by cruisers, but Germany's pre-war naval spending had concentrated on battleships for the North Sea to the detriment of its global capacity to wage a *guerre de course*. The biggest surface threat to British trade at the outset of the war, Spee's East Asiatic Squadron based at Kiaochow, was destroyed at the battle of the Falklands on 8 December 1914. Frustration at the inability of the High Seas Fleet to engage the Royal Navy on reasonable terms produced pressure from some Navy Ministry officials, the press, and business interests for submarine attacks on allied seaborne commerce. Alfred Ballin, the Navy Ministry under-secretary, best encapsulated the tenor of these arguments: Germany had to undertake 'the most brutal carrying out of a submarine blockade'. On 1 February 1915, Wilhelm II and his senior civilian and military advisers decided that German submarines, not surface vessels, would carry out 'a commercial blockade' of allied shipping.

Germany possessed only thirty-nine submarines during the first months of the war. As the operational importance of these warships began to dominate Berlin's naval strategy—they could be built faster and more cheaply than surface craft—Wilhelm II's government diverted greater funding and resources to their development. Between the autumn of 1914 and the spring of 1915, 103 submarines were ordered from German shipyards. By early 1915, the German navy was conducting operations in the Atlantic and North Sea approaches to Britain and France and off Flanders. These attacks had a limited impact on allied imports. For example, in March 1915, only 21 merchantmen out of 5,000 leaving or entering British ports were sunk. But on 7 May 1915, a British liner that had departed from New York, the *Lusitania*, was sunk off Ireland. Although German intelligence believed the *Lusitania* carried war materials and the German embassy in the United States published warnings in American newspapers that such ships would be subject to

Weather Forecast: FAIR.

ETTING THE PACE!
WORLD ADS LAST JANUARY—
MORE Than The Herald.
WORLD ADS LAST FEBRUARY—
More Than The Herald.
WORLD ADS LAST MARCH—
More Than The Herald.
WORLD ADS LAST MONTH—
More Than The Herald.
ful is the Big SUNDAY WORLD To-Morrow!

The World.

"Circulation Books Open to All."   "Circulation Books Open to All."

VOL. LV. NO. 19,618.   ★   NEW YORK, SATURDAY, MAY 8, 1915.   ••   PRICE { ONE CENT in Greater New York and Jersey City. TWO CENTS outside of Greater New York, Jersey City and on trains.

Copyright, 1915, by The Press Publishing
Co. (The New York World).

DON'T FORGET!
Reasonable Photos of Warships. Men
Who Man Them, &c., WE Will the
NAVAL REVIEW Edition of the
Eight-Page Pictorial Supplement of
The Sunday World To-Morrow!

TWO TORPEDOES SINK LUSITANIA; MANY AMERICANS AMONG 1,200 LOST; PRESIDENT, STUNNED, IN SECLUSION.

LUSITANIA, HER CAPTAIN, AND PLACE WHERE SHE WAS HIT

S. S. LUSITANIA

CROSS SHOWS where the LUSITANIA WENT DOWN.

ptain W. T. TURNER

HINGTON, SILENT, AWAITS
ADVICES ON AMERICANS' FATE

m, After Receiving Official News From Queenstown Say-
g "Probably Many Survivors; Rescue Work Progressing
vorably," Leaves White House in Drizzle—Calls No
unsellors or Conferrees on His Return—Situation Most
ense Since Spanish-American War—"Strict Accountabil-
Note" to Germany Is Recalled.

(Special to The World.)

ASHINGTON, May 7.—The White House and State Department at
night received this message from Wesley Frost, the American Con-
Queenstown, Ireland:

usitania sank at 2.30. Probably many survivors. Rescue work pro-
favorably."

message also asked the State Department if Consul Frost should
a list of the American survivors, to which the department replied
ch a list should be sent immediately.
It appeared to him, because earlier messages had given out,
that no passengers had been lost, and therefore America could not
lly involved.
minutes later the Secret Service men, who were on guard at
ouse, were surprised when a puffing policeman, who guards the
oor at the White House, rushed in and told them that the President
t left the house unaccompanied.
The Secret Service men rushed through the parking they saw the
nt cross Pennsylvania Avenue and take a course due north
Sixteenth Street. He appeared to be oblivious to the light drizzle
was falling, and in the newsboys who scampered through the streets
g "Extra, extra! many lives lost on the Lusitania!" Americans
the dead?"
President appeared to be deep in thought as he walked through

(Continued on Fourth Page.)

CUNARD OFFICES CLOSE AS
LIST OF THE DEAD GROWS

Action Unexplained, but an Official Said at 11 o'Clock Only
509 Had Been Accounted For, and Four of These Were
Dead—Hoped to Hear of 200 More by Morning.

The New York offices of the Cunard Line, after giving out a series of
bulletins during the early evening, were unexpectedly closed shortly after
11 o'clock last night. All the line officials, however, remained on duty,
although reporters and other outsiders were shut out. No explanation
was given for this action, nor would officials reply to the question whether
their sudden decision was due to either even worse news than given out,
or to a hint from the British Government that the censorship would in-
terpose.
A high official of the local staff of the Cunard Line, however, although
refusing to allow his name to be used, stated that up to that point but 509
of the ship's company had been accounted for, at least four of these being
known to be dead.
"We hope for a couple of hundred more in the morning," he said.
Eight persons so far are known to the Cunard officials by name as
having been saved. They are Mrs. Bretherton of Los Angeles, Cal., and
her two children, one and two years old; Mrs. H. B. Lafetter of Sydney,
Australia, and her son, F. Lafetter; George A. Kessler of New York,
Miss Jessie Taft Smith of Braceville, O., and Miss Irene Paynter of Los
Angeles, Cal.

3 Years' Work—Cost, $8,000,000;
Sunk by Torpedo—Cost, $4,000

The following estimate may serve to present to the readers of The
World a mental picture of the giant liner Lusitania in comparison with
the small but deadly submarine torpedo that destroyed her:

Average length of a torpedo	16 feet
Length of the Lusitania	790 feet
Average cost of a torpedo	$4,000
Approximate cost of the Lusitania	$8,000,000
Time required to make and test a torpedo	3 months
Time required to build the Lusitania	3 years

AND
TIME REQUIRED TO DESTROY THE LUSITANIA
WITH A TORPEDO................15 minutes.

Liner Attacked Supposedly by German Submarine Off the Irish Coast, and
Goes Down in Fifteen Minutes—Luncheon Being Served at the Time—
Survivors Picked Up From Lifeboats and Taken to Queenstown, Forty
Miles Distant—Regarding 1,254 Passengers and 850 of Crew Aboard,
Cunard Line Says: "First Officer Jones Thinks 500 to 600 Are Saved"—
Ship Left New York Last Saturday With Many Americans, Including
Prominent New Yorkers, Who Disregarded German Warning Not to Sail.

(Special Cable Despatch to The World.)

LONDON, May 8.—The Cunard liner Lusitania was torpedoed, supposedly by German submarines,
shortly after 2 o'clock yesterday afternoon, ten miles off the Old Head of Kinsale, on the south coast
of Munster, Ireland.
She sank fifteen minutes later. The company states that no warning was given her.
Passengers and crew, the Lusitania carried 2,104 persons when she sailed from New York, on May 1.
The meagre, confused reports so far received make it uncertain how many of these have been saved.
A steward of the first boat that reached Queenstown—forty miles by sea from Kinsale—with survivors
from the liner, said he feared that 900 lives had been lost.
This despatch came from Queenstown at 1.10 A. M.:
"The tug Stormcock has returned here, bringing about 150 survivors of the Lusitania, principally
passengers, among whom were many women, several of the crew and one steward.
"Describing the experience of the Lusitania the steward said:
" 'The passengers were at lunch when a submarine came up and fired two torpedoes, which struck
the Lusitania on the starboard side, one forward and the other in the engineroom. They caused terrific
explosions.
" 'Capt. Turner immediately ordered the boats out. The ship began to list badly immediately.
" 'Ten boats were put into the water, and between 400 and 500 passengers entered them. The
boat in which I was approached the land with three other boats, and we were picked up shortly after 4
o'clock by the Stormcock.
" 'I fear that few of the officers were saved. They acted bravely.
" 'There was only fifteen minutes from the time the ship was struck until she foundered, going down
bow foremost. It was a dreadful sight.'
"Two other steamers with survivors are approaching Queenstown."
An official statement issued by the Cunard Steamship Company said:
"First Officer Jones thinks from 500 to 600 were saved. This includes passengers and crew, and is only
estimated."
A despatch to the Chronicle from Queenstown says that "seven torpedoes were discharged from the
German attacking craft, one of them striking the Lusitania amidships."
This would indicate that at least two submarines were arrayed against the liner. Even the new-
est type of the undersea boats carries but six tubes, and most of them have only four.
A despatch coming from Kinsale at 7 o'clock says that at 3.30 two lifeboats were intercepted six
miles off Old Head by the motorboat Elizabeth and convoyed by a Cork tug, which took from one 63 passengers and from the other 16, most of them women and children. They were taken to Queenstown instead of to Kinsale, whither they were bound.
These survivors said that the Lusitania got two torpedoes, the first of which struck her on the port
side. She canted toward the land, and received the second on the starboard side.
They said a heavy list to port followed, and the Lusitania remained afloat for only ten minutes, and
only six lifeboats could be launched. These contained about 300 passengers.
Other reports say that the first of the torpedoes struck the liner near her bows, the second tearing
its way into her engine room. Terrific explosions followed, and great volumes of water poured in
through the rents.
A midnight report to the Chronicle says that the number of survivors at Queenstown is 520.
An Admiralty report said that between 500 and 600 survivors have been landed at Queenstown, "Including many hospital cases, some of whom have died."
In this report it is added that some were also landed at Kinsale, "the number not having yet been received." Private telegrams say that "several hundred passengers" have been landed at Clonakilty, not
far from Kinsale.

Hospitals at Queenstown Caring for Lusitania's Survivors;
Dead and Wounded Arriving on Boats From Scene of Disaster

Cork newspapers say that the number taken to Clonakilty was 509.
Official figures make the number at Kinsale eleven.
The only figures so far offered by Queenstown account for 505 survivors and 4 dead. Of these the tug Stormcock was reported to have
brought in about 150, passengers and crew; the trawlers Dock and Indian
Empire have about 200, the tug Flying Fish about 100 and three torpedo
boats 45 and 4 dead.
In making these figures known, the Admiralty announced that it was
not withholding any verified facts, but that it would decline to pass de-
spatches based merely on rumor.
The naval and military hospitals at Queenstown are receiving the
wounded as they arrive. The survivors are being cared for at hotels and
boarding houses, and "because their immediate wants must be given our
first consideration," neither the Cunard officials nor the Admiralty will
attempt to make up any list of them to-night, it is announced.
The first word that Queenstown had of the disaster was when she
picked up this wireless call from the liner:
"Want assistance. Listing badly."
What this meant needed no definition. During this week alone twenty-

eight vessels had been sunk or damaged in the war zone that Germany
had established about the British Isles.
Admiral Coke lost not a moment, therefore, in despatching to Kinsale
every available tug and steam trawler. The tugs Warrior, Stormcock and
Julia led the procession, with two trawlers and a tug-towed lifeboat in
their wake. Steamers in the vicinity picked up the fleet's calls and
started to her aid.

Sank Quickly After Being Struck.

From the signal station at the Old Head of Kinsale, the Lusitania was
seen at 2.12 o'clock to be in distress. At 2.33 she had completely disappeared, according to reports.
It was officially announced last night that she remained afloat at least
twenty minutes after being torpedoed. At that time it was added
"twenty boats were on the sea."
How many of those were the Lusitania's own lifeboats there is yet no
way of determining. It has been stated, however, that she had time to clear
most, if not all, of them away. She carried boats and rafts enough far at
least 500 more persons than she had in her company.
At midnight the Admiralty was still without information as to the

submarine attack, over 1,000 passengers died, including 120 Americans. The American government, led by President Woodrow Wilson, issued a strong protest that suggested the United States might intervene in the war against Germany.

Through complicated diplomacy—and after more American lives were lost when another vessel was sunk in August—Washington's protest and the chance that American resources might be fully committed to the allied alliance saw the German government adopt a policy of restricted submarine attacks: neutral merchantmen and all passenger liners would be exempt from attack. In large degree, the German submarine offensive went into suspended animation until January 1917. But the German navy's frustration redoubled after the failure to break the Royal Navy's stranglehold on the North Sea in the battle of Jutland. The chief of the Admiralty staff claimed that U-boats could sink 600,000 tons of shipping per month, and that the adoption of unrestricted submarine war would knock Britain out of the war within six months. The navy was supported by the army, devastated by the battles of *matériel* of 1916 and persuaded that they rested on the economic and industrial might of the United States. The failure of the peace negotiations in December 1916 dented the arguments of those more concerned to keep America neutral. Germany reckoned that the war would be won or lost before the United States' military contribution could take effect.

Beginning in February 1917, German submarines conducted the kind of operations envisaged by Ballin and others two years before. Through the

Allied naval forces, especially the Royal Navy, utilized a number of operational tactics to combat German submarine attacks against both naval vessels and merchantmen carrying essential supplies and industrialized goods to and from allied Europe. Along with the use of convoys, smoke screens were one such tactic.

spring and summer of 1917, this German offensive saw mounting shipping losses for Britain and its allies—1,505 merchantmen (2,775,406 tons) in six months. However, supported by the United States navy, the Royal Navy responded with effective defensive measures: heavily protected convoys, improved employment of depth charges and mines, and better use of intelligence. By late 1917, although the British had to ration food, and some basic commodities were in short supply, Germany's ability to disrupt allied economic life via the submarine offensive abated (617 sinkings in five months). Attacks on allied shipping continued into 1918 with limited effectiveness, but the Central Powers had lost this critical element of the economic war by the time the Germans forced the Bolshevik Russian regime to sign the Treaty of Brest-Litovsk and embarked on their great, and ultimately unsuccessful, offensive in 1918.

Because of the unexpected duration of the struggle, the operational side of economic warfare for both alliances was balanced by their diplomacy towards the neutral powers. The reason was simple: the onset of total war meant that the allied and the Central Powers' economies required agricultural products, industrial raw materials, and specialized machinery, plus financial assistance, that could come only from neutral sources. Although belligerent foreign policies considered a series of minor issues touching the neutrals, like Spain's desire to trade with Germany, London, and Berlin were each preoccupied with their alliance's relations with Sweden and the United States. The turning point for both of these problems occurred in mid-1917 with the collapse of the tsar's regime and American entry into the war against the Central Powers. The result was a diplomatic victory for the allied powers that strengthened their ability to disrupt the Central Powers' war effort.

The effects on neutral powers

The most important European neutral power for both the Central Powers and the Entente until mid-1917 was Sweden. This situation stemmed from several factors: the Swedish government's avowed neutrality after August 1914; the pro-German and anti-Russian proclivities of the Swedish court, armed forces, and political and intellectual élites; and the geographical importance of the country respecting trading routes to both Germany and tsarist Russia. In August 1914, the Swedish government simultaneously declared its neutrality and its intention to continue its commercial links with Germany—in this, it had American support until April 1917. Just as crucial in this period, Stockholm had a decided diplomatic advantage of its own. The only effective trading route for tsarist Russia was overland from Swedish ports like Gothenberg to the Russian grand duchy of Finland; the Turks closed the Dardanelles, and a rail-line from Nikolaev on the Murman coast south was not yet completed. In difficult negotiations in early 1915, and despite an even more restrictive British order-in-council (March 1915), the Swedish government forced the allies to accept the principle of transhipment: for every ton of goods of either Swedish domestic production or foreign manufacture that crossed Sweden bound for Russia, the Swedes could export an equivalent amount to Germany.

Though distasteful to the Admiralty and other ministries in London, this arrangement was supported by the British minister in Stockholm, Esme Howard, and the Russian government. Transhipment was the price to ensure that adequate supplies reached Russia, permitting the tsar's regime to maintain its armies against Germany and Austria-Hungary on the eastern front. A Russian military collapse or a separate peace treaty would free 80 to 100 German divisions that, if transferred west, could allow Germany to break the military stalemate in France. Added to Howard's concern was a veiled Swedish threat that, if pushed too hard over blockade, Sweden would join the war on the side of the Central Powers. Such an event could drive Russia from the war. This does not mean that Howard approved of transhipment—he did not. But the dictates of *realpolitik* had to guide allied policy, and Crowe and the Contraband Department grudgingly supported Howard's application of blockade policy in the north.

The United States was the most important neutral power for both the allies and the Central Powers. American policy concerning the belligerent's economic warfare after August 1914 was based on a demand for 'freedom of the seas' or, more prosaically, neutral trading rights. Wanting access to American goods and capital, both alliances warily approached the Americans. The Wilson administration's success in neutering Germany's submarine offensive after the *Lusitania* sinking has already been discussed. Less effective was American resistance to the British orders-in-council, prize courts, and other elements of the allied blockade. Washington's opposition to these measures was driven home to the British and their allies in a series of formal protests between late 1914 and the end of 1916. Strong pro-allied and Anglophile sentiments were held by a number of prominent Americans, including Wilson and the financier J. P. Morgan, Jr., whose firm served as Britain's banker in the United States. But Anglo-American relations were severely strained in the first two years of the war as, backed by the power of the Royal Navy, London refused to modify the blockade to meet American grievances. By late 1916, when American presidential elections were held, the possibility of a rupture between the two English-speaking powers seemed possible. Wilson won re-election in November on promises to keep out of the war and ensure the 'freedom of the seas'. The tangible manifestation of American sensitivity towards the allied blockade came with the passage of a bill in Congress in December authorizing the construction of a navy 'second to none'. A major crisis seemed imminent.

But then came Germany's announcement of unrestricted submarine warfare. On 3 February 1917, American repugnance to this major assault on neutral trading rights led to a severing of relations with Germany. American anti-Germanism grew during the next two months and, nurtured by issues like the Zimmermann telegram, led to the American declaration of war against Germany on 6 April 1917. United States entry into the war came at a

propitious moment for the allies. A month earlier, the tsar's regime had been overthrown by moderates seeking a constitutional government. The resultant chaos in Russia, which led to a disastrous offensive in the summer and the Bolshevik *coup d'état* in November, saw Russia's withdrawal from the war. Germany's chance to break the stalemate in the west had arrived; its offensive there began in March 1918. These events in the year after April 1917 meant that allied economic warfare entered a new phase. This phase was marked by heightened economic pressure on the Central Powers that, simultaneously, led to a weakening of the German submarine offensive, further material shortages, and increasing domestic unrest in Germany and Austria-Hungary. Additionally, with the United States a belligerent, the neutral powers, chiefly Sweden, had lost their most powerful ally in seeking to mitigate the impact of the blockade.

Indeed, the United States navy joined with the Royal Navy in enforcing the blockade against both the Central Powers and their neutral suppliers, and it did so with unexpected vigour. After the collapse of Russia's war effort, Sweden's threat to intervene in the war on Germany's side disappeared; Howard, Crowe, and the Ministry of Blockade now turned the economic screws on

The effectiveness of the allied blockade made money of little value within the German economy. Barter, thus, became crucial for the survival of the average German, especially in the cities. This photograph shows Berliners bartering potato peelings for firewood in 1917.

Economic warfare and final victory

Sweden—and Germany—as tightly as they could. Finally, American supplies and loans flowed more easily across the Atlantic to aid the allied armies in meeting the renewed German threat on the western front. It is not surprising that, within a month of the American declaration of war, Arthur Balfour, Grey's successor as foreign secretary, went to the United States to arrange new loans and increase American material assistance to the allied war effort. The American Expeditionary Force played a minor role in the final defeat of the Germany and its allies in November 1918. Yet, strengthened by the United States navy and with full access to American economic and financial resources, allied economic warfare in the final eighteen months of the conflict helped hasten the collapse of the Central Powers. Allied blockade policies pursued from August 1914 to April 1917 had disrupted the German economy, increased food shortages, and created domestic unrest that led to worrying civil disturbances like the food riots. After mid-1917, more effective allied economic warfare accentuated these problems for Germany

The economic dislocation in Germany caused by the allied naval blockade created political unrest, including anti-government demonstrations. This photograph shows anti-government rioters, in the midst of street fighting in Berlin, stopping to butcher a dead horse with pocket knives while the fighting goes on around them.

and its confederates. When the great German offensive failed to deliver the anticipated knock-out blow by the late summer of 1918 and its three allies sought separate armistices, Wilhelm II's government realized that it lacked the military and economic capability to continue the struggle. The result was the collapse of the imperial regime, the advent of its republican successor, and the German surrender on 11 November 1918.

Economic warfare was of decided importance in the course of the First World War. Overall, the ability of each alliance coalition to disrupt the enemy's economy and cripple its financial health became as crucial in the pursuit of victory as success on the battlefield. When quick victory proved illusory, the strategies of economic warfare on both sides became more precise and more brutal. The allies proved ultimately more adept at practising this element of the art of total war, something seen in the legal basis of their blockade, the establishment of the Contraband Department and Ministry of Blockade, their anti-submarine skills, and their pragmatic diplomacy towards the neutral powers before and after mid-1917. Conversely, the Central Powers' conduct of economic warfare was simplistic: find material supply from neutrals and captured territory whilst using submarines to attack allied and neutral shipping. When German leaders opted for unrestricted submarine warfare, they drove the United States into the allied camp, weakened friendly powers like Sweden, and, because of added shortages in essential commodities, saw a rise in domestic discomfort amongst their populations that struck at the political strength and cohesion of the German and Austro-Hungarian states. Although not solely responsible for the Central Powers' defeat, the allied approach to the economic side of the struggle 'disheartened' the Central Powers and helped undermine their ability to wage total war.

CHAPTER 10

Economic Mobilization: Money, Munitions, and Machines

HEW STRACHAN

The short war illusion

We are often told that soldiers marched off to war in August 1914 believing that they would be home before the leaves fell—or, at worst, by Christmas. That is no more than a comment on human nature. Wishful thinking in the face of adversity is one of the mechanisms by which people cope. It is not necessarily an insight into pre-war assessments concerning the war's duration or its nature. Popular conceptions should not be mistaken for expert opinion.

When Helmuth von Moltke succeeded Schlieffen as Germany's chief of the general staff he told the kaiser that the next war 'will not be settled by a decisive battle but by a long wearisome struggle with a country that will not be overcome until its whole national force is broken'. In so saying he was doing no more than repeating the wisdom of his distinguished uncle. Nor was he alone. When Kitchener became secretary of state for war in Britain in August 1914 he advised the cabinet to ready itself for a war that would last three years.

Soldiers had three reasons for anticipating a long and indecisive war. First, they knew, in so far as anyone could know, the likely impact of the revolution in firepower that had taken place since 1871. This appeared to favour the

134

defensive and was likely to make attacks protracted and costly affairs. Secondly, the widespread adoption of universal military service did more than create abundant reserves on which a long war could feed; it also, in a more democratic age, ensured that states would only fight when the cause was deemed both just and popular. Such a war, once started, would by definition be difficult to stop. Thirdly, the alliance blocs of 1914 meant that a decisive victory over one power would not of itself settle the outcome of the war.

The problem for Moltke, as it had been for Schlieffen, was that the German army could not live with the implications of this analysis. Britain, France, and Russia had a combined national income 60 per cent greater than that of Germany and Austria-Hungary; even in terms of peacetime military expenditure, the three Entente nations comfortably outstripped the Central Powers. A protracted war promised defeat for Germany.

It was therefore precisely because he recognized the danger of a long war that Schlieffen developed an operational plan for a short and decisive campaign against France. But since he knew that tactical and strategic logic vitiated his own solution, he used arguments that were economic and financial to buttress his position. He argued that the war would be short because the powers could not afford it to be long.

A large body of informed economic opinion took a similar line. Indeed one of the best-known analyses of future war written before 1914, that by I. S. Bloch, a Polish banker, was not so out of step with the then-current orthodoxy as some would have us believe. Bloch anticipated a long and indecisive war, and reckoned that even the advanced nations would have considerable difficulties in funding it. His conclusion was as irrationally optimistic as the popular mood of August 1914 itself: he contended that the costs would deter nations from going to war.

Bloch's military analysis was correct, his financial calculations totally wrong. Even the poorest European powers were not forced out of the war by financial imperatives. Indeed the Ottoman empire sustained the longest war of all, since it effectively began fighting in 1912. The treasuries of Europe saw their task not as one of restraint but of enablement. Typical was Karl Helfferich, Germany's finance secretary from February 1915 to May 1916, who rejected thrift; the watchword in Germany was that 'money plays no role'. In Britain, the chancellor of the exchequer at the war's outbreak, Lloyd George, had—in the opinion of J. M. Keynes—not the 'faintest idea of the meaning of money'. In general the belligerents took the view that the bulk of the war's costs would be paid after the war was over.

Taxation therefore played a minimal role in funding the war as it was being fought. Most states' taxation systems in 1914 relied on indirect revenue, principally customs and excise, and these receipts declined as international trade diminished. Britain alone had an effective system of income tax in place in 1914, although only 1.13 million of the total population of 46 million paid it. During the war 2.4 million entered the system for the first time, and the con-

Financing the war

Crowds assembled in cities throughout Europe on the eve of war but many did so not to support or oppose the conflict but to withdraw cash from their banks. What they wanted was hard currency, not notes. Here in France, 1,500 million francs were withdrawn in four days, prompting the very moratorium the queues had aimed to anticipate.

tributions of waged members of the working class multiplied 3.7 times. But taxation still only covered about 20 per cent of Britain's war costs. The prime function of taxation was to curb inflation—generated in part by the fact that money incomes were rising while the availability of consumer goods was falling—and to sustain international credit.

The reason why so many financiers had anticipated a short war was that they had underestimated the state's ability to borrow. The war was financed primarily by credit. Loans were raised in three ways. First and most significant was the issue of short-term treasury bills, which gradually took the place of gold in securing a state's note issue. Thus the cash in circulation increased in step with the government's borrowing, so stoking inflation. Between 1914 and 1918 note circulation in Germany rose 1,141 per cent, in Britain 1,154 per cent, and in Austria-Hungary 1,396 per cent. The inflationary effects meant that the increase in money supply became a form of compulsory domestic borrowing.

By contrast, the second form of borrowing, publicly issued war bonds, was subscribed to voluntarily. Buying bonds became an indication of faith in ultimate victory and thus a form of popular mobilization. It was also a means of consolidating the floating debt created through the expansion of the note issue. As the war went on, much of the war loan stock was, like the treasury bills, taken up by financial institutions. France was the most successful of the belligerents in mobilizing private investors.

France did not issue its first war loan until November 1915, and Britain issued only three war loans in all. The difference between the borrowing patterns of these two powers and those of other belligerents can be explained by their comparatively greater reliance on overseas credit—the third form of borrowing. This is not to say that foreign borrowing was unimportant to the Central Powers: Germany advanced credits to Austria-Hungary in exchange for gold, and in its turn Germany passed gold to Turkey in exchange for Turkish treasury bills. Thus the people of Germany, not the people of Turkey, funded increases in currency in the Ottoman empire. But Germany was not able to lock into the most important neutral money market in the world, that of New York. German imports from the United States were restricted by the Entente's blockade. Thus its demand for dollars was also limited.

By contrast the Entente, and particularly Britain, paid for goods in the United States with money raised in the United States. Initially, much of this effort was directed towards the needs of Russia. Because Russia lacked the international financial credibility possessed by Britain, the latter acted on its behalf. Over 70 per cent of American funds advanced to Britain and France up until April 1917 were destined for Russian use. But in 1915 Britain also became banker to Italy's war effort, and in 1916 increasingly to France's. By 1 April 1917 Britain was spending $75 million a week in the United States, and it had borrowed $358 million against total securities of $490 million.

Predictions of a short war therefore rested on the presumption that the orthodoxies of peacetime financing would continue to prevail in war. Economic analysts could envisage running out of cash; they found it harder to imagine running out of munitions. But in the event the maximization of resources, not the management of money, came to dominate the economic policies of the warring powers.

Shell shortage

In 1914 Europe was in the grip of a land arms race which had grown in intensity since the second Moroccan crisis of 1911 and had been stoked by the Balkan wars. The consequent level of mobilization within the arms industry even in peacetime confirmed the beliefs of those who expected a long war, not a short one. And yet the first major economic crisis of the war—apart from the initial problems of liquidity consequent on mobilization—was not one of funding but one of production.

Shell shortage was a phenomenon common to all the armies by the winter of 1914–15. Most had built up stocks which they thought would be sufficient for a minimum of three months' fighting, and in some cases six months'. But they ran out of shells much faster than that. The French were short of shells by mid-September, and the Germans, British, and Russians by late October. Thus the cause of shell shortage was not that the war was longer than they had expected but that its nature was different.

The principal precipitant of shell shortage was trench warfare. If shell

The real strength of the British ministry of munitions lay not in London—for all Lloyd George's trumpeting of his own achievements—but in the regions. National shell factories and national shell-filling factories, the second of which were commemorated for the Canadian War Memorial Fund by Charles Ginner, were administered by area boards made up of local businessmen.

shortage arose in manœuvre warfare it tended to be transitory—the result of horse-drawn supply not keeping pace with the fast-moving armies in the field. Once the front became static, the line of communications between factory and battery became secure. If the guns ran short of shells in trench warfare, they did so not because of transport problems but because the rate of fire exceeded the rate of production. Furthermore fixed positions enabled the guns to identify more targets. This not only increased shell consumption, it also generated a demand for a different type of shell from that with which most field artillery batteries were equipped in 1914. Shrapnel, which burst in the air scattering fragments in a forward projection, was the preferred munition against dispersed infantrymen advancing over open ground. But high explosive was deemed more appropriate against men who had dug in. Generals anxious to explain their failures in 1914 were quick to attribute all to a lack of high-explosive shell. In doing so they only exacerbated the shortage of which they complained, effectively discouraging the search for tactical and operational solutions in favour of that for economic and industrial ones.

The pursuit of methods by which to increase shell production in 1914–15 was the outward manifestation of a fundamental reorientation of industry, from peacetime needs to wartime priorities. Given the requirements of domestic consumption and of international trade, no power could contemplate such a dislocation in advance of war itself. Although the political dimensions of the change varied according to local circumstances, the economic realities were broadly speaking comparable. Three specific issues arose immediately—the need to secure raw materials, the demand for labour, and the availability of plant.

The most immediate cause of shortages in raw materials was invasion. France's output of coal, iron ore, and steel was slashed by the loss of its northeastern territories in August; Austria-Hungary's Galician oilfields were under Russian occupation until May 1915; and as Russia evacuated Poland in the same summer it lost a fifth of its coal and a tenth of its iron ore. More delayed in its effects was blockade. Russia, its Baltic and Black Sea exits closed, and its western frontier a battlefield, found its remaining maritime links—Vladivostok, Archangel, and Murmansk—too distant and too poorly served by railways to sustain the imports it required.

The fear of British involvement in the war had caused the German navy to stress the vulnerability of the Ruhr to a blockade of imported raw materials as early as 1906. Although little was done before 1914, Germany's response in August was immediate: a raw materials office was set up under the aegis of the Prussian war ministry. The office was an agent of collectivism, its task being the central allocation of raw materials. But its staff, including its parent and first head, Walther Rathenau of AEG, were mostly drawn from large companies. The capitalist ethos was evident in the fact that the ownership of raw materials remained vested in individual businesses.

Such paradoxes were not confined to Germany. All the industrially more advanced belligerents relied on businessmen to staff their war economies. In Russia, where the issue was less the conversion to war production and more the advent of industrialization *per se*, industry effectively mobilized itself. In June 1915 the association of trade and industry called for full industrial mobilization and created a central war industries committee. By 1916 the Russian economy had grown 21.6 per cent over 1913. At the opposite extreme was Austria-Hungary. Alone of the belligerents it had collectivist legislation in place before the war began: the 1912 emergency war law allowed the state to take over war-related businesses, and made their employees liable to military law. On the one hand entrepreneurial flair seemed to be snuffed out, and on the other the state's supervisory apparatus was fragmented by interministerial disputes and by Hungary's refusal to co-operate with what it saw as an Austrian arrangement. None the less, by 1916 key production indices showed an improvement over 1913; they fell in 1917 and collapsed in 1918.

Britain, its maritime links robust until 1917, was more worried by the management of labour than by the acquisition of raw materials. Lloyd George, who became the first minister of munitions in June 1915, was determined to

'Please let us know, as soon as possible, the number of tins of raspberry jam issued to you last Friday.'

Waste was a consequence of industrialized war, particularly for the better-supplied Entente armies on the western front. The salvage of equipment kept 50 men in continuous employment in one Australian division in 1917. Another approach to waste management was tight accounting, which required harrassed front-line officers to fill in countless forms in seemingly pettifogging bureaucracy.

curb the power of the trade unions, and particularly the right to strike. Munitions workers found themselves committed to compulsory arbitration. Nor were they free to change employment: by mid-1915 the recruiting of the New Armies had deprived the arms factories of 16 per cent of their workforce and the chemicals and explosive industries of 23.8 per cent. Vickers initiated the policy of 'badging' their workers, to enable them to resist the imputation that their lack of uniform indicated a lack of patriotism. 'Dilution'—the use of unskilled labour in automated processes—was some compensation for the loss of skilled workers, but it was fiercely contested by the trade unions, and eventually adopted as a wartime expedient only.

These problems were less acute in countries with conscription. In France, Albert Thomas, appointed a junior minister with responsibility for munitions in May 1915, shared with Lloyd George a radical pedigree, but like others elsewhere set out to boost production through the enlistment of capitalism rather than through the espousal of collectivism. Workers' rights were secondary. A law of August 1915 established the notion of 'military workers', men released from the army for the needs of war production, but who thereby lost the freedom to change jobs and also effectively forfeited the right to strike. When Britain eventually adopted conscription—in early 1916—it was as much a device for apportioning the nation's workforce as a whole as it was a means to get men for the army.

The third problem—that of plant—was one that afflicted all powers. Most routine arms orders before the war were handled by state ordnance factories. The work of private business in peacetime was restricted to the construction of warships (where there was effectively over-capacity in the context of the immediate needs of 1914–15) or to the satisfaction of specific but often short-term demands. To prevent plant lying idle, arms firms either diversified into other businesses or pursued export markets. What they could not do was sustain in peacetime the level of plant which wartime orders would demand.

Thus, when the belligerent nations turned to private industry with massive orders for guns and shells, the specialized arms manufacturers were unable to respond in short order. Many of them were also cautious: the construction of new factories and the acquisition of fresh machinery would leave them with excessive capacity at the war's end. What resulted was a *de facto* division of labour. The pre-war arms manufacturers—including Krupps in Germany, Schneider-Creusot in France, Skoda in Austria-Hungary, and Vickers in Britain—concentrated on the most sophisticated end of the market. They built heavy artillery which required precision engineering using highly specialized machine tools. The production of other weaponry was reconfigured in such a way that businesses with no background in arms manufacture could be rapidly enlisted.

Trench warfare helped. It promoted a reversion to 'old' technologies, the mortars and grenades of siege warfare—neither of them sophisticated devices and both means of drawing in new firms to arms production. In Russia Fabergé abandoned jewellery for grenades. Shell manufacture was simplified. In Germany and France shells were made of cast iron rather than compressed steel so that factories equipped with simple turning lathes and milling machines (rather than hydraulic presses) could be brought into service. Thus automobile manufacturers like Louis Renault were able to enter the munitions business. But the turning process could not fashion the nose-cone of the shell, and Renault's shells had to be made in two parts, so earning the nickname 'bi-blocs'.

The short-term consequence of increased output was a fall in quality. Inspection standards were lowered, and the performance of the new shells did not match that of the old. France lost over 600 field guns in 1915 through premature explosion. On the Somme in 1916 30 per cent of the shells fired by British guns proved to be duds. Not until after 1916 would the defects inherent in rapid expansion of production—the lowering of inspection standards, the incorporation of ill-qualified firms, the dilution of skilled labour—be overcome. In the last two years of the war the belligerents, and especially the Entente powers, enjoyed both quantity and quality.

The battle of matériel

Between 1914 and 1916 the major land powers of Europe were in some senses running hard to stay in the same spot. They had committed themselves to the formation of mass armies before the war began. Thus much of their productive effort was devoted to making good the gaps which the opening battles made in their massive arsenals. France, for example, became preoccupied with 75-mm. guns and shells to the virtual exclusion of heavy artillery. But Britain did not enter the war with a mass army. Its munitions crisis was driven to a lesser degree by the problems of replacement and replenishment and to a much greater degree by those of rapid expansion. In equipment terms it was less constrained by what it already had. Furthermore both services had come to rely on a margin of technological superiority—in the navy as means to sustain its overall supremacy, and in the army as compensation for its numerical inferiority in the operations of colonial conquest. In 1904 Britain was the first power to standardize the distribution of machine guns; in 1905 it spearheaded the dreadnought revolution. In 1915, therefore, it continued to seek a qualitative edge and to use technology to complement, or even to substitute for, manpower. One outcome was the development of the tank. But much more significant was a sequence of programmes developed for the production of heavy artillery, not field artillery, and which set targets in excess of Britain's manpower capabilities. Britain hoped to win the war in 1917 by the systematic application of industrial power to the battlefield. In the event alliance considerations brought this timetable forward to July 1916, too early for this arsenal to be fully available or for the imperfections in its employment to be resolved. Moreover, the effects of Verdun on the French army meant that British manpower took the larger share of the Somme battle. Britain would not experience the full benefits of its artillery superiority until 1917–18.

By 1916 both Britain and, to a lesser extent, France had accepted a considerable degree of control and centralization in the direction of their war economies. But in Germany the chancellor, Bethmann Hollweg, remained resistant to anything that smacked of corporatism. Such convictions were challenged by the impact of Verdun and the Somme: the British artillery, in the opinion of some observers, broke the old German army and loosened, if not shattered, its morale. The Germans employed a new vocabulary to describe what they saw as a new type of warfare, a 'battle of *matériel*'.

Not the least of those whose views were reshaped was the new chief of the general staff, Hindenburg, whose first exposure to the fighting on the west-

ern front this was. On 31 August 1916 Hindenburg launched his so-called 'programme', to double the supply of munitions and to triple the output of machine guns and artillery by May 1917. The main effect was rhetorical. The targets were little different from those already established by the Prussian War Ministry, and in any case they were not met. What had set the pace of gun production in Germany was the output of powder for the shells; the German chemical industry was reliant on imports of cotton, camphor, pyrites, and saltpetre in 1914. It developed alternative processes to compensate for these, but there remained little point in having more guns if there was nothing to fire from them.

Moreover, the Hindenburg programme treated the arms industry in isolation from the economy as a whole—despite the fact that the message of 1916 was that the two were indivisible. In part this was a reflection of bureaucratic confusion. For the general staff to state its munitions requirements was unexceptionable; for it to do so in direct collusion with its industrial suppliers and without the involvement of the Prussian War Ministry was not. In October 1916 the supreme headquarters proposed the creation of an economic command that would be under its control and independent of the War Ministry. In the event the new authority, called the War Office, was incorporated within the framework of the existing War Ministry, but duplicated many of its functions.

Austria–Hungary's iron and steel industries were slow to modernize, and their output lagged far behind that of the other major European powers before the war. The empire never overcame the deficit, and by 1918 its steel production had slumped to half the 1916 peak of 3.3 million tons. Church bells were collected in the Vienna arsenal for conversion into munitions.

What had set industry against the existing War Ministry was the management of labour. Industry wanted to direct Germany's workforce in its own interests. The War Ministry was more sensitive to other concerns—not only the army's need for men but also the recognition of workers' rights. The Hindenburg programme exacerbated these tensions, as its achievement depended on the release of skilled workers from the army. Industrialized war demanded a labour policy that was comprehensive in its acknowledgement of the needs of the army, industry, and labour. Thus the vision that impelled the War Office's Auxiliary Service Law, approved by the Reichstag in December 1916, was genuinely corporatist. In conscripting all males aged 17 to 60, Germany accepted the principle of compulsory arbitration and accepted the role of trade unions in the management of labour.

At a parochial level what is striking in both measures is that Germany's legislation was introduced four years after Austria-Hungary's emergency war law and about eighteen months after comparable steps had been taken in Britain. Even then the controls which were imposed were less extensive.

In March 1915 the British trade unions had insisted that the corollary of the loss of rights for those in munitions industries should be a limitation on employers' profits. The Munitions of War Act had therefore set a ceiling on the profits of armaments firms, and in September 1915 an excess profits tax was imposed in those businesses engaged in other activities. Italy followed suit in November, Austria-Hungary in April 1916, and France in July. The British tax was far from perfect, and both Austrian and French businesses were able effectively to postpone payment until after the war: Citroën showed a profit of 6.1 million francs between 1914 and 1917, but paid only 60,000 francs in tax. But in Germany, although it too introduced a war profits tax at the end of 1915, the government gave sufficient notice to enable evasion, and thereafter firms could avoid liability by transferring their profits to their reserves or by acquiring government war loans. Firms set prices on delivery and thus the state (as the principal consumer) became the main payer of the tax. The trade unions demanded the tax be tightened as part of their acceptance of the Auxiliary Service Law, but failed. Wilhelm Groener, the first head of the War Office, found himself forced out of his job when he took a similar line in 1917. In 1916 the Daimler motor works distributed a dividend of 35 per

In November 1914 France's daily output of 75mm shells was the same—13,000—as it had been at the outbreak of the war. It reached its January 1915 target—80,000—in July. Thereafter, by following a policy of standardization and large-scale production, Citroen overhauled Renault as France's principal private shell manufacturer, producing 24 million shells by 1918.

FABRICATION DES OBUS SHRAPNELLS

ANDRÉ CITROËN

POUR LA FRANCE LA RUSSIE L'ITALIE ET LA ROUMANIE

cent, and the most successful steel and mining firms showed an eightfold increase in profits on 1912–13 over the first three years of the war.

It was argued then, and has been since, that the profit motive was the best method of mobilizing industry for the war effort. But this argument could not apply if high profits went hand in hand with falling productivity. German industry's preoccupation with labour reflected its belief that it was the key input in determining production. But the concentration on manpower deflected its attention from machinery. During the war automation declined rather than advanced: Daimler employed 1.8 workers per machine in July 1914 but 2.4 per machine in autumn 1918.

These figures bear testimony to the ability of industry to extract labour from a man-hungry army. But they also indicate the failing powers of workers in the central European lands. Short of food, lacking disposable cash for clothing, their strongest taken for military service, workers found their output falling despite longer working days. In Austria-Hungary in 1916 the output per worker from blast furnaces was 365 tons; in 1917 it was 225 tons. In the Donetz basin in Russia the annual output of coal fell from 146 tons per worker in 1914 to 122 tons in 1916, and of iron from 347 to 202.

In the second half of the war, therefore, the fundamental issue in resource mobilization was the trade-off between machinery and manpower. If automatic weapons, light machine guns, flame-throwers, tanks, and—above all—artillery could substitute for men with rifles, then labour could be released from the army to increase the production of those munitions. Thus the ratio of fire to men at the front line would go up, while at the same time the wheels of industry would be accelerated rather than slowed.

Machinery versus manpower

Herein was the theoretical solution to the conundrum of industrialized war sustained over a long haul. At the beginning of the war an allocation of two machine guns per battalion was standard across all armies. In March 1918 each German division of nine battalions had 54 machine guns and 144 automatic rifles, and each French division 72 machine guns and 216 automatic rifles. The British division, which had 64 machine guns and 192 light machine guns, was in the throes of being reduced from twelve battalions to nine, so immediately increasing its weapons-to-manpower ratio. For the attack at Amiens in August each British battalion, which in 1916 had averaged 1,000 men and been equipped with 4 light machine guns and 1 or 2 light trench mortars, carried 30 light machine guns, 8 light trench mortars, and 16 rifle grenades for its 500 men: it was also preceded by 6 tanks.

At the end of 1917 the British army in France reckoned it would be short of 250,000 men by March 1918, but a cabinet committee on manpower placed the army's manpower needs beneath those of shipbuilding, aeroplane, and tank production. In Germany the Hindenburg programme drained the army of a million men. Between September 1916 and mid-July 1917 the number of workers exempted from military service rose from 1.2 million to 1.9 million, and by January 1918 had reached 2.3 million.

The implications of such decisions were more manageable for the Entente powers. When the Germans attacked in March 1918, the British were reinforced by the French and in due course by the Americans; furthermore, they derived immense benefit in manpower terms from the empire. But the Germans lacked such resources. The German army's holdings of artillery peaked at 7,130 guns in February 1917. By December 1917 they had fallen to 6,353 and by November 1918 to 5,000. The decline was deliberate—a reflection of the lack of men (and horses) available to service them. When confronting collapse in October, the cry of the supreme command was not for munitions but for men.

Manpower was of course not the only variable in determining the relationship between battlefield performance and industrial productivity. Ultimately the Central Powers could not evade for ever the raw material shortages which had preoccupied them at the war's outset. On the whole these constraints were not felt directly at the front—principally because the war economy gave the needs of the armed forces priority. Where they had become most evident by 1918 was in transportation. In 1917 coal production in Germany fell for lack of labour. When labour was released from the army, the availability of coal highlighted the consequences of sustained underinvestment in rolling stock and rail track. The denial of maritime transport and the expansion of territory through conquest increased the load which the railway networks had to bear. Austria-Hungary, as a net coal importer before 1914,

Static fronts made railways better able to supply mass armies than would have been possible in more mobile operations. But by 1918 this gleaming British engine, with its tender full of coal, would have found little reflection in the strained networks of the Central Powers. Insufficient maintenance and inadequate fuel were bringing their locomotives to a halt.

was even more vulnerable to these pressures. By 1918 demand for coal in the Dual Monarchy exceeded supply by 27 per cent. As the war ended the Central Powers were literally grinding to a halt: the movement of coal depended on the railways but the railways themselves were consuming the coal that was produced.

The effect of the blockade in creating these particular resource constraints was indirect at best. Its focus became not contraband narrowly defined—munitions of war and the means for their production—but foodstuffs. However confused the administrative arrangements which the Central Powers adopted in response to food shortages, they at least ensured that those most vital to the war effort—soldiers at the front and workers in heavy industry at home—received priority. The blockade's principal victims, therefore, were those least essential to war industry. None the less, in the eyes of Entente financiers, economic warfare had one decisive, if unintended, effect.

America's entry to the war

On 28 November 1916 the United States' Federal Reserve Board advised its member banks against the purchase of foreign treasury bills, and warned private investors to consider carefully the nature of their overseas investments. Allied shares fell, and $1,000 million was wiped off the stock market in a week. The American economy, fuelled by allied orders, had become too dependent on the war itself and on an ultimate Entente victory for the Board's comfort. Moreover Entente dependence on the United States' money market for access to its industrial capacity created a possible lever with which the United States could act as the broker in peace negotiations.

During the winter of 1916–17, Britain shipped $300 million in gold to buoy up the exchange rate, and so manage the costs of its American imports; it also accumulated an uncovered debt of £358 million with its New York bankers. But it refused to panic. Arguably the economic dependence of the two powers was mutual: the United States could not now afford to countenance an Entente defeat.

That too was the calculation in Berlin. From Germany's perspective the United States, although nominally neutral, had become a covert belligerent in economic terms. Thus it could calculate that the decision in February 1917 to adopt its own form of economic warfare, the unrestricted use of submarines, had no penalty. But in reality Britain could not see how it could continue to pay for the war beyond April. Germany knew of Britain's financial plight, but had so downgraded the significance of money in the war effort that it could not appreciate its potentially decisive implications.

The resource constraint that worried Britain most in the last two years of the war was money. Its own debts to the United States were offset by the debts the allies had incurred in London. But Russia looked likely to default, and neither France nor Italy was as fiscally rigorous as Britain would have liked. When unrestricted U-boat warfare triggered America's entry into the war, the British Treasury breathed a collective sigh of relief. Moreover, the effect of American entry was also to tighten and clinch the blockade of Ger-

Facing: The rape of Belgium in 1914 remained a powerful propaganda tool even in October 1918 and even in the United States. But America's war loans proved unpopular with private investors: the interest rate of 4.25 per cent seemed low in relation to a long period of inconvertibility. The banks took 83 per cent of the third and fourth Liberty Loans.

many, since the belligerents were now freed of any undue regard for neutral opinion.

None the less, it would be wrong to conclude any analysis of the war economies by suggesting that the Entente won because the United States threw in its lot against the Central Powers. First, American financial aid after April 1917, though crucial, was grudging, and ultimately recalled. Secondly, the creation of an American mass army diverted American munitions production from the support of the armies of Europe to that of its own. Thirdly, much of the most sophisticated equipment required for the American armies was provided by the Entente powers—particularly in the shape of artillery from France. Undoubtedly the First World War helped promote New York as a financial centre to rival and eventually overtake London, but the decisive nature of American might in the Second World War should not be projected back on to the First.

CHAPTER 11

Women, War, and Work

GAIL BRAYBON

Within months of the outbreak of war, journalists, politicians, social scientists, and other commentators across Britain, France, and Germany began to talk of its impact on 'society'. With surprising rapidity, the idea took hold that military and industrial mobilization would have a permanent, possibly radical, effect on class, sex, and familial relations. Debates on women workers' future were ironically fuelled by writers from widely differing political backgrounds. Feminists sought to show that women's new skills must now be recognized by all, and that they should be rewarded with 'the Vote'; the patriotic right (and government commentators) used 'women's wonderful work' as propaganda, proof that the nation was united against the enemy; other writers, from a variety of backgrounds, warned that women workers might not want to go 'home' after their experience of new jobs and higher wages, a fear played upon by some trade unionists, concerned with the possible danger of cheap female labour. In many ways, women became a focus for both anxiety and hope amongst those who looked forward to the post-war world.

Contemporary interest in women's role was by no means surprising, given the essential nature of their war work, and their sudden visibility on the urban scene, performing a wide variety of tasks 'normally' done by men, from window cleaning to clipping train tickets. What is perhaps more intriguing is the extent to which so many recent social historians have also accepted the idea

The variety of women's experience

Facing: This American poster, produced shortly after the USA entered the war, was designed to encourage support for the allied war effort, and remind the public of what the French people were going through. The grimness of the factory, and the sight of heavy work being done by women, were designed to elicit sympathy, but ironically reflected reality for many European munitions workers.

that the war was a social and political 'watershed' for women, and even that it marked the 'emancipation' of women. The enduring myth that women's wartime jobs led to dramatic social change can be summed up by this quotation, from a book about the war's impact on world history:

The social behaviour and dress of women altered concomitantly with these changes of status. Women and girls frequented the night clubs that had sprung up during the war, and single women dined in restaurants without escorts. Women began to smoke in public, and their drinking increased. They took up the free use of cosmetics, the bobbing of hair, and the wearing of short skirts or slacks and uniforms at work. Their new social freedom encouraged freer sexual relations, the consequences of increasing promiscuity and illegitimacy.

This is patronizing, misleading, and so inaccurate as to be unworthy of further discussion, but it is a fairly typical piece of hyperbole. There are two main problems with this kind of approach. The first is that it makes assumptions about 'social change' based solely on apparent changes in women's employment patterns—which, as we shall see, have been much exaggerated. Such generalizations do justice neither to the complexities of arguments about women's work, nor to the variety of women's wartime experiences. Secondly, it assumes 'Women' were some kind of coherent group, with a uniform set of aims, ambitions, and experiences. This was not the case. Women's wartime lives were as varied as men's; they were influenced by class, age, marital status, trade, geographical area. Such immediate issues as food rationing, fuel prices, rents, and even local censorship also had an impact. Consider the lives of the following individuals: an Italian peasant woman, running a farm on her own; a Russian nurse on the eastern front; a Scottish fish gutter, unemployed in 1914; a French car worker; a Berlin housewife, sewing uniforms at home; a Woolwich Arsenal worker, forced to leave work because of TNT poisoning. These women had very different wartime experiences, and one can be quite certain that they had more on their minds than bobbing their hair, night clubs, and smoking.

Before 1914

The political and economic structures of Britain, France, and Germany were quite different, yet the role of women in industry before the war was strikingly similar. Most women workers were single, and they always earned considerably less than men, even when working on similar jobs. Usually, there were rigid demarcations between 'men's work' and 'women's work', and any skilled trade which required apprenticeship or long training was almost by definition 'men's'. It was widely assumed that women would leave work on marriage; this encouraged women themselves to view their work as temporary, and employers to under-utilize their skills. They were often viewed with suspicion by trade unions, which tended to cater for skilled men, and saw any suggestion of using female labour as a threat to wages, status, and jobs. Women were also said not to 'need' job security or higher wages, as they were not the primary breadwinners. In reality, however, many working-class wives did move in and out of work according to financial need, and their presence in industry was underestimated by official figures. They took in washing, went out cleaning, did childminding for neighbours, worked for a few hours in the corner shop, or took in lodgers. Middle-class wives, on the other hand, seldom worked after marriage. The rapidly expanding numbers of white-collar jobs in offices, banking, and government departments were taken up by young single women. There were also increasingly large numbers of women in teaching, though only up to a certain level, as they were still barred from many universities.

There was one big difference between Britain and mainland Europe, however, and this was the extent to which women worked on the land. France and Germany still had a large number of peasant farmers, including millions of women, while in Britain, with its large farms and extensive use of agricultural machinery, most rural workers were men.

Russia too had an enormous peasant population, but there were few similarities between this vast, under-industrialized nation and the other three countries. This was an autocratic and strongly patriarchal society, in which women's status was very low. In rural areas, they were completely under the control of husbands or fathers, and confined to hard and unskilled work. Domestic violence was both common and acceptable. Urban dwellers were a small minority—only around 3 million out of a total of 170 million worked in industry in 1914—but in Russia's towns and cities working conditions were worse than anything found in western Europe, where factory inspectors and limits on hours and night work went some way towards curbing the worst exploitation in major industries. All wages were low, but women's were far lower than men's, and those who campaigned for workers' rights risked imprisonment or exile. Housing conditions too were worse, with women factory workers often billeted in barracks attached to workshops. There were also few jobs available for educated women, as white-collar trades were not expanding as fast as in western Europe.

Two other facts are worth noting. The first is that all four countries had feminist movements, although these were of varying size, organization, and militancy. Britain's feminists were by far the most active, but there were high hopes for women's suffrage across western Europe—though Russia seemed to have little prospect of gaining democratic rights for either men or women. The second is that the largest single trade for women was still domestic service. Numbers were declining by 1914, as other job opportunities arose, but service remained the only waged work available for the majority of working-class girls.

Life during wartime

Although the enthusiasm with which Europe's civilian population greeted the outbreak of war has probably been much exaggerated, it is true to say that one of the first casualties of the conflict was the women's peace movement. Valiant attempts were made by a number of feminists (many German and American) to campaign against the war, and force the combatant governments to see sense before it was too late. A peace conference was organized for The Hague, but many feminists turned their back on the movement. As one German feminist said, 'Whatever they may bring, whatever they take, these years represent the solemn peak of the lives of our generation.' A French feminist averred, in 1915, 'French women . . . united with those who battle and die . . . do not know how to talk of peace.' The 'summons to the Daughters of Russia' issued by the League for Women's Equality revealed another aim, which could conveniently go hand in hand with patriotism:

We women have to unite: and each of us, forgetting personal misfortune and suffering, must come out of the narrow confines of the family and devote all our energy, intellect, and knowledge to our country. This is our obligation to the fatherland, and this will give us the right to participate as the equals of men in the new life of a victorious Russia.

Mrs Pankhurst, leader of Britain's militant suffragettes, could not have put it better when she called for 'women's right to serve'. Even those far less enthusiastic about the war than the Pankhursts soon realized that women could prove once and for all that they were worthy of civil and political rights. Most women, however, were neither ardent patriots nor pacifists. They simply accepted the inevitability of war.

As workers, women were newly 'visible' in the towns of Britain, France, and Germany from an early stage in the war, as they took over the jobs of fathers, husbands, and sons who had been called up, or volunteered. Within a few months it was common to see women road sweepers, lamplighters, delivery van drivers, or shop assistants. Their labour was also required across mainland Europe to bring in the harvests of the autumn of 1914. However, it was not until 1915 that the serious recruitment of women to major industries began. As casualty figures rose, more men were withdrawn from civilian life to replace the dead and maimed. A competition for men began between Europe's voracious armies and the war industries, now under pressure to deliver munitions on an unprecedented scale. Third in line for human resources were the civilian industries. Employers turned first to boys, old men, 'colonial' or foreign labour, and even prisoners of war—but in the end they had to accept that women would be necessary to keep both war and civilian factories operating.

The increase in women's industrial employment between 1915 and 1918 seems at first sight astonishing. In Russia, by 1917 it was estimated that women made up 43.2 per cent of the industrial workforce. In the German chemical industry alone, the number of women workers rose from 26,749 in 1913 to 208,877 in 1918; in the machine industry, numbers rose from 74,642 in 1913 to 493,374 in 1918. A single armaments firm, Krupps, employed only 2,000–3,000 women before the war, and 28,000 by January 1918. In France, it was calculated that women made up 33 per cent of the total labour force in munitions by spring 1918. Yet such figures can be misleading, as a closer look at the British statistics reveals. A contemporary analyst calculated that in

1914 there were around 3,276,000 women in full-time employment in industry, finance, and the professions, with another 1,600,000 in domestic service. This is certainly an underestimate, given the number of women in casual work, but is a useful starting point, giving a total of nearly 4.9 million women in waged work. By 1918, the same analyst estimated that there were 4,808,000 women in industry, and 1,200,000 in domestic work, a total of 6 million women workers. Two things are obvious. First, the total number of waged women only increased by about 1 million during the war, and secondly, a large number of domestic servants took the opportunity to find better jobs. (This shift was noticeable all across Europe—and indeed in the United States, where white domestic servants often found factory work, and many black women moved from the land to service in their place.) What seems to have happened in Britain was a transfer of women *from* low-paid 'women's work' *to* the war industries and transport, particularly trams and trains. Their reasons for taking such work varied. The jobs were usually better paid, they were often more interesting, and many women felt that they would like to 'do their bit' in supporting the troops as well. Numbers were further increased by girls entering work straight from school, and by married

A smartly dressed woman railway worker, in Britain. Transport was one of the major employers of women across Europe, but there were often disputes about what work they should do. Women clerks, cleaners, and platform staff were common, but only Russia used women as train drivers, and not extensively. Women also worked as conductors on buses and trams, and as drivers in Britain.

women—of all ages—whose labour was, for once, in demand. At this point, therefore, we can dispense with one of the most abiding myths of the First World War. Contrary to propaganda reports at the time, there was no enormous influx of non-working women into men's jobs: millions of working-class women in Britain moved into *different* trades when the opportunity arose. Furthermore, most women in industry and transport were working class. Although propagandists waxed lyrical about the idea of duchesses or colonels' daughters in the workshop, in reality there were few middle- or upper-class volunteers in the factories.

Women's move into industrial and transport jobs followed a similar pattern in France and Germany, although the amount of state interference varied from country to country. In Britain, the government managed many private factories for the duration of the war, as well as its own shipyards and arsenals. The introduction of women here was done with the co-operation of both employers and trade unions. Negotiations in 1915 culminated in a series of agreements about women's work on 'men's jobs' in munitions and engineering. It was to be temporary, they would not be trained up as 'fully skilled tradesmen'; and they would be paid equal wages on work 'customarily done

Woman at a turning machine at Armstrong Whitworth, Elswick. Working in a modern engineering workshop, wearing a neat uniform, she is clearly doing what many saw as 'men's work', like many other women in Britain, France and Germany. Whether she was paid 'men's rates' would have depended largely upon union negotiations and local practice, particularly whether she did her own tool setting.

by men'. In practice, women rarely achieved equal pay, even on very similar work, while in the filling factories they were still classed as doing 'women's work' and paid accordingly, in spite of the risk of explosion or TNT poisoning. Women's wages in most jobs remained low compared to men's, but high compared to those in traditional women's trades like service or dressmaking.

Women were needed in industry, but they were seldom accepted with enthusiasm, despite labour shortages. The British government was forced to dispatch 'Dilution officers' around the country, armed with glowing testimonials and photographs of the variety of work women could do. In other trades, a combination of management doubts and union hostility often kept them at bay for as long as possible. For example, in 1914, the Women's Institute approached the London Postal Service to suggest that women be used for sorting mail. The Controller wrote back, turning the idea down on the grounds that (1) women would need separate rest rooms, which meant the building would need major structural alteration; (2) women would need separate offices, as they could not work next to men; (3) sorting mail was too arduous for them, and they would need seats—special seats, as the height of the sorting boxes was unusual; (4) women could not do night work, and much sorting was done at 4 or 5 a.m. Only five months later, labour shortages were such that the Post Office had to think again, and all these obstacles to women's employment were easily overcome. Other civilian industries, competing with the superior wages on offer in munitions and engineering, were forced to follow suit, modify working practices, and allow women into some areas of men's work.

There was less government intervention in France and Germany. It was usually left to employers and trade unions to sort out the terms on which women would be admitted. But many employers, like those in Britain, were cynical about women's capacities, and anticipated laying them off as soon as the war was over. Certainly many trade unions maintained a hostile stance. To quote the French metalworkers' words of 1917: 'the systematic introduction of women into workshops is entirely at odds with the establishment and maintenance of homes and family life.' Yes in spite of much rhetoric about the health and welfare of mothers, future and actual, governments, employers, and unions paid little attention to the practical problems of women working in the war industries. Crèches and canteens, though appearing later in the war, remained uncommon; regulations on the supply of nursing rooms in French factories were seldom followed, and no allowance was made for the time women might need to spend queuing for food. Protective legislation had been largely suspended in 1914, leaving women open to exploitation and exceptionally long hours in munitions. Industrial injuries occurred in all munitions factories in all countries. In France, for example, there were 69,606 reported industrial accidents in 1917, resulting in 59 fatalities, and thousands of permanent disabilities. It gradually dawned on each government that exhausted workers were inefficient workers, and the eight-hour shift returned in the later years of the war—although there was always over-

time to add on. Women in civilian industries like transport often fared better, earning improved wages but facing fewer risks to health.

This much, women had in common. But at the same time there were major differences between the experiences of women in different areas of Europe. For example, in Britain the increase in domestic food production during the war years was achieved largely without additional female labour—older men, boys, prisoners of war, soldiers, and machinery were enough. The Women's Land Army arrived late in the day, and offered some skilled support in ploughing, gardening, and milking, but employed only a few women in farming. In contrast, the peasant farms of mainland Europe depended heavily on women's labour, often leaving younger girls to take care of the housework. Yet even peasant women's experiences were not uniform. In France, farm incomes rose, and women experienced a new level of prosperity in nearly all regions. Incomes were further raised by the state allowances paid to soldiers' wives and parents (which many Italian or Russian peasant women, for example, did not have.) Local observers frequently commented on the positive effects of this small extra guaranteed income. A schoolmaster reported: 'Never before has the wife of a day labourer, the mother of three children, received 82.50F per month, the amount of her allowance . . . More than one mother of a family, whose husband has been called up, is now able to buy things she had wanted a long time.'

As always, there were also those who disapproved of women earning more money than usual, complaining of women's 'profligacy, laziness and drunkenness', or even their 'debauchery' as a result of such untold wealth. While many rural areas prospered, food prices rose in towns, causing bitter complaint, yet there were no real food shortages in France—or in Britain.

In contrast, Germany, suffering from the effects of the allied blockade, was increasingly short of food (and fuel) from early in the war. The average daily calorie input for a civilian adult dropped from around 1,500 in 1915 to below 1,000, in the winters of 1916–17 and 1917–18. Life for urban dwellers became increasingly miserable with even turnips, acorns, and horse chestnuts rationed. An Australian woman living in Leipzig in 1917 wrote:

Coal has run out. The electric light is cut off in most houses (I have gas, thank Heaven!), the trams are not running, or only in the very early morning, all theatres, schools, the opera, Gewandhaus and concerts and cinematographs are closed—neither potatoes nor turnips are to be had—they were our last resource—there is no fish—and Germany has at last ceased to trumpet the fact that it can't be starved out. Added to that the thermometer outside my kitchen window says 24 deg. Fahr. *below zero*. I have never seen that before.

Rates of pneumonia and tuberculosis increased, and the death rate per thousand women went up from 11.2 in 1914 to 17.8 in 1918. The situation in Austria was similar. These deteriorating conditions had a dramatic effect on women's willingness (and ability) to do a great deal of industrial work. Not only did women have to queue for food on a daily basis, but at the weekend thousands of them took trains into the country in search of black market supplies. Many wives took in homework (poorly paid as usual) but would not work full-time in munitions, needing time to search for food instead. Ironically, the separation allowances paid to soldiers' wives actually discouraged women's full-time work by topping up part-time wages. This in turn exacerbated labour shortages. Life in the factory was, in any case, quite hard enough. One visitor to an armaments factory wrote:

The working conditions were like what they must have been under early capitalism. There was always 'something wrong'. Especially during the night shift. Never a night passed without one or more of the women collapsing at their machines from exhaustion, hunger, illness . . . On many days in winter there would be no heating, the workers stood around in groups, they could not and would not work . . . In the canteen there were almost daily screaming fits by women, sometimes even depressing fights between them, because they claimed 'the ladle had not been filled'.

Facing: This picture, of healthy, good-looking Land Army volunteers (significantly wearing breeches), could only have been taken in England. The Land Army offered middle and upper-class women an opportunity to learn new skills in market gardening and agriculture, but their numbers were tiny compared with the millions of women peasant farmers who maintained food production across Europe.

These girl labourers in an Italian munitions works are an enormous contrast with the women in the previous picture. Their youth is not unusual, as children were widely used in the war industries across Europe, but their poverty is striking. Italy was barely industrialised in comparison with her allies, and working conditions were notoriously bad.

Russia's wartime factory conditions were inevitably even worse, given how little protective legislation was in force, and the fact that workers had no rights at all. Women carried a major burden in both town and country, yet had to survive on the lowest wages in Europe.

In these deteriorating circumstances, existing divisions in society—between town and country, between classes, and certainly between government and governed—grew wider. Britain and France managed to maintain a relatively united home front during the war, aided by good food supplies and maintenance of trade with the rest of the world, in spite of the German naval threat. Strikes, over wages and rents, increased as war-weariness spread, but morale never really plummeted. In contrast, the working classes of both Germany and Russia grew ever more desperate. It is no coincidence that so many strikes were led by women in 1917, and that looting of food shops was often done by mothers and children who had little to lose. (This happened in Italy too, where threats to send strikers to the front could hardly be used against women.) As a German military commander commented, the women's behaviour in 1917–18 was understandable: 'they are supposed to work and cater for their hungry families and see that they are powerless to do so.'

The front line

Women also experienced the risks of the war more directly in the occupied territory of east and west. Here they faced eviction from their land, even industrial conscription, and the threat of violence to themselves or their families. The years 1914–18 were years of both privation and fear.

Other women made a choice to see war at closer quarters, and participate. Thousands signed up to support the medical services. Many of these were nurses, but women doctors too volunteered—although they frequently found that their offers of help were more favourably received by small nations like Serbia, which had a less fixed notion of what was suitable work for women. Some also worked as ambulance drivers close to the front. The most famous of these were the 'Women of Pervyse', Elsie Knocker and Mairi Chisholm, who risked their lives in no man's land daily to rescue wounded soldiers and stretcher them back to safety. They kept working until a serious gas attack which injured them both in 1918.

However, the idea of women fighting was another matter. Britain reluctantly allowed the establishment of women's army, navy, and even air corps, but although these women wore uniform and lived under military discipline there was no suggestion that they should bear arms. Their role was to support the armed forces by doing clerical work, driving, and catering, 'releasing' men for the front. In Russia, a few hundred women did join the army, and fought alongside men, but Russia's allies found the idea of women fighting or

WAAC cooks in France, 1917. Another group of army auxiliaries, showing the extent to which women in the British forces were doing classic domestic work. Work in mass catering was hard, and the pay was lower than in other army trades. The war work of a cook may have been very different from that of Flora Sandes, fighting in the Serbian Army, but was no less essential.

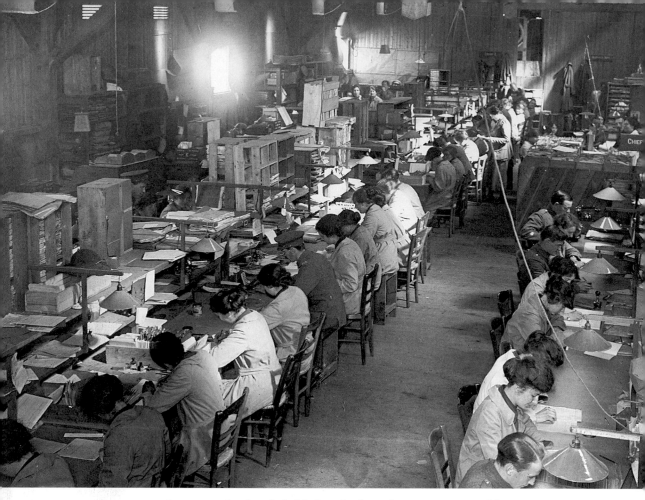

WAAC clerks at a transport depot in France, 1917. This gives some indication of the enormous bureaucratic structure which lay behind the fighting forces in each nation. Having already proved successful substitutes in banking, insurance and the civil service, women were now used for clerical and administrative work in the army to 'release' men for the front line.

dying on the battlefield deeply disturbing. Maria Bochkaraeva's Women's Battalion of Death was the most famous group of female soldiers. Its formation was encouraged by the Provisional Government of 1917, which hoped that the sight of women fighting might encourage the demoralized Russian troops. Women's reasons for joining Bochkaraeva's battalion were various. The volunteers were interviewed in 1918, and it was reported that:

The former stenographers, dressmakers, servants, factory hands, university students, peasants, and even bourgeois ladies who surrounded her said they joined 'because they believed that the honour and even the existence of Russia were at stake and nothing but a great human sacrifice could save her'. But [the interviewer] added that others came because 'anything was better than the dreary drudgery and the drearier waiting of life as they lived it'.

Life must indeed have been hard if the dangers of the eastern front in 1917 seemed preferable.

Britain's one female combatant was Sergeant Flora Sandes, a middle-class woman who began as a nurse, and finished by fighting in the Serbian army. Her fame led to much soul-searching in the British and American press about women's role in wartime. As one journalist wrote in 1917: 'But if women were to be taken into our armies . . . what is to become of our ideas, of chivalry and of all that has grown out of them?' Flora herself discovered that those men she fought with found it hard to relate to her when she dressed as a woman—and that the close friendships she experienced during the war faded once she ceased to be soldier and returned to civilian life.

At the end of the war, there was a general desire that life should return to 'normal'—in so far as this was possible for victors or vanquished. (Clearly there was no possibility of 'normality' in Russia after the 1917 revolutions.) Women's task, in this post-war world, was to rebuild the homes of Europe. In Britain, women's ostensible 'reward' for their work was suffrage for those over 30, though in truth the extension of franchise had probably been delayed rather than accelerated by the exigencies of war. In France, the feminists, who had been so convinced that they were on the verge of winning changes in the civil code and franchise, were now told that 'While women did give immense service to France during the war, they did so for love of *patrie*, not in the expectation of reward: it would be an insult to pay them for their patriotism.' Although the Chamber of Deputies passed a bill granting women's suffrage, the Senate voted against. It was in France that women bore the brunt of 'pro-natalist' legislation. Their role now was 'to give birth and give birth and give birth once again. A woman who refuses to bear children no longer deserves the rights she enjoys.' In 1920, a law was passed against the dissemination of information about birth control, and this was followed three years later by anti-abortion legislation. Penalties were large fines and imprisonment. In spite of much talk about encouraging motherhood, no other country was so aggressively pro-natalist—though significantly, the French birth rate remained low.

The aftermath of war

In the new post-war climate, women industrial workers were dismissed with alacrity. Even legislation was widely used to remove them from 'men's jobs'. They were supposed to go back to their old jobs, or their husbands—if these were still alive. A notice on the wall of one French munitions factory advised that, 'Now you may best serve your country by returning to your former pursuits, busying yourselves with peacetime activities.' Many women were shocked by the treatment they received, after years of being told that their labour was essential to the war effort. As one wrote to the French paper *La Vague*: 'My husband has been in the army for the last six years. I have worked like a slave at Citroën during the war. I sweated blood there, losing my youth and my health. In January I was fired, and since then have been poverty-stricken.'

Those still in work encountered abuse in the streets and criticism in the papers for their selfishness, while the unemployed faced a concerted effort by labour exchanges to get them back into 'women's trades'. One German exchange reported in 1919 that 'the reluctance to accept positions in domestic service has not diminished', and another confirmed that it was 'extraordinarily difficult to return these groups to their earlier occupations or to re-educate them to new circumstances'. These words were echoed by officials in France and Britain. The 1920s were to prove difficult years for many women workers. Married women were often barred from both white-collar and industrial jobs, and female workers were nearly always first in line for short-time working or redundancy. Some said that life was harder than it had been during the war, when at least work was easy to find.

Although women strongly resisted the pressure to return to domestic service (and numbers never returned to pre-war levels) it was clear by the early 1920s that the old patterns of male and female employment had reasserted themselves. White-collar trades and light industrial work continued to use increasing numbers of female workers, but these trends had been established before the war. The world, it seemed, had not been turned upside down by the millions of women who worked in munitions factories, or on trams and trains.

Yet although one might conclude that the war's influence on women's employment prospects was broadly neutral, this fact should not be allowed to overshadow the importance of the war's wider effects—good or bad—on women as individuals. Furthermore, as we have seen, women's work cannot be viewed in isolation: their feelings about their work were inevitably influenced by the social, economic, and political environment in which they lived. There were those, particularly in Britain, who felt that these were the most exciting years of their lives, giving them a sense of purpose and companionship, with the added bonus of good wages. There were others, particularly in Germany, for whom the war marked a new level of poverty, hunger, anxiety, and exhaustion. In Russia, meanwhile, memories of war were soon overtaken and dwarfed by revolution.

Furthermore, the progress of the war itself affected women deeply, often pushing all thought of work or ambition into the background. For many of them, the most important thing was whether the men they knew survived. We know that there were millions of war widows, many of whom were young, and had children. We cannot even guess at the numbers who lost fathers, brothers, sons, and friends. Nor was death the only legacy of the war. Other women had to learn to live with men who returned mentally or physically scarred, including those too ill or badly injured to work again. This experience did not end in 1918.

CHAPTER 12

The Challenge to Liberalism: The Politics of the Home Fronts

JOHN TURNER

P re-war Europe was dominated by four large industrial societies—Britain, Germany, Italy, and France—and two sprawling and largely agrarian empires—Austria-Hungary and Russia. The war which broke out in August 1914 presented three challenges to these political systems. First, internal conflicts had to be resolved so that the warring powers could fight their enemies. Second, civilian politicians and soldiers had to renegotiate their relationship after years of peace. Third, states had to expand their powers to mobilize people and materials for war. Different countries met these challenges at different times and in different ways, with different long-run consequences. None could escape the storm of war. Most found that the regimes of 1914 were very fragile indeed.

The industrial workers on whom late nineteenth-century European society depended for its wealth and power were numerous, concentrated in small areas, and increasingly well educated. They could not be relied on to accept the subordination which well-ordered society and well-ordered industry required. Intimidation was useless; natural deference was disrupted by rapid

The political context

163

social change and personal mobility. Governments everywhere were forced to confront the challenge of mass politics and the working class.

This problem was common to political systems which in other ways were bewilderingly diverse. One major European society—Britain—had been industrializing steadily for more than a century. America, France, and Germany had grown rapidly from the middle of the nineteenth century and made huge leaps forward in its last decade; while Italy and Japan began to grow suddenly in the 1890s and a reluctant Russia in the same period was hustled somewhat unsuccessfully towards industrialization by its rulers. The social and political balance between industry and agriculture therefore varied, and with it the size and composition of the middle classes which were as much the product of industrialization and prosperity as the working classes.

The governing systems of the powers also varied. Though all (except France and the United States) were monarchies and all (except Russia) had representative assemblies which were elected by widespread or even mass suffrage, these terms meant very different things in practice. In central and eastern Europe, mass politics had had relatively little impact on the structures of government. The German government was dominated by the kaiser and his court. The chancellor and his ministers, appointed without reference to the Reichstag, ruled with the help of a powerful landed aristocracy, an efficient bureaucracy, and the army. The political parties had little influence. The Austro-Hungarian empire had a foreign and military policy run by the emperor's ministers, who largely ignored the 'Delegations' (from the Austrian and Hungarian parliaments) which constituted the representative assembly of the empire. The Austrian parliament represented the nationalities of the Austrian part of the empire reasonably well on the basis of a wide franchise and active political parties; the Hungarian parliament was dominated by Magyars and the Hungarian government was autocratic and repressive. In Russia the concentration of power in the hands of the tsar and his advisers was even more extreme, and the Duma, set up hurriedly after a minor revolution in 1906, was in any case easily suspended altogether.

In the west, governing structures more closely reflected the plural nature of society. Italy was a constitutional monarchy in the hands of a political class which dominated the assembly and the executive government, but political parties were weak and disorganized. Partly because of this disorganization, the state itself had little impact on Italian society. In Great Britain, another constitutional monarchy, political parties were highly organized and well able to establish robust governments, but again the state laid only a light hand on society. In France the Chamber of Deputies had a quite remarkable power to make or break governments (of which there were sixty between 1871 and 1914); the executive government itself was constitutionally weak; parties were ill-disciplined; and yet the hand of the state rested rather more heavily on French society than it did in Britain or Italy.

The main political victim of the Great War was a style of government and an attitude to politics which was characteristic of the late nineteenth century and the decade before the war. In any European political system there were some people who believed that countries should be run by constitutional governments; that these governments should be responsive to the majority of the populations which they governed; that social and political change was a fact of life; that it was the duty of governments to put right at least some social wrongs; and that on the whole it should be possible for nation states to coexist peacefully in a prospering world. These were liberal attitudes. Liberalism represented the balance between what the historian Arno Mayer has called the 'forces of order' and the 'forces of movement'—roughly, conservatism and socialism. Liberalism also implied belief in free markets, free speech, and the protection of individuals' rights against the state. It offered the hope that if reactionary conservatism was curbed the insurgent forces of the working class could be held back from demanding revolutionary change. Most European societies had one or more political parties which embodied at least some of these values, and the practices of constitutionalism, flexibility, and responsiveness together comprised a style of government which could be adopted by parties or regimes which had little interest in the other core liberal values. Liberalism represented the acceptance of a plural society, and the hope that social differences did not ineluctably mean damaging conflict.

In some countries, notably Britain, liberal attitudes were dominant before the war, influencing even the parties of the right, and the Liberal Party itself had held power in Britain since 1906. In Germany and Austria, and even more so in Russia, Liberalism was espoused by political parties with no hope of governing, and the idea of an open, responsive, and constitutional government was merely a notion sometimes discussed by ministers as a technique for managing awkward situations. In Italy the liberal regime saw itself not only as a barrier against the advance of socialism, but also as defender of constitutional and secular values against Catholic authoritarianism and strident nationalism. Diverse as they were, these liberal positions reaped the benefit of accelerating social political and economic change across Europe from the late nineteenth century onwards, which had tended to reinforce the apparent advantages of liberalism in the competition with conservatism and socialism. The war tested these advantages to destruction.

Almost everywhere in Europe the immediate political consequence of war was an outbreak of apparent social and political unity. In Britain the main political controversies of 1914 died down, at least for a time. In the absence of conscription, men rushed to volunteer for a patriotic war. Industrial unrest visibly ebbed and civil war in Ireland was averted. On other matters the two main parties, Conservative and Liberal, declared a 'political truce' to which the minor parties, Labour and Irish Nationalist, largely conformed. The prime minister, H. H. Asquith, was moved to comment with only the slightest irony that the outbreak of war had been one of the characteristic strokes of luck in his political career.

In France a similar popular welcome for the war was the background for a party-political truce within the Chamber of Deputies. Coalitions were not unusual in French politics. The *union sacrée* cabinet of August 1914 was none the less remarkable for including, besides the prime minister, René Viviani, Alexandre Millerand (still a socialist), Aristide Briand (like Viviani, a former socialist) and the conservative Republican Alexandre Ribot. This government lasted until October 1915, and was succeeded by a cabinet under Briand which included representatives both of the Catholic right and of extreme anticlericalism. Although the *union sacrée* cabinets were no less fragile than other governments of national unity, the idea of national coalition persisted well into 1917.

Giovanni Giolitti, Italian prime minister 1903–1914, represented the old order of pre-war, middle-class Liberalism. His opposition to Italian participation in the war ruined his own political career and split Italian Liberalism beyond repair.

The French and British political truces—neither of which lasted until the end of the war—contrasted starkly with the experiences of Italy, Germany, Austria, and Russia. The Italian decision for war was made by a handful of cabinet ministers without reference to the military authorities, let alone the National Assembly. Consequently the war itself was a matter of political contention. Giovanni Giolitti had been a Liberal prime minister for most of the period from 1903 to 1914. He was succeeded in March 1914 by Antonio Salandra, who was more open to the right. When Salandra took Italy into the war, Giolitti won considerable support among deputies for an anti-war position until he was outmanœuvred. Giolitti's supporters were stigmatized as anti-patriotic, and linked to the Socialists, who had been labelled anti-patriotic since their opposition to the war against Libya in 1912. There was no strong popular support for the war, either at its beginning or during the long years of Italian humiliation at Austrian hands which culminated at Caporetto in 1917, and the regime was the only one among the victorious powers which actually fell in the aftermath of war.

The German case differed even more radically, largely because Wilhelmine Germany had political parties which could not compete for power in the manner familiar elsewhere. Most of the Social Democrat Party, which held a majority in the Reichstag, abandoned their traditional opposition to an aggressive foreign policy, but the imperial ministry did not in any case need their approval to carry on government during wartime. The practical result was the *Burgfrieden*, essentially a consensus between the parties that the left would support the war in return for unspecified reforms to the system. The first phase of war saw a growing confidence on the part of the extreme right, which was determined both to commit the government to ambitious war aims in both east and west, and to reinforce the authoritarian potentialities of the regime. At the same time, the need to mobilize the economy for war led naturally to greater state intervention, much of which was managed by the leaders of industrial Germany, such as Alfred Hugenberg, who had been kept at arm's length by the pre-war regime and who were prominent in right-wing politics.

In Austria and Russia, the monarchies responded to the outbreak of war by trying to forget pre-war political problems and to govern by decree. The problems proved to be too great to ignore. National 'minorities' throughout the Austrian empire resented a call to arms on behalf of a distant dynasty. Calls for self-determination were heard across the Slavic territories, especially those governed by the Hungarian parliament. War policy was so centralized in the imperial government that the leading politicians of Austria and Hungary only learned in December 1918 that Count Czernin, responsible for the empire's foreign policy, had advised in April 1917 that the empire was bound to dissolve if the war continued. In Russia the disaffection was general, and sprang from dislike of a regime which was ruthless in its demands on the army and civilian workers, yet demonstrably inefficient as an organizer of industrial warfare. But dissatisfaction of this sort, and on the scale which eventually overturned two great empires, was quite slow to reach its full effect.

The 'left' in pre-war Europe was a mixture of socialist groups, usually with middle-class leadership, and trade unions whose main interest was in industrial matters. Union leaders were often socialists, and socialist parties were correspondingly associated with union interests. But the relationship was rarely easy. Many union leaders rejected socialist political aims such as the replacement of capitalism by socialism, the extension of welfare systems, or the quest for economic equality, in favour of concentration on their members' direct interests. In Britain, an extreme example, the Labour Party was brought into being in 1900 not as a socialist party but as a parliamentary pressure group to defend the legal privileges of trade unions in the market place. The 'working-class movement' was thus a fragmented thing, which tried to organize and represent a large number of people, many of whom did not recognize the existence of a class struggle or seek to change the distribution of industrial ownership or, except at the margin, the distribution of wealth. Socialist rhetoric was nevertheless the lingua franca of European socialist parties and trade unions. Many of them acknowledged a common identity in the Socialist International (the Second International) which organized international gatherings and fostered the idea that working-class solidarity was stronger than national loyalties.

War brought class conflict into focus across Europe. Would trade unions and socialist parties put class-consciousness before patriotism? If they did,

The incorporation of the left

would the mass of the industrial population follow them, or support the middle-class and aristocratic governments which had stumbled into war? Across Europe socialist parties divided, with the majorities supporting their national governments and minorities keeping faith with internationalism. In France the labour movement's support of the war was swiftly expressed and almost unambiguous. Léon Jouhaux, secretary-general of the Confédération Générale du Travail (CGT), undertook that French workers would 'sound the death-knell' of the monarchical regimes of Austria and Germany. In Britain the Labour Party and the Trades Union Congress also accepted, with rather less enthusiasm, that this was a war between democracy and autocracy in which labour should take the Entente side. Arthur Henderson became secretary of the parliamentary Labour Party, succeeding Ramsay MacDonald who had resigned because he wished to keep faith with the internationalism of the Independent Labour Party (ILP) of which he was a founder member. The consistent scepticism of the ILP was the core of Britain's untypically strong anti-war movement, but it was emphatically the minority view in a movement whose official line was that 'the victory of Germany would mean the death of democracy in Europe'. In Germany the corresponding rationalization was that Germany was threatened by uncivilized Slavic hordes and by the manipulative governments of France and Russia which had exploited a Balkan quarrel for imperialist ends.

The rhetoric of August and September 1914 could not commit whole classes and political movements for the duration. The problem of working-class participation became more acute as governments tried to allocate scarce manpower and resources between different elements of the war effort. The demands of trench warfare forced governments to squeeze the workforce which remained at home making munitions and growing food. To varying degrees, strike action was banned or discouraged, wages were regulated, workers were directed to particular industrial sectors, and the traditional practices which had given workers some control over the labour market and the very process of work were forcibly abandoned. Women and unskilled men without apprenticeships entered the factories to replace skilled workers who had gone to war; skilled men, accustomed to some degree of choice in their employment, were ordered to work where the state required them. Whether this was done under military authority, as increasingly it came to be in Germany, or under the extended powers of the civilian government, as it generally was in Britain, France, and Italy, it had the potential to provoke a damaging backlash, especially when the immediate agents of change were the employers.

French and British governments therefore made an explicit bargain with the trade unions. Trade unionists would take part in the local committees which tried to set wages and distribute labour, in return for acquiescence in conscription, wage control, and the widespread employment of women and the unskilled. Workers' representatives were given places in coalition governments: Arthur Henderson joined the first British coalition in April 1915 in an ornamental role, while Albert Thomas, a leading member of the French socialist movement, was in charge of the French munitions effort from October 1914 until September 1917. But this contrivance did not make class conflict or industrial unrest go away. Shop-floor workers who felt that their officials were collaborating with the class enemy were ready to follow leaders who would fight harder for their interests. Major strike action was first threatened in Britain in the late summer of 1915 in protest against plans to introduce conscription; widespread stoppages were seen in engineering industries in the spring of 1916 and again in 1917. These movements were led by 'shop stewards', who challenged both the collaborationism of union and party leaders and the sectarian craft exclusivity of traditional union organization.

Far from neutralizing conflict, the incorporation of labour leaders in the workings of the state contributed to a split in the labour movement and the hardening of left-wing attitudes, which in due course threatened the continuation of the war. In September 1915 a number of minority socialists from most belligerent countries met at Zimmerwald in Switzerland for a conference which denounced the war but for the most part rejected the strategy of 'revolutionary defeatism' urged by Lenin. War-weariness eventually took up where Zimmerwald had failed. Strikes in 1916 and 1917 were about much more than the industrial interests of the workers. Although working-class real incomes in general went up during the war in all the industrialized countries, the lack of sophisticated economic management meant that price rises sometimes ran ahead of wage rises: this led to acute local discontent. Conscription and housing conditions were key factors in 1915 and 1916; by 1917 the shop stewards in Britain were calling for a negotiated peace to spare the country further civilian hardship.

The first Russian revolution and the emergence of the soviets of soldiers and workers in opposition to the Provisional Government both inspired and terrified western labour movements. Arthur Henderson, returning from a visit to Russia in July 1917, warned his partners in the recently formed Lloyd George coalition government that an early negotiated end to the war had to be considered lest the industrial working classes should rise up and stop the war. His cabinet colleagues duly sacked him, and he returned to the bosom of the labour movement. By the end of the year both right and left in the Labour Party were strongly critical of the government's refusal to contemplate negotiations. This led to some reconciliation between the opposing wings of the party and even some meeting of minds between shop stewards and the official trade union hierarchies.

Similar developments were seen across Europe. The abandonment of working-class claims to better wages, improved working conditions, and a greater share of political and social power could only be temporary and conditional. There was always doubt about the wisdom of giving up hard-won advantages; and the failure of governments to reciprocate ensured that when the going got rough—as it did in most belligerent states by 1917—the full-blooded socialist opposition discussed in Chapter 17 became a real threat. In France the conflict between 'minority' and 'majority' socialism was personified by the *minoritaire* A. Merrheim, secretary of the metalworkers' union (and a *Zimmerwaldien*), who insisted in December 1916 that 'where national defence begins, there socialism and syndicalism disappear' in opposition to Jouhaux's *majoritaire* claim that the interests of the nation were the interests of labour. German workers and socialists were by then similarly dividing between majority Social Democrats (now led by Friedrich Ebert), Independent Socialists (led by Hugo Haase) who were openly critical of the war, and Spartacists (Karl Liebknecht and Rosa Luxemburg) further to the left who enthusiastically embraced the message of the Russian revolutions.

The incorporation of the left and the working class into the political process had a lasting effect on working-class movements, and it made socialist governments an imaginable possibility in post-war Europe. On the other hand, the *breakdown* of incorporation in the latter years of the war institutionalized class conflict, and this was perhaps the more important legacy of war.

The resurgent right

Right-wing politics in pre-war Europe were as diverse and fractured as left-wing politics. The lines of cleavage can be defined socially, politically, and economically. Everywhere but France, and even there to some degree, a conservative landowning aristocracy with close connections to the military was an important political force. Also ranged generally on the right were the representatives of industrial capitalism: trade and employers' associations, leagues pressing either for free trade or tariff protection, and societies for the defence of property rights. The political parties which embodied these right-wing positions were, understandably, quite often in disarray because they contained contradictory elements. In Germany, for example, the Prussian aristocracy dominated the court, the imperial bureaucracy, and the army, but also had a large representation in the Reichstag because the electoral system was weighted heavily towards the representation of the agricultural regions; the businessmen of Rhine-Westphalia were marginalized. In Britain the landed aristocracy was manifestly in retreat because its economic position was collapsing, but it was still influential in the Conservative Party, whose leaders it had provided until Arthur Balfour (nephew of the 3rd marquess of Salisbury, who had retired as prime minister in Balfour's favour in 1902) was ousted by Andrew Bonar Law (a Glasgow businessman) in 1911; and in Britain the Liberal Party still appealed to many businessmen.

Aristocracies were inclined to conservatism wherever they were found, because they had something obvious to conserve, but they were never the easiest allies for industrial capitalists. German, French, Italian, and to some extent British businessmen felt themselves excluded by aristocratic influence from the political power to which they thought they were entitled. Just as anxious to challenge the left in mass politics, they tended to prefer different tactics. Stridently nationalistic appeals to working-class patriotism were common, though in most countries where this tactic was energetically used it appealed to the lower middle classes and farmers rather than to industrial workers. Another, closely related political stance was 'social-imperialism'—the promise of full employment and some measure of welfare, conditional on expansion into colonial territories which would offer markets and raw materials. Some of these positions were incompatible with others. Armaments and military expansion usually meant taxes, mostly paid by the rich. Welfare meant state intervention in society. Compromises made by the industrial and aristocratic élites of pre-war Europe to fend off the left—a notable example being the tariff policy which served the interests of Prussian landowners and Ruhr industrialists in Bismarckian Germany—were often fragile.

The war was an opportunity for the right to regain the initiative. In Germany the 'pan-German' movement, particularly associated with heavy industry and the militarist pressure groups favoured by arms manufacturers, became more and more strident. The pan-Germans were quick to complain that the Social Democrat Reichstag deputies who had voted for war credits had claimed undue merit for taking a patriotic position which would have been forced on them in any case. The right raised the stakes by demanding a set of expansionist war aims which were quite incompatible with the socialists' idea of a war of patriotic defence. The intensification of political conflict continued as the trench war came to a standstill in November 1914 and the war of manœuvre on the eastern front became ever hungrier for men and ever more unpredictable. By the middle of 1916 the right and the army high command—supported by the centre parties including the National Liberals who had by now completely forgotten their pre-war affection for international peace—were pressing for an all-out war to dominate not only Europe but also the colonial world. Political initiative on the right fell to the high command itself, personified by Field Marshal Paul Hindenburg, victor on the eastern front, and General Erich Ludendorff. The Social Democrats, recognizing that German industry and German workers were suffering without clear hope of success, began to retreat from their support for war credits and even proposed peace negotiations on the basis of an equitable compromise with the Entente. This political battle was fought over the rather bemused heads of the chancellor, Bethmann Hollweg, and the kaiser, who both recognized that a pan-German peace was impossible to attain but could not stomach the apparent defeatism of the Social Democrats' 'Scheidemann peace' or the demand for constitutional reform with which it was associated.

The complete collapse of constitutionalist politics soon followed. The high command pressed for unrestricted submarine warfare which inevitably brought America into the war. After this failure to bring the Entente to its knees, the left-wing parties in the Reichstag proposed a 'peace resolution'. Ludendorff threatened to resign his military post because he could no longer work with Bethmann Hollweg. Because the Reichstag parties refused to support Bethmann at all, even against the army, the chancellor was sacked and replaced by Michaelis, an army puppet. Michaelis faced an effective pro-peace coalition majority in the Reichstag between the Social Democrats, the left-wing Liberals, and the Catholic Centre Party. A peace resolution was duly passed and ignored. Behind Michaelis was the army, which within three months replaced him with Count Hertling, who was no more able than Bethmann Hollweg or Michaelis either to respond to what the Reichstag wanted or to prevent it from expressing dissent. The right set up the Vaterlandspartei in September 1917, which stood for everything pan-German, and Hindenburg and Ludendorff tightened their hold on German government.

The autumn of 1917 was in fact a bad moment for liberalism in most European states, though each liberalism met its nemesis in a different way. In France the successive *union sacrée* cabinets had stumbled on through military setbacks and civilian unrest until the disastrous Nivelle offensive of spring 1917, which had been followed by widespread mutinies. The Briand government fell in March 1917 just before the Nivelle disaster; and the Ribot government then took the full brunt of attacks from the left, wanting peace, and the right, wanting a more vigorous prosecution of the war. Ribot fell at the end of August; Painlevé lasted until November 1917, when he was succeeded by Georges Clemenceau, who finally put an end to the *union sacrée* by turning out the Socialists. Clemenceau has gained a reputation as a vigorous oppressor of labour and an enemy of freedom. This is probably excessive, but he certainly had a brutal way with political opponents, the most outspo-

David Lloyd George (the Goat) and Georges Clemenceau (the Tiger) were the victorious beasts of wartime politics. Each began his career as a radical; each won power by sacrificing pre-war political commitments for the sake of victory. Beside Lloyd George stands Colonel Sir Maurice Hankey, the war cabinet secretary who masterminded the creation of a centralized, secretive governing machine.

ken of whom risked jail, and he had little time for the Chamber. Clemenceau's strength, which kept him in office for the rest of the war, was that he had popular support to set against his critics in the Chamber, and this made him unassailable. French politics was reduced to an argument for or against victory, in which the odds were heavily stacked.

There are marked similarities between Clemenceau's situation and that of David Lloyd George in Britain. Lloyd George had been minister of munitions in the Asquith coalition which was set up in April 1915. Asquith presided over a cabinet which was dominated by Liberals, but the government accepted the necessity of military conscription and of extending state control of the civilian economy. This lost them the support of Liberals and Labour in the House of Commons, without winning the affection of the Conservative Party, which fundamentally did not believe that Asquith or his Liberal colleagues (except for Lloyd George) were really committed to the war. Asquith finally fell in December 1916, to be succeeded by a Conservative-dominated coalition under Lloyd George. The Lloyd George coalition extended state control of economy and society. Lloyd George believed that he held power only because public opinion supported him against the House of Commons; and after May 1917 he was constantly manœuvring for a general election in which he would lead a coalition of right-wing pro-war Liberals and moderate Conservatives against an anti-war opposition consisting of Asquith, left-wing Liberals, and the Labour movement. He finally succeeded in splitting the Liberal Party by associating it with 'defeatism'. The anti-war movement was outwitted in January 1918 by a shift in the government's ostensible war aims to acknowledge the 'democratic peace' urged by President Woodrow Wilson of the United States. While this made little difference to war policy, it was an admission that the anti-war movement was politically dangerous, but at the same time an affirmation that robust politics would overcome 'pacifism'.

Lloyd George's government faced another typical challenge from the right. Not satisfied with military victory, most belligerent states were preoccupied in 1917 and 1918 with the possibility of an 'economic war after the war' in which the victorious powers would achieve the commercial dominance by force of arms for which they had striven before the war. In Britain this meant the triumph of the tariff reform wing of the Conservative Party and the reversal of generations of Liberal free trade doctrine; in Germany it was part of the victory of pan-Germanism; in France it represented yet another move towards the nationalist interests of big business and away from socialist internationalism. It had become a serious political issue on the Entente side with the Paris Economic Conference of 1916, and its acceptance in Britain and France by liberal and socialist politicians was yet another blow for pre-war liberalism.

We have already seen the profound effects of military intervention on German politics. Even in Britain, a country with a strong tradition of constitu-

Political soldiers

173

tional politics, the military hierarchy was politically very strong, partly through the Conservative Party, partly through a sympathetic press, and partly because Asquith was prepared to make a point of 'backing the generals' in order to embarrass the former colleague who had ejected him from office. The general staff had played a large part in the fall of the Liberal government in 1915 by blaming civilian politicians for military failure by means of the 'Shells Scandal'; and their work was completed by the noisy resignation of Admiral Lord Fisher over the plan for a naval attack in the Dardanelles. With Conservative help, they had browbeaten the Asquith coalition into imposing conscription at the end of 1915, and deflected criticism of their strategy of concentrating on the western front.

Though Lloyd George was an advocate of conscription, against most of his Liberal colleagues, he had always questioned the strategic wisdom of the British army, and finally lost patience after the Somme. One of his principal objectives as prime minister was to curb Robertson, the chief of the imperial general staff, and Sir Douglas Haig, the commander in France, in their desire to use more troops on futile offensives. Ironically he was prevented from sacking Haig in March 1917 by the Conservative political allies who had put him in office, and this forced him to accept Haig's plan for the Flanders offensive which led to Passchendaele. Robertson was only sacked in February 1918 as part of the establishment of the Supreme War Council, and Haig survived until the end of the war.

Lloyd George was not alone in having to tolerate unbiddable generals. In Italy General Cadorna refused to discuss strategy with civilians, banned politicians from the war zone after August 1916, and tried in 1917 to force the dismissal of Orlando, the interior minister, though without success. He could only be removed after the disaster of Caporetto, when Orlando became prime minister and replaced him with General Diaz. The French went through four principal commanders. Joffre championed the costly offensives of 1914 and 1915, though it was Briand's government which forced on him the equally costly defence of Verdun and finally dismissed him when he asked for another offensive for 1917. Briand was then taken in by Nivelle, whose spring 1917 offensive broke the morale of the French army. Pétain, who restored the army as much by inactivity as by strategic insight, was effectively superseded in March 1918 by Foch, who preserved his reputation by rallying the allied armies on his appointment as generalissimo after the German offensive. Like their British counterparts, French generals showed a remarkable capacity to outlast their political masters, manipulate popular opinion, the press, and parliamentary

Vittorio Emanuele Orlando struggled to rescue Italian politics after the defeat at Caporetto in 1917. As prime minister he outflanked his generals and survived to sign the Treaty of Versailles, but he could not stem the collapse of Italian parliamentarism after the war.

faction to their own ends, and protect the mystique of military insight from a sceptical civilian gaze.

In other chapters we have seen the important social and economic changes of war: massive intervention in industry, a large though temporary transformation of the role of women, the decline of social deference, and thus a realignment of class relations. An important and distinctively *political* manifestation of these changes was the expansion of the state in diverse ways at the expense of the privacy and autonomy of its citizens. As we have noted, this process began at different starting points in different countries but it moved in only one direction, and the principal victim was the pre-war liberal order.

State and civil society

An essential corollary of war was the suspension of individual rights against the state. In Britain military conscription was introduced for the first time, with a corresponding outcry which continental Europeans, accustomed to compulsory military service even in peacetime, found difficult to understand. Perhaps more significant in the longer term was the development of machinery for domestic political surveillance. The political police of tsarist Russia were well known as a symptom of Russian political backwardness, but inevitably less was known about the French military intelligence officers who spent the war observing prominent anti-war intellectuals such as Romain Rolland, or the work of British Special Branch policemen who turned their attention from Irish nationalists to shop- stewards and later to potentially disgruntled ex-servicemen. It was a short step from there to the organization of covert anti-left and strikebreaking machinery which was characteristic of the inter-war period.

A different but no less important part of the interface between state and society was in taxation. Wartime increases in public expenditure related mostly to munitions expenditure and the cost of armies; they were financed either by taxation—which was unpopular everywhere and much less used than most citizens believed—or by raising war loans, or by printing money and causing inflation, a technique which was almost universal. But the form of public expenditure which survived the war, and contributed most to the maintenance of high-spending government throughout Europe after the war, was transfer payments: expenditure on social welfare targeted at particular social groups either because their need was great or because they posed a political threat. Unemployment benefits and public housing programmes were typical examples. Liberals disliked both the extra taxation this implied and the distortions it created in the free market for labour.

European states also learned from the war to intrude on the private behaviour at least of the working classes. The British state made sure that soldiers' wives who were paid separation allowances by the War Office only got the money if they remained faithful to their husbands and conscientious in the rearing of their children; the French state, soon after the war, strengthened its already fiercely pro-natalist policies by banning birth control. In general, this corresponded to the transfer to the state of a moral oversight which

before the war had been exercised by voluntary, middle-class philanthropic agencies such as, variously, the Charity Organization Society in Britain or the Catholic Church in France.

Finally, the boundaries between the state and the rest of society were permanently blurred, but probably expanded, by wartime changes in industrial relations. Pre-war welfare systems, except in Germany, had depended heavily on trade unions as friendly societies, a form of organized self-help. In Britain and France, moves were being made before the war to integrate this into state welfare systems, for example in the British 1911 National Insurance Act, and much political heat was generated by the need to preserve the independence of the trade union movement. At the same time there were struggles between unions and employers for control over welfare schemes. On both sides of industry the loudest voices wanted to keep the state out, though some employers wanted the state brought in to bear the escalating costs and many trade unionists realized that their mutual societies were not enough to provide all that was wanted. State, unions, and employers could be regarded as three independent entities, with the first holding the ring (and maintaining public order, which was rarely an impartial action) in the conflict between the other two. This was characteristic of the pre-war liberal state.

During the war, as we have seen, governments embroiled both unions and employers in the process of running the war. As well as official union participation, governments relied on businessmen as individuals—such towering characters as Walther Rathenau, who managed German war production, or Eric Geddes, a railway manager who did various jobs in British government—and on employers' associations to manage the huge civilian war effort. Powerful 'peak organizations' grew up in Britain, such as the Federation of British Industries (FBI), which paralleled the Central Association of German Industrialists and similar big-business bodies in France and Italy. Both employers' associations and the peak organizations were ambivalent about state intervention in the economy, taking a position not dissimilar to the trade unions which saw the benefits to themselves of participation but feared that a sell-out to government would lose them the support of their members. Trade associations were particularly interested in economic warfare and wanted to influence government policy; by and large, governments listened to them but also tried to negotiate the terms on which such benefits would be extended. The result was an unexpected interpenetration of private and public activity.

The tendency to associate government, employers, and trade unions in a common enterprise reached its furthest extent in the rather short-lived agreements between German unions and industrialists, the so-called Stinnes–Legien agreements, which foreshadowed an acceptance by the post-war German government that economic policy would be made by tripartite agreement; this held until the Great Inflation of 1923–4. In Britain the equivalent effort was the National Industrial Conference in 1919, which was addressed by the prime minister and made a number of recommenda-

Facing: The Signing of Peace in the Hall of Mirrors, Versailles, 28 June 1919, by Sir William Orpen.

Front: Dr Johannes Bell (Germany) signing, with Herr Hermann Müller leaning over him.

Middle row (seated, left to right): General Tasker H. Bliss, Colonel E. M. House, Mr Henry White, Mr Robert Lansing, President Woodrow Wilson (United States); M. Georges Clemenceau (France); Mr D. Lloyd George, Mr A. Bonar Law, Mr Arthur J. Balfour, Viscount Milner, Mr G. N. Barnes (Great Britain); the Marquis Saionzi (Japan).

Back row (left to right): M. Eleutherios Venizelos (Greece); Dr Alfonso Costa (Portugal); Lord Riddell (British Press); Sir George E. Foster (Canada); M. Nikola Pašić (Serbia); M. Stephen Pichon (France); Colonel Sir Maurice Hankey, Mr Edwin S. Montagu (Great Britain); the Maharajah of Bikaner (India); Signor Vittorio Emanuele Orlando (Italy); M. Paul Hymans (Belgium); General Louis Botha (South Africa); Mr W. M. Hughes (Australia).

tions accepted by both the Trades Union Congress and the FBI, but in Britain there was a rift between the FBI, mostly concerned with trade policy and tariffs, and the National Confederation of Employers' Organizations, mostly concerned with wage-bargaining, and there were no long-lasting results of co-operation. Nevertheless the practice of trade unions and trade and employers' associations *separately* talking to government was much more securely established than before the war in both France and Britain, and this represented a new form of political action little known in the pre-war liberal state.

Liberalism defeated

In the simplest sense, European political systems in the Great War saw a flight to the extremes of left and right, and this was a blow to pre-war liberal and centre-left parties everywhere. For the most part, the left won in the defeated nations. Violent revolution overthrew the monarchical regimes of Germany and Russia. The Austro-Hungarian empire shattered into fragments. The Ottoman sultanate succumbed to the nationalist and secular insurgency of Kemal Atatürk. It is hardly surprising, then, that the collective memory of war has often reflected the Russian Bolshevik dictum that war is the 'mother of revolution'.

For the victorious powers, though, there was no such inevitability. Britain and France retained their regimes into the inter-war period, with right-wing political forces much strengthened. Italy responded to a botched peace by moving to a right-wing authoritarian regime with no left-wing interlude. Even Spain and Portugal managed to hang on to their somewhat feeble monarchies, also with strong right-wing movements. Though there were substantial changes in political culture in all these societies, sometimes involving greater mass participation in politics, the First World War cannot simply be identified with 'progress', or movement to the left, or movement towards democracy.

But the liberalism which was lost in the Great War was not just the moderate soft centre of early twentieth-century politics. Whether post-war states moved to the right or to the left, they spread their influence further into society, and became a different sort of political entity. Even on the left, internationalism was in abeyance. Political conflict was more directly focused on conflicting class interests and on economic policy because governments during the war had taken responsibility for economy and society in a way which was unusual before 1914. Under pressure of war the state had become active, not only on behalf of its citizens but also in defence of its own existence. The 'mother of revolution' had also given birth to reaction, leaving pre-war liberalism as the Cinderella of inter-war politics.

CHAPTER 13

Eastern Front and Western Front, 1916–1917

ROBIN PRIOR AND TREVOR WILSON

For the German high command, war on the eastern front in 1916 was meant to be anything but total. The Russian retreat of 1915 had placed the tsar's forces far from the German frontier. So Falkenhayn would direct his endeavours where, in his judgement, combat counted: the western front. This did not mean that the German command would disregard strong defensive action on the Russian front in 1916. But there would be no major German attack.

Meanwhile, at a conference at Chantilly (Joffre's headquarters) in December 1915, the allied commanders were endeavouring to co-ordinate strategy for the coming year. As soon as could be managed, the armies of France and Britain and Russia and Italy would move as near simultaneously as possible against the Germans and Austro-Hungarians. Thereby they would deny the enemy the opportunity of employing interior lines to transfer forces to whichever front required them.

Russia's intended role in this great movement envisaged only minor action on the south-western front against Habsburg forces, and then only after major operations against the Germans on Russia's western and northern fronts had got under way. Correspondingly, manpower and weaponry for the offensive

The Brusilov offensive

179

would be concentrated against the Germans. The campaign was timed for June, when the tsar's forces would have recuperated and been resupplied.

Given past experiences, not all of Russia's military command were eager for renewed operations against the Germans. And their misgivings were reinforced when, following a sort of success late in 1915, Russian forces around Lake Narotch mounted an attack towards Vilna on 18 March 1916. It had been intended to go ahead some weeks earlier, taking advantage of the frozen lakes and firm ground of late winter. Delays in the concentration of men and weapons caused it instead to coincide with the start of the thaw, thereby depriving it of any chance of success. One consequence was a further waning of enthusiasm for a summer offensive against the Germans.

So when, in April, the Russian commander-in-chief endeavoured to set in motion preparations for a June campaign whose main target would again be Vilna, his army commanders on both his western and northern fronts dragged their feet. They would act, they said, but only when supplies of heavy ammunition had reached formidable levels—a response, it may be added, not without its merits.

What eventually persuaded them to agree to act was the intervention of the newly appointed commander of the south-western front. General Brusilov urged that his scantily supplied armies should attack the Austro-Hungarians simultaneously with operations against the Germans. This would pin down enemy forces and improve the prospects of success to his north. Brusilov's proposal was accepted, with the proviso that his forces would receive no additional resources in men or ammunition. Thereby an agreement (of a sort) was reached that all three Russian commanders would attack in the summer in line with the Chantilly arrangement.

The outcome was, in one respect, a widely hailed success. As it happened, Brusilov moved in advance of the two northern armies, which were still awaiting the abundance of resources they had stipulated. Responding to an appeal by the Italians for relief from an Austro-Hungarian attack in the Trentino, Brusilov struck on 4 June. His manner of proceeding ran counter to current orthodoxy. Instead of concentrating his less-than-adequate weaponry and man-

Brusilov proved the most effective Russian commander of the war, although perhaps only because he was engaged against the forces of the fragile Habsburg empire. His offensive against Austria-Hungary in June 1916, intended as the lesser part of a great Russian campaign, enjoyed dramatic if transitory success, capturing one-third of a million prisoners and much territory and inducing Romania to enter the war.

A highly evocative depiction of the
Flanders landscape during the Third Ypres
battle, and of the misery and resignation
to which defending troops as well as
attackers were reduced. Otto Dix's bleak
portrayals of the war brought him into
disfavour with the Nazis and caused him
much difficulty once they came to power
in Germany.

The women of America were urged to follow the militant example of Joan of Arc and buy War Savings Stamps. Few would remember the embarrassing detail that it was the English who burned Joan at the stake.

'Japan joins in the fight against the barbarians', this French poster affirms. Japanese naval strength did help transport Allied troops to the Mediterranean, but only after repeated requests from the Allies. They managed to overcome Japanese fears that sending their fleet to the European theatre would be leaving the Pacific open to the expansion of American naval power.

power against a particular sector, he attacked right along the front. Had he been operating against the Germans, it needs to be said, this could only have been a prescription for disaster (a point that usually goes unnoticed). Against Habsburg forces that were not only severely demoralized but seriously undermanned (because of the diversion to the Trentino), it was, to begin with, remarkably successful. The first weeks of June witnessed almost un-relieved progress for Brusilov, bringing him huge numbers of prisoners and large acquisitions of territory.

Such success could not be maintained. The Russian high command's con-centration of resources on the northern fronts, and the wide distribution of Brusilov's attacks, gave him the advantage of surprise but no reserves whereby to exploit it. And he soon found himself confronting mounting num-bers of Germans, as the kaiser's eastern command accepted that the plight of the Austro-Hungarians was so serious that German reinforcements must be hurried south.

The Russian command, meanwhile, was dithering about whether to con-tinue preparations for the offensive towards Vilna or to divert resources to Brusilov. At last, early in July, the Russian offensive against the German front got under way. In short order, it was stopped dead in its tracks. Hereafter, all went wrong not only for Russia's northern offensives but on the Habsburg front as well. The Romanians, anticipating the collapse of Austria-Hungary, entered the war (with lamentable results) on Russia's side. This diverted Brusilov's forces into the Carpathians and involved them in Romania's rout. Before long, Brusilov had been forced to relinquish—largely under German pressure—all his gains. Overall, his casualties were 1.4 million.

A summing-up of this episode is called for. Brusilov, while seeking to achieve one purpose—the provision of powerful flanking support for opera-tions to his north—had momentarily appeared likely to achieve quite another: the elimination of Austria-Hungary as a combatant power. Instead he simply reaffirmed the message proclaimed on the eastern front from the opening months of the war. If Russia could not defeat the Germans, it could not win anywhere.

The opening of 1917 on the eastern front promised a rerun (with slight vari-ations) of the year before. The German high command again opted to stand on the defensive in the east (while in the west, the U-boat campaign was expected to provide a happier alternative to a land offensive). Events within Russia reinforced this decision. As enthusiasm for the war wilted there, the German command was loath to revive Russia's fighting spirit by going on to the attack.

On the other side of the front, the Russian army, according to plans made at the turn of the year, was yet again to embark on operations against Ger-mans and Austro-Hungarians, but this time with the prime target being the south-western front and the vulnerable Habsburg forces. All the plans, how-ever, became speedily overshadowed by events on the Russian home front.

The July 1917 offensive on the eastern front

181

The spread of revolutionary sentiments, and mounting disenchantment with the war—evidenced by 2 million desertions in March and April 1917—called into question the Russian army's capability for a further offensive. Yet the Provisional Government (formed in the aftermath of the collapse of tsarism) concluded that only an allied victory could preserve the new regime, and that only a great offensive could restore the army's enthusiasm.

So, with Brusilov now commander-in-chief, a great endeavour was launched in June and July. Shock troops were employed to spearhead the attacks, followed up by forces of doubtful reliability. All along the front, these operations (despite brief initial success) expired in a couple of weeks. The shock troops speedily became casualties. The follow-up forces either refused to budge or readily gave up.

Brusilov was sacked and succeeded by German Kornilov, who called off the offensive and devoted himself to conspiring against the civilian government—thereby aggravating the demoralization of his army. Russia's role as a combatant in the Great War was at an end. Hereafter the western allies would have to persevere in the absence of Russian endeavours.

Artillery and the western front

If 1916 and 1917 on the eastern front went well for the kaiser's army and ill for the tsar's, events on the western front proved more ambiguous. The three offensives launched by British and French forces did not (on the kindest view) prosper. But, equally, Germany's offensives against the western allies, on land in 1916 and from beneath the sea in 1917, held little joy for the Central Powers.

Allied plans for the western front in 1916, deriving from the Chantilly Conference of late 1915, proposed a great Anglo-French offensive in midsummer astride the river Somme. But they were pre-empted in February 1916 by a vast endeavour on the part of the Germans, against the great ring of fortresses which constituted the French stronghold of Verdun.

The contrast is often made between the purposes of the two campaigns. The Franco-British offensive on the Somme was intended to rupture the German line on a 20-mile front and to pour infantry and cavalry through the gap and into open country. This has been deemed fanciful. The German purposes at Verdun, by contrast, seem positively level-headed. Falkenhayn, the German commander-in-chief, did not aspire to a breakthrough. His purpose was attrition, in the sense of killing vast numbers of Frenchmen without his own forces suffering comparable loss. He would first eliminate enemy forces where they stood, then move forward his own troops and artillery, and after that eliminate enemy reinforcements as they appeared. So bit by bit he would both overrun the French stronghold and drain his adversary's army (but not his own) out of existence.

Falkenhayn's intentions have since seemed—in contrast to Haig's wild ambitions—chillingly realistic. Actually, they were nothing of the sort. The differences in the two commanders' intentions were not of long-term importance to the course of their campaigns. In fundamentals, Falkenhayn and Haig shared the same insights, and were gripped by the same delusions.

The crucial insight was that the weapon of victory had now proclaimed itself. It was not poison gas, which had failed in 1915. It was not the tank, which held only limited promise and anyway would become available only late in 1916. The weapon of victory was the high-explosive shell. Other noteworthy weapons of this war, like the machine gun and barbed wire, might be primarily of value to the defender. The shell, if employed in vast quantities, did not take sides. Defenders under shelter would, like troops in the open, succumb to its wrath.

This was Falkenhayn's insight, and it was Haig's. The war, ultimately, would (with qualifications) prove them right. The victories of 1918 were, in the main, accomplished by artillery. The western allies, among other reasons, won the Great War because, on the battlefield, they brought to bear appropriately immense quantities of shell, developed the most effective means of delivering them, and divined what constituted feasible and profitable objectives. But 1918 was not 1916. By the fourth year of the war, guns and shells and the skills to use them were present in abundance. In 1916 they were not.

Both Falkenhayn and Haig declined to notice this qualification when they planned for Verdun and the Somme. They observed the vast accumulation of shells they were stockpiling, and deemed it unprecedented. Quite illogically, they went on to conclude that those shells would be sufficient for the large purposes they had in mind: be it the bleeding white of the French army, or the rupturing of the German line.

Falkenhayn did at least endeavour to limit the frontage which he was attacking, in order to deliver a bombardment so intense that it would extinguish life in the target area. Even then, his artillery experts questioned whether his bombardment would be intense enough for his purpose. But more important, by choosing to attack only a limited front (8 miles on the right bank of the Meuse), the German commander was having to disregard the likely response of French gunners on the left bank, outside the area under his bombardment but well within its range.

Haig, by contrast, foresaw the menace that fire from the flanks might constitute for troops trying to advance. He chose to obviate it by attacking on a 20-mile front, thereby placing his advancing infantry and cavalry in the centre beyond the range of fire from the flanks. He thereby fell into the opposite trap from that which ensnared Falkenhayn. For so wide a front, he had nowhere near the guns and shells required to subdue the enemy defences straight in front of him—so, in the event, his forces would be swept away by enemy artillery and machine guns which his bombardment had been too feeble to eliminate.

This failure by both commanders to confront the crucial issue of how much weaponry they actually possessed for the tasks it was supposed to accomplish caused the Verdun and Somme campaigns, despite apparent differences of planning and intent, to proceed with mounting similarity. Huge casualties were sustained by both sides, trivial amounts of ground changed hands (sometimes only temporarily), and neither operation advanced attacker or defender markedly towards victory.

Verdun

Falkenhayn launched the Verdun campaign on 21 February, with a devastating bombardment. There followed a stunning early success—the capture of Fort Douaumont. Thereafter the operation became bogged down, and never recovered momentum. The attacks were checked in part by what survived of the resistance ahead, but far more by flanking fire from the left bank of the Meuse. In short order Falkenhayn was obliged to reorient his operations. He turned his attention to the left bank of the Meuse, thereby widening his front and losing his sense of direction. Not until late in May, after intensely bloody fighting for both sides, did he achieve his purpose of eliminating French artillery concentrations on the other bank of the Meuse and so manage to return to his original targets. In June he accomplished his second (and last) capture of a French fortress. Thereafter the approaching allied campaign on the Somme gave Falkenhayn cause—or perhaps only excuse—to call off the battle.

The French army, fighting with grim determination for most of this cam-

The detonation by the British of this mine on 1 July 1916 was captured on moving film and has become an enduring image of war. The fact that mines could be dug from one front line to the other for the purpose of placing explosives under enemy positions is evidence of the static nature of the war. Only once did mining contribute on a large scale to an attack: at Messines in the Ypres salient on 7 June 1917 (see p. 188). Thereafter, the detection of mining by listening devices got the better of this form of activity.

paign but with noticeably waning morale towards the end, had suffered atrociously. But Germany's losses were almost as great (about a third of a million casualties each.) And at the last Falkenhayn had come away empty-handed. His attempt to drain away the manpower of the French army without significant loss to himself, and to acquire a prestigious territorial objective into the bargain, had proved entirely barren.

By the time the Anglo-French operation commenced on 1 July, French losses at Verdun had rendered the Somme a predominantly British offensive. The onus of planning and direction, correspondingly, fell mainly on Haig as commander-in-chief and Sir Henry Rawlinson as chief of the 4th Army.

The Somme

Haig and Rawlinson had fought together in all British actions on the western front in 1915. They had had the opportunity to learn important lessons: that only huge concentrations of artillery could batter down well-prepared defences; that no feasible measure of success for the attacker opened the way to a breakthrough; and that attacking infantry needed to proceed at speed, utilizing cover and employing mutually supporting fire-and-movement tactics. (Even newly arrived Kitchener units had proved capable of employing these tactics.)

Planning for the Somme barely embraced this accumulated wisdom. Rawlinson's ideas for limited attacks were set to one side, and the whole British plan focused upon breakthrough and cavalry exploitation, so dictating a front of 20 miles and initial penetration to a depth of 4,500 yards. Haig's 400 heavy and 1,000 field guns were quite inadequate to overwhelm such an area. Equally, the wisdom acquired about infantry tactics was set aside. Instead, attacking forces would proceed across no man's land in rigid, slow-moving waves.

As a consequence, the first day of battle (1 July 1916) was an inevitable disaster. Trench defences were not eliminated, and enemy batteries scarcely even engaged. By the end of the day, 57,000 of the 120,000 attacking troops had become casualties, including 20,000 dead. Only in the southern part of the front was even a modest amount of territory taken. There, aided by lavish French gunnery on their right, the British and French captured the German front line and advanced some way towards the second. In the north and centre of the attack, by contrast, no gains at all were made. There was no question that this inauspicious start would halt the battle. Commitments to allies and all of Haig's inclinations dictated a continuance. Three phases of the subsequent operations can be identified: July–August, September, and October–November.

In the first phase Haig and Rawlinson exercised little direction over day-to-day events. A typical battle-day saw small formations of troops attacking on narrow fronts and at different times. This method allowed the Germans to concentrate their firepower on one attack at a time. Most failed at heavy cost. Just occasionally, affairs were handled better. On 14 July a crushing artillery bombardment enabled a considerable section of the German second line to

However intense the artillery bombardment which preceded and accompanied an offensive, the moment had to come when the attacking infantry must leave the comparative security of their trenches and advance across open ground. Unless the artillery had done its job exceptionally well, these infantry would be exposed to fire from rifles, machine-guns, mortars, and shells.

be captured. But this provided no model for other operations. Between 2 July and the end of August the British lost 82,000 casualties for hardly any more ground than had been gained on the first day. The French, tied to the British, could only keep pace on the right.

In September, prospects for the offensive seemed to improve. British artillerymen were now capable of firing a moving curtain of shells in front of advancing infantry. This 'creeping barrage' proved most effective in neutralizing trench defenders (but not enemy artillery). Moreover, a new weapon in the form of the tank was at hand. In the event, when first used (on 15 September) the new weapon and the new artillery technique were mishandled. Gaps were left in the creeping barrage so as not to hit the tanks. As many of the latter broke down before arrival, the infantry in some areas received protection from neither tanks nor artillery. In any case, Haig had once more spread his artillery over too wide an area so as to get the cavalry through. Hence on 15 September the debut of the tank produced only small inroads into the German defences. Ten days later a more substantial success was obtained. All the tanks were for the moment out of action, so just artillery protection was provided for the infantry. Moreover, Haig's objectives were quite modest. The third German defensive system was finally overrun.

As it happened, this proved of limited utility. A fourth, fifth, and sixth German line had by this time been constructed between Haig's armies and Bapaume. Rain was falling. The campaigning season was drawing to an end. The imperatives to call a halt were plain. Haig pressed on. Seven times between early October and mid-November, he launched his troops against the German fourth line. In impossible conditions of mud and slush, all failed. With reserves of manpower running low, the campaign was finally halted on 14 November, 6 miles short of Bapaume (the objective set for the first day).

The Somme had cost the British 450,000 casualties, the French in their flanking operations 200,000. The Germans had suffered less—400,000 casualties. Haig and Joffre announced that the campaign would resume in the new year.

In the event, the plans of Haig and Joffre for 1917 did not come to fruition. The French government had no intention of sanctioning a rerun of the Somme. They sacked Joffre and replaced him with General Robert Nivelle, the successful commander of a recent limited-objective attack at Verdun.

Nivelle's plan for 1917 was deemed a real alternative to what had gone before. In the first instance the British (having been placed under Nivelle's direction) were called on to draw in the German reserves by attacking at Arras. Then Nivelle would strike the main blow on the Chemin des Dames. Such was intended to be the violence of his attack that the French were expected to break through the German positions and obtain a great strategic victory. This would occur within forty-eight hours, or the operation would be halted.

The political leadership in France and Britain were initially enthusiastic about Nivelle's conception. For the French it seemed far removed from Jof-

The Nivelle offensive

The despair to which French soldiers had been reduced by unrelenting and unrewarded frontal assaults is encapsulated in this painting by the distinguished French artist Pierre Bonnard. The next stage after disillusionment was a refusal to participate any further in such assaults.

187

fre's costly 'nibbling'. For the British prime minister, any French general seemed preferable to Haig. Unfortunately for the allies, these wishes were not fulfilled. In February 1917, seeking to conserve manpower, the Germans had withdrawn their armies to the shorter and more defensible Hindenburg line, so reducing the salient against which Nivelle intended to strike. The first attack at Arras on 9 April did capture Vimy Ridge and some territory to the south, but thereafter the British attack bogged down. On the Chemin des Dames, Nivelle's great strike on 16 April made initial gains, but there was no breakthrough and heavy loss. Ominously, there was also no halting of the offensive.

For many French soldiers (whose hopes had been raised by Nivelle's extravagant promises) this proved intolerable. Some units out of the line announced that they would return only to defend the trenches—they would not take part in further attacks. Others refused to return at all. The worst period came at the end of May when possibly 35,000 soldiers were involved in acts of 'collective indiscipline'. The French government was equally disillusioned. Nivelle was sidelined. Pétain, his replacement, called off the offensive and promised improved conditions for his troops. He also court-martialled 3,400 ringleaders and sentenced 450 to death. (Only about fifty of these sentences seem to have been carried out.)

The Germans never discovered the extent of French unrest. Almost certainly, they were in no position to take advantage of it anyway. Gradually calm was restored. But one thing was clear. The French army was incapable of another sustained offensive that year. If the allies were to attack again in 1917, it must be a British affair.

The third battle of Ypres

With the French failure at the Chemin des Dames, the British supporting operations at Arras served no purpose. Haig, restored to command of his army, opted for another offensive, but in the north. He would attack out of the Ypres salient and propel his forces towards the Belgian coast. The submarine bases in that area would be captured and the whole German position in Belgium unhinged.

First, however, Haig needed to capture the Messines Ridge, to prevent the Germans observing his preparations for battle in the salient. This was accomplished by General Plumer's 2nd Army on 7 June. Over the preceding two years, 1 million pounds of TNT had been placed under the German lines on the ridge. Nineteen mines were detonated at zero hour, and this, together with the domination of German artillery by Plumer's counter-batteries, secured him the ridge at modest cost.

To direct his main northern attack Haig chose not Plumer but the inexperienced (if compliant) 5th Army commander General Gough. Inexplicably, Gough was not to launch his attack until six weeks after Messines. This gave the Germans time to rush their defensive expert, Colonel von Lossberg, to the area and convert the salient into one gigantic defended zone. Gough's

troops, attacking at last on 31 July, faced the most formidable defences on the western front.

The British assault went in after a bombardment without precedent in history. Nevertheless, because of the ambitious nature of the plan, it was insufficient to reduce all aspects of von Lossberg's system. Moreover, some ground initially gained fell to counter-attacking formations held back beyond the range of British artillery. Most significantly, little ground was gained on the vital Gheluvelt Plateau, from where the Germans could overlook the battlefield. Nevertheless, Gough did gain some 3,000 yards on a 14,000-yard front—decidedly better than the unambiguous failure of 1 July 1916. The remainder of the battle is conveniently considered in three periods: August, September, and October–November.

August was the first mud phase. Rain started on the afternoon of 31 July and hardly let up during all of August. Most of the low-lying ground became a swamp. This did not deter Gough. He attacked six separate times during the month. By its end, for a total of 60,000 casualties, he had barely advanced the line at all. At times the going was so bad that the troops could hardly clamber out of their trenches, let alone mount a coherent attack. Finally Haig

The state to which the Third Ypres battlefield was reduced by constant shelling, by the wrecking of the delicate drainage system in this low-lying area, and by constant rain in both the August and the October–November phases of the battle, is powerfully revealed in this illustration. Equally evident is the inappropriateness of trying to employ tanks over such a battlefield.

acted. Gough was relegated to northern flanking operations. Plumer's 2nd Army took over the seemingly intractable problem of the Gheluvelt Plateau.

This inaugurated the September period. Plumer waited for fine weather. Then, in a series of three limited-objective attacks on 20 and 26 September and 4 October, he advanced a total of 4,500 yards across the Gheluvelt Plateau. That brought his troops within hailing distance of the Passchendaele ridge, one of Gough's original objectives on the first day of battle.

The commencement of rain in early October ushered in the third phase. The rain converted the already sodden battlefield into a moon-like quagmire. Haig's army also found itself advancing into an ever narrowing salient. This gave it insufficient room to deploy its own guns, and laid it open to heavy enfilade fire from the south. Common sense demanded that the campaign must end. Neither Haig nor Gough accepted this. Nor, more surprisingly, did Plumer. Without cause, all British commanders declared the Germans to be at the end of their tether. All hankered after the Passchendaele ridge and the green fields beyond. The battle continued.

So on 8 October the expectant cavalry were once more massed behind the front. No breakthrough awaited them. In conditions that at times reduced the infantry to crawling into battle, the series of attacks slowly gained ground towards the Passchendaele ridge. On 10 November Passchendaele village was at last captured and the campaign ended. The hapless troops now found themselves in a salient so pronounced that it was recognized to be untenable against a concerted counter-attack. (In the German spring offensive of 1918, all the ground gained in 1917 was evacuated in three days.)

The campaign cost the British 275,000 casualties, the Germans considerably fewer—200,000. It weakened the largest reliable army left to the allies, and it robbed Haig of the reserves needed to stem at the outset the German onslaught in the coming spring.

There was one last flicker of activity on the western front in 1917. While the Passchendaele campaign was in its last phase, Haig collected troops for an attack on a thinly held section of the Hindenburg line at Cambrai. The attack, commencing on 20 November, achieved nothing of permanence—on the 30th the Germans recovered all the ground they had lost. However, in two ways this battle pointed ahead. First, tanks were used in mass. Although too mechanically unreliable to persevere, they did in the initial phase help the infantry forward while minimizing losses. Secondly (and of greater importance) new artillery techniques were employed. Sound detection located enemy guns with great accuracy, allowing British batteries to remain silent until zero hour and then blanket German guns with fire. Surprise was thus restored to the battlefield. In 1918 artillery accuracy and surprise, occasionally assisted by tanks, would open the way to battlefield victory.

CHAPTER 14

Mutinies and Military Morale

DAVID ENGLANDER

Discipline and morale

Military thinking before 1914 assumed that success in battle was primarily a matter of morale, an action-based, group-centred concept that summarized the relative combat-willingness of individuals and units. Its focus was upon the problem of unit cohesion and group solidarity, upon the subordination of self and the formation of a loyalty that outweighed all personal considerations. Battle was conceived as a contest between two opposing wills, a clash of moral powers, and only secondarily as a collision between material forces. Tactical effectiveness thus required a secure moral basis. Drill, training, and military education provided the means for its attainment. Discipline supplied the overall source of integration. The revolution in firepower in the late nineteenth century did little to undermine these views. The soldierly spirit, properly cultivated, would still enable the soldier to cross the fireswept zone and close with the enemy. The military found no need to modify the volitional vocabulary in which its ideas were habitually expressed. Foch's famous formula 'Victory = Will' was representative of opinion among military professionals throughout Europe.

Morale was separate from the influences that produced or sustained it. Chief among these was discipline. Its primary function was to enable the soldier to conquer fear and do his duty in spite of it. Questions concerning the aims, objects, and forms of discipline, posed by extended firing lines and the isolating effects of the new technological battlefield, remained unanswered

191

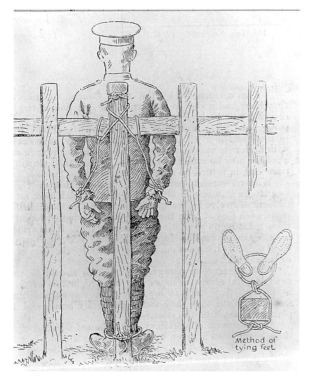

Method of tying feet

Field Punishment No 1: The most controversial of summary punishments, Field Punishment No 1 was applied extensively in British and Dominion Armies. The offender was placed on public display and left tied to a post or the wheel of a gun carriage in order to shame and humiliate him. It aroused anger among servicemen and dismay among civilians who first became aware of its application in 1916. Revised regulations in due course made it less of a public spectacle.

Soldiers, subjects, and citizens

before 1914. The idea of the intelligent and responsible soldier capable of individual initiative and rational corporate action in the main took second place to traditional concepts of mechanical obedience based on punishment and fear. All armies retained the capacity to inflict brutal, degrading, and often highly visible punishments upon enlisted personnel. Russian officers supported their authority by verbal and physical abuse coupled with excessive punishments. British officers left the coarse language to NCOs and denied themselves the right to strike subordinates but were equally free with humiliating summary punishments, at least until the second half of the war, when civilian pressure compelled greater circumspection. In this respect, they were more canny than their German counterparts who never ceased to lament the Reichstag intervention which made the penal laws more lenient and prohibited the soldier under 'close arrest' from being tied to a fixed object. The imposition of summary executions, authorized by French commanders, was also brought under formal control. Commanders in the Italian army, by contrast, were placed under no such restraints and relied on brutality and summary execution to maintain discipline. Capital punishments, though, were dished out with a variable liberality by all commands. Table 1 shows the number of death sentences dispensed by military courts during the First World War. Allowing for variations in army size, it will be seen that the Italian soldier was more severely dealt with than any other combatant but that British and Belgian soldiers were more at risk than either their French or German counterparts.

TABLE 1. Death sentences, *1914–1918*

Armed forces	Capital convictions	Number executed
Belgian	220	*18*
British	3,080	*346*
French	2,000	*700*
German	150	*48*
Italian	4,028	*750*

Morale and discipline, as traditionally conceived, were essentially the expression of the hierarchical view of the professional officer. Soldiers as automatons were required only to act, not to think. European armies thus reserved no place for politics. Voting rights were generally denied servicemen and the scope for political participation minimized. The soldier was represented as an object rather than an agent, capable of responding to the physical and instinctive but devoid of independent thought or judgement. The professional soldier, in short, embodied little more than a basic animality. Servicemen well understood this role. *Hommes et chevaux* (men and horses), inscribed on troop trains on the western front, thus became a parody of a particular power relationship rather than the summary of a freight manifest.

By the close of 1916 traditional habits of thought in respect of troop management were in urgent need of revision. Modern mass armies, so far from total institutions on which authority could freely stamp its will, were found to be teeming with assertive individuals who resisted the prescribed roles for which they had been cast. Soldiers of the Great War, however, were more than a mass of civilians in uniform with no fixed identities. Urban recruits were, with the notable exception of the British, in the minority in all European armies. Peasant soldiers, though, were not an undifferentiated mass without distinctive traditions or differing priorities. The Russians, for example, could think of nothing but returning to the land; whereas the Germans could think of nothing but abandoning it. The tsar's soldiers also brought to

Allied military co-operation helped to overcome deficiencies in equipment and training. Here a British officer teaches the rudiments of the mortar to his Russian ally in Galicia, 1917.

the army a distinctive conception of authority and a tradition of rebellion which sanctioned action against a weak centre but submission to a strong one. Many, indeed, came with first-hand knowledge as both rebels and repressors. More than one in three of the troops mobilized in 1914 was a veteran of the turmoil of 1905–7. Many, too, were heads of households and authoritative figures with experience of self-management in their villages. Peasants, if illiterate, were not unthinking.

Imperial armies invariably included irredentist elements of uncertain loyalties. Subject peoples and nationalities supplied much of the military manpower for the Romanov and Habsburg armies. Poles and Danes contributed to the German army in much the same way as the Senegalese and Zouaves served the French or the Indians served the British. The mutiny and surrender of a Czech infantry regiment on the Carpathian front in the winter of 1914–15 underscored the formidable management difficulties posed by the mobilization of minorities with distinct national identities. In general, high commands were careful in the management and disposition of their troops. Alsatians and Lorrainers serving with the German army were thus sent to the eastern front, while the Habsburg high command managed to postpone the breakdown of its multinational forces until the closing stages of the conflict.

Regional and class identities were equally marked. Flemings, for example, who made up more than two-thirds of the Belgian army, were profoundly influenced by the multiple deprivations, social, cultural, and material, experienced within a francophone-dominated state and its armed forces. Peasant localism, too, found expression in the homesickness and depression among conscripts posted to distant battlefields. The Sicilian dispatched to northwest Italy simply lacked a feeling comparable with that deep-rooted republicanism which the *poilu* found so sustaining. Cadorna's authoritarianism was a reflection of Italy's relative backwardness and attempt to secure by coercion that which had elsewhere been accomplished by the processes of economic development and cultural change.

The harshness of the disciplinary code, which never allowed soldiers to forget the basis of their subordination, also served to maintain class feeling. Inequalities in the terms and conditions of service, as in its rewards, appeared to replicate class privileges which the experience of discrimination— in respect of restaurants, barber shops, and bordellos—seemed to reinforce. The gulf between officers and men, though widest in the caste-ridden continental armies, was everywhere sufficient in breadth to ensure that the changes in class relations brought about by war service were minimal.

Obedience and resistance

Soldiers, in short, declined to accept an identity imposed by tradition and the command culture of the military. Soldiers, it was found, were not manipulable from above in accordance with the precepts of the training manuals. The relationship between the soldier and the military authorities was necessarily ambiguous, involving both an accommodation and rejection of the rules of his subordination. Soldiers, though ready to fight and endure, were often

unwilling to proceed on the terms chosen by their commanders. Resistance took many forms. Personal survival strategies ranged from keeping a low profile to feigned illness, self-mutilation, and the wilful commission of imprisonable offences. The repertoire of resistance that was available to the individual might also include failure to advance, premature retirement, desertion, or voluntary surrender. Not all defensive strategies were personal. Spontaneous fraternizing, for example, was an endemic feature of trench warfare which allowed for a mutually agreed limitation on violence rather than a suspension of hostilities. Tacit truces of this sort need not be soldier-led. Easter truces and other forms of fraternization were tolerated by the Central Powers on the eastern and southern fronts where the intention was to depress and demoralize the enemy, but regarded with concern by high commands on the western front where such arrangements were taken as evidence of a want of control.

Fraternization, whatever the source, was a striking reminder that obedience was conditional and could not be taken for granted. Line officers quickly discovered that leadership required a measure of consent, and that the sanctions of the disciplinary code were not a substitute for the acquisition of appropriate management skills. Regimental officers in their everyday encounters soon learned that subordinates were neither silent nor submissive, and that grousing was a flexible form of social interaction by which officers and other ranks defined and redefined their relationship within an otherwise unworkable framework of discipline. Grousing was, in fact, the principal means by which soldiers communicated their concerns, verbally or visually, to a commanding officer who could, without loss of authority, choose

German and Russian soldiers: troops also fraternized to celebrate the cessation of hostilities. The armistice of November 1917 relieved the Russian soldier from further participation in useless offensives and allowed the German soldier to contemplate the possibility of being discharged even before victory in the West had been secured.

to ignore them, to penalize them as insubordinate, or to accept them as valid criticism and modify his conduct accordingly. Grousing, a universal feature of war service, was not, however, the only means by which the allegedly hapless soldier could assert himself.

Morale: measurement and assessment

Recognition of the soldier as a moral being found institutional expression in the creation of an extensive intelligence network for the monitoring and control of service opinion. All armies developed elaborate systems for the gathering of information on the activities and attitudes of enlisted personnel. Postal censorship grew from a narrow concern with security issues into a powerful instrument of social research concerned with charting changes in troop morale as an aid to the improvement of combat efficiency. Letters were opened, the content analysed, and the sources of grievance laid bare. Postal control had an acute understanding of the interactive nature of the home front and fighting front and of the ways in which shifts in opinion were influenced by the two-way flow of information between them. Troops, it was found, were as much influenced by domestic as by military developments. They were particularly unsettled by news of privations at home. Soldiers on leave also played a key role in the formation of civilian opinion and and were equally influential in the units to which they returned. High commands, then, were well informed on the changing mood of the men.

Armies in fact were huge bureaucracies. In addition to postal surveillance, commanders received regular reports on the nature and distribution of indiscipline and on variations in sickness wastage, sometimes supplemented by other surrogate morale measures such as the uptake in war loan. How these were read and evaluated remains to be established. What is clear, however, is that from the beginning of 1917 all the key indicators began to point downwards. Three years of inconclusive fighting and 17 million casualties left servicemen increasingly restive. Armies were becoming more difficult to manage. Some form of political education was deemed necessary. The Central Powers were the first to create and deliver new schemes of patriotic instruction for the ideological remobilization of their armies. Ludendorff's order of July 1917 provided for the establishment of *Vaterlander Unterricht* (patriotic instruction) to root out idle talk of peace and pessimism. Sixty minutes of each day were allocated to a 'love-the-fatherland' slot in which unit officers denounced peace proposals and other enemy attempts to undermine the morale of the victorious German forces. The British, who, like the Austrians, had hoped to get by on voluntary methods boosted by the contribution of the padres, followed suit with comparable measures. The Italians, whose approach hitherto is generously described as Neanderthal, posted propaganda units to each regiment. The need for political education, however, was less pressing than the need for a revision of tactics and strategy.

Mutiny and disorder

The French armies experienced widespread mutinies in the spring following the failure of the Nivelle offensive on the Chemin des Dames. The 250 acts of collective indiscipline reported between April and June 1917 involved 68 divisions or two-thirds of the French army. Soldiers, fed up with futile offensives, struck against the conduct of the war and refused to advance until less suicidal tactics were introduced. Mutinies among homesick and hungry troops in Ravenna and Catanzaro in March and July resulted in the execution of eighty-six soldiers. During the summer the Belgians were shaken by mass desertions—5,603 in 1917 compared with 1,203 in the previous year—and the British affected by the growth of disobedience and disorder. In September 1917 the training establishment at Etaples was convulsed by large-scale disturbances which were put down by force after three days. Unruly incidents at British base camps, however, were small beer by comparison with the mass desertions and large-scale mutinies that preceded the rout of the Italians at Caporetto in the autumn. The Austrian offensive on the Isonzo—the twelfth battle in a grisly war of attrition—almost cost Italy the war, as discipline broke, panic ensued, and soldiers deserted in droves. Three hundred thousand were taken prisoner in what was as much a moral slump as a military defeat. Most spectacular of all, though, was the Russian collapse into revolution.

The revolution that swept away the Russian autocracy began when the Petrograd garrison refused to crush civilian demonstrators in February 1917. The revolution then proceeded from the city to the front as a soldiers' revolt against the system of command authority. It was driven by the hopes and fears of the peasant conscripts who accounted for the vast majority of the tsar's soldiers. These his generals used with great callousness and extraordinary carelessness. Of the 15 million who by early 1917 had passed through the ranks, an estimated 1.8 million were dead, 3.9 million wounded, and 2.4 million taken prisoner. Ill-equipped, ill-treated, and ill-used, the Russian soldier had had enough. The mutiny by the Petrograd garrison in March 1917, carried to the front with telegraphic rapidity, prompted the abolition of traditional forms of discipline and the vesting of authority in the newly formed soldiers' councils or soviets. Soldier radicalism escalated thereafter as hitherto inarticulate masses of grey-coated *muzhiks* became conscious of their collective capacity to bend events to their will.

Order No. I, issued by the Petrograd Soviet, which provided for the democratization of discipline, and the subsequent introduction of civil rights into the army, did not cause military breakdown. Soviet order, the only order that was available, prevented disintegration. No mass exodus from the trenches took place in the first half of 1917 while the soldiers waited on the progress of peace negotiations. The July offensive made it clear, however, that peace would only be secured by the soldiers themselves. Consciousness of that imperative found expression in the self-demobilization that preceded the collapse into revolution in October.

Soldiers' soviets did not supply a model for ready imitation. Troops in other armies, however, were not without creative means of self-expression. Flemish separatism, for example, displayed resource and imagination in asserting

197

Demonstrations, as at Petrograd in April 1917, gave expression to soldiers' demands for recognition of their own humanity and their aspirations for an honourable peace followed by a better life for themselves and their families.

its claims. Its instrument, the Front Party, was a clandestine military organization, the outgrowth of a soldiers' study circle which had been proscribed by the authorities in 1917. It was organized under the leadership of a secondary school teacher with the assistance of an army committee made up of delegates from each division. The core of the 5,000-strong membership, though, seems to have been concentrated among the artillery. Its defeatism and related demands were broadcast through trench newspapers, anonymous tracts, placards, and graffiti, and supplemented by demonstrations of an increasingly serious nature. Regiments and divisions were convulsed by a series of carefully orchestrated strikes and protests throughout 1917–18. Protest demonstrations were held at dusk, lasted for thirty minutes, and generally involved between 100 and 400 Flemish soldiers. Unarmed except for protective sticks, the latter would chant slogans and slip away before the authorities could intervene. The movement reached its climax on 13 March 1918 when five of the six Belgian artillery divisions were shaken by a co-ordinated set of strikes. But thereafter the German army from which so much had been expected itself began to crumble.

The spring offensive of 1918 brought the German soldier to the limits of his endurance. Up to 10 per cent of men deserted in the preparatory stages *en route* from the eastern front. Those who survived the subsequent holocaust became more and more resistant. Refusals to obey orders and attack were the prelude to an undeclared soldiers' strike as hundreds of thousands sought by means of evasion to avoid further service during the summer and autumn. Before Ludendorff's decision to sue for an armistice that September, the German army stood almost as defenceless as the French had been during the mutinies of the previous year. The formation of soldiers' councils in November did not, however, signal a revolutionary outburst similar to that which convulsed the Russian armies. In Germany defeat made for the departure of the monarchy, but there was no fundamental collapse comparable with the breakdown of the state machine in Russia. The role of the soldiers' councils was correspondingly different. Social democratic in mentality and make-up, the soldiers' councils were disciplined, restrained, and preoccupied with the commanding problems of demobilization, above all with the maintenance of public order and continuity in production. Proletarian spontaneity spent itself in containing the destructive energies unleashed by military defeat, economic disruption, and social dislocation.

Service radicalism displayed extraordinary diversity. Apart from differences in time and space, there was considerable variation within and between branches of the armed forces. Technical and support staff, for example, were generally considered more susceptible to political activity than front-line soldiers. Navies were, in this respect, particularly vulnerable. The substitution of coal for canvas and the mechanization of firepower made fishermen sailors redundant and caused admirals to seek recruits from among the most advanced sectors of the urban working class. They brought with them industrial and political traditions which ill-accorded with the discipline and submission expected by their officers. Sailors, too, were more open to civilian influences and less exposed to combat than soldiers. The deadening effects of trench warfare gave place to long periods of inactivity and frustration and created a milieu in which revolutionary politics could flourish. Sailors were prominent in the Russian Revolution of 1917 and in the German Revolution of 1918 and visible in the generalized unrest of the closing stages of the war and its aftermath.

Naval unrest

The politicization of naval unrest seemed striking. All the principal fleets were affected. The Russian and German navies moved from mutiny to revolution. The French and Austrian fleets developed a dangerous list to the left. And within the Royal Navy the spirit of 1797 was abroad. The revolutionary character of naval unrest, however, should not be overstated. The root cause in all cases was to be located in deficiencies in man-management, pay, leave, and cognate grievances. The precise combination varied. The caste spirit and social exclusiveness that so antagonized officer–men relations in the Russian and German navies was less pronounced in the British and French fleets where other issues were more prominent. French naval radicalism was essentially that of disgruntled seamen politicized by their retention for service against the Russian Revolution. The radicalism of the British lower deck, by contrast, was professional rather than political. Naval democracy within

199

the British fleet, and the elaborate unofficial organization of death benefit societies that sustained it, represented the claim of the regular rating for a career and not a bid for state power. The soviet idea never fired the imagination in Rosyth as it did in Reval.

The limitations of naval radicalism were by no means a peculiarity of the British. The imperial German navy mutinies of 1918, for example, were a sailors' rebellion rather than a socialist rising. Sailors at Kiel rose against their officers rather than embark upon a suicidal mission against the British to vindicate *Junker* conceptions of honour. The socialism of the mutinous French Black Sea Fleet in the following year was also more a matter of protest than ideology. Even in the Russian navy, the most revolutionary of all, there existed a discrepancy between the sovietist sailors of the Baltic Fleet and the Bolsheviks who came to be regarded as the usurpers of their revolution.

Distinctions of this nature, though, were lost on naval commanders, who usually out of ignorance, and sometimes out of convenience, tended to attribute a political character to all forms of unrest. Generals were no better. Projection and displacement gave a political coloration to their anxieties. Notwithstanding the intelligence resources at their disposal, deficiencies in troop morale or failure in the field continued to be explained in terms of subversion and external agitation.

Explanations and meanings

If defeatist agitation is rejected, what, then, caused the mutinies? One explanation presents military breakdown as a function of a specific level of casualties. The case, baldly summarized, is that disintegration occurred when the number of battle deaths equalled the fighting strength of the armies on the outbreak of war. The argument, for all its sweep and simplicity, is too mathematically exact and too restrictive in respect of human agency. But it was precisely their collective capacity to control their destiny that drove soldiers' radicalism in the Russian armies. Front-line soldiers, so far from the dark, brooding masses of popular representation, were active supporters of the revolution. They sought direction from the new government and were intensely suspicious of information circulated by their officers, particularly by high-ranking officers, whose uncertain loyalties made them liable to arrest. The recasting of the command structure on democratic lines through the abolition of old regime symbols of caste distinction, and the insistence that officers treat their subordinates with the respect due to citizens, provides striking confirmation of the awareness and understanding of the soldier masses. Mutinous Russian soldiers, unlike their French counterparts, were not primarily concerned with the conduct of the war and not willing to resume their place in the trenches. The tactical adjustments which pacified the *poilu* were irrelevant to the *muzhik* whose greater alienation and larger ambitions required a more comprehensive control over his commanders. Equally striking was the growth of representation and creation of a coherent structure of soviets. The soviet idea not only expressed a vision of land, peace, and social liberation, but was also the most potent symbol of the soldier's sense of power. His politics were determined not by fixed party allegiances, but by a shifting assessment of those policies that were most likely to advance peasant-soldier interests. Support for Bolshevism was thus never unconditional. The bastardized version with which the soldier came to identify had little in common with socialist transformation, but much to do with agrarian reform, the liquidation of the *ancien régime*, and the peace necessary for their realization.

Soldier strikes, mutinies, and disorders arose primarily from the circumstances of the war. Soldier grievances invariably were concerned with the conduct of the war in respect of themselves and their families. Apart from questions concerning food and drink, soldiers were exercised by issues respecting pay and allowances, clothing and comforts, shelter, warmth, and rest. Dominating all was the question of leave and family income support. Soldiers lived and died in the trenches while directing their conscious life homewards. Civilian society, though the object of criticism, was never rejected. Soldiers continued to look to family and friends to satisfy their emotional and psychological needs rather than to an imaginary counter-culture of the trenches. The war experience was less of a discontinuity than is sometimes allowed. The Flemish movement in the Belgian army was thus fuelled

Cleaning kit, 1917: a universal feature of military service, the cleaning of kit was perceived as a burden that was essential to the maintenance of combat efficiency. Soldiers were encouraged to cherish their rifle as they would a bride!

by an ongoing experience of discrimination and inequality. Domestic priorities likewise influenced the relative radicalization of soldier unrest. Questions of citizenship and land reform, which had been settled in France 100 years earlier, for example, meant that the issue of peace did not preoccupy the *poilu* in the same way as it drove the *muzhik*. For the former it implied relief from incompetent generals; for the latter it meant deliverance from oppression. The French army mutinies of 1917 were a revolt against a particular way in warfare; the Russian against a particular way of life.

The theme of continuity finds further illustration in the limited radicalism of the British soldier. The absence of large-scale mutinies and disorders comparable with those among contemporaries does not mean that the British army was free from indiscipline. It was not. Command authority was contested individually and collectively. Soldier protest, indeed, readily appropriated both the imagery and vocabulary of revolution. Soldiers' soviets in the British army—at least three were reported in 1917–18—were, however, a vehicle for the dramatic registration of protest. Hoisting the Red Flag was a signal to the authorities, a bargaining counter, which came readily to those who brought to the most proletarian of European armies the customs and outlook of the most disciplined labour force in the world. Cultural continuities, moreover, were sustained by the character of morale management which, in certain respects, was light years ahead of allies and enemies alike. The self-sufficient nature of British military organization, with its ready concession to popular taste in the provision of rest, entertainment, and refreshment, helped steel the soldier against defeat and disintegration. Even so, it was a close-run thing.

Conclusion

Discipline and authority relationships in the First World War were less mechanical than is sometimes suggested. The obedient and unquestioning subordinate was an imagined soldier quite unlike those encountered by line officers, who soon found that authority was more than a matter of issuing orders. Senior officers, if slower to learn, were also brought to a realization that a greater measure of agreement was required than was formally allowed. High commands in consequence were compelled to adjust their tactics and stand on the defensive, as in the case of the French after the mutinies, or engage in direct negotiations with the rank and file, as with the Russians. The Belgian and British authorities, confronted by soldier unrest, likewise took remedial action. Even the Italians, following the mass defections at Caporetto, liberalized leave arrangements, improved rations, and sanctioned the introduction of trench newspapers. In general, though, concession and coercion went hand in hand. 'Ringleaders' were identified and punished, and the gap between command and consent closed. Historians have in recent years begun to reopen it. What they have found is that soldiers of the Great War were rather less helpless than was previously thought and that some choices remained possible even in the most extreme situations. The idea that soldiers were simply manipulated from above will no longer do. Farm boys or factory hands, clerks or craftsmen brought to war service a set of specific ideas and interests and of values, beliefs and attitudes, which, try as it might, the military could not ignore. Those customs, habits, and outlooks, moreover, were not left behind on enlistment but continued to inform the conduct, motivation, and self-perception of the soldiery. War service thus gave a new dimension to pre-existing class and civilian identities without transforming either.

CHAPTER 15

War Aims and Peace Negotiations

DAVID STEVENSON

This chapter will reconsider the First World War in the light of the celebrated insight of the Prussian theorist Carl von Clausewitz that war is a 'true political instrument, a continuation of political activity by other means'. It will focus on the problem of what, politically, the struggle was about, through an analysis of the two sides' war aims: the conditions that they intended to impose on their enemies. The incompatibility between these aims blocked all efforts to halt the fighting by negotiation even after it became far longer and more costly than any government had envisaged in 1914. This political approach is only one possible interpretation of the central dynamic of the conflict, but it is among the most illuminating, and the history of war aims and peace negotiations provides a backdrop against which the military operations can be better understood. What follows will be divided into three parts: the development of war aims between 1914 and early 1917, taking the Central Powers and the allies in turn; the failure of the 1917 attempts at peace through compromise; and the decision-making in 1918 that brought the conflict to an end.

Germany's war aims

Our knowledge of wartime diplomacy has been transformed by the opening of the relevant archives, and a formidable body of literature is now available. But the trailblazing book that opened up the topic was Professor Fritz Fischer's *Germany's Aims in the First World War*. Although telling criticisms have been made of Fischer's work, it remains the starting point for all subsequent discussion.

Fischer contended that German war aims exhibited 'monolithic' continuity, and enjoyed support from much of German society and almost all the political class. Both assertions must be qualified. Certainly, the Germans took their war aims seriously. They had begun hostilities with little thought of their objectives, beyond the hope that overwhelming France and Russia would assure their security within Europe and bring opportunities for expansion outside. But within days deliberations started in the office of the chancellor, Theobald von Bethmann Hollweg, and soon there was continuous planning in the relevant ministries, combined with periodic high-level conferences and a wider public debate.

Fischer's most sensational discovery was the 'September programme', approved by Bethmann on 9 September 1914. 'The general aim of the war', it stated, was the 'security of the German Reich in west and east for all imaginable time'. On the western frontiers it envisaged that Luxembourg would be annexed and Belgium become a 'vassal State', giving 'the advantages of annexation without its inescapable domestic political disadvantages'. Germany would take Liège, as well (the Navy Office later advocated) as the Bruges–Ostend–Zeebrugge triangle as a naval base. The rest of Belgium would be occupied until far into the future, it would enter monetary and customs union with the Reich, and its railways would come under German control. From the French the main annexation would be the Briey–Longwy basin, which accounted for nine-tenths of their iron ore output. Otherwise, although France would pay a heavy indemnity to impede its rearmament, on condition that it broke loose and made peace separately from its allies it would escape relatively lightly. If it did not, much more severe exactions, possibly including the northern coalfield and the Channel ports, would be in order.

It is true that the western aims set out in the September programme remained relatively constant through the war, though by 1917 there was some willingness to moderate them. A second consistent ambition, promoted by the Reich Colonial Office, was a colony from coast to coast in Central Africa, to be carved out from French and Belgian possessions. A third was the navy's drive for bases in the Mediterranean sea and in the Atlantic and Indian Oceans, which in combination with the Flanders strongpoint would menace Britain's imperial communications. The two remaining strands of German objectives, however, showed less continuity. The first—and the primary economic goal—was *Mitteleuropa*, a customs union encompassing the west and centre of the continent, intended in the September programme to 'stabilize Germany's economic domination over Central Europe'. Bethmann saw it primarily as another means of controlling Germany's neighbours politically, and much of the business community doubted its value if it meant exclusion from markets outside. Later in the war, as the allied blockade tightened, regaining access to world trade became the crucial commercial objec-

DAVID STEVENSON

tive. *Mitteleuropa* persisted as a more restricted plan for a military pact and preferential tariffs with the Austrians, whose justified wariness impeded its realization.

The final strand was eastern Europe. Although the September Programme envisaged that 'Russia must be thrust back as far as possible . . . and her domination over the non-Russian vassal peoples broken', the Germans' objectives in this theatre were slower to crystallize, until during 1915 Russian Poland fell under their and Austria-Hungary's occupation. Before the war the three eastern empires had shared an interest in keeping Poland down, but now its future divided not only the Central Powers from Russia but also Berlin from Vienna. At first Bethmann agreed to Russian Poland being incorporated into the Habsburg monarchy in return for the latter accepting *Mitteleuropa*-style economic and security ties, but the Brusilov offensive in the summer of 1916 underlined the danger of depending on the Habsburgs. It was decided instead that Russian Poland should be nominally independent but in monetary and customs union with Germany and under German occupation: thus extending further the Belgian formula. A similar combination of

'Of Two Evils the Lesser', from *The Bystander* (London), 27 December 1916. David Lloyd George, newly installed as British prime minister, rejects the Central Powers' December 1916 peace note in preference for the more austere attractions of continued war.

nominal independence with indirect control was approved for the Baltic provinces of Courland and Livonia, and by 1917 was envisaged for the Ukraine.

Despite the continuity in objectives against the western powers, those in the east therefore expanded as Germany's armies advanced. War aims were not set in concrete, and were continuously debated. Nor were they necessarily absolute demands, on which no compromise was possible. Bethmann called the September programme 'provisional notes' towards a western settlement that, with German forces skirting Paris, seemed imminent. Within three months of it, however, he agreed with Erich von Falkenhayn, the new commander-in-chief, that complete victory over all the allies was unlikely, and that Germany faced being worn down in a prolonged confrontation with stronger enemies. From now on he considered his main objective as being to split the opposing coalition. To achieve it, he and Falkenhayn were willing to jetti-

206

son more specific aims. Both considered the most promising target to be Russia, to whom peace feelers were extended in 1915, and the blows struck against it in Poland and the Balkans were meant to encourage a response. The Germans initially planned to annex only a 'frontier strip' of Polish territory (from which, however, Slavs and Jews would be cleared), and their more extended eastern goals after 1916 reflected their disappointment with Petrograd. Likewise, they hoped the Verdun campaign would force Paris to yield. But by the end of 1916 neither Russia nor France had shown interest, and Falkenhayn's successors, Paul von Hindenburg and Erich Ludendorff, were less convinced that Germany must compromise. Encouraged by Austria-Hungary and foreseeing a confrontation with America over submarine warfare, Bethmann won approval for a joint declaration in December that the Central Powers were willing to propose terms, but he would have been unable to offer much even had the allies responded to the initiative, which in fact they indignantly rejected.

German policy was torn between the war aims programmes and the imperative of dividing the allies. It aspired to expansion by means of buffer states and economic dominance, given its reluctance to absorb large subject populations: but the outcome would still be continental hegemony. In public the authorities referred to their objectives as 'securities' and 'guarantees', rather than spelling them out. None the less, an imperialist settlement was desired by powerful forces in German society, including the right and centre in the Reichstag and much of heavy industry, agriculture, and the intellectual élite, as well as by Wilhelm II himself.

If Bethmann wished to part the allies, they were determined to remain together. A leading issue in the conflict became the pattern of international alignments. Germany had already felt encircled by the Triple Entente of Russia, France, and Britain before 1914, and went to war partly in order to smash it. Its enemies recognized that to let it do so would destroy the balance of power that preserved their independence, and in the Pact of London of September 1914 they undertook to make no separate peace or negotiate unilaterally. There was a basic difference between the two coalitions. Germany was clearly the strongest among the Central Powers, and if it chose to make peace its partners would have to do likewise. But among the allies, Britain, France, and Russia were approximately equal in their contributions to the common effort, and all developed ambitions that cut directly across the Central Powers' objectives.

Britain combined fixity of purpose outside Europe with characteristic uncertainty within. It intended that a defeated Germany should lose its battle fleet and colonies, which were seen as threats to British sea lanes and overseas territories. But inside Europe Britain's one clear commitment was to restoring Belgium to its pre-war independence and integrity. Beyond this, British leaders hesitated to weaken Germany too much economically (in recognition of its importance as a trading partner), or to exact crushing repa-

War aims and the cohesion of the Entente

Facing: 'A Japanese View of Peace', from *Jijo* (Tokyo), reproduced in the *New York Tribune*, 23 January 1917. The allies (represented here as essentially British) show disdain for the Central Powers' December 1916 peace appeal. By the time this cartoon was printed in New York the allies had also rejected American mediation.

rations; nor did they desire to weaken it too much strategically to France's and Russia's benefit. They hoped democratization might make it feasible to maintain a united Germany while reforming its behaviour—and that defeat itself would teach that aggression did not pay. The French favoured a more robust approach. They committed themselves at once to regaining Alsace-Lorraine, lost in 1871, which would give them iron ore, phosphates, steel, and a Rhine frontier, as well as satisfying nationalist sentiment. They wanted Belgium and Luxembourg to agree to a customs union and security collaboration after the war. Moreover, in February–March 1917 they made a secret arrangement with Tsar Nicholas II (the Doumergue Agreement) to support Russian demands in Poland in return for a free hand on the left bank of the Rhine. The latter would be divided into buffer states under French occupation, most of the Saar coalfield being annexed along with Lorraine. The remainder of Germany would pay reparations and be disarmed. Whereas for Britain and France the main enemy was always Berlin, however, for the Russians Austria-Hungary and Ottoman Turkey were almost equally important adversaries. They proclaimed in 1914 that they would unite under their sovereignty all the areas of Polish inhabitation (including Poznán from Germany and Galicia from Austria), but did not commit themselves beyond this against either Berlin or Vienna, and soon experienced such grave military setbacks that their planning fell into abeyance.

Between 1914 and 1917 the allies wove a spider's web of treaties in order to attract new partners and to hold existing ones in line. In the process they further complicated peacemaking with the Central Powers, by making it harder to detach Germany's subordinates. Japan, which entered the war in August 1914, was promised support for its claims to Kiaochow (Germany's lease in China) and to Germany's Pacific islands. Italy, which did so in May 1915, negotiated beforehand the Treaty of London, which promised it Habsburg territory in the Trentino, the South Tyrol, Istria, and Dalmatia. Romania, in return for entering in August 1916, was also promised gains at Austria-Hungary's expense. A still more intricate network of undertakings resulted from Turkish intervention. The Russians demanded Constantinople and the Asiatic shore of the Bosporus, which Britain and France conceded in the Straits Agreement of March–April 1915. Before the Arab revolt of June 1916 the British promised an independent Arab state in the McMahon–Hussein correspondence, and the prospect of the uprising hastened an accord with Paris. The Sykes–Picot Agreement carved out spheres of control and influence in Turkey-in-Asia, conferring British predominance in Mesopotamia, and French in Syria and the Lebanon. Further understandings in 1916–17 assigned Russia predominance in Turkish Armenia and Italy in southern Asia Minor. More generally, at the Paris Economic Conference of June 1916 the allies agreed to discriminate against German commerce after the war while making their own bloc as self-sufficient as possible. Finally, on 10 January 1917, in reply to an invitation to both sides from the American president to state their war aims (to which Bethmann responded confidentially), the allies publicly specified their objectives with unprecedented, if misleading, precision.

If we compare the opposing coalitions, the points of conflict are evident. Britain and Germany clashed over Belgium and over colonies; France and Germany over Alsace-Lorraine and the Rhineland; Russia and the Central Powers over who would dominate Poland; Austria-Hungary and Italy over the Alps and Adriatic. Germany and France had rival projects for tariff blocs. But few peace feelers in 1914–16 reached the point of substantive discussion. Germany's hope of dividing the allies was frustrated by their solidarity, and a diplomatic impasse over war aims joined the strategic impasses on land and at sea. The war could be ended neither by compromise nor by military breakthrough: nor by revolution, while the combatants and the home fronts held firm. From the first battle of Ypres until the overthrow of Nicholas II, this triple stalemate was its dominating feature.

(From Jiji, Tokio)

Of the three elements in the stalemate, it was the cohesion of the home fronts that most altered during 1917. The fall of the tsar inaugurated a wider challenge to the established order, including strikes in Germany and Britain, riots in Italy, and the French army mutinies. But the eastern European belligerents, Russia and Austria-Hungary, were under the greatest strain, and from them came the impetus that helped make 1917 the climax of attempts at a negotiated settlement. They failed, however, to win more than cosmetic changes in either side's war aims, and the other major development, American intervention, initially reinforced the stalemate and prolonged the conflict.

There were changes of leadership in both Petrograd and Vienna, the advent of the Russian Provisional Government being paralleled by the death of Franz Joseph and the accession of the Emperor Karl, with Ottokar Czernin as his foreign minister. As national separatism in the Dual Monarchy gathered momentum, and supplies to its cities deteriorated, Karl and Czernin were desperate to make peace soon. Karl went behind the back not only of his ally but also of his minister, secretly contacting the French via Prince Sixte de Bourbon and offering in writing to support their 'just claims' to Alsace-Lorraine. France and Britain, who had no territorial quarrels with Austria-Hungary, were sorely tempted, but felt unable to abandon Italy. In any case, Karl wanted a general rather than a separate peace, and was neither willing to desert the Germans nor able to lure Bethmann into compromise. On the contrary, the chancellor, although still looking to split his opponents, was being badgered by Hindenburg and Ludendorff to make his aims more

The peace initiatives of 1917

rigid. Even when in July the Reichstag passed a 'peace resolution' condemning annexations and indemnities, its authors did not extend the condemnation to the autonomous buffer states that were the hallmark of German planning. Simultaneously with the passage of the resolution Bethmann was forced to resign, but his successor, Georg Michaelis, was the candidate of the high command rather than the legislature. He accepted the peace resolution only 'as I understand it'.

Russian pressure within the allied coalition was scarcely more effective. Like Karl and Czernin the Provisional Government drew back from a separate peace. The Erzberger–Kolyschko conversations with Germany in March–April gave it little encouragement to conclude one, as it seemed that Poland and the Baltic coast would be the price. The government called for an inter-allied war aims conference, but when Britain and France stalled it did not insist. More dangerous to Russia's partners was the proposal for a meeting in Stockholm of all socialist parties, which was vigorously espoused by the Petrograd Soviet. Although the initiative led nowhere, it helped to radicalize the left in France and Britain. The line against compromise was held, and the Dumont resolution passed by the French Chamber of Deputies in June repudiated annexations as equivocally as did its German counterpart.

If peace would not come from below, nor would it come from exchanges between governments, as new contacts in the autumn demonstrated. The starting point was an appeal by the Pope, Benedict XV, who urged a settlement based broadly on the pre-war status quo. Although both sides rejected his note, the British inquired via the Vatican for clarification of Germany's position over Belgium. Meanwhile news reached Berlin of meetings between the Austrians and the French (the Armand–Revertera conversations), in which the latter had offered German territory if Vienna would abandon its ally. Michaelis's foreign minister, Richard von Kühlmann, perceived a menace to the unity of the Central Powers, and decided to respond in kind. The British inquiry confirmed his view that London was the allies' weak link, and he intimated via a Spanish intermediary, Villalobar, that he was ready to exchange views.

Kühlmann's message was forwarded in September, at the same time as information reached Paris that a German official in Brussels, the Baron von der Lancken, was willing to meet in Switzerland with Aristide Briand (the French premier from October 1915 until March 1917) and that Briand was willing to go. Both western European powers now faced critical decisions. Briand's successor as French premier, Paul Painlevé, doubted that his people would go on fighting if they were offered Alsace-Lorraine. Painlevé's foreign minister, Alexandre Ribot, outmanoeuvred Briand and prevented the Swiss visit. In fact the Germans were prepared to restore only a few border villages, although Michaelis was willing to drop the annexation of Longwy–Briey in return for guaranteed access to the iron ore. As for Britain, at the Bellevue crown council the German leaders agreed to sacrifice the navy's demand for the Flanders coast, but their other aims in Belgium remained intact. David

Lloyd George himself was willing to contemplate a peace at Russia's expense, but the majority of his cabinet insisted that Britain must consult its partners. The Foreign Office therefore did so, with the result that Kühlmann was invited to communicate with the allies as a whole, a suggestion he ignored.

The Germans were not offering nearly enough to make either Britain or France split away, as would have become obvious had negotiations started. Underlying the calculations of both sides were assessments that the war could still be won. Hindenburg and Ludendorff believed that with Russia's collapse they could gain the upper hand; Ribot and Lloyd George that they could survive the onslaught and secure their war aims with American aid. US Treasury loans had rescued the British within weeks of bankruptcy, and enabled the allies to continue purchasing essential steel, wheat, and oil. America's entry promised hundreds of thousands of new recruits at the very moment when Russia faltered. Even so, its assistance would be sufficiently delayed and limited to offer the Central Powers one final opportunity.

The reasons for this were not just logistic but also political. President Wilson had broken off diplomatic relations with Germany in February 1917 when the latter resumed unrestricted submarine warfare. But it is unlikely that he would have declared war in April had he not intended to exert decisive influence on the post-war settlement and believed that only by becoming a belligerent could he do so. He harboured a grand design to restructure international relations between the industrial countries, under the auspices of his proposed League of Nations. Because the militarists in Berlin were a fundamental obstacle to that design, Germany must be defeated and democratized. Yet the British, French, Italian, and Japanese leaders were also suspect to him as imperialists.

In the short term, Wilson opposed a compromise that would leave Wilhelm II's regime intact. He rejected participation in the Stockholm Conference and rebuffed Pope Benedict's appeal. He did not meddle with his allies' objectives, although they tried to humour him by endorsing the League. Similarly, in November 1917 the British issued the Balfour Declaration in favour of a 'national home' for the Jews in Palestine in part because they knew that Wilson was sympathetic and they hoped for goodwill from American Zionists. The French narrowed the economic war aims of the 1916 Paris Conference, concentrating on signing up the president for continuing controls over world trade in commodities after the end of the war. Yet none of this cut much ice. Wilson kept his distance, adhering to neither the secret treaties nor the Pact of London, and remaining not an allied but an 'associated' power, at liberty to conclude a separate peace. He welcomed his partners' growing financial dependence, and cultivated European radicals and socialists, making ready to put pressure on their governments when the time came. In the culminating drama, Washington was reserving for itself the role of arbiter.

In 1917 the stalemate had been shaken, but not enough to enable compromise. In 1918, the war was ended both in east and west by military might. In **Brest-Litovsk and its consequences**

DAVID STEVENSON

the eastern theatre the Bolshevik revolution for the first time brought to office in a great power a regime willing to conclude a separate peace. An armistice ensued in December 1917, and the Treaty of Brest-Litovsk three months afterwards. This was not Lenin's original intention, which was rather that revolution should spread to Germany. When it failed to do so, however, the survival of Bolshevik power became the priority, which made it essential to halt the war. Yet by publishing and repudiating the inter-allied secret treaties, and denouncing annexations and indemnities in a 'Decree on Peace', the Bolsheviks in some ways aligned themselves with Wilson, and they challenged internal consensus everywhere.

The consequence was a propaganda battle. Kühlmann and Czernin perceived an opportunity to divide the Bolsheviks from the west through the agency of their 'Christmas Declaration', in which they purported to repudiate annexations and indemnities on condition that their enemies did likewise. However, the allies and the Americans would not content themselves with a status quo ante peace, as Lloyd George made clear in his Caxton Hall speech on 5 January and Wilson in his Fourteen Points address on the 8th. Both men appealed to a triple constituency: to socialists and trade unionists in the Central Powers and to their own domestic left, as well as to the Russians. For Wilson this meant presenting a reformist alternative to Lenin's, and he promised open diplomacy, free navigation of the seas, non-discrimination in commerce, arms limitation, and an 'impartial adjustment of all colonial claims', in addition to the League. But he also supported a carefully limited version of the allies' war aims, including restoring Belgium, redressing 'the wrong' done to France over Alsace-Lorraine, and awarding Italy territory of indisputably Italian ethnicity. Austria-Hungary and Turkey should grant autonomy to their subject peoples but would not be partitioned, and Russia must be free to decide its own destiny.

The Central Powers seized on this pretext to assert that the Christmas Declaration was invalidated, and proceeded to make peace with a separatist government in the Ukraine. The Russians, declaring 'no war, no peace', withdrew from the negotiations, but were helpless before the subsequent German advance. Lenin overcame the majority in the Bolshevik Central Committee that favoured revolutionary war and won it round to accepting terms. At Brest-Litovsk the Bolsheviks ceded

'The Russian Cake', *Le Journal* (Paris), 2 March 1918. A French comment on the peace negotiations between Bolshevik Russia and the Central Powers. Wilhelm II cuts a tiny portion for his ally, remarking, 'Here is your share, young Austro-Karl, and learn that in German arithmetic two halves are never equal'.

sovereignty over Poland, Courland, Lithuania, and the Ukraine, and evacuated Finland, abandoning one-third of the tsarist empire's population and agricultural land and much of its industry. In May Romania, which had been left helpless, agreed in the Treaty of Bucharest to sell to Germany its wheat and oil surpluses and accepted an indefinite occupation. Still the German troops moved forward, and in a supplementary agreement in August Lenin abandoned Livonia, Estonia, and Georgia. The Central Powers enjoyed such total preponderance that they could impose their conditions without restraint, and with support from most of the Reichstag deputies who had voted for the 1917 peace resolution. The German ambition of a chain of eastern satellite states seemed close to realization.

In addition, the Russian ceasefire enabled Ludendorff to gain numerical superiority in France for the first time since 1914, and to unleash his devastating spring offensives. Victory helped to reunite the home front and to lessen the friction with the Habsburgs. Moreover, in the so-called 'Czernin incident' in April 1918, the French premier, Georges Clemenceau, published Karl's secret letter of the previous year to Sixte de Bourbon, thereby forcing Karl to pledge to Wilhelm that there would be no more independent diplomatic initiatives. Negotiations for future collaboration between Germany and Austria-Hungary moved into higher gear, and it seemed that

Signature of the treaty of peace between the Central Powers and Romania at Bucharest, 7 May 1918. Austro-Hungarian foreign minister Count Stephan von Burián is seated second from left; German foreign minister Richard von Kühlmann third from left.

213

Berlin was consolidating not only its dominion in the east but also its ascendancy over Vienna.

Peace without victory?

None the less, within months of this apparent apogee in their fortunes the Germans accepted defeat. The main reason was the turnaround on the western front. Ludendorff's attacks were held, and by July American troops were arriving at top speed and the allies had regained the initiative. On 28 September, with Bulgaria suing for peace, the Turkish armies routed, and the British overrunning the Hindenburg line, Ludendorff decided that he too must seek a ceasefire. However, his armies had nowhere yet retreated to German soil, he soon recovered confidence that he could resist for many months, and the appeal that went out on 4–5 October was directed not to the allies generally but to Wilson alone, requesting not only an armistice but also a peace based on the president's principles. An accompanying broadening of the government's composition, with Prince Max of Baden being appointed chancellor, created an impression of democratization. Germany was trying to settle while it still had cards to play, and, yet again, to split its enemies.

The difference from 1917 was that the United States was advancing towards comparable primacy in the allied camp to Germany's in its own, and that Wilson saw a chance to implement the next phase in his design. In contrast with the treatment of earlier such approaches, he responded publicly without consulting Clemenceau and Lloyd George, agreeing to a Fourteen Points peace. But at the same time he insisted on such stringent ceasefire terms as to place Germany at its enemies' mercy. When Ludendorff tried belatedly to object, Wilhelm, in a rare display of assertiveness, insisted on the general's resignation while requiring Hindenburg to stay. His action came too late to save his dynasty, for during November revolution spread through Germany's cities and on the 9th Wilhelm abdicated in favour of a socialist-led Provisional Government. Later Nazi claims to the contrary notwithstanding, the German collapse at home came after and in consequence of the decision to seek peace, a decision initiated by the high command. The November revolution left Germany helpless to resist: but the armistice terms were settled before

France ought to have Alsace-Lorraine

Carl

the kaiser fell, at an inter-allied conference in Paris. The big losers were the Austrians, against whom the western powers had hardened their line since the Czernin incident, deciding that the Dual Monarchy was irretrievably lost to German domination and that it was better to turn to its subject nationalities. New undertakings had been given to Polish, Czechoslovak, and Yugoslav representatives, and when Vienna appealed for a settlement based on the Fourteen Points Wilson declared that these no longer applied. Partly because of his pronouncement, nationalist revolutions finished off the Dual Monarchy days before the socialists took power in Berlin. Against Germany, however, Wilson obtained his partners' agreement to a peace based on his principles, and to this extent the Germans won easier terms than they would have done from France and Britain alone. None the less, the Fourteen Points were accepted only with reservations (the British refused commitment on the freedom of the seas, and broadened the potential for reparation claims), and the military and naval clauses of the armistice gave the allies powerful assets. Germany's colonies stayed under British occupation, it handed over most of its navy, and Belgium was evacuated. The French moved into Alsace-Lorraine and the Saar, and the allies garrisoned the Rhineland. The Italians occupied the territories promised them in 1915, while the Germans evacuated Russia and cancelled their treaties with the Bolsheviks. Whether Wilson would indeed be able to impose his global vision remained to be settled at the peace conference.

Both the Central Powers and their adversaries had fought to safeguard their security against external danger, and had portrayed the conflict to their peoples as a war to end war. But defensive objectives were to be attained by expansionist methods, and although both sides were wary of outright annexations both sought to carve out spheres of influence and permanently restrict their enemies' sovereignty. There was truth in Lenin's observation that the war was an imperialist one. This is not necessarily to say that it was pointless and futile, or that the ordinary citizens who suffered so grievously for their leaders' objectives were duped. By 1917–18, after the Russian Revolution and American entry, the struggle pitted relatively liberal states against authoritarian ones, and western statesmen warned with justice that a compromise with a Germany in which Ludendorff held such prominence was unlikely to last. The 'peace without victory' that Wilson advocated while still neutral would have been a fragile basis for stability. The Versailles Treaty, for all its faults, contained enough to have maintained the peace of Europe for much longer than twenty years if it had been vigilantly defended. Instead, the inter-allied unity that Germany had tried so hard to shatter splintered anyway in the 1920s and the 1930s, clearing the road to a second world war.

CHAPTER 16

Propaganda and the Mobilization of Consent

J. M. WINTER

Wars of persuasion: the political dimensions

Every combatant nation in the Great War set up agencies to control the flow of information and to monitor and influence public opinion. The first task was hardly original: armies have always drawn a veil over the details of military deployment, the timing of operations, and casualties incurred in them. The second task did require new initiatives. In earlier conflicts, writers and artists, priests and lay notables, had rallied around the flag, but in the Great War, appeals had to reach the nation as a whole. Consent was an essential element of mass warfare; propaganda helped shore it up over the fifty months of the conflict.

The Great War spawned the most spectacular advertising campaign to date. Its product was justification of war. Its language was moral and replete with the symbolic forms within which notions of justice and injustice were inscribed in popular culture. Because of the excesses and exaggerations of this effort, the term 'propaganda' has come to mean 'lies'. During the war, propaganda entailed more than this. The best way to understand its mixture of moral outrage, selective reporting, and misleading or untrue assertions is to see propaganda as a state-dominated lawyers' brief, pleading the cause of the nation before its population and that of the world.

State-dominated does not mean state-directed. Yes, there was manipulation from above, but that is far from the end of the story. One of the key features of propaganda is its dual character. It mixed political polemic with appeals originating in the private sector. The power of state propaganda was a function of its synergistic relationship with opinion formed from below. When common sense on the popular level diverged from state propaganda, the official message turned hollow or simply vanished. But when propaganda coincided with popular feeling, independently generated and independently sustained, then it had a real and profound force.

Between 1914 and 1916, both sides emphasized the defensive nature of the war. Each had been provoked and attacked; each was simply defending its soil and its national greatness. In this first phase, the military played a predominant role, through such monitoring bodies as the German Kriegspresseamt or the French Maison de la Presse. But from 1917, civilian agencies came to the fore. The reason for the change is clear: when the political character of the war changed, so did propaganda. The two Russian revolutions of 1917 and the entry of the United States into the war in April 1917 transformed the conflict. Now war aims became central to propaganda. What kind of peace, indeed what kind of post-war world, were questions at the heart of the appeal to public opinion in the last two years of the war.

'Do you want four Alsace-Lorraines?' is the rhetorical question on this Austro-Hungarian war poster. To avoid the dismemberment of the empire into small and unstable ethnic fragments was reason enough to carry on the war.

Within each European combatant, the dormant socialist movement revived, establishing its outlook on the future of Europe. Moderate socialists wanted the perpetuation of state control of the command economy; it had provided decent wages and eliminated unemployment. Lenin and the Bolsheviks had another set of answers to these questions: the war was an imperialist plot. To prove the point, they published documents from the tsar's Foreign Ministry about the deal made between Russia, Britain, and France over future control of Constantinople. Is that why millions had died? American President Woodrow Wilson had still another point of view: the sacrifices had to be justified by the creation of a democratic international order presided over by a League of Nations.

This turbulent period clearly required a new approach to the orchestration of the chorus of public opinion. The European powers were much more conservative than any of these new voices of 1917. David Lloyd George (British prime minister from December 1916) and Georges Clemenceau (French premier from December 1917) did not want what either Lenin or Wilson was selling. The German high command was even more resistant to the spread of democratic ideas. Alternative justifications of the war effort had to be constructed. Consequently, the main European combatants stream-lined their propaganda effort. New public agencies and new approaches appeared. The German high command hitherto had run the war without much thought as to the state of public opinion. Now, under Hindenburg and Ludendorff, there was a new sensitivity to counter the growing grumbles over the need for a compromise peace. The same scattered but persistent doubts as to the wisdom of a fight to the finish impelled the British government to create a Ministry of Information—the first in British history. Lloyd George turned to two press magnates—Lords Beaverbrook and North-cliffe—and handed them the assignment of managing propaganda abroad and at home. Thus, by the last phase of the war, propaganda became a sepa-rate and essential element of war policy. We will examine its effects below.

The political history of propaganda does not disclose its full significance within the history of the twentieth century. This story lies more in the cultural and social history of mass mobilization. Here propaganda produced much that has characterized political and social life throughout this violent century.

The mobilization of the imagination: cultural dimensions

Propaganda contributed to the cementing of the solidarities essential to the endurance required by four and a half years of war. It did not shorten the war, or win it; rather propaganda helped transform the societies that waged it into more effective tools of war. Since 1914, alongside the mobilization of men, munitions, and labour, alongside war against civilians, came the mobilization of minds. This phenomenon was one of the most striking and disturbing fea-tures of the Great War. Here the boundaries between the private and the public realms, between individual expression and thought control, were redrawn or obliterated.

As we have noted, state propaganda in wartime is only part of the story. The propaganda efforts of both sides stretched from atrocity stories to bar-baric caricatures to children's tales to outright lies. The most powerful pro-paganda did not come from the centres of power, but rather from within these societies themselves. The politics of hate was mass politics; it was as much visual as verbal, and it was effective. It worked because it drew on images and notions broadcast from below, through commercial advertising, through cartoons, through posters and postcards, through sermons, through sentimental songs and the amateur poetry which flourished in wartime.

One particular class of images deserves special attention. The Great War mobilized sacred images and words on behalf of the cause. This is hardly sur-prising, given the anxiety felt by millions at home about the welfare of their loved ones in uniform. Thanks to the Virgin for the survival of individual sol-diers, in the form of *ex voto* plaques placed in churches throughout France, hint at the upsurge of religious language from the earliest days of the war. This was a 'holy war', one consecrated by every established church and most unconventional ones too.

At the same time, within these nations at war, religious divisions began to fade. Other boundaries were crossed in important ways. In France this had profound consequences. Much of Catholic opinion before the war had been hostile to the Republic. In turn, the moderate Radical Party in power waged war against the privileges of the Church, formally separated from the French state in 1905. In a cultural (rather than institutional) sense, the Great War nationalized Roman Catholicism.

And not only in France. The great celebration of German victory over France in the war of 1870–1, Sedan day, was, in many parts of Germany, an anti-Catholic festival. After 1914, German Catholics could show how German they were. As in France, their language of sacrifice and martyrdom infused wartime culture. The patriotic spirit of Jews in all combatant countries did much, at least for a time, to eclipse endemic anti-Semitism. Everywhere, sermons were preached proclaiming the righteousness of the cause, and invoking God's protection for the nation's men at arms. Within each nation, war was an ecumenical event.

Propaganda entered every home. There was a vast array of stirring messages for children, and, to judge by the essays of French children written during the war, the citizens and soldiers of the future shared in the culture of wartime. And that meant first and foremost hatred of the enemy.

The ancient and distinguished martial traditions of German history supported the men in the trenches, according to this wartime poster. Germania embodied the nobility of arms, and the invincibility of the men who bore them.

Children stood as images of bravery and victimhood as far back as the Napoleonic period. But after 1914, they not only suffered, they also killed, and waited for the time when they could wreak vengeance on the enemy. One British children's ditty captured this new mobilization of children in total war. Accompanying a drawing of a devastated house, a child intoned:

This is the house that Jack built.
This is the bomb that fell on the house that Jack built.
This is the Hun who dropped the bomb that fell on the house that Jack built.

This is the gun that killed the Hun who dropped the bomb that fell on the house that Jack built.

This time, it was the child who carried the gun and intended to use it.

At the outset of the war, propaganda was more verbal than visual. Notables in all major combatants put pen to paper to denounce the enemy and ennoble the cause of national defence. A galaxy of German scientists and humanists threw back at the allies the accusation that German troops had behaved barbarically in Belgium. It was not Germany, the professors opined,

Above, left: Morale in all armies depended on the maintenance of strong links between front and home front. Here a German wife embraces her husband's helmet, and trusts that his military service will protect the homeland from the predators surrounding it.

Above, right: Here is a more risqué version of the maintenance of ties between front and home front. This French woman prepares for 'the assault' on her man, home on leave and in need of close support.

but the allies who brought black troops to subdue European soldiers. Later in the war, British and French intellectuals, artists, and writers descended to similar depths of vilification of an enemy whose very culture, they believed, had spawned the disease of 'Prussianism'.

As mobilization spread, the appearance of learned pamphlets tracing the mendacity of one side and the moral probity of the other became a marginal exercise. More central to propaganda was the cultivation of visual forms, especially in caricature and in poster art. Newspapers in all combatant countries moralized the conflict by producing stereotypes of the enemy: the mad or animal-like Hun corresponded to the fat, grasping British businessman, lusting after Germany's wealth and treasures. In France, a rotund, cunning, and bloodthirsty Brünnhilde stood for Germany; a lithe, joyful, though naïve Marianne for France.

These cultural icons came in many forms, aside from caricatures. What French scholars call the 'banalization of the war', its capacity to settle into daily life as a normal set of events, is nowhere more visible than here. Hindenburg doilies, Foch ashtrays, and Kitchener beer mugs mixed patriotism and profit, trivializing the struggle in a manner consistent with its unending continuation. The Pellerin firm, based in the city of Epinal in eastern France, specialized in cheap posters illustrating the glories of combat. Its banalities and absurdities created an entirely imaginary war, far from the mud and blood of the conflict. Perhaps this very unreality helped its sales: they were gigantic and worldwide.

Wartime patriotism sold, especially when it came in sanitized forms. Picture postcards, the essential medium of correspondence between home and front, carried all kinds of patriotic messages. In France, sexual innuendo mixed with appeals to repopulate the country after the carnage of the war.

Trivialization was anything but trivial. In effect, the power of these ephemeral objects derived from their rehearsal of a national script about the war. It went on, so the message said, because the cause was just. That cause was not so much political—an area in which honourable people could disagree—but rather moral. Those who thought the war should be brought to an end through negotiation, or a compromise peace, were supping with the devil, and thereby risking the betrayal of the men at the front and the men who had already fallen. This kind of propaganda from below, therefore, was a powerful tool helping to muzzle dissent. Governments did their best to prevent pacifist messages from spreading in wartime, but a much more powerful agent of conformity was the cluster of images spread throughout wartime societies in a host of visual forms, refined and vulgar alike.

By the middle of the war, the film industry emerged as the most important vehicle for projecting the meaning of the war as a struggle of Good against Evil. This cinematic effort took many forms, from comedy to melodrama to tragedy. Much of this film output was neither inspired by nor organized through governments, though state funding was frequently involved. To be sure, the censor was active; but here again the private sector took the lead. On the screen, kitsch and popular entertainments came into their own, broadcasting messages with evident mass appeal about the virtues of one side and the villainy of the other. Music hall, melodrama, and the gramophone industry all chipped in, selling (at a profit) anodyne or uplifting images and songs to increasingly fatigued, anxious, and irritable populations.

Film, propaganda, and moral rearmament

No wonder film was so popular during the war. It satisfied longings for the mundane at an extraordinary moment: it lampooned the dreariness of military life, and it added a large dose of outrage directed against the source of all the troubles—the enemy. This was a situation tailor-made for Charlie Chaplin. A British-born music hall performer, he had joined Mack Sennett's Keystone Company in December 1913. He was already a celebrity in 1914, and contributed to the war not by joining up but by staying put in California and making films.

Chaplin's service to the allied war effort on the screen far outweighed the advantages of putting him in uniform. He was an iconic figure, a man both terribly vulnerable and somehow able (sooner or later) to plant his boot on the seat of authority. He was the great survivor, 'the tramp'—the title of one of his most successful films of 1915—the little guy whose decency almost gets trampled, but whose resilience is indefatigable. No wonder some British Highland Light Infantryman stole a cardboard figure of Chaplin and brought it over to the western front.

More unusual was the effect Chaplin's photograph had on shell-shocked soldiers. A physician serving with the US army said that an autographed photo of Chaplin did wonders for the men in his care. 'Please write your name on the photos', Dr Lewis Coleman Hall wrote to Chaplin, 'the idea being that nearly everyone has seen you in pictures. I will show your picture to a poor fellow and it may arrest his mind for a second. He may say "Do you know Charlie?" and then begins the first ray of hope that the boy's mind can be saved.'

Some of his films were explicitly propagandistic. He used film to promote Liberty Bonds, and followed this up with public appeals. On 8 April 1918, his appearance with Mary Pickford and Douglas Fairbanks on Wall Street in New York drew an estimated 30,000 people. After clowning with Fairbanks (and standing on his shoulders), he told the crowds that 'This very minute the Germans occupy a position of advantage, and we have to get the dollars. It ought to go over so that we can drive that old devil, the Kaiser, out of France.' In Washington, he repeated the same pitch: 'The Germans are at your door! We've got to stop them! And we *will* stop them if you buy Liberty Bonds! Remember, each bond you buy will save a soldier's life—a mother's son!— will bring this war to an early victory!' He then promptly fell off the platform and (in his words) 'grabbed Marie Dressler and fell with her on top of my handsome young friend', who happened to be the then assistant secretary of the navy, Franklin D. Roosevelt. He met President Wilson, and, for his British audiences, he appeared with the British music hall star Harry Lauder, whose son had been killed in 1916.

But his major achievement on the screen was to produce the war film to end all war films, *Shoulder Arms*. It premiered on 20 October 1918, and received instant acclaim. Drawing on a tour of US army training camps, the story lampoons the rigours of boot camp. After a hopeless spell of drill, exhausted, Chaplin falls asleep and wakes up on the western front. He captures a German unit by single-handedly surrounding them, masters the arts of camouflage by turning into a tree, and manages to capture the kaiser himself (played by his brother Sydney).

Chaplin was in a class of his own during the war: the comic genius of his time. Film worked on many different registers during the conflict. Many films distributed during the war had nothing to do with the conflict, sticking to escapist themes. But others returned to the war, and used film to spread explicit moral messages in the hope of stiffening public morale. When we look at these films, we see some of the ways in which, in many countries at war, consent was fortified and the inevitable anxiety of military conflict softened by the gentle and reassuring images of cinematic comedy.

Many Germans, too, believed that their cause was just, and that their civilization was based on values higher and nobler than the decadence of France or the crass commercialism of Britain and the United States. In Germany, too, film was there to spread the message. There were over 2,000 cinemas in Germany in 1913, with over 200 in Berlin alone. This national total was only

Facing: The iconic figure of the early cinema, Charlie Chaplin conquered all in his 1918 feature film *Shoulder Arms*. A London-born comic trained in the late Victorian music hall tradition, Chaplin spent the war in the United States, and vividly led the cinematic charge against the Germans in the last year of the war.

223

half that of the British cinema industry, but with Danish and American imports, German film was booming on the eve of the war.

Initially, the film industry was ignored by the high command as an annoyance, but with the accession of Eric Ludendorff to the post of quartermaster general in 1916, film suddenly found many powerful backers. When, in 1917, American newsreel imports were banned, into the breach stepped the domestic industry, producing newsreels for the mass audience with an insatiable appetite for images of the front. Alfred Hugenberg, director of the armaments firm of Krupp, took a leading part in this effort, which in late 1917 gave birth to 'Ufa' (Universum Film AG), a consortium of film companies, one-third owned by the German state bank, and under indirect military control. With such backing, Ufa's viability was assured. But like so much of the German war effort, it emerged not from within popular culture, but from within the political and industrial élite.

The tie of the film industry to the authorities restricted its freedom of action and its effectiveness. But the popular demand for film was recognized by the high command. Cinema houses were given priority for coal and electricity in the hard months of 1917–18, producing consistently high attendance throughout Germany and in occupied Belgium.

The army had its own cinema industry. There were 900 field cinemas in 1917, featuring the great stars of the German cinema, Henny Porten and Asta Nielson. They specialized in comedies and melodrama, but were conscious of marrying profit and patriotism, thereby establishing a strong domestic film industry by the end of the war. The German film industry then came into its own both as a viable economic enterprise and as a vehicle for daring experimentation. The legacy of film propaganda in the 1914–18 war was there for the Nazis to exploit *en route* to the Second World War.

Outcomes

Did propaganda help shorten the war? Almost certainly not. Germany capitulated when its army was beaten in the field and for no other reason. Embittered men tried to blame allied propaganda—seductive and misleading—for the defeat, but only those with the blinkers of Adolf Hitler and his entourage took this argument seriously. Historians of the First World War have dismissed this charge out of hand.

The same exaggerated claims have been made about the effects of allied propaganda on the entry of the United States into the war in April 1917. There was indeed a massive and sophisticated British and French propaganda effort in the United States. German propagandists were there too, though their work bore the same marks of bungling and clumsiness evident elsewhere in the German war effort.

The British approach to 'publicity' was indirect. Recognizing the strength of American isolationism, British propagandists, under Canadian-born Sir Gilbert Parker, tried to reach influential people through direct mailing. Sir Gilbert's card came along with the pamphlet or reprint, adding a personal touch. They arranged interviews in the press with prominent Englishmen and always answered press criticism with polite letters to the editor. Film newsreels brought positive images of the allies to a wider public, reached too through a host of public meetings. In January 1917 Sir Gilbert Parker returned to Britain and handed over his post to his successor, Professor W. M. Dixon of Glasgow University.

From that point on, the German cause in the United States self-destructed. First came unrestricted submarine warfare: a direct threat to American ships bringing privately funded American seaborne aid to the allies. Then came the February Revolution in Russia, eliminating one of the embarrassments of the campaign upholding 'democracy'—that is, the allies—against 'militarism'—that is, Germany. Then came the mad approach of the German Foreign Ministry to Mexico, offering large parts of the south-west of the United States as the potential fruits of joint action in the war. British intelligence intercepted this message, and saved it for just the right moment, when newly re-elected President Woodrow Wilson would be forced to act. He did so on 6 April 1917, as the United States entered the war.

The strength of allied propaganda was to control, neutralize, though never completely eliminate, isolationist and anti-British opinion. The United States went to war not because of propaganda but because of multiple direct German threats to American lives and American interests.

Within the European theatre of operations, there were sources much more powerful than propaganda which account for the capacity of the allies to withstand the pressures of war better than the Central Powers. The allies had at their disposal the finance and the raw materials which came out of a century of imperial expansion. Germany had no such second, third, or fourth line of reinforcements. Propaganda was a marginal source of defeat, when compared to these massive imbalances of power.

In the war of words and images, Germany had another disadvantage. The state rested not on the consent of the governed, but on the invincibility of the army. That myth sustained public opinion for four years. The men who had won the spectacular victory at Tannenberg in August 1914—Hindenburg and Ludendorff—were in charge of the war effort four years later. They stood for a proud and defiant military tradition that had held the world at bay for fifty months. When the German line bent and moved back in the summer of 1918, when everyone in Germany came to see that the war could not be won, then the exaggerated notion that Germany was invincible made the bitterness of the defeat even worse.

Propaganda did not create the bitter pill Germany had to swallow in 1918. It helped sustain allied civilians and soldiers through the dark periods of the war. It did so by sticking to a simple message: the armies were in the field because Germany was a menace and had to be stopped. For the French army fighting on French soil, and for the Belgians, this was evident. But the same sentiment existed among American, British, and imperial forces far from home, and among their families in the rear. Propaganda did not create this belief; the German invasion of Belgium, and the ruthlessness and harshness of the German war effort since 1914, did so. The lengthening casualty lists added to the bitterness on the allied side of the line and to their determination to see the war through to total victory. The *Kaiserreich* dug its own grave, and later attempts to divert attention from this fact gave Great War propaganda a military significance it did not deserve. Its fundamental effects were cultural, not political; they pointed to an even darker future, and to the mobilization of hatred in an even more terrible war.

CHAPTER 17

Socialism, Peace, and Revolution, 1917–1918

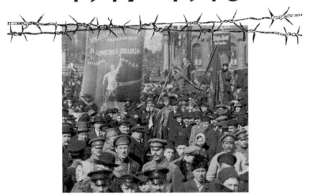

JOHN HORNE

B y 1914, war and peace, as well as revolution, had long exercised the imagination of socialists. When, in November 1912, Europe seemed poised on the brink of war over the Balkans, the leaders of the socialist Second International met in Basle, Switzerland. As the great bells of the cathedral where they gathered tolled in warning, they issued a declaration that the likely price of war would be a revolutionary catastrophe for the ruling élites that unleashed it. Logically, perhaps, in an organization committed by its principles to socialist revolution, such a prediction should have been a matter of welcome, not warning. Some on the far left, such as Lenin and Rosa Luxemburg, indeed saw war as a possible path to revolution. A new theoretical emphasis in pre-war socialist thought on the latest stage of capitalism as one of economic imperialism, in which conflict between international economic forces would lead to continuous wars and eventual revolution, tended in the same direction. Lenin was to provide the most famous formulation of this idea in *Imperialism, the Highest Stage of Capitalism*, written in 1916.

But, by and large, European socialists were remarkable for their resolute hostility to the idea of war and for the detachment of the question of war and peace from that of revolution. Developments since the founding of the International in 1889 had underlined the importance of the national circumstances within which each constituent party evolved as well as the complexity of economic and political change. The Second International had undeniably developed a distinctive and profoundly internationalist culture, shaped above all by the Marxism of the dominant German Social Democratic Party (SPD) and of its chief philosopher, Karl Kautsky. But the 'revolution' envisaged was broadly one in which proletarian unity would be forged by inexorable historical forces. Reducing the social cataclysms of Marxist theory to abstractions, this culture was infused with an optimistic rationalism which turned socialism into the most advanced expression of 'civilization'.

With rising international tension, socialist custodianship of humanitarian values made the prevention of war—which was seen not just as the product of capitalism but also as the antithesis of 'civilization'—an overriding concern. True, by 1914 there was a certain pessimism as to whether the working class, or even organized labour, would obey the International's order to refuse to fight a war, not least because the competing national allegiances which divided socialist parties had prevented any agreement on what form such a refusal would take. But this only made it all the more important to prevent war occurring.

War and socialism, August 1914– February 1917

War broke out none the less, dealing a double blow to socialists. It revealed the impotence of the Second International, though it was the occasion more than the cause of this. It also challenged socialist views on war since the conflict arose not from economic rivalries but from a nationalist conflict in the Balkans, where the International prided itself on having restrained conflict in 1912. As war triggered a chain reaction of invasions, socialists rapidly rediscovered an older language of justifiable participation in national defence to safeguard their own future. The argument had emerged in the influential book *L'Armée nouvelle* (The New Army) (1910), written by the French socialist leader Jean Jaurès, in order to reconcile international proletarian action to prevent capitalist and colonial wars with the right of the working class to defend the nation, an idea rooted in the French republican tradition. Ironically, Jaurès himself was assassinated by a fanatical nationalist on the eve of French mobilization, a martyr to war hysteria. But across Europe, not only socialists but also anarchists and revolutionary syndicalists accepted that workers did have a fatherland, and, by an explicitly left-wing logic, they supported (and even participated in) wartime national governments.

Initially, any semblance of normal political life was suspended as the military effort and a speedy victory pre-empted everything else. But as the trenches stabilized, socialists, like others, confronted the radical novelty of an extended, industrial war. This affected them in several ways. First, a long war required the mobilization of all the ideological and cultural resources of the nation behind the war effort. This process inevitably raised the question of the purpose of the war and its sacrifices, and enabled the currents of socialism backing the national effort to demand greater equity in its prosecution. In the light of the sweeping economic mobilization which the war also required, it generated a distinctive wartime reformism among majority labour and socialist leaders in countries such as Britain, France, and Germany by which the lessons of national mobilization and a controlled wartime economy were projected into a post-war future of political and social 'reconstruction' along socialist lines. In effect, the war confirmed the national vocation of socialism. Secondly, the revelation that munitions were needed on an unimagined scale made the industrial worker as important as the soldier for victory. As the industrial mobilization geared up, and especially as wartime economic conditions depressed living standards while giving labour considerable economic leverage (despite attempts to control it with new forms of industrial discipline), workers became not only vital to the war effort but also increasingly militant. In the major munitions centres, radical local industrial movements developed which cut across established trade union and socialist organizations. Thirdly, as casualties rose and the military effort sank deeper into stalemate, voices in all the belligerent powers queried the need to fight the war to the bitter end, as opposed to cutting it short by negotiation. Socialism, as the most important oppositional political movement, was especially open to these doubts.

The combination and effect on socialists of these different aspects of the war varied considerably by country. Where the legitimacy of the pre-war regime, and hence of the wartime national mobilization, were broadest, as in Britain and France, the potential socialist opposition to the war was mildest. It also helped that in these two countries the economic impact of the war on workers was less serious than elsewhere (though still significant) owing to government efficiency in supplying the civilian population and fuller access to world food supplies. In Germany, harsher economic conditions and a more contested regime, evolving towards military authoritarianism during the war, resulted in greater disaffection and a socialist opposition which, in April 1917, split to form an Independent German Social Democratic Party (USPD). Yet the majority SPD, the largest party of the pre-war International, remained powerful and still committed, in some form or other, to the national effort. It was in countries like Italy and especially Russia, where the narrow pre-war state and its weak mediating links with society (and especially with the working class) had been profoundly destabilized by the brutal economic and military impact of the war, that popular dissent from the war effort was greatest and socialist hostility to the conflict most pronounced. For all these differences, war-weariness was common to most combatant states by 1917, with strikes, protests, and mutinies variously suggesting a deep longing for peace.

Peace, no less than war, acquired new weight and meaning for socialists through the experience of the world conflict. The young German Social Democratic deputy Karl Liebknecht refused to vote for war credits in December 1914, in a gesture that received instant, international celebrity. By early 1915, minority voices in most European socialist parties and many trade

Peace and revolution, February–September 1917

War as catastrophe. 'Le Jour des Morts' ('All Souls' Day'), 1 November 1918. Mass death devastates all the belligerent nations (symbolized by their soldiers' headwear), while a mourning woman expresses her moral revulsion. This cartoon appeared in the French minority socialist and pacifist paper, *La Vague,* whose editor, Pierre Brizon, attended the anti-war socialist conference at Kienthal, April 1916.

union movements had begun to question support for the war and seek an end to the fighting. Since hostility to war, on class and humanitarian grounds, was so deeply embedded in the values of the pre-war International, it was logical to revive at least the spirit of the International in order to oppose the war. The permanent bureau of the Second International (which had moved from Belgium to neutral Holland on the German invasion) was paralysed by hostility between mainstream socialists supporting their national efforts, so it was neutral socialists who informally took the lead. Both moderate Dutch and Scandinavians and more radical Swiss and Italians organized international meetings. In particular, dissident socialists and trade unionists from France, Germany, and the diaspora of exiled Russian socialism (including Lenin and Trotsky), as well as from neutral countries, met in two obscure Swiss villages, Zimmerwald (September 1915) and Kienthal (April 1916), to oppose the war.

The language of the resolutions resulting from these two meetings remained that of conventional pre-war Marxism. The war was seen as the product of capitalism and imperialism. International labour and socialist unity was the way to oppose it. Only revolution would definitively end imperialism and militarism, and hence war itself. But peace, not revolution, was the goal. Although the two terms coexisted in the same semantic field, there was a significant difference of emphasis between them. The Zimmerwald resolution stressed the importance of achieving peace, not revolution (despite a minority declaration drafted by Lenin), and although the tone hardened at Kienthal, in 1916, peace remained the principal aim, opening the way for the 'final triumph of the proletariat'. Lenin was keenest to emphasize revolutionary action. In 1914 he considered the old International to be dead, and he gradually moved towards a policy of splitting the hard-line revolutionaries from the rest, including moderate pacifists, thus subordinating peace to revolution.

But it was the reverse emphasis on peace rather than revolution that prevailed in the socialist and trade union opposition to the war, and the moral aversion to war, so clearly present in the pre-war International, kept breaking through the socialist rhetoric. The leaders of the emergent minority in Germany (Bernstein, Kautsky, and Haase) described the war as combining 'the cruelty of barbaric ages' with 'the most sophisticated tools of civilization' in their statement of June 1915, *The Demand of the Hour*, and the same terms were used elsewhere. The Zimmerwald resolution (drafted by Trotsky) explained that 'the war which has provoked this chaos is the product of imperialism', but it prefaced this with a description of the chaos itself:

Millions of corpses cover the battlefields. Millions of men will remain mutilated for the rest of their days. Europe has become a gigantic slaughter-house for men. All the civilization created by the labour of previous generations is destined to be destroyed. Savage barbarism is today triumphing over everything that heretofore constituted the pride of humanity.

A pamphlet issued by Committee for the Resumption of International Relations, the French organization that publicized the Zimmerwald and Kienthal meetings in 1916, seized on the anguish of women waiting for news of their loved ones at the front: 'Oh women, with sensitive hearts, you who were made to procreate and love, do you not see the horrors of the battlefield, do you not hear the cries of pain from your sons, your husbands, your brothers?' No doubt much of this reflected the high moral language of socialist activists, and even intellectuals, rather than that of ordinary soldiers, workers, and war-weary civilians. But it also represented an attempt by socialists to grasp and respond to the radical novelty of industrial war and a scale of destruction that strained the terms of conventional class analysis.

Events in Russia in February 1917 (March by the western calendar) might seem to have placed the notion of revolution decisively back on the agenda of socialists everywhere. The fall of tsardom was a dramatic occurrence, and in the longer run the Russian cataclysm could not fail to redefine socialist understanding of what was meant by revolution. But in 1917, its immediate significance was perceived above all in terms of current concerns with war and peace. Naturally, the revolution had its own, strictly Russian logic. The collapse of military confidence, the disintegration of tsarist legitimacy, deep economic dislocation, and the one-sided polarization of society against the state were not paralleled in other countries in 1917, whereas they had been rehearsed in the earlier Russian revolution of 1905, following defeat in the war with Japan. But contemporaries, especially socialists, were not always aware of how specific the crisis was as they sought to divine its implications.

The Provisional Government (composed of the liberal opponents of the regime), which was the first, and weaker, of the two forms of power that replaced tsardom, was committed to continuing the war. The second, and stronger, source of political authority (in what contemporaries called the system of 'Dual Power') consisted of a highly varied movement of popular protest, including workers, peasants, and increasingly soldiers, which formed a myriad of local committees and 'soviets'. The most influential of these, the Petrograd Soviet, expressed socialist and popular disaffection with the war and, from the outset, called insistently for general negotiated peace, though without abandoning the national defence.

Since the dominant historical model of revolution available to contemporaries was the French Revolution, which had produced war (and not been produced by it, like the Russian Revolution), there was a widespread belief among allied (and especially French) opinion that the February Revolution would create a democratic, national mobilization for war on the Jacobin model. Indeed, a number of pro-war socialists (including Arthur Henderson,

Всенародный праздникъ 1-го Мая 18-го Апрѣля 1917 г. въ Петроградѣ. Дворцовая площадь.

Celebrating the revolution, 1 May 1917, on Winter Palace Square, Petrograd (18 April, old-style). The mixed composition of the popular movement in the major Russian cities in 1917 is shown clearly in this contemporary postcard. Women, men, workers, and soldiers enjoy the festival of labour and the arrival of spring after an exceptionally bitter winter throughout Europe.

leader of the British Labour Party, and Albert Thomas, the French minister of armaments) were sent by their governments to Russia to encourage precisely this outcome. The Provisional Government did indeed attempt to implement the Jacobin model and relaunch the war effort as one of national liberation, though the result (under Kerensky, a right-wing socialist) was the failed offensive of the summer of 1917 and final disintegration of the army.

But it was the popular revolutionary demand for a negotiated peace which electrified European socialists and explains much of the wider influence of Russian events. For the revolution embodied the hopes for peace which accompanied the crises of morale afflicting nearly every belligerent nation in 1917. The identification of the message with the soviets and other forms of revolutionary representation gave a sense of controlling fate which contrasted with the feeling of powerlessness induced by the military stalemate and wartime social conditions. 'Take your destiny into your own hands,' a revolutionary pamphlet celebrating the Russian Revolution declared to Leipzig workers during the strike of April 1917. The example of the soviets encouraged radical industrial militants everywhere to see their local power as a means of pressing for peace. The most serious popular upheaval of the war in Italy, the insurrection in Turin in August 1917, was partly triggered by a visiting delegation from the Petrograd Soviet, greeted by 40,000 Turinese socialists and metalworkers crying, 'Long live the Russian Revolution, long live Lenin!' Although caused by bread shortages and bitter hostility over industrial discipline, the Turin rising rapidly adopted the demand for peace. In

France, where the political culture of labour drew on a broad revolutionary tradition, the Russian Revolution strengthened the tendency for economic and political protest, including the demand for peace, to be expressed in revolutionary language and imagery. 'The Russian Revolution has occurred just when the peoples [of Europe] are weary of spilling their blood to satisfy the appetites of the Tsar, the Kaiser, and Poincaré' declared the French socialist deputy and Kienthal signatory Pierre Brizon in March 1917. 'The revolutionaries will impose peace, which will bring the regeneration of humankind and abolish all frontiers.' Even in Britain, where the political culture of labour was generally anything but revolutionary, the prestige of the February Revolution gave a fillip to the yearning for peace. An extraordinary meeting of socialist opposition groups, held in Leeds in June 1917, called for the establishment of 'Councils of Workers and Soldiers' throughout the country.

The centrality of peace for European socialists outside Russia in 1917 (with revolution important above all as a richly symbolic vocabulary for expressing this) was demonstrated clearly by the plan for a major socialist conference to be held in Stockholm. This project was the culmination of the neutral attempts to revive international contacts between belligerent socialists, but without the endorsement of the Petrograd Soviet it would never have been more than a blueprint. Pro-national defence socialists were rarely apologists for war but their commitment to the logic of ultimate victory made it hard for them to condemn the particular horror of the trench stalemate. Extreme revolutionaries (such as Lenin and the Zimmerwaldian left) saw the war as symptomatic of the crisis rather than as the crisis itself. It was therefore a broad coalition of pacifists, widely divergent on other criteria (such as reform and revolution), who generated the mood of hope that surrounded the planned conference and who sought to provide a socialist voice for the popular currents of war weariness in 1917. The founding of the German USPD in April 1917—including the revisionist Bernstein, 'pope' Kautsky, and elements of the extreme left Spartacist movement led by Liebknecht and Luxemburg—epitomized the political realignment forced by the question of peace. The same dynamic was at work elsewhere. It drew in both revolutionaries (hoping to use peace to win converts) and also pro-national defence majorities who, even if they remained sceptical of a negotiated peace, insisted, in a reflection of the deepening human misery of the war, that their own nation's aims should be non-expansionist and dedicated to abolishing international conflict.

Yet the failure of Stockholm demonstrates how illusory any socialist consensus on peace was in 1917. In the end, the conference, which was eventually scheduled for early September, was never held. The French and British governments feared that public opinion might take the allied socialist presence to be a sign of weakened resolve to win the war, and they forbade their national socialist and Labour delegations to attend. But even without this, the impossibility of socialist agreement on the terms of a compromise settlement for ending the war doomed the conference in advance. The logic of

conflicting national war aims remained too powerful. The SPD was trying to distance itself from the radical expansionism of the military government, but it still considered the war justified as one of German national defence. The British and French majorities remained convinced that Germany had been responsible for the war, and in part they wished to use Stockholm to confront the SPD with its complicity in this, thereby helping keep Russia, and especially the Petrograd Soviet, in the conflict. When the conference failed to take place, the Zimmerwaldian left (predominantly Bolsheviks and Spartacists) met at Stockholm to bury the attempted revival of the International and unequivocally to harness the peace movement to revolution.

Between moral revulsion against the catastrophe of the war, with its human slaughter, and agreement on how to end it and thus on its political outcome, lay a gulf in which the Stockholm project foundered. It was the same gulf which, outside Russia (and perhaps Italy), prevented movements of industrial and popular protest with their anti-war overtones from turning into outright rejection of the national war effort. Indeed, even the popular revolutionary movement in Russia only moved towards this last position with the failure of the final offensive in June 1917, in the upheaval of the July Days. As the French minority socialist leader and pacifist Jean Longuet commented during the German spring offensive in 1918: 'Before such a danger . . . for the liberty of the world, there is no socialist, or internationalist, who would express any other thought . . . than that of resistance . . . in the face of the Germanic onslaught.'

Revolution and peace, October 1917–November 1918

The failure of socialists to agree on peace at Stockholm in September was immediately followed by the success of the Bolsheviks in carrying out a revolution in October (November by the western calendar). The future of the new regime was highly insecure and it took nearly three years of internal conflict, civil war, and repulsion of external aggressors before the October Revolution was confirmed in power, in the summer of 1920. None the less, from the moment the near bloodless coup of October 1917 placed the Bolsheviks in control of Russia's destiny, the first successful socialist revolution in the world could not fail to exert a powerful influence on the politics of other socialist movements and on the image of revolution itself.

The view of its severest detractors that the October Revolution was no more than a putsch did little justice to the importance of the Bolsheviks as a political force. Under the decisive guidance of Lenin, on his return from his Swiss exile in April 1917, the Bolsheviks, more than their sister Marxist party the Mensheviks, or the populist Socialist Revolutionaries (SRs), had managed to express the popular urban movement's principal grievances—the demand for improved food supplies and an end to the war. They had also endorsed the upheaval of land seizures by peasants which, in any event, they were powerless to prevent. The Bolsheviks' influence was reflected in the majority position that they achieved in the Congress of Soviets by October. But when the party leaders hesitantly seized power from the paralysed Provisional Government under Kerensky, they reshaped both the revolutionary process and socialist theories of revolution.

Most importantly, the Bolsheviks rapidly implemented a one-party state. As a distinct minority in the rural mass of Russian society, they cancelled the classic process (derived from the French Revolution) of electing a constituent assembly by universal suffrage to elaborate a constitution, a process which had been set in train by the February Revolution. Having thus dissociated 'proletarian power' from conventional western norms of democracy, they conflated the notion of the 'dictatorship' of the proletariat with the rule of the Bolshevik party itself, especially once bitter disputes developed with their initial partners in revolutionary government, the Mensheviks and left-SRs. Acutely conscious that carrying out an advanced, socialist revolution in a backward, barely industrialized society was, in terms of Marxist theory, a deeply paradoxical act, they quickly relied on the tight discipline which had long been the hallmark of the party in order to deal with other revolutionary parties, to control the popular movement, and to oppose the counterrevolution. Even so, by the first anniversary of the October Revolution, there was a deep contrast between the image of orderly but sweeping transformation projected by the new regime, which saw itself as creating a modern industrial society in Russia via socialization and collective ownership, and the reality of chaos and bitter conflict resulting from wholesale economic requisitioning, the improvisation of a Red Army, and civil war.

Internationally no less than domestically, the implications of the October Revolution were fraught with paradox. Faced with the stark alternatives of remaining in the world war by launching a Bolshevik national mobilization against Germany or taking popular, anti-war feeling to its logical conclusion by opting out of the conflict altogether, Lenin chose the second course, despite opposition by extreme elements of the revolution and the reluctance of some of his closest colleagues, such as Trotsky. By the Treaty of Brest-Litovsk in March 1918, revolutionary Russia made peace with the German military and withdrew from the war. The price was heavy, with the loss of the western portion of the former Russian empire to German control. One solution to this immediate humiliation lay in a world revolution, of which Russian events would be merely the first act. This was also the answer to the larger

Facing: Another revolutionary, another revolution. Rosa Luxemburg (seen here walking in Berlin in 1914) rejected Lenin's authoritarianism but believed as fervently as he did in the possibilities of violent revolution. She paid the price in the brutal repression of the Spartacist uprising in Germany, in January 1919.

235

conundrum of a Marxist revolution in a backward country. As argued especially by Trotsky, revolution might well begin in the weakest link of global economic imperialism, but could only survive if it spread to the advanced industrial heartlands, such as Germany. This understanding of the revolutionary process placed a premium, for the Bolsheviks, on a 'permanent revolution', which they believed to be under way but which they also fostered through a new, revolutionary International.

By subordinating peace to revolution in the dramatic form of the Brest-Litovsk Treaty, the Bolsheviks significantly reduced the appeal of revolution for socialist movements still caught up in the war. This was particularly so with the former allies. French and British socialists in general judged the Bolsheviks harshly for unilaterally withdrawing from the war and allowing the Germans to launch their western spring offensive in 1918. Even some German socialists criticized the Bolsheviks for strengthening the hand of militarism and reaction in Germany. But there were also more principled objections. It is not surprising if these came above all from German socialism, since the implications of the Bolshevik seizure of power were most serious for the mainstream Marxism of the Second International of which the SPD had seen itself as the particular custodian. In an influential book published in mid-1918, *The Dictatorship of the Proletariat*, Karl Kautsky rejected the Russian revolutionary model, arguing that any attempt to implement socialism before the working class formed the vast majority of society necessitated violent dictatorship and negated the democracy on which socialism's success, and even survival, depended. In effect, Kautsky considered the synthesis of liberal democracy and collectivist socialism embraced by much of the SPD, and even of the breakaway USPD, to be the antithesis of Bolshevism. In late 1918, Rosa Luxemburg, who in December was to preside over the conversion of the Spartacus League into the German Communist Party (KPD), published a no less trenchant critique. Like Lenin a key radical of the pre-war younger generation that attacked the comfortable rhetoric of the Second International, she had long imagined the revolution as a cataclysmic wave of mass action, which revolutionary politics would guide, not dominate. She therefore criticized the Bolshevik 'dictatorship' for stifling the creativity of the revolutionary process—before being killed with Karl Liebknecht in January 1919, as her brand of more spontaneous revolutionary violence was brutally crushed by the post-war restoration of order in Germany.

Despite such critical reactions, however, Bolshevism exerted a gravitational pull on the extreme left of European socialist movements, realigning it on the issue of revolution. The wariness of the early KPD was not matched by the radical fringes of French socialism and revolutionary syndicalism, and still less by an Italian socialism bitterly opposed in its vast majority to the Italian war effort. Helped by the scarcity of news, each group could project its own fantasy (for syndicalists, the general strike, for anarchists, self-governing soviets) onto an October Revolution that was above all an idealized image. Yet for the bulk of central and western European socialists, peace not revolution remained the defining issue while the war lasted. The Stockholm fiasco had ended any serious hope of short-circuiting the bloody conflict by socialist consensus and diplomacy. But this only made it more important than ever to ensure that the true meaning and outcome of the war should be the impossibility of such a conflict ever recurring. 'Never again' was no post-war rationalization but a call which came from the war itself. This in turn meant directing the moral thrust of wartime pacifism and of socialist patriotism alike into the project of creating a new world order, to ensure that 'the war to end all war' became a reality. The ideas of liberal internationalism—universal disarmament, arbitration, and a League of Nations—had already surfaced in the Second International before the war. But now they acquired a totemic status, uniting the broad centre ground, both programmatically and through the outpouring of socialist and popular support for a 'democratic' peace settlement. This vision was expressed most influentially by the American president, Woodrow Wilson. Wilson briefly acquired an iconic status, as shown by his welcome from British and French Labour and socialist leaders when he arrived in Europe in December 1918. In the final year of the conflict, 'Wilsonism' was undoubtedly more influential than 'Leninism' among European socialists. Not surprisingly, given its length and human cost, the war fostered eschatological beliefs in a transcendent future, not only among socialists but more widely. Belief in world peace, even more than world revolution, seemed to many the only ideal capable of redeeming the horror of the conflict.

Peace did not remake the world. Socialist parties everywhere condemned the peace treaties and the League of Nations as a travesty of their wartime hopes. The aftermath of war brought crises of transition in various defeated or newly founded states. In Germany, the revolution of November 1918 swept away a monarchy discredited by defeat, but was itself polarized between a socially reforming liberal democracy and a radical socialist minority. The former only managed to suppress the latter with the aid of militarized elements of the old regime, compromising the future Weimar Republic from the outset. But by 1920 the waves of radicalism were receding everywhere. Communist Russia, though isolated, exerted an even stronger influence on the image and politics of revolution. Socialist criticisms of Bolshevism intensified accordingly, until the divergences fragmented the International between a Communist Third International (founded in 1919) and two Socialist Internationals, which eventually amalgamated.

The events of 1914 had exploded the political culture of the Second International. But the long process of disintegration was shaped by the experience of the war, including the changing significance of peace and revolution. The Bolsheviks derived their revolutionary credentials in part from the claim that they had consistently rejected the war, and their founding mythology included a demonized history of the war and the 'treason' of the pro-war socialists. Pacifism, as a moral discourse, continued to serve the revolution-

Conclusion

237

The founders' approval. Lenin speaking at the unveiling of a temporary monument to Marx and Engels in Revolution Square, Moscow, 7 November 1918. Very different kinds of revolutionary claimed to be the only true interpreters of Marxist doctrine.

ary purposes of post-war communism, until the threat from fascism changed attitudes to war in the 1930s. Reformist socialists, by contrast, considered Bolshevik authoritarianism part of the more brutal world the war had created. Their own gradualist paths to post-war socialism excluded the chaos of the October Revolution. With the conflict between national defence and pacifism now resolved, democratic world peace became central to what in effect was a reformulation of the humanist values of pre-war socialism. This was a process which helped reconcile reformists with some of the non-communist currents of revolutionary socialism which flourished immediately after the war. Long after it was over, the war continued to redefine the division of socialism which it had occasioned.

CHAPTER 18

The Entry of the USA into the War and its Effects

DAVID TRASK

T he United States intervened in the Great War with reluctance, and largely unprepared to engage powerful European armies. President Woodrow Wilson tried to avoid belligerency, instead attempting to mediate the conflict, itself a striking departure from the historic policy of isolation. When finally he joined the allies he did so, so that he could dictate the post-war settlement to all the other warring nations.

The declaration of war (6 April 1917) was the culmination of long-term foreign policy trends that gradually aligned the nation with the countries opposed to the Central Powers. For the pre-war generation a certain Anglo-American *entente* had come into being and at the same time a less evident German–American antagonism. These political changes reflected the shifting interests of the republic as the nation became a great power and as the international equilibrium came entirely apart. Like Great Britain and other insular nations the USA had a vital interest in preventing hegemonic enterprises by any land power in Eurasia. The agglomeration of power that might result if one nation gained control of all or a great part of Eurasia could pose desperate security problems for the New World in general and North America in particular. If such a catastrophe took place, the civilization associated

The decision to fight

239

with American government—of, by, and for the people—might come to an end, contrary to the traditional assumption that democracy on the Yankee model would eventually spread throughout the world.

Events during the period of American neutrality (August 1914–April 1917) vastly accelerated the nation's instinctual preference for the Entente powers, the anti-hegemonic coalition. The undersea warfare of Germany against non-combatant and neutral commerce on the high seas came to symbolize the aggression of the Central Powers. On 1 February 1917, when this naval campaign blossomed fully into unrestricted submarine warfare, a violation of traditional neutral rights, public opinion grudgingly became convinced that the USA must assist the Entente.

Wilson deplored this necessity: he hesitated for two months before asking Congress to declare war. He had spent over two years in an extensive effort to make himself the mediator between the opposed coalitions, hoping that the war would end without requiring American belligerency. This attempt failed because during 1915–16 neither the Entente nations nor the Central Powers were prepared to accept mediation. On the contrary: as the war progressed, the stakes were increased manyfold, and both sides committed themselves to total victory.

Wilson's attempt to arrange US mediation, initially a secret diplomatic initiative, became public in December 1916, when he asked the belligerents to state their war aims as a basis for making a negotiated peace. Neither coalition responded satisfactorily. The German answer, unrestricted submarine warfare, bespoke defiance of American wishes. Wilson now faced an insoluble dilemma. He must choose between intervention on behalf of the Entente or reversion to passive neutrality.

Wilson chose intervention. It was the only way to force international acceptance of an extraordinary new world order. For Wilson sought not simply to mediate; he had in mind an ambitious international programme for the future. This Wilsonian grand design reflected the nation's interest in a stable international setting and also progressive elements of its ideology, especially the democratic values reflected in anti-militarism and anti-imperialism. Wilson detected fatal defects in both coalitions. The choice of which side to join reflected the nation's natural opposition to expansionist powers in Eurasia. At the war's end he hoped to constrain the allies as well as the Central Powers in so far as their behaviour violated fundamental aspects of his agenda for the future.

Wilson's preferred solution rested on two pillars, an equitable territorial settlement based on national self-determination and a league of nations built on collective security. The league would have a council devoted to peace-keeping in which the great powers, including the USA, would predominate. It would also sponsor all manner of international reforms through various agencies that reflected the nation's vision of a peaceful and prosperous future for all peoples. This programme ignored the 'secret treaties' to which the allies had bound themselves. These confidential agreements dealt exten-

President Woodrow Wilson is pictured in December 1918 with the French President Raymond Poincaré, when the American leader encountered enthusiastic welcomes as he prepared to participate in the post-war peace conference. His popularity rapidly declined when it became known that he opposed many war aims of the allies.

sively with post-war territorial arrangements, often without regard for national self-determination.

Wilson was no pacifist, although he sought to explore all options short of war before condoning armed intervention. His decision to fight stemmed from his conviction that only a peace settlement like that he described publicly in his greatest oration, the 'peace without victory' pronouncement of 22 January 1917, could suffice to restore stability and opportunity for all, including peoples in Africa and Asia dominated by various European powers. The members of the Entente were imperialist powers. Thus Wilson meant to reform the allied coalition as well as the enemy camp, reflecting the ancient American notion of a Manichaean division between the decadent Old World and the pristine New World. The New World would redeem the Old.

The difficulty was insufficient military and naval strength. The USA was unprepared for a major conflict because Wilson did not anticipate belligerency. His mind was fixed on mediation. By 1916 he recognized that his failure to force mediation stemmed in part from the lack of powerful armed forces. He needed sufficient strength to support his ambitious diplomacy. At this juncture he became a convert to 'preparedness'. Congressional legislation in 1916 provided for 'a navy second to none' and much-improved land forces, but the intervention came before this dramatic change in national security policy could have an effect.

How could the USA assist its new 'associates'? (Wilson never used the term 'allies', honouring the national abhorrence of entangling alliances.) It

America at sea

could extend loans to provide much-needed supplies for the home fronts and the armed forces of the Entente. It could also make an immediate naval contribution because a considerable number of vessels were ready for action. The rub came elsewhere. The army consisted of a mere 130,000 regulars and a reserve of 70,000 national guardsmen. General Peyton C. March aptly described the situation. This force had 'no practical military value as far as the fighting in France was concerned; it was scarcely enough to form a police force for [domestic] emergencies'.

The German leadership endorsed unrestricted submarine warfare, knowing that it would probably lead to American intervention. They assumed that the USA could not mount a significant effort before the Entente powers were forced to capitulate. Berlin adopted a radical maritime strategy, undersea interdiction of maritime commerce, because they decided that their army could not force a decision in France, although Germany had all but defeated Russia. It would now stand on the defensive until the navy won the war.

For the moment Wilson avoided discussions of post-war arrangements with the allies, knowing that such exchanges might stimulate distrust. He planned to resume his diplomatic campaign for self-determination, collective security, and international reforms after the USA had made a significant contribution to the allied cause. To Colonel Edward M. House, his closest adviser, he wrote: '*England and France have not the same views with regard to peace that we have* by any means . . . When the war is over we can force them to our way of thinking because by that time they will, among other things, be financially in our hands; but we cannot force them now, and any attempt to speak for them or to our common mind would bring on disagreements which would inevitably come to the surface and rob the whole thing of its effect.'

The United States made fundamental decisions during the early months of intervention that guided its war effort thereafter. Means of sustaining the financial positions of Great Britain and France were agreed upon. Also it was decided to accept the naval strategy of the allies, which stressed containment of the German surface fleet and an economic blockade of the Central Powers. The U-boat offensive endangered these objectives.

The prime immediate necessity was the dispatch of American antisubmarine craft, especially destroyers, to help contain the undersea threat. After brief hesitation the USA suspended the huge naval building programme of 1916 that had been intended to create a 'balanced fleet' capable of attaining command of the sea according to the specifications of the naval propagandist Alfred Thayer Mahan. Dire necessity forced a distasteful naval strategy. Instead of capital ships US shipyards would construct antisubmarine vessels and also merchant ships. A squadron of six destroyers was immediately sent to Queenstown, Ireland, where it conducted operations commanded by a British admiral. Others were sent when they became available. One squadron of American coal-burning battleships joined the British

Grand Fleet in 1918, the only significant departure from the emphasis on anti-submarine warfare.

Admiral William S. Sims, who was dispatched to London, strongly supported the British plea for anti-submarine reinforcements. Although Sims's endorsement of British views raised hackles in the Navy Department, where the ancient dislike of the Royal Navy still lingered, his recommendations generally gained approval. There was no alternative, although the chief of naval operations, Admiral William S. Benson, and others were loath to postpone construction of a Mahanian fleet, arguing that post-war conditions would require a powerful navy capable of operations against any Eurasian fleet, including those of Britain and Japan. If necessary, the building programme could be resumed later.

Some controversies marred generally successful naval co-operation. The Navy Department persisted in its view that the coalition should take 'offensive' action against submarines and submarine bases. Convoy appeared to be a defensive tactic. This attitude eventually produced widespread American support for mining operations in choke points through which submarines must manœuvre to reach the open sea. Such a location lay between Norway and Scotland. In 1918 the USA spearheaded massive mining to close this exit from the North Sea. Like other such efforts in the Strait of Dover and the Strait of Otranto, this measure failed. The convoy system decided the undersea war, containing the U-boats sufficiently to preserve necessary communications.

Another maritime dispute arose in 1918, when the USA began to dispatch many troop transports to Europe. The British did not want to weaken escorts for convoys of merchant ships. The Americans naturally wished to provide extensive protection for their men. Fortunately the coalition maintained enough vessels to escort both merchant ships and troop transports. No loaded American transport was sunk *en route* to Europe. Although the loss of merchant tonnage continued throughout 1918, the volume decreased significantly.

Land strategy posed many problems because the army was so small. How **The US army** would the nation mobilize its army? Where would it serve? How would it be employed? One possible means of sending manpower quickly to the battlefield would be to send combat troops formed in regiments or divisions to operate under experienced Entente staffs and commands, using the allied logistical system to maintain these 'amalgamated' units. The USA consistently opposed proposals to send Americans to 'secondary theatres' such as Salonika and Palestine. US preparations presumed a 'western strategy'; the War Department never deviated from the view that concentration for victory in France would decide the war most efficiently.

Allied missions sent to advise the USA broached the possibility of amalgamation on the western front, but it was immediately rejected. It would constitute an affront to national pride, and the military would naturally oppose it, preferring to serve under its own flag. There was also a cogent political consideration: amalgamation might undermine support for Wilsonian diplomatic initiatives after the war.

Instead of using its manpower to replenish French and British formations, the USA decided to mobilize a huge independent army, fighting under its own flag, commanded and staffed by its own officers, supplied through a separate logistical organization, and employed in its own sector of the western front. When formed, this army would strike a decisive blow and underwrite post-war political goals. General John J. Pershing was sent to France with this approach in mind, and the War Department lent undeviating support. Secretary of War Newton D. Baker voiced the most important consideration: 'It was necessary at all times to preserve the independence and identity of the American forces so that they could never be anything but an instrument of the policy of the United States.'

Pershing enjoyed a degree of autonomy from civilian interference rarely achieved in military history. His influence was so considerable that the War Department came to see itself as an extension of the general's staff in France, whence came extensive guidance for the mobilization. General Tasker H.

Marshal of France Ferdinand Foch, the generalissimo of the allied armies in France, devised theatre operations plans for the defensive warfare of March–July 1918 and the successful inter-allied offensive that followed during August–November. General John J. Pershing, hoping to command an independent American army on the western front, often resisted Foch's proposals for the use of American troops.

Le Bon Français

Travaille pour nos soldats

The war intensified the division of labour. Women entered
war work, but men remained vital for production as well as
fighting. This poster seeks to reassure the French that the
male munitions worker is just as much a patriot as the soldier
at the front, and perhaps to remind the worker that his patriotic duty prohibits strikes and pacifism.

ЗАЕМЪ СВОБОДЫ

The revolutionary Provisional Government of February 1917
attempted to remobilize the nation for the war. In this war
loan poster, army and people are one. The banners read
'Victory over the enemy', War until victory', Freedom', and
'Do not let the enemy take away the freedom you have won'.
The attempt failed with the disastrous offensive of June
1917.

Night was a time of vigilance in the salient.
Star shells are bursting to illuminate No
Man's Land in case of enemy patrols or
raids. In the foreground, three soldiers are
on the fire step, watching for movement.
In the background, three other soldiers
are repairing wire defences in the salient's
water-logged area.

Bliss, the army's chief of staff until 1918, saw his role as 'Assistant Chief of Staff to the Chief of Staff of the AEF' (American Expeditionary Forces). Bliss's successor, General Peyton C. March, attempted to regain control of theatre forces, but Pershing preserved much of his influence. Nevertheless the president kept control of policy, ensuring that professional military decisions were consistent with his larger political objectives. Command arrangements did not threaten civilian control because Pershing did not choose to influence basic policy and strategy. He concentrated on training and operations, emphasizing from first to last the creation of an independent army.

The decision to mobilize a huge independent army entailed considerable risk. Such a force could not conduct extensive operations until 1919, and perhaps even 1920. The American approach meant that the allies must hold without appreciable military assistance until the AEF had been fully recruited, equipped, trained, and transported to the western front. Given the extraordinary demands of the conflict, no one could be certain in 1917 that the allies could resist long enough to benefit from American combat operations. Wilson's patent idealism did not mean that he was incapable of expediency as a means to his ends.

The mobilization of the army proceeded rapidly if chaotically during 1917. The administration adopted conscription, enhancing the efficiency of the build-up and its equity. Local dignitaries served on draft boards, a means of legitimizing the process. Training cantonments were hastily erected, and industry converted to the production of equipment and supplies, Nevertheless only four divisions were sent to France in 1917, and none was as yet prepared for full-scale combat.

The mobilization surpassed all previous efforts, but the nation did not immediately adopt the extensive institutional changes made in Europe to wage total warfare. The cautious Wilsonians sought to make the necessary effort with minimal violence to existing methods. The establishment of an effective War Industries Board to rationalize procurement did not occur until 1918, and essential administrative structures were only slowly developed in the War and Navy Departments. Consequently the USA did not make the fullest possible use of governmental authority. The USA entered the desperate year of 1918 with much to do before its army could take the field.

A series of disasters befell the western coalition in 1917, among them the U-boat depredations, the failure of French and British offensives in France, the defeat of Russia, the Bolshevik revolution, and the Italian débâcle at Caporetto. These blows forced the western coalition to adopt unprecedented measures of inter-allied co-operation. A Paris conference in December 1917 created the Supreme War Council to provide overall political-military direction. A Naval War Council was also founded to co-ordinate naval activity. Other inter-allied organs were set up to deal with shipping, production, finance, and land transport.

**Wilson and
Bolshevism**

The USA was strongly supportive of these changes provided nothing was done to interfere with Wilson's post-war plans. To avoid entanglements that might limit the nation's freedom of action, Wilson did not send a political delegate to the Supreme War Council. Nevertheless he appointed General Bliss to the Council's advisory group of Permanent Military Representatives to press for needed military co-ordination, particularly unity of command. Wilson proved reluctant to support initiatives of the Supreme War Council that he deemed unsound or threatening to his post-war intentions. For example, he consistently opposed allied schemes intended to destabilize the new Bolshevik regime in Russia. He decried efforts to disrupt Lenin's government, but not because he was pro-Bolshevik. Wilson deemed such measures violations of national sovereignty. He assumed that the defeat of the Central Powers would undermine the Russian radicals, and he opposed major military commitments elsewhere than on the western front. In July 1918, responding to extreme pressure, he grudgingly condoned strictly limited expeditions to north Russia and eastern Siberia to protect supplies stockpiled at Murmansk, Archangel, and Vladivostok and to help expedite the rescue of captive Czech soldiers.

Responding to the Bolshevik challenge and recognizing the enlarged American role in the war, Wilson eventually broke his silence on war aims. On 8 January 1918 he announced his Fourteen Points in a message to Congress, a unilateral pronouncement made without consultations with the allies. Similar statements were issued in February, July, and September, so that the eventual American programme contained twenty-seven distinct points, by far the most detailed public exposition of post-war political objectives made during the war. The principal goals remained constant: he defined an equitable territorial settlement based on self-determination and a system of international organization based on collective security. Wilson acted because he recognized that the allies were now dependent upon the USA and were in no position to protest. For the moment he made no attempt to gain inter-allied endorsement of his peace plans, recognizing that his bargaining power would continue to strengthen. In this manner the USA gave public notice of its broad intent to both belligerent coalitions without prejudicing its relations with the allies. Wilson hoped that his moderation and ingenuity would stimulate international support for the Fourteen Points and associated statements after the war.

**US troops in
France**

Early in 1918 the German duumvirate of Ludendorff and Hindenburg realized that unrestricted submarine warfare had failed, and they also recognized that they must force a decision before the American reinforcements altered the balance of forces in France. The result was a decision to achieve a breakthrough on the western front intended to crush the French and British armies and thereby end the war before American troops appeared in great numbers.

When the German army launched the first of their five powerful offensives on 21 March 1918 only 300,000 American troops had arrived in Europe. The new German strategy forced the allied and associated powers to set up a unified command under the French general Ferdinand Foch to improve coordination between the several armies in France, including the Belgian army and the nascent American army, a move which the USA strongly supported. The German offensives also forced the USA to modify its effort to field an independent army. The patent need for manpower in France revived interest in the temporary amalgamation of American combat troops by small units into the allied armies, at least for training and also for limited combat exposure. It would allow the AEF to help thwart the German offensives while continuing to build an independent army. Pershing was loath to permit amalgamation in any form, fearing that it would delay development of a distinct American army. The result was that while American divisions began to arrive in increasing numbers in France (800,000 men during May–July 1918), for the most part they were assigned to quiet sectors for training. This measure made experienced allied troops available to bolster the defence. The allies carried the brunt of the German offensives, although some of the most experienced American divisions lent useful assistance, notably during the fourth German offensive in June and the brief final offensive in mid-July.

Pershing's resistance to amalgamation, which he condoned only for brief periods in return for additional shipping from the allies, earned him broad unpopularity. Unlike Sims, who maintained excellent relations with the allies without undermining his nation's interests, the self-righteous and overbearing Pershing alienated the military and political leadership of the Entente, especially Premier Georges Clemenceau of France, by adopting an unduly rigid interpretation of his mandate to create an independent army.

A compromise that would have permitted temporary amalgamation of more American divisions, especially for training, might have hastened American preparations for separate operations, although Pershing remained convinced that such concessions were designed to interfere with his plans. He feared that allied generals would exhaust American divisions, leaving them unfit for independent actions. General Bliss at the Supreme War Council was inclined to agree with the allies, although he supported Pershing loyally. Tensions eased somewhat during the summer, when the German attack was finally stemmed and General Bliss assumed much of Pershing's role as military intermediary with the allies. Moreover, Pershing gained the authority to form the US 1st Army and to conduct independent operations beginning in September. This force would be far from self-sufficient, lacking sufficient artillery, armour, air, and logistical support, which the allies had to supply. It was the price paid to encourage extensive American combat operations.

Foch devised a plan for offensive operations beginning in July that would unroll in two phases during the remainder of 1918. First there would be a series of limited offensives intended to eliminate various salients along the western front, a means of assuring efficient mobility. Such enterprises would strengthen the morale of the French army, still not fully recovered from the

Gunners of the AEF are shown firing a 37-mm gun on the western front. The late entry of the United States into the war forced the US Army to rely heavily on France and Britain for weapons and munitions during 1918.

devastating defeats of 1917. It would help prepare the British and American forces for a second phase of the 1918 campaign, a general offensive designed to expel the Germans from their conquests in Belgium and France and assure a decision in 1919.

Foch's series of limited offensives proved uniformly successful. The British army achieved a significant breakthrough at Amiens in August. It forced Germany to consider ending the struggle. Meanwhile, French troops, assisted by several American divisions, made important gains in the Oise–Aisne–Marne region. The US 1st Army conducted the last of the limited offensives in September, reducing the Saint-Mihiel salient in Lorraine where Pershing's staff had always planned to undertake major operations.

The 1st Army's attack on the Saint-Mihiel salient took place on 12–16 September. The German army had occupied this position since 1915, but, recognizing its vulnerability, the German command planned to withdraw from it to strong defensive positions along its base. The American attack hastened and confused the withdrawal, leading to the jest that the Americans had relieved the Germans in the salient. Although Pershing hailed the operation, victory obscured some painful realities, especially the inexperience of commanders and staffs. The reduction of the Saint-Mihiel salient by no means proved that the 1st Army could overcome determined defenders.

The American triumph completed Foch's preparations for a general counter-offensive, which was launched late in September. Unlike Clemenceau, Foch was prepared to propitiate Pershing sufficiently to ensure American assistance. From the beginning of his mission in France, Pershing had planned to conduct his first major offensive in Lorraine eastward towards the fortified city of Metz. His staff believed that the capture of Metz would interdict German communications, allowing the independent American army to impose a decision. He constructed his services of supply and training facilities to support this ambitious operation. Pershing failed to recognize that the seizure of Metz would not close an alternative route some distance east of the city. Foch, on the other hand, planned to breach the Hindenburg line, which protected the railroads used to supply the German front line. His objective was the railway section between Maubeuge–Aulnoye to the north and Mezières–Sedan to the south; success here would enable the allies to interdict essential communications between Lille and Strasbourg and necessitate a German withdrawal to at least the line Antwerp–Meuse. Foch therefore ordered an American attack northward as part of a co-ordinated drive to the Aulnoye–Mezières district. The 1st Army would make an important contribution but share victory with the allied armies.

Marshal Foch's co-ordinated thrust succeeded immediately. The British strike eastward in Picardy toward Saint-Quentin, Cambrai, and beyond broke through the Hindenburg line and exposed the Aulnoye–Maubeuge area. Several American divisions served effectively with the British 4th Army, an indication that temporary amalgamation was feasible. This victory finally broke the German leadership.

The American 1st Army did not make gains at all comparable with those of the British or even the French. Pershing's massive attack beginning on 26 September between the Argonne forest and the river Meuse with fifteen divisions, equal to thirty European divisions, in concert with the French 4th Army of twenty-two divisions driving northward to the west of the Argonne forest, took place on a front of 44 miles. The strong German position between the Argonne and the Meuse was initially manned by only five divisions at perhaps a third of their normal size. Elevations west and east of the Meuse provided excellent locations for artillery and machine guns. Pershing's frontal movement across difficult terrain was supposed to overwhelm several fortified lines quickly and open the way to the Mezières–Sedan area. The 1st Army relied upon surprise to gain its objective, the line Grandpré–Dun-sur-Meuse, a means of compensating for its inexperience.

At first the attack of 26 September went well, but, after reaching the second line of enemy fortifications, the 1st Army became bogged down. It had failed to achieve surprise, and German reinforcements quickly arrived. Only two inadequate roads provided access to the front, which led to huge traffic

jams. Infantry movements, artillery relocation, and logistical support became exceedingly difficult. During October the 1st Army made little further progress but suffered heavy losses. At the armistice about 120,000 of the 1.2 million troops engaged had become casualties, of whom 25,000 were killed.

Pershing claimed that his operations pinned down German units that otherwise would have reinforced beleaguered German forces elsewhere, but this accomplishment was far from the decisive victory that had been envisaged earlier. As Haig and others had feared, inexperienced commanders and staffs proved inefficient, and the tactics of 'open warfare', which Pershing insisted upon, were inappropriate in the area under attack. The vastly outnumbered defenders poured murderous fire on advancing waves of massed infantry. The outcome amounted to a severe check if not defeat while the allies achieved victory elsewhere.

On 10 October, Pershing made Major General Hunter Liggett the commander of the 1st Army and formed the US 2nd Army under Major General Robert Bullard. The 2nd Army was ordered to prepare for an attack eastward, an indication of continuing interest in Metz. Pershing became commander of the American group of armies. Liggett spent several weeks retraining his shattered divisions, finally introducing tactics that had proven effective elsewhere on the western front. These measures benefited the 1st Army in later operations north toward Sedan.

The discouraging Meuse–Argonne campaign did not prevent President Wilson from exploiting the German desire to seek peace. The new chancellor, Prince Max of Baden, recognized that the American peace plan was much less devastating than that of the allies. Accordingly he sent a note to Wilson, received on 6 October, proposing peace negotiations based on the Fourteen Points and related statements. Wilson's response of 8 October led to further bilateral exchanges between Washington and Berlin that culminated on 27 October, when Prince Max accepted Wilson's requirements. Throughout this period Wilson did not consult the allies, who manifested considerable irritation. There remained a final step, an inter-allied conference in Paris to decide whether the suspicious Entente powers would accept this arrangement.

On 1 November, Foch launched another general offensive, seeking to complete the movements that had begun on 26 September. The stricken German army had no alternative but to retreat. At last the US 1st Army breached the fortifications between the Meuse and the Argonne and participated in the thrust that soon interdicted the enemy's rail communications and completed Foch's planned operations. Pershing still dreamed of the Metz offensive, but he never gained an opportunity to launch it. By the armistice of 11 November the Americans had advanced 34 miles and occupied 580 square miles, a real but modest gain compared with those of the allies.

Meanwhile Colonel House, representing Wilson, participated in the inter-

Soldiers of the AEF make use of a German-made field telephone in 1918. Telephones, telegraphs, and radios became essential modes of communications on the western front, an effort to improve command and control in battles dominated by extraordinary firepower.

allied discussion of the American deal with Germany. Although various disputes arose, particularly over the US demand for freedom of the seas and the French desire for indemnity, Wilson forced the frustrated allies to accept almost all of his grand design. The Germans were then required to sign terms of armistice that guaranteed against resumption of hostilities.

Although the US army never attained the decisive victory envisaged for it, the overall American reinforcement provided the margin of victory. The AEF fought bravely for the most part, but it never matured into an effective independent force. Ironically some of the best combat service came from American divisions temporarily assigned to allied forces, especially those attached to the French 6th and 10th armies during the Aisne–Marne offensive of July–August 1918 and to the British 4th Army during the decisive British operations in Picardy during September–November. The war ended before American commanders and staffs could attain full proficiency, adjusting their training methods and tactics to meet the demands of the western front. Pershing's flaws as a commander mirrored those of many European officers who learned earlier from bitter experience the best available means of fighting a modern war. He benefited from the changes in command during October that placed his most competent generals in command of the 1st and 2nd armies.

President Wilson dominated the post-war peace negotiations. Although forced to compromise on various issues, he obtained the consent of the allies to territorial arrangements that generally respected self-determination and allowed the creation of a league of nations system that would keep the peace and sponsor healing international reforms. The miscarriage of the Wilsonian peace during the inter-war years stemmed from the refusal of the president's countrymen to accept international leadership. The peace settlement could not work without energetic American support. Wilsonian principles eventually triumphed, but not until the world had suffered through the Second World War and then the long Cold War that endured until almost the end of the century. These struggles to prevent German and then Russian hegemony in Eurasia were extensions of the imbalance that existed in 1914 and whose repair failed between 1918 and 1939.

CHAPTER 19

The German Victories, 1917–1918

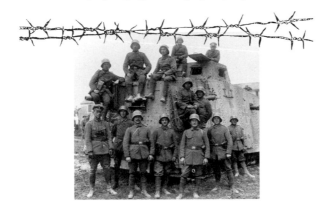

HOLGER H. HERWIG

Prospects for the Central Powers were bleak at the end of 1916. Kaiser Franz Joseph of Austria-Hungary had died in November and little was known of his successor, Kaiser Karl. General Franz Conrad von Hötzendorf's 'punitive expedition' against Italy had foundered along the Isonzo river, and in the east General A. A. Brusilov's breakthrough offensive at Lutsk had shattered the old imperial and royal army. War industries were short of every kind of raw and war materials. Starvation ravaged Vienna and other urban centres. Food riots and industrial strikes were on the rise.

In Germany, General Erich von Falkenhayn had yielded at the general staff to Field Marshal Paul von Hindenburg and General Erich Ludendorff after the twin débâcles (800,000 casualties) of Verdun and the Somme. The new men opted for a long-term 'strategy of annihilation' to bring the war to a victorious conclusion. For 1917, they adopted a defensive posture: to withdraw from advanced salients such as the 'Ancre knee' between Arras and Soissons in France; to construct massive defensive fortifications soon to be known as the Siegfried (or Hindenburg) line; to retrain the army along the lines of Captain Willy Rohr's storm battalions; and to break Britain's 'hunger blockade' by renewing unrestricted submarine warfare. The 'turnip winter' of 1916–17 left the home front demoralized and on the point of starving. Still, Hindenburg and Ludendorff sought to gear both industry and nation for 'total war' by 1917–18.

German defences prepared 1916–1917

Operation 'Alberich' became the war's greatest feat of engineering. An army of half a million German reservists and civilians as well as Russian prisoners of war laboured for four months to create five separate concrete and steel reinforced defensive positions along the line Arras–Laon. Ludendorff, remembering the Russian 'scorched-earth' policy in Poland in 1915, laid waste all abandoned territory so that the allies would 'find a totally barren land, in which their manœuvrability was to be critically impaired'. Cities and villages within 10 miles of the Siegfried line were destroyed. All war materials were removed. Trees were felled, streets mined, and wells poisoned. With one bold stroke Ludendorff surrendered about 1,000 square miles of land won at the cost of tens of thousands of soldiers over the past three years. Perhaps the brilliant masterpiece in Ludendorff's art of operations, 'Alberich' shortened the German front by nearly 30 miles and thus released ten divisions and fifty artillery batteries.

Ludendorff next reorganized existing formations. The division, already elevated to semi-independent status, was given control over its artillery and divided into three regiments of three battalions each. Each division was equipped with 54 heavy and 108 light machine guns. Four of the Reich's eleven cavalry divisions were dismounted.

Doctrine also was revised. On 1 December 1916 Captain Hermann Geyer drafted the *Principles of Command for the Defensive Battle in Position Warfare*. Designed to 'husband one's own forces' while allowing the enemy 'to exhaust himself and to bleed' heavily, the *Principles* featured not soldiers but 'preponderantly machines (artillery, trench mortars, machine guns, etc.)'. Defences were to be constructed 'in depth'—that is, with a killing zone consisting of at least three lines between 6 and 8 miles deep. The 'defence in depth' received 'elasticity' in so far as the outpost zone was to be thinly manned and to 'evade' the main assault, which would then expend itself in the battle zone dominated by machine guns with interlocking zones of fire. Small groups of combined-arms units in the rear zone would recapture lost territory. Artillery sited on reverse slopes and directed by aerial spotters would initially engage hostile artillery, and thereafter enemy infantry (now beyond the range of their own guns).

Ludendorff next turned his attention to training what Ernst Jünger called the new 'workers of war'. One-month long instruction courses in Geyer's *Principles* were introduced for all company and battalion commanders; special 'war schools' for the best and brightest staff officers followed at Solesmes, Valenciennes, and Sedan; and nine artillery schools were created by Ludendorff to train his artificers to lay down Colonel Georg Bruchmüller's rolling barrages ('steel wind') to cover the infantry's advance. By January 1917 four- and then six-week courses were introduced to train soldiers in the ways of Rohr's storm battalions. A typical *Sturmbataillon*, led by a captain and four lieutenants, consisted of 24 light machine guns, 8 trench mortars, 8 light mortars, 8 flame-throwers, 4 light artillery pieces, heavy machine guns, hand grenades, and a signal horn.

The new workers of war: Captain Willy Rohr's stormtroopers in full gear. Armed with machine guns, trench mortars, flame-throwers, and hand grenades, the *Sturm-bataillon* was to infiltrate allied lines quickly and deeply; new units were to leapfrog ahead of exhausted ones to maintain continuous momentum.

In terms of material, Ludendorff by way of the 'Hindenburg programme' instructed the Prussian War Ministry to double the output of ammunition and trench mortars and to triple that of artillery and machine guns—measures actually already enacted by the Prussian War Ministry. 'Men—as well as horses—must be replaced more and more by machines.' An Auxiliary Service Law sought to mobilize all males between the ages of 17 and 60 and to bring females into the industrial labour pool. A special War Office was created under General Wilhelm Groener to oversee this attempt at 'total war'. Groener estimated that production rose only 60 per cent. Shortages of rolling

HOLGER H. HERWIG

stock and coal as well as rail yards and bridges proved bottlenecks to enhanced production, as did the severely strained transportation system. Nor did Hindenburg's wish to see urban youths and women enrolled in labour battalions reach fruition. But Ludendorff and his minions at least faced up to what the German army had avoided before 1914: that modern industrialized wars fought by millions of combatants and fuelled by the labour of millions of industrial workers could not be fought with the organizations and tools of the Napoleonic era.

Entente attacks 1917

For most of 1917, then, the German army braced itself against expected and concerted allied attacks, as outlined in the Chantilly conference in the winter of 1916. In the west, Anglo-French assaults ran up against the Siegfried line. On 16 April 1917 General Robert Nivelle unleashed a massive French assault against the gigantic German salient that stretched from Arras southward to Soissons and then eastward to Reims. But the Germans had abandoned the salient as part of Operation 'Alberich' and, secure behind the concrete and steel forts and blockhouses of the Siegfried line, they blunted Nivelle's offensive within four days. To the north, Sir Douglas Haig from 7 June to 21 July launched a major attack in Flanders against Messines and Ypres. Once more lacking the elements of surprise and concentration and advancing over ground recently scorched by the retreating Germans, Haig's armies scored initial gains, only to get stuck in the mud and blood of Flanders. Undaunted, Haig on 31 July launched the third battle of Ypres. Haig's men advanced across a swamp: 400,000 casualties attested to the strength of the German elastic defence-in-depth. While shocked at the horrendous casualty lists from Passchendaele, Hindenburg and Ludendorff nevertheless were pleased with the success of their defensive strategy along the western front.

In the east, the Russian front also erupted in an inferno of activity. On 1 July 1917 General Brusilov launched the vaunted offensive named in honour of the war minister, Aleksandr Kerensky. The assault by the Russian 7th, 8th, and 11th armies was designed to retake eastern Galicia. At first, all went according to plan as the Habsburg 2nd and 3rd armies retreated from the Dniester river. But then the Germans counter-attacked, and by 19 October had crushed Brusilov's forces near Zloczów. Thereafter, General Max Hoffmann's troops advanced through Galicia and the Bukovina as rapidly as the Russians could retreat. Lack of supplies, summer heat, and exhaustion finally ended the advance. German troops conquered Riga in September and the Baltic islands of Ösel, Moon, and Dagö in October. Bolshevik leaders under V. I. Lenin, who earlier had been transported from Switzerland to Petrograd by the German army, seized power in the Russian capital between 6 and 8 November 1917.

Finally, the Italians, in accordance with the joint allied strategy laid down at Chantilly, hammered at Austro-Hungarian positions along the Isonzo river in May and June, and again in August and September 1917. General Luigi

Cadorna's armies suffered 159,000 casualties in the tenth battle of the Isonzo, and an additional 168,000 in the eleventh. And while Habsburg forces endured only half of these losses, civilian as well as military leaders in Vienna conceded that the Dual Monarchy could neither continue this human haemorrhaging nor win the war without German help. Although Vienna viewed the Italian front as 'its war' and Kaiser Karl decreed that only his 'own troops' would strike 'the hereditary enemy' Italy, in the end Vienna had no choice but to turn to Hindenburg and Ludendorff for succour.

In fact, Ludendorff, determined that his forces not remain entirely on the defensive throughout 1917, in September had dispatched his expert on Alpine warfare, the Bavarian General Konrad Krafft von Dellmensingen, to the Julian Alps. Convinced that Austro-Hungarian forces could not survive another Italian attack, Krafft von Dellmensingen recommended an Austro-Hungarian-German assault along a narrow 30-mile front between Flitsch and Tolmein. In its centre stood the small village of Caporetto (Karfreit). The Bavarian rejected the customary Habsburg tactic of storming and then advancing along the Alpine ridges in favour of broad sweeps down the mountain valleys. He termed the operation 'difficult, dangerous, and uncertain'— but possible.

Caporetto

Ludendorff concurred. He appointed General Otto von Below to head the new 14th Army, with Krafft von Dellmensingen as his chief of staff. Beginning on 20 September, more than 2,400 trains hauled heavy artillery, howitzers, and air units from the Baltic front to Carniola and Carinthia. Over the next month, Below assembled his composite forces in steady rain in well-camouflaged jump-off positions on the southern slopes of the Julian Alps. The troops moved by night and over circuitous routes. Wireless deception and close air cover hid their movements from Italian spotters. The Germans undertook gruelling training patrols and mock attacks to ready themselves for mountain warfare. Lengthy artillery shelling was eschewed in favour of hurricane saturation bombardments, followed by creeping artillery barrages. The final advance into jump-off positions was undertaken by night and supplied by pack animals with muffled hooves.

At 2 a.m. on 24 October 1917 Below's 14th Army unleashed a devastating blue cross and green cross gas-shell attack from 2,000 barrels in dense, grey fog. The gas was highly effective in the fog- and snow-shrouded narrow Alpine valleys; primitive Italian gas masks offered Cadorna's troops no protection. Below's trench mortars next switched to shell and wreaked material and morale damage on the Italian first line, which held the majority of Cadorna's combatants and machine guns. Around 6.30 a.m. the Germans concentrated heavy mortar fire directly against Cadorna's first and second lines of defence. Finally, between 8 and 9 a.m., German and Austro-Hungarian infantry advanced in thin columns behind a creeping barrage. Flitsch, Tolmein, and Caporetto were quickly seized and numerous units advanced 10 miles that day. Captain Erwin Rommel's regiment, part of the

Württemberg Mountain Battalion, in quick order stormed the heights of Monte Cragonza, Monte Kuk, and the Matajur, taking more than 3,000 prisoners of war. The 'stone wilderness' of the Isonzo with its sharp-angled limestone cliffs offered little shelter to the Italians. Ten regiments surrendered *en masse* in a blinding snow storm on Monte Maggiore.

A rout ensued. General Luigi Capello's Italian 2nd Army, consisting of twenty-six divisions, was smashed in the opening phase of the battle. By late October, 1 million men of the Italian 1st and 2nd armies, along with their gear, streamed from the Isonzo to the Tagliamento river. Cadorna in four days abandoned all the territory that he had seized in the past thirty months at a cost of 300,000 dead and 740,000 wounded. His entire 100-mile-wide defensive front between Monte Peralba and the Adriatic Sea was destroyed. Austro-Hungarian units crossed the Tagliamento on 2 November and Below, in the heat of victory, ignored Ludendorff's orders to halt at the river. Torrential downpours and the lack of cavalry and motorized units finally blunted the Austro-Hungarian-German advance at the Piave river—70 miles behind the original Isonzo front. The Allies rushed six French and five British divisions from the western front to the Piave. Cadorna and Capello were sacked. The new Italian commander, General Armando Diaz, promised a fighting retreat as far south as Sicily; the French general, Ferdinand Foch, acerbically suggested the Piave river as a starting point.

The battle of Caporetto was one of the Great War's most spectacular operational successes. What had begun as a limited campaign designed to relieve Italian pressure on the Austrians had expanded into an advance of 80 miles in seventy days. In the process, the Central Powers' front with Italy had been narrowed by more than 200 miles. The Italian army had sustained staggering losses: 10,000 dead, 30,000 wounded, and 293,000 prisoners of war, along with 3,150 guns and 1,730 howitzers; more than 350,000 deserters roamed the countryside. The victors suffered between 65,000 and 70,000 casualties.

But Caporetto also revealed shortcomings in the German and Austro-Hungarian art of military operations. Starving troops had revelled for days in bountiful Italian food and wine depots—a harbinger of things to come in France in 1918. Lack of tanks and motorized transport had slowed the advance and eventually had halted it at the Piave river. Inter-allied cooperation had been minimal. Habsburg generals argued that Ludendorff had curtailed the operation too early and accused German commanders of denigrating the performance of Austro-Hungarian units. The Germans replied by casting aspersions on the 'dash' and 'valour' of their Austrian colleagues and by suggesting that success was due solely to Below's 14th Army. Above all, Ludendorff had mounted the operation as an end in itself rather than as part of a broader strategy.

The 1918 offensives

The new year 1918 offered Ludendorff the prospect of finally ending imperial Germany's two-front nightmare. Taking advantage of Lenin's revolution, more than fifty German divisions renewed the war in the east on 18–19

February. Foreshadowing the assault of 1941, a northern force marched from Pskov to Narva; a middle contingent headed for Smolensk; and a southern force occupied Ukraine. General Hoffmann termed the campaign a leisurely stroll by train and car. The Bolsheviks entered into armistice discussions with the Germans on 3 December 1917. After some desultory wrangling, Lenin agreed to terms at Brest-Litovsk on 3 March 1918—while German forces stormed the Caucasus and the Crimea as well as Finland. Two months later, Romania in the Treaty of Bucharest was reduced to a German vassal state. Proponents of the *Mitteleuropa* (central Europe) dream were delighted that Germany was on the way to economic hegemony on the basis of 'indirect' expansionism. Visions of unlimited grain and oil reserves danced before their eyes. Few noticed (or cared) that 1 million German troops had to remain in occupied Russia to police and to exploit this vast region.

In fact, while Ludendorff was redrawing the borders of eastern Europe with reckless abandon, his field commanders and staff were assessing the Reich's prospects for 1918. They were not bright. The last reserves had been called to the colours; industry lagged behind the targets set in the Hindenburg programme; roughly ten to fifteen American divisions were expected to arrive in France by May or June 1918; and the unrestricted U-boat campaign of 1 February 1917 had turned into a 'wild-goose chase'. The western front remained decisive, Britain the primary adversary. Major Georg Wetzell, head of operations at the supreme command, put it bluntly: the only option was 'to deliver an annihilating blow to the British before American aid can become effective'. At Mons on 11 November 1917 Ludendorff decided on the gambler's last throw of the dice: Kaiser Wilhelm II was apprised of Operation 'Michael' on 23 January 1918, and Hindenburg issued formal orders for the attack on 10 March. Many staff officers spoke of the operation as the Reich's 'last card'.

Imperial Germany geared up for one final, desperate effort to win the war. More than 10,400 full-length trains ran day and night between 15 February and 10 March to move men and material to the front. Ludendorff divided his forces into three categories: 44 'mobile' divisions with full-strength battalions of 850 men each armed with machine guns, flame-throwers, and trench mortars; about 30 'attack' divisions designated as first-line replacement units; and more than 100 'trench' divisions stripped of their best weapons and designed merely to hold territory gained. Captains and majors from the 70 'mobile' and 'attack' divisions underwent eight-day training courses in the art of the attack at Sedan and Valenciennes. Speed, timing, and concentration were decisive. Artillery was resupplied and air forces beefed up to 126 squadrons of roughly 2,600 planes. Troops moved up to the front by night and a special decoy plan was instituted to confuse allied spotters.

Infantry once more was highlighted as the queen of battle. In January 1918 Captain Geyer produced a new tactical assault doctrine, *The Attack in Position Warfare*. It stipulated that small combined-arms units were to infiltrate (*durchfressen*) enemy lines, bypass centres of resistance, and 'penetrate quickly and deeply' into the enemy's rear. Reserves were to exploit ruptures in enemy lines. Units were not to halt and resupply but to drive forward until exhausted. Fresh formations would then leapfrog ahead of them. 'The surprised adversary should not be allowed to regain consciousness.' Tactical virtuosity had replaced strategy at the supreme command. In fact, Ludendorff refused to allow the terms 'strategy' or 'operation'. 'I object to the word "operation". We will punch a hole into [their line]. For the rest, we shall see.'

The German plan called for the 17th, 2nd, and 18th armies to drive through Field Marshal Haig's 3rd and 5th armies in a pincer movement and trap British forces in the Cambrai salient. Thereafter, these German units would follow the Somme north-west to Arras-Albert and throw the remaining units of the BEF into disarray. The area chosen for the attack consisted mainly of flat sweeps of heavy clay soil, dissected by the narrow, swampy valleys of the Ancre and Somme rivers as well as the Crozat canal. The main attack zone between Albert and Montdidier had been devastated by the Germans during Operation 'Alberich' in 1917.

At 4 a.m. on 21 March 1918 the western front erupted in a hurricane of fire and thunder as 6,608 guns and 3,534 trench mortars announced the start of Operation 'Michael'. Five hours later, the artillery changed from gas to explosive shells and laid down a creeping barrage for the roughly seventy assault divisions. Berlin was bedecked with flags and bells rang out in anticipation of victory.

March 1918: the last throw of the dice. Massed units of General Oskar von Hutier's 18th Army advance through the devastated streets of St Quentin against the 'Haig position' along the Somme river near Foreste and Péronne.

Initial reports from the battlefield pleased Ludendorff. Within forty-eight hours, General von Below's 17th Army and Georg von der Marwitz's 2nd Army linked up in the direction of Bapaume and stormed Haig's third line of defence as well as his artillery park. Elsewhere, General Oskar von Hutier's 18th Army crashed through the 'Haig position' and advanced toward Foreste. Ludendorff quickly reinforced Hutier's army and drove it forward near Péronne on the Somme. In two days, German forces had shattered General Hubert Gough's 5th Army and driven the BEF almost 40 miles behind the Somme and the Crozat canal. Haig had lost 290,000 men and 1,300 guns.

Without a strategic or even operational concept, Ludendorff exploited Hutier's success by ordering the 17th Army on to Doullens and the 2nd and 8th armies in the direction of Miraumont–Lihons and Chaulnes–Noyon. He hoped to drive a wedge between the French and British at the vital rail link of Hazebrouk. For three days, Ludendorff pushed his forces over the old Somme battlefields of 1916. Haig and the French commander-in-chief Philippe Pétain feared that the allied front might collapse. While the over-

Too little, too late: the German A7V medium tank. With a best speed of 5 miles per hour and range of 15 miles, it lacked manœuvrability. Nor were the 10 tanks assigned to Operation Michael a match for their 800 allied counterparts.

extended 5th Army fell back, British attention was devoted to the 3rd Army's efforts to hold the northern shoulder of the consequent salient around Arras and Vimy Ridge. To the south, the French moved twenty-four divisions to plug the gap, but their movement was slow. Moreover, Pétain was as anxious as Haig not to drop his guard elsewhere along his front. Wariness engendered distrust. Both were thus more accepting than hitherto of the idea of a supreme allied command to co-ordinate their responses. At a conference at Doullens on 26 March Foch—although it required further meetings to define his powers more clearly—was appointed allied generalissimo with responsibility for the entire western front. Foch correctly identified Amiens as the key to frustrating the Germans. On 28 March General John J. Pershing agreed to release American formations to buttress allied lines. A week after launching 'Michael', Ludendorff was committed to a series of small attacks with limited objectives against both the French and the British. In the process, he weakened the momentum of the assault. German units, fanned out across the region between the Oise river and the English Channel in a giant radiating movement, were soon exhausted and demoralized. One-half of German reserves had been ground up in the advance, as had one-third of German artillery. By 27 March the offensive had degenerated into position warfare.

The Young Turks on Ludendorff's staff decried the lack of a strategic plan or even an operation goal behind 'Michael'. Some stated that Ludendorff had 'lost his nerves'. Others lamented the lack of tanks (10 German against 800 allied) and trucks (23,000 German iron-rimmed against 100,000 allied rubber-tyred vehicles). Still others shuddered that German troops all too often stopped to loot bountiful allied food depots and wine cellars. And when general staff officers reminded Ludendorff on 27 March of his earlier claim that the fourth day of 'Michael' would tell whether it had been a success, the first quartermaster general acidly replied: 'What is the purpose of your croaking? What do you want from me? Am I now to conclude peace at any price?'.

Rather than admit defeat, Ludendorff shifted the campaign's centre of gravity. On 9 April he struck in Flanders, on the river Lys, again making rapid initial gains and prompting Haig to issue, on 12 April, an order of the day reminding the British troops that they stood with their 'backs to the wall'. The allies lost Messines by 10 April, and Mont Kemmel to the north of the Lys on 25 April. But by the 26th they had stabilized their front, and three days later the battle was closed down.

On 27 May Ludendorff shifted his line of attack once more, the Aisne river. The breakthrough battle of the Chemin des Dames ('Blücher') was designed to threaten Compiègne, Reims, and eventually Paris, in the process drawing French reserves away from Haig, the real target of the assault. General Hans von Boehn's 7th Army rolled over the French 6th Army and reached Fismes on the Vesle river on the first day of battle. Ludendorff exploited this limited tactical success by expanding 'Blücher' into the great battle of Soissons–Reims. In five days the Germans took 50,000 prisoners, cut the vital Paris–

Nancy rail link, and advanced to Château-Thierry on the Marne river. Early in June German soldiers were in many of the same positions that they had abandoned in September 1914. Paris once more seemed in danger, and as many as 1 million people fled the capital in panic. From the forest of Crépy, modified 21-cm. Krupp naval guns brought Paris under fire.

Ludendorff faced what became his last major offensive decision in the war: should he widen the Marne salient and storm Paris, or should he now shift his forces north and drive the British against the English Channel? To avoid any loss of immediate impetus, he chose the former, more tantalizing option. On 9 June Hutier's 18th Army and Boehn's 7th Army attacked ('Gneisenau') in heavy fog between Noyon and Montdidier, just west of the Marne salient. Two days later General Foch launched a spirited counter-offensive at Château-Thierry and Belleau Wood, supported by 'tanks' as well as by the American 2nd and 3rd divisions. Once more the German army halted just outside the gates of Paris, bloodied and exhausted. It had lost 209,345 men in June.

While the Germans marched against Paris, Conrad von Hötzendorf, now Habsburg commander in the Tyrol, persuaded Kaiser Karl to mount another offensive against the 'snake' Italy. On 15 June 1918, after almost a week of steady rain, Conrad attacked along a 50-mile front between Astico and the Piave river; concurrently, Field Marshal Svetozar von Boroevic advanced in

On to Paris: German stormtroopers advance through the village of Pont Arcy in May 1918, having just crossed the Aisne river. For all but the most discerning eye, this picture could as well have been from the Second World War.

the direction of Oderzo–Treviso. While Conrad dreamed of entering Venice, Boroevic set his sights on Padua. Instead, the battle of the Piave, in the words of the Austrian historian Peter Fiala, proved to be the *Götterdämmerung* of Habsburg military fortunes. By 16 June Conrad's 11th Army was back in its original positions, low on food, ammunition, and morale. At the same time, Boroevic's 6th Army was shattered by allied air forces and the rising waters of the Piave. In just over a week, the Austro-Hungarian army had lost 142,550 men. It ceased to be a fighting force as almost 200,000 soldiers deserted in the next three months.

Conrad's defeat in the battle of the Piave and Ludendorff's aborted final assault against the eastern side of the Marne salient in mid-July 1918 forced the armies of the Central Powers on the permanent defensive. Deep in their heart of hearts, both Ludendorff and Conrad knew that the initiative in the war had passed to the allies. Victory was no longer a possibility.

CHAPTER 20

The War in the Air

JOHN H. MORROW, JR.

T he late nineteenth and early twentieth centuries witnessed an explosion of technology and industry, from cars and chemicals to dynamos and dynamite. The era of powered flight dawned with the invention of the dirigible in France in 1884 and of the aeroplane in the United States in 1903. Dreams of flight expressed in the myths of Daedalus and Icarus long antedated powered flight, and visions of aerial warfare preceded the First World War in the air. Aviation quickly captured the rapt attention of civilians, and aerial achievements measured the greatness of nations early in the twentieth century.

Air war prefigured

The images of aerial warfare conjured up by human imagination did not necessarily presage the reality that followed. In 1883, one year before the invention of the dirigible, Albert Robida's book *War in the Twentieth Century* envisaged a sudden crushing air strike, while Ivan S. Bloch's treatise on warfare written in 1898 expected bombardment from airships. The evolution of German Count Ferdinand von Zeppelin's giant dirigibles in 1908 and 1909 threatened fulfilment of such dire predictions.

In Britain flight portended a new avenue of assault on an island nation immune in modern history to the threat of invasion. Press magnate Alfred Harmsworth, Lord Northcliffe, had recognized that 'England was no longer an island' when Albert Santos-Dumont flew in France in 1906. His conception of the threat as 'aerial chariots of a foe descending upon England' indicated a classical, if unrealistic, appraisal of its nature.

Writers speculated on the potential effect of powered flight on war. H. G. Wells's work of 1908, *The War in the Air*, inspired by Zeppelin flights, predicted an interminable world war conducted primarily by airships that would

265

ultimately cause the collapse of civilization. Other European authors proclaimed that aviation would bind nations together and make war too horrible to endure; still others equivocated, declaring flying machines useful for peace or war.

Across Europe popular interest in aviation, often spurred by government officials, surged in 1908 with a twelve-hour Zeppelin flight, Henri Farman's first cross-country flight in an aeroplane, and Wilbur Wright's two-hour closed-circuit flights. In 1909 Louis Blériot's flight across the English Channel and the Reims air meet further stimulated public enthusiasm for flight. As the flights of airships and aeroplanes impressed the European public, military aviation leagues and aero clubs formed in France and Germany and then across Europe. These extraparliamentary pressure groups for aviation, which emulated the naval leagues that had preceded them, included prominent military, political, and industrial leaders, developed their own press organs, and encouraged parliamentary representatives to support military aviation. Highly placed patrons, such as Prince Heinrich of Prussia, Grand Duke Alexander Mikhailovich of Russia, and First Lord of the Admiralty Winston Churchill in Britain, sponsored military aviation.

These bellicose popular attitudes encouraging the militarization of aviation formed the context for the development of European aviation to 1914. The United States, lacking this impetus, rapidly fell behind Europe in the development of land planes, although Glenn Curtiss excelled in the development of seaplanes and flying boats. By the end of 1909, France and Germany were forming military air services, and in Germany the press and public actually helped to prod the army to accept the Zeppelin before it met military performance stipulations.

After the Moroccan crisis of 1911, Europe expected war. Finally responding to continental progress and warnings of Zeppelin attacks from the Aerial League of the British Empire and the British Aero Club, the British government formed military and naval air services in 1912. The German army, playing upon chauvinistic notions of cultural supremacy to bolster military aviation, effectively controlled civilian aviation through its pervasive influence in German society. In 1912 government and industry organized a national aviation fund that bought aeroplanes for the army, trained military pilots, and funded airfield construction and an aviation research institute.

Other European countries also established such funds. Sport aviation languished as the era of great races and tournaments ended and accidents cooled public enthusiasm for air transport. In the absence of substantial sport or commercial markets, the supporters of military aviation moulded popular attitudes to benefit their cause. Aircraft manufacturers, indissolubly tied to the military through contracts by 1912, sponsored civilian aviators, whom the press lionized as defenders of national honour. Designers and manufacturers like the Farman and Voisin brothers, Louis Breguet, and Louis Béchereau of SPAD in France; Anthony Fokker, Robert Thelen, and Ernst Heinkel in Germany; Geoffrey de Havilland and T. O. M. Sopwith in Britain; and engine firms like Gnome and Renault in France and Daimler in Germany would form the nucleus of the wartime aviation industry.

The competition for national superiority in aviation had cultural and imperial overtones. Germans believed that the Zeppelin symbolized their presumed cultural supremacy, while Frenchmen presumed that the initiative necessary to use aeroplanes accorded with traditional Gallic audacity. British aerial advocates like Rudyard Kipling viewed the aeroplane as a tool to unify the empire and to impress white superiority and control on non-white, colonial populations. While the British contemplated using aircraft to police the empire, the French and Italians actually used aeroplanes in campaigns in North Africa in 1911 and 1912. Flight thus assumed nationalist, imperialist, and militarist characteristics by 1914.

The Zeppelin generated unrealistic expectations in the German general staff that its minuscule fleet of some ten airships could deliver a telling first strike against enemies. The aeroplane had generally inspired much popular excitement but not such apocalyptic expectations, since mass destruction clearly lay beyond the capabilities of the fragile craft of the day. Yet designers Gianni Caproni in Italy and Igor Sikorsky in Russia were creating multi-engined craft capable of bombing by 1914.

The literature of the pre-war era foretold nearly every role that aircraft would play in the First World War, including the potentially devastating impact on national morale of bombing civilian targets. Such attitudes anticipated Italian aerial theorist Giulio Douhet's post-war advocacy of the bombing of civilian populations to force nations to defeat. The intimate connections between the civilian and military arenas in aviation provided an appropriate context for a weapon that would both galvanize and directly threaten civilians in the coming war.

The public of the pre-war era already considered aviators heroes, masters of technology in the conquest of the heavens. A new warrior élite arose in the air services of Europe, exemplified by the dashing and audacious 'Lieutenant Daedalus Icarus Brown', Royal Flying Corps pilot of 'fame and renown' proclaimed in British doggerel.

Most armies (and navies) emphasized the development of slow, stable aircraft for reconnaissance. Pre-war civilian and military experiments had practically ignored the realm of aerial combat in favour of reconnaissance and bombing. Ironically the coming war would catapult the pre-war sport aviator's small, speedy, and manoeuvrable aeroplane, now armed, back into the forefront of public imagination, as the vehicle of the war's greatest individual heroes, the air aces, the heirs of pre-war daredevil sport aviators. Wartime air combat would reintroduce aspects of sport aviation that the pre-war military had sought to eradicate—the emphasis on individual exploits and the high performance aeroplane occasionally dangerous even to its own pilots.

In August 1914 the European powers went to war with rudimentary air services, each comprising at most a few thousand personnel and 200–300 air-

Reconnaissance 1914

267

Aircraft in use in 1915, a German Fokker monoplane fighter (foreground) and a French Caudron bomber, on display in Paris in 1917. All sides in the conflict displayed captured aircraft as trophies in museums or in public.

craft, and embryonic aviation industries. During the war of movement on the western and eastern fronts, aeroplanes delivered valuable information. When the conflict on the western front settled into a trench stalemate, the aeroplane became the sole mobile means of reconnaissance and artillery spotting, although it required further advances in photography and wireless telegraphy to enhance its observation capability. The aeroplane further demonstrated potential for bombing and aerial combat in the hands of aggressive British and French pilots, who were not content merely to perform their military duty of observation.

Logistics and production proved critical, as everywhere the war's onset disrupted both for some two months. In the west units moved by rail and primarily by truck. In the east Russian and Austro-Hungarian units often used horse or oxcarts for transport—pairing the most modern of inventions with the most ancient means of conveyance. The French responded most rapidly to the challenge of the unexpectedly high attrition of men and machines by standardizing types and placing priority on aircraft and particularly engine production in the autumn. The Germans followed suit in the winter. British production remained small scale, more comparable to that of Russia or Austria-Hungary, though the two eastern empires lacked Britain's industrial potential.

In October 1914, a French artilleryman, pointing to a German plane near Albert, commented to a British reporter, 'There is that wretched bird which haunts us.' The bird of war had spread its wings, casting its shadow over the battlefields of Europe. In 1915 it would transmogrify into a bird of prey with fierce talons, transforming the skies, like the earth and seas below, into an arena of mortal combat.

In 1915 air arms became more sophisticated, adapting types to perform specialized functions at the front and requiring greater technological and industrial mobilization to meet the demand for new and improved *matériel*. Bombardment and pursuit, the air arm's new roles, necessitated the adaptation of the most suitable aircraft types available—light planes such as Moranes, Nieuports, and Fokkers for fighting and heavier ones such as Voisins and Aviatiks for bombing. Russia, Italy, and Germany had a few operational large planes—Sikorskys, Capronis, and Gothas—whose range and load indicated their potential for development as strategic bombers with more powerful engines.

Yet in 1915 only the German dirigible could carry enough bombs and climb fast and high enough to evade aerial interception, thus making strategic raids possible. England consequently experienced its first air raids. The giants were still vulnerable to ground fire and weather, and they failed to deliver a telling blow, similar to the failure of an inadequate submarine fleet to drive Britain from the war in 1917. The German army removed the costly monsters—irresistible targets for enemy artillery—from the western front and relegated them to the less populous skies over the broader eastern front. The German navy continued to use dirigibles successfully as scouts for the fleet. All powers, including Italy, which entered the war in May 1915, employed seaplanes or flying boats over the North, Black, and Adriatic seas.

The major aerial development of 1915 was the beginning of fighter aviation, heralded first by Frenchman Roland Garros's use of a fixed forward-firing machine gun with only a deflector to protect his propeller, and then Fokker's adaptation of a synchronizing gear to mount a gun on his monoplane. By the end of the year an effective fighter required speed and manœuvrability as well as fixed forward-firing machine guns. The early pursuit pilots—Max Immelmann, Oswald Boelcke, Georges

Bombers and fighters 1915

A Fokker advertisement depicting a close-up view of a German fighter pilot in his Fokker monoplane, its synchronized machine gun and propeller, with Germany's highest medal, *le pour le mérite*, in the top left corner.

Guynemer, and Lanoe Hawker—though varied in temperament, displayed tenacity, determination, courage, and aggressiveness. This new breed of technological warrior evolved new fighting tactics and recommended improvements for pursuit planes. Their efforts would make the skies over Europe's battlefields far more dangerous in the coming year.

The advent of true aerial warfare 1916

A post-war photograph of marshal of the Royal Air Force Sir Hugh M. Trenchard, wartime commander of the Royal Flying Corps from 1915 to 1917 and then of the RAF's independent bombing force in 1918, reviewing RAF apprentices.

Historians have considered 1916 a watershed in the First World War, as the battles of Verdun and the Somme dashed both sides' hopes for imminent victory. These battles also marked the true beginning of aerial warfare, as both sides committed themselves to the development of larger air arms to attain aerial superiority. Aerial warfare in 1916 was as much a technological and industrial as a military affair. Although political and administrative friction marred the aviation mobilization of all the powers, France was winning the race for industrial mobilization. Its aero engine production far outdistanced all other powers because of its early and extensive mobilization of the automotive industry to build a diversity of engines, in particular the revolutionary Hispano-Suiza V8. Germany, strapped by material and manpower shortages, could not match the Entente's industrial superiority in general and its engine

production in particular. It could only hope to counter through superior aircraft technology, such as Hugo Junkers's all-metal aeroplane with cantilever wing and the gigantic R-planes of 1915, and the Albatros fighter of 1916.

The aerial strategies of the major powers on the western front reflected these industrial realities and their basic military strategies. British and French air policies were offensive, and Royal Flying Corps chief General Hugh 'Boom' Trenchard pursued the air offensive more unrelentingly and inflexibly than the French. The Germans husbanded their resources, fought defensively, and concentrated their aviation forces to seek an aerial mastery limited in time and space.

In 1916 the air services provided Europe with its most revered heroes—youthful aces who epitomized the national will to sacrifice. Boelcke, a master flier and codifier of aerial tactics, crashed to his death in October with forty victories, occasioning national mourning and eulogies emphasizing his role as an inspiration to German youth. The era of the individual ace would last into 1917, but the individual would have less impact in the growing war of attrition in the air. In 1917 industrial mobilization would become even more critical for aviation, for the aeroplane had become indispensable to the conduct of the war.

In 1917 the aeroplane became a multifaceted weapon of war, with the evolution of massed fighter tactics over the western and then the Italian fronts, of close air support and tactical raids, and of the German strategic bombing campaign against Britain. The Royal Flying Corps, in its effort to carry the fighter and bomber war to the Germans, suffered cruel losses among inadequately trained new aircrew in the spring and summer, epitomized in the 'Bloody April' of legend. The Royal Flying Corps command played down the significance of the high losses, while touting them as proof of the service's contribution to the war effort. It replaced the losses with men from the dominions, took delivery of three new fighters—the Sopwith Camel, the SE5, and the Bristol Fighter—that would serve well to the end of the war, and surmounted the crisis by the autumn.

Attrition in the air 1917

The French pursued a more circumspect policy in order to conserve dwindling manpower, as the army confined itself to limited offensive actions after the Chemin des Dames débâcle of May 1917. Still, élite fighter units like the Cigognes (the Storks) relentlessly pursued the 'Boche'. Yet the French fighter pilots' concept of air combat as a solo knightly affair became increasingly detrimental to the effectiveness of their fighter units. In the aerial environment of 1917, very few individuals were capable of surviving, much less killing, alone, as the demise of lone aces Albert Ball, Guynemer, and Werner Voss demonstrated. The great British and German aces who survived into 1918—Edward Mannock, James McCudden, and the 'Red Baron' Manfred von Richthofen—were expert squadron leaders. The great French aces, like Charles Nungesser and René Fonck, remained loners, surviving and killing against the odds. But mass, not individuals, determined the course of the war in the air as it did on the ground. British and German fighter pilots might acknowledge the notion of being a new military aristocracy. Yet British fighter pilots combined this with a faith in teamwork derived from the public schoolboy's perception of aerial combat as a team sport, while the Germans, many of whom were professional soldiers, believed in discipline. Such cultural attitudes facilitated an effective transition to mass aerial combat, epitomized in German fighter 'circuses' comprising as many as four squadrons with sixty aeroplanes.

By 1917 the German and British commands judged ground attacks from low-flying aircraft to be a powerful weapon in battle. British fighters assumed the responsibility of ground attack along with army co-operation planes in random, uncoordinated, and individual strikes. Such attacks failed to affect the mass battlefield despite high losses of aircrew. The Germans developed specialized armoured ground attack planes and highly manoeuvrable two-seater fighters flown by non-commissioned officer crews in masses of up to thirty planes for devastatingly effective trench strafing.

In 1917 attrition and shortages forced increased aircraft production, accompanied by heightened political strife in Britain and France. Among the

The 'Red Baron,' Capt. Manfred von Richthofen (centre), surrounded by squadron mates (*from left to right*) Sergeant Major Sebastian Festner, Lieut. Karl Emil Schaefer, Manfred's brother Lothar, a lieutenant, and Lieut. Kurt Wolff, early in 1918. Only Lothar would survive the war, to be killed in an aeroplane crash in the 1920s.

lesser aerial powers, Italy's aerial mobilization emphasized rigorous standardization to compensate for severe material shortages. The Russian aerial effort, never substantial except for the squadron of Igor Sikorsky's giant four-engined reconnaissance bombers, disintegrated in revolution. Austria-Hungary, beset by overwhelming shortages, slid toward collapse. An aerial presence for the United States, which entered the war in April, lay in the future, and only with the help of its allies in training and aircraft.

The evolution of air power demonstrated the signal importance of aero engines in 1917. All three major powers suffered crises of engine production. France solved its problem of perfecting and producing *en masse* higher horsepower versions of its vaunted Hispano-Suiza V8 engine which powered French SPAD and British SE5A fighters. Neither Britain nor Germany could overcome more fundamental problems of inadequate engine production, and consequently by the end of the war France would manufacture as many engines as Britain and Germany combined.

The French and British administrations of aviation were highly politicized. French governmental instability and bureaucratic bifurcation between the high command and the War Ministry condemned aviation to constant changes and conflicts, until Georges Clemenceau as prime minister and Philippe Pétain as commander-in-chief achieved stability in the late autumn

A Royal Air Force SE-5A squadron at the front, including pilots, ground crew, and pets, including a goat. The SE-5A, powered by a variety of engines but preferably the Hispano Suiza V8, was the RAF's standard first-line single-seat fighter plane throughout 1918.

of 1917. In Britain the War Office and the Admiralty struggled fiercely for aviation resources. Ultimately, Lloyd George's government formed a separate air force to resolve the conflict and to give the prime minister an ally in his struggle with the generals over strategic policy. Consequently, in April 1918 the Royal Air Force, which included an Independent Force intended for strategic bombing, became the first autonomous air arm, although in practice its operations changed little.

Compared with those of the constitutional governments, the German military aviation bureaucracy was a paragon of stability, as the same officers—Colonel Hermann von der Leith-Thomsen and Lieutenant Colonel Wilhelm Siegert, with the addition of General Ernst Wilhelm von Hoeppner in 1916 as commanding general of the air forces—continued in control of aviation to the end of the war. Facing irremediable shortages of material and manpower, the German air arm followed the army's Hindenburg mobilization programme of autumn 1916 with another of its own, the *Amerikaprogramme* of 1917, in anticipation of ever worsening odds.

Over the western front, the lack of co-ordination between the British and French enabled the German air arm to survive despite the Entente's increasing numerical superiority in 1917. Yet the entry into the war in April 1917 of a United States woefully unprepared in aviation necessitated a more co-ordinated allocation of all resources in order to equip an American air service for future action.

Air power's contribution to final victory

In 1918 aviation played a significant role in the outcome of the war. The sheer numbers of aircraft on the western front in 1918, more than 8,000 in total on all sides, indicated that the air war in general, and aerial combat in particular, had become a mass struggle of attrition. Air services had grown to 90,000–300,000 men and 2,000–3,000 aeroplanes at the front in 1918, while national aviation industries employed hundreds of thousands of workers to manufacture thousands of planes and engines monthly.

Not only had the basic tactical units such as the squadron expanded, but also these units were subsumed under increasingly larger ones, like the German fighter circuses of sixty planes, in the attempt to achieve aerial superiority. In 1918 France achieved ultimate concentration with its aerial division of more than 700 bombers—the superlative Breguet 14, fast, sturdy, and well armed—and fighters, the powerful SPAD 13, intended for aggressive tactical raids over German lines. Even German formations equipped with the legendary Fokker D7, the war's ultimate fighter produced in quantity, could not prevent the incursions of such Entente numerical superiority. Over the Italian front, waves of thirty to forty Caproni trimotored biplane bombers supported infantry attacks or staged long-distance raids across the Adriatic, sometimes flying only 12 yards above the waves to evade anti-aircraft defences.

These air arms did not determine the outcome of the war; that was decided on the earth's surface. Fighters, except when pressed into service for ground attack, played an indirect role in the ground war by protecting or attacking reconnaissance planes and bombers, while strategic bombing remained too embryonic to affect the outcome of the war.

The aeroplane established its real significance in support of the army on the battlefield. Reconnaissance made it difficult for armies to achieve surprise and forced the movement of men and *matériel* behind the lines at night. The French and British two-seater biplanes that performed these missions were obsolescent and thus fell prey to enemy fighters until the arrival in 1918 of types like the Salmson 2A2. The Germans, in contrast, sent expert crews

Installing a French Renault 300 hp twelve-cylinder engine in a Breguet 14 air frame. This combination of superlative engine and airframe gave the French Aerial Division of 1918 a powerful and effective tactical day bomber.

alone and at high altitude in superior Rumpler and DFW biplanes, formidable opponents even for highly skilled fighter pilots. In 1917 and 1918 aircraft staged increasingly aggressive strikes against troops and supplies on and behind the battlefield. German battle fliers, in concentrations of thirty aircraft operating at 100 yards altitude, attacked enemy batteries, strong points, and infantry reserves with machine guns, grenades, and light fragmentation bombs.

Control of the skies over the battlefield had become essential to victory in the First World War. Aircraft had served on all fronts. Politicians and commanders such as the British minister of munitions, Winston Churchill, the German first quartermaster general, Erich Ludendorff, and the French commander-in-chief, Philippe Pétain, recognized the 'capital' importance of air power when used in mass. The war ended with the British poised to begin bombing Berlin with the giant Handley-Page V-1500 bomber. The value of strategic bombing remained unproven, but the notion that the bombing of civilians could undermine their morale and potentially end wars was established in the minds of some practitioners and theorists of aviation. The fighter pilots of 1914–18 evolved the basic techniques of aerial combat still employed today and some became the commanders in the second Great War. In both strategy and tactics the air war of 1914–18 portended the larger aerial struggle of 1939–45.

Within two years of the war, all of the aviation arms had been demobilized, the losers by the treaties of peace, the winners by the absence of war. The aviation industry shrank with the diminishing orders from the military. Some fliers and industrialists refocused on civilian air transport which the military in some countries had helped to initiate; others remained in the military air arms of Britain and France that concentrated on policing the far reaches of their empires.

The legacy of wartime aviation, in the sole official history of the air war, the English multi-volume work, *The War in the Air*, and in biographies, combat reminiscences, and popular works, reinforced the emphasis on the heroic and individual. The eulogy of aerial heroes and the concentration on individual aerial combat harked back to ideals of pre-industrial warfare and mythical warriors of the past that had been popular just before the war and made the war and its modern technology easier to accept. The romanticization of the exploits of this new warrior élite enabled an extension of national myths into the warfare of the industrial era, in which the new military élite came primarily from the middle class.

The very circumstances of the First World War encouraged a mythologizing of the air war into a single image of individual combat. Mass slaughter on an unprecedented scale rendered individuals insignificant. Aerial heroes provided a much-needed, though misleading, affirmation of the importance of the individual and of youth in a slaughter of both. The fighter pilots consequently became not only the symbols of aviation but also the ultimate heroes of the First World War.

Unlike the French, Germans or Americans, the British tended to eschew mass cemeteries in favour of smaller, more intimate plots, redolent of country churchyards. The massive memorials to the missing on the Somme and at Ypres were therefore unusual. The latter, Reginald Blomfield's Menin Gate, commemorates over 54,000 British soldiers who have no known grave, and was unveiled in 1927.

Although the conduct of the war was shaped by industrialization, its commemoration more often relied on rural motifs. The poppy, found on both sides of the line on the western front, was appropriated by the British. In 1933 the Women's Co-operative Movement produced white poppies to symbolize the dead of both sides and as a pledge for peace.

Yet the concentration on individual exploits gave an archaic, anachronistic image to the newest combat arm, which epitomized the new 'total warfare' in its meshing of the military, political, technological, and industrial sectors. It also tended to obscure the extent of the casualties in the war of attrition in the sky. Of more than 18,000 aircrew trained in France between 1914 and 1919, 39 per cent fell casualty, while more than 50 per cent of 22,000 British pilots became casualties. German casualties, if harder to document, were certainly similar. French infantry losses in the first six months of 1918 totalled 51 per cent of effectives, while French pilot losses reached 71 per cent. The greatest sources of casualties were accidents at the front and training in the rear.

Combat flying was no sport or game. It was a deadly, ruthless, and capricious business, in which a man's life depended not only upon his skill and luck, but also on aeroplanes whose engines failed, guns jammed, and wings broke with distressing frequency. Occupational hazards like nerves and flying fatigue reflected the stress of war flying. The Irishman Edward Mannock, Britain's highest-scoring ace, suffered so severely from nervous strain in 1918 that he was often sick before patrols. Shaking hands and tearful outbursts disclosed Mannock's stress, occasioned not only by his conviction that he would die and his fear of burning to death, but also by recurring problems with his aeroplane. He was shot down in flames from ground fire in the summer of 1918. Aerial combat was exhilarating and intoxicating, but nerve-racking and frightening as well.

The emphasis on individual combat also masked a further legacy of the war, the myth of strategic bombing of civilian populations. The air weapon was truly the child of the era of total war, which conflated civilian and military targets and deemed the bombing of women and children an acceptable means of winning a war. The experience of the First World War provided little evidence of civilian collapse under aerial bombardment beyond some panic in London during early German air attacks. Yet the presumption of civilian vulnerability to aerial bombardment persisted. These images—the romantic idealization of individual aerial combat rooted in the past and the brutal vision of massive civilian destruction foreshadowing the future—constituted a dual legacy for air power in the twentieth century.

CHAPTER 21

The Allied Victories, 1918

TIM TRAVERS

A t the beginning of 1918, the balance of the war shifted against the allies. The Russian Revolution, the defeat in Italy at Caporetto, the French mutinies of 1917, declining allied manpower, and the exhaustion of British forces after Passchendaele, all pointed to considerable problems. So, in early 1918, the French and British decided to go on the defensive on the western front, and wait for sufficient Americans to arrive, together with greater production of tanks, planes, and other mechanical means, before once more going on the offensive. But this future decisive offensive was generally expected to take place in 1919. How then did the allies essentially win the war on the western front in 1918?

The allied victories on the western front in 1918 really occurred in six critical stages. These were, first, halting the massive German 1918 spring offensives; secondly, mounting the decisive French counter-offensive at the Marne on 18 July; thirdly, the successful Australian/Canadian/British Amiens offensive of 8 August; fourthly, the continuing arrival of the American Expeditionary Force (AEF); fifthly, the sweeping allied offensives of late September; and lastly, the final allied pursuit of the retreating German army in October and early November, leading to the armistice of 11 November 1918.

Counter-attack on the Marne

The German spring offensives between March and June all ran out of energy after initial successes. General Ludendorff, at German headquarters, con-

ceived of these offensives as drawing allied reserves away from the Flanders region, where he intended to launch the war-winning 'Hagen' attack and drive the British Expeditionary Force (BEF) into the sea. Now, Ludendorff tried again, with an offensive in the Marne area, planned for mid-July, threatening Paris and Reims. However, time was now critical, since by the middle of June the AEF already consisted of 20 large-size divisions in France, and more American troops were pouring into Europe at the rate of 250,000 per month. Very shortly the German advantage in numbers was going to be reversed, but at the Marne in July, there were still 33 French divisions facing 45 German divisions, although these were under strength. Moreover, the German army was starting to run out of artillery, so that training batteries had to be included in the 6,353 guns assembled for the Marne offensive. Even so, the German superiority of 2 : 1 in artillery was the lowest of any of the previous German attacks. More significantly, the French army, commanded by General Pétain, soon learned the 15 July date of the German attack through intelligence sources, and surprise was lost through the sheer difficulty of concealing an offensive which required an artillery ammunition approach route every 125 yards. Pétain had also learned the need to adopt a defence-indepth system, and he persuaded the French 4th Army commanded by General Gouraud to accept this, although the French 5th Army did not. Meanwhile, the French artillery readied a counter-preparation against the German infantry, rather than on the German batteries, since there were not enough guns to do both.

The British retreat during the German March offensive. The date is 24 March 1918 at Omiecourt, and British soldiers have set stores and huts on fire. In the foreground, horse teams are moving to hitch up the guns and pull out. Despite the bustle, there is order and no sign of panic.

On the night of 14 July, soon after midnight, one of the first German shells cut the power to General Gouraud's headquarters. Despite the darkness, Gouraud was pleased, for the shell confirmed the accuracy of French predictions: 'Never has a cannon shot given me so much pleasure.' The German offensive rapidly became bogged down, and then, on 18 July, the French counter-offensive began. This attack had been in preparation for some time, originally simply a limited assault on Soissons, but then developed by General Mangin, of the 10th Army, into a major offensive against the flank of the Marne salient.

Ironically, the limited German success of 15 July benefited the French counter-offensive by further deepening the salient. The French attacked with 10th and 6th Armies (including American and British divisions), 750 tanks, and a 2:1 superiority in artillery. The attack was a surprise, without previous artillery registration, but with a thick creeping barrage to support the infantry, and made strong initial gains. Artillery was the key to success, with one heavy shell per 1.27 yards of ground, and three field artillery shells per yard. As with all other operations, later attacks were more difficult, but French and allied divisions continued the offensive until early August.

The French counter-offensive was decisive in shifting the balance of the war against the German army. It is notable that on 20 July Ludendorff called off the 'Hagen' offensive, and on 24 July General Foch, now commander-in-chief of allied armies on the western front, directed his armies to go on the offensive. The tide had turned, and the German army would remain on the defensive to the end of the war. However, 18 July has been overshadowed by the subsequent Amiens offensive of 8 August, and historians have tended to underrate the fighting ability of the French army in 1918. Yet French casualties between 15 July and 5 August amounted to 95,165, and another 100,000 in August. The French 10th Army, spearhead of the 18 July attack, suffered over 108,000 casualties between 18 July and the end of the war, including 13,000 killed. Between 1 July and 15 September, total French casualties amounted to around 279,000. BEF casualties were higher, and the French army was still influenced by the mutinies of 1917, but it was not a spent force in 1918.

Nevertheless, other statistics tell an even more important story in regard to the German army. The result of the German offensives between March and July was primarily the capture of ground, which all had to be defended. Moreover, the strain on the German army was very great, and total German casualties for this period amounted to nearly 1 million men, including 125,000 dead, and 100,000 missing. Just as difficult for the German army was a steep decline in morale. German soldiers, short of supplies, plundered enemy supplies and alcohol where possible, while many German soldiers took the opportunity to desert or avoid front-line duty. Then, in June and July, the influenza epidemic hit the German army, with more than half a million cases. The result was seriously depleted German divisions by July 1918, so that on 1 August the German 2nd Army reported that, of its 13 divisions, 2

THE ALLIED VICTORIES, 1918

were fit, 5 were only good for defence, 3 could hardly defend, and 3 needed relief. Battalion strength was down to around 200 rifles, with some 15 to 20 light machine guns, and few NCOs and officers. It can be argued, therefore, that the German army on the western front really lost the war between March and July through the costly failure of its own offensives. This certainly did not mean that the German army stopped fighting; indeed another 420,000 Germans were killed and wounded between July and the armistice. As part of this process, the Amiens offensive of 8 August was another large step toward German defeat.

The next stage of the allied victories, therefore, was the Amiens infantry, artillery, tank, and air offensive of 8 August. Organized in the 4th Army by General Rawlinson, Amiens showed what a carefully planned combined-arms assault could achieve. Deception measures and strict secrecy produced surprise, especially important because the Australian and Canadian Corps were spearheading the operation, and the German army knew these units as the premier attack troops in the BEF. The infantry were supported by more firepower than before, in the shape of Lewis guns, mortars, machine guns, and smoke grenades. The artillery calibrated behind the lines, and pre-registered onto enemy batteries and other targets with accurate survey methods developed in 1917. Ninety-five per cent of the German guns had been identified before the battle began, so that German counter-preparation would not be a problem. Around 1,900 planes gained air supremacy, and partially covered the noise of 342 Mark V tanks, 72 Medium A tanks, plus troop-carrying and supply tanks, as they arrived at the start line. Mist, smoke, and darkness covered the 4.20 a.m. start, which began with the crash of 2,000 guns and howitzers. The attack was also assisted by a German relief rotation during the night, low German morale, and sparse German defences.

Lieutenant Colonel Cy Peck, commanding 16th Battalion in 1 Canadian Division, recalled the moment: 'Dense fog hung over the land. Bn. sprang forward with eagerness at zero hour . . . Little opposition for first mile. Very thick pall of smoke . . . Piper Paul killed beside me. Bn. moved steadily ahead, capturing ridge after ridge. Temporarily held up at Aubercourt. Tank relieved situation. Final objective captured about 7.15 a.m.' In fact, the attack was amazingly successful, advancing 6 to 8 miles on the first day, although progress on the flanks was much slower. On the following days, further progress was made, but at greater cost, as Foch and Haig, the BEF commander-in-chief, pressed Rawlinson to make the battle a deeper one than he wished. Tanks and planes were sacrificed to keep the attack going: for example, only 38 tanks were 'runners' on the fourth day, while 96 planes were lost on 8 August, and 45 the next day, largely through attempts to destroy the Somme bridges.

In fact it was on 10 August that Captain West, flying a contact patrol near Roye, earned a remarkable Victoria Cross: 'Just as he [West] turned to fly back to our lines he was attacked by 7 Fokker biplanes. With almost his first

Amiens, 8 August 1918

Mark V 5th Battalion tanks going forward on 10 August 1918 to support the allied offensive at Amiens. Due to the heat and gases inside, some of the tank crews are outside and the hatchways are open. A dead horse and its cart block the road, an officer directs traffic, and German prisoners move to the rear.

burst, one of the hostile machines . . . shot his left leg off . . . with three explosive bullets. In spite of the fact that Capt. West's leg fell helpless amongst the controls, and he was wounded in the right foot, he managed to fly his machine back and land it within our lines.' On landing, Captain West also insisted on making his report before receiving medical help.

Hurried and uncoordinated starts at Amiens on the days following 8 August produced heavier than necessary infantry casualties. Moreover, the attack was reaching the old Somme battlefield, where advances were difficult. Finally, eighteen German reserve divisions had moved in to support the defence. Therefore, under pressure from the Canadian Corps commander, Currie, Rawlinson persuaded Haig to end the offensive on 11 August. However, the Amiens success was not exploited on the flanks, where the BEF's weak III Corps to the north ran into serious problems, while Debeney's French 1st Army to the south did not press forward. Also, Rawlinson's 4th Army headquarters held back the only available BEF reserve, 32 Division, until too late to make a difference. On the other hand, 8 August produced a strong reaction at German headquarters. Ludendorff termed it the 'black day' of the German army, while the official German monograph stated: 'As the sun set on the 8th August on the battlefield the greatest defeat which the

German Army had suffered since the beginning of the war was an accomplished fact.'

Following Amiens, Foch now pressed for a series of allied attacks, to be achieved as rapidly as possible. Before the war, Foch had been the apostle of the attack at all costs, and now the situation and the idea seemed to finally coincide. But how to attack? Foch wished for offensives against specific objectives, while Haig was more interested in a general advance along the line. Later in August, Haig suggested converging offensives toward Mezières in the south, and Saint-Quentin/Cambrai in the north, which Foch accepted. But the reality of the situation was that, until the Americans were ready, the strongest allied forces were in the centre of the line, primarily the BEF armies, and therefore that is where the major blows had to be struck. So, to exploit the damage done by Amiens, the BEF's 3rd and 1st armies, and the French 10th and 6th armies, took part in large-scale attacks in the Albert/Bapaume area from 21 August. Notable feats of arms included the Australian

Breaking the Hindenburg line

A scene during the opening day of the Arras offensive of 21 August 1918. This railway line near Achiet-le-Petit in the Bapaume area has been hit by British artillery fire, and a dead soldier lies beside the tracks. The debris of battle marks a heavily contested German defence line.

capture of Mont Saint-Quentin on 1 September. This awkward village was taken via a half-hour storm of mortars and howitzers, then a rush by the infantry, armed with Lewis guns and rifle grenades. And in early September, the Canadian Corps took the Drocourt–Quéant line through an extremely heavy barrage of 740 guns, tank support at critical moments, heavy fighting by the infantry armed with Lewis guns and rifle grenades, and poor morale among some of the defenders.

Now the war was poised to move to the next critical stage of storming the Hindenburg line, which was to be part of a sequential series of four large-scale allied offensives in late September. Foch followed Haig's 'converging offensives' idea, focusing on the Laon bulge in the centre, but Foch also wanted to spread out the German defence to the greatest extent, so that German reserves could not be shifted around. Thus, Foch ordered a giant drive forward from the Meuse to the North Sea. On 26 September, the American 1st Army and the French 4th would attack towards the Mezières–Sedan area. On 27 September, the BEF's 1st and 3rd armies would attack towards the Cambrai area. On 28 September, the Flanders group of Belgian, French, and British armies would aim at Ghent and also move along the coast. Finally, on 29 September, the BEF's 4th and French 1st armies would attack towards the Busigny area.

In such a massive undertaking, only certain scenes can be picked out. The first scene concerns the successful reduction of the Saint-Mihiel salient by the AEF between 12 and 18 September, and then a shift over to engage in the less fortunate Meuse–Argonne offensive, from 26 September to the end of the war. Perhaps the AEF did not win the war for the allies, but they provided the vital edge in manpower, with over 2 million American troops in France by the end of November. It was the anticipation of this steady accumulation of AEF troops that forced the German army into their ultimately ill-fated spring offensives. The arrival of the AEF produced an enormous psychological boost for the allies, and ensured an eventual allied victory, even if the raw and inexperienced performance of the AEF in the field was understandably flawed at times.

A second scene involves the Canadian Corps of the 1st Army, and their assault on the Canal du Nord on 27 September. Currie, the corps commander, planned a risky rush across the 2,600-yard dry part of the canal by two divisions, then a fan out by two more divisions. Despite efforts by his army commander General Horne to get him to change the plan, Currie refused. The attack was launched at 5.20 a.m. (early attacks were now the rule, making use of darkness to shield the troops from machine guns), and relied heavily on the artillery. Counter-battery fire achieved an 80 per cent success rate, against 230 German guns, while the zero hour creeping barrage paralysed the German defences. As one gunner noted: 'all you could see for miles and miles along the front was the flashing of guns, and Fritzie's line was a mass of smoke and bursting shells.' The infantry found the canal no obstacle: jumping down to the dry bed they set up scaling ladders on the far side and clam-

bered up the bank. Where there were not enough ladders, the men simply climbed on each other's shoulders.

Few tanks were available, so machine guns were suppressed by the barrage and by Lewis guns and rifle fire. By evening, most objectives had been reached, and the Canal du Nord line was broken. German defence was patchy, and morale was low in some areas. One observer recalled 'As the barrage was lifting back like the rolling away of a mist I could see Germans coming on the run toward our lines and lifting their hands to each man they met.' A German prisoner shouted in English to his captors: 'You don't know it, but the war's over.' This was clearly premature since the next day saw German counter-attacks, and, as the Canadian Corps struggled forward in somewhat disorganized attacks over the next few days, the German machine gun defence often decimated them. 'We have never known the Boche fight harder,' wrote Currie on 4 October, although Cambrai fell by 9 October. The fighting was really attrition warfare, and the Canadian Corps took 30,806 casualties between 22 August and 11 October. This stage of the war was being won, but at a high cost.

A third scene concerns the key offensive by the 4th Army on the Hinden-

Infantry of 4 Canadian Division move steadily forward on 27 September 1918 during the Canal du Nord offensive. Canadian and Australian troops were often used as the spearhead of allied offensives during the late summer and autumn of 1918.

burg and Beaurevoir lines, including the Saint-Quentin canal, on 29 September. The attack was organized by the Australian Corps commander, Monash, whose corps formed part of the 4th Army. Like the Canal du Nord, Monash planned an ambitious 6,000-yard dash across the narrow covered portion of the canal by two American divisions, and then a fan-out, as well as a drive through the centre by two Australian divisions who would leapfrog through the Americans and capture the final Beaurevoir line. Unhappy with the plan, Rawlinson doubled the frontage to 10,000 yards by including 46 Division to the south, who would have to cross the water-filled portion of the canal by means of life rafts, life belts, ladders, boats, and ropes. Then, 32 Division would pass through and exploit. Rawlinson also nearly doubled the number of tanks allotted, to 162 (general headquarters had reserved most of the tanks for the 4th Army), and added Whippet tanks and armoured cars. Because the Hindenburg line featured five lines of trenches, which were heavily wired, the artillery preparation by 1,637 guns would be deliberate, over four days, in order to cut wire, break down defences, especially opposite 46 Division, and suppress enemy artillery and machine guns. Also used for the first time by the BEF were 30,000 BB shells (mustard gas). Finally, a captured map of the German defences gave the artillery a valuable number of specific targets.

Across most of the covered part of the canal at 5.50 a.m. on 29 September, the heavy creeping barrage and the tanks helped the infantry to gain their objectives. But the later leapfrog Australian divisions faced heavy machine gun fire, as reported by tank B53 at 6.30 p.m. on 29 September: 'During my progress the front of the tank was swept by a hail of MG bullets from numerous positions both in the trench positions in front of [Cabaret Wood] Farm and from the Farm itself . . . My left gun using case shot knocked out a MG & gunners in rear of trench, my right gun using steel shot kept down fire of MGs and Field Guns & I observed many hits from my own front Machine Gun among the enemy in trench. During my progress . . . my tank was hit twice in the R. Sponson, taking the door away.' In fact, it was not unusual for there to be 200 German machine guns or more covering individual villages and strong points, and these could rarely be destroyed by the artillery. So it was up to the tanks or infantry to deal with these formidable defences. Further south, the unusual crossing of the water-filled canal by 46 Division was a remarkable feat of arms. Assisted by a very good creeping barrage, and dense mist, the leading infantry brigade cleared its way to the canal and then stormed across, followed by other brigades and 32 Division. Then, for the next six days, the battle continued, with too much rush and too many uncoordinated attacks, so that losses were heavy. Indeed, between 8 August and 5 October, the Australian Corps, as part of the 4th Army, had taken 25,588 casualties, and there was Australian resistance to their constant attack role. Thus they were withdrawn from the line on 5 October.

With the breaking of the Hindenburg line and other defences by the late September offensives, the allies moved into the final stage of the war on the

Facing: Canadian troops advancing through the ruins of Cambrai on 9 October 1918. Allied infantry had entered Cambrai during the night, and now the main concern was to defuse mines and booby traps, as well as fighting fires that may have been set by German demolition teams.

Ludendorff seeks an armistice

western front. But already on 28 September, Ludendorff had decided that an armistice was necessary to save his dwindling army, and Field Marshal Hindenburg agreed. The day before, 27 September, Germany's ally Bulgaria had asked for an armistice following the battle of Monastir-Doiron. Then, in late October, the Italian front, stable since the failed Austrian Piave offensive in June, went into action. The joint Italian-French-British offensive of 24 October saw a double envelopment at Vittorio Veneto that hastened the Austrians to defeat and an armistice on 3 November. Turkey also agreed to peace terms, on 30 October.

Germany's allies were falling fast, but on the western front there was still the final stage of the pursuit from mid-October to the eventual armistice line. The enemy went into a general retreat, especially in front of the BEF's 1st, 3rd, and 4th armies. Normally, there was a daily German retreat, with German field and heavy guns covering each other's retirements, while machine guns, single guns, and mortars covered the infantry withdrawal. The allied response was to rely on their artillery, as one officer wrote: 'The Infantry have no difficulty in reaching their objectives up to the limits of the creeping barrage. The Germans are then captured, killed, or have retreated to the next offensive line, possibly 6,000 yards in the rear. The Infantry then advance this far . . . and are then brought to a standstill against the next line.' Allied problems included logistics, and war-weariness, as a soldier from the French 5 Division recalled: 'Everyone was depressed, because we knew that the Boches had asked for an armistice and we were hoping that news would come before our turn came to go back in line. Alas, there was none, and each of us, feeling the end near, was afraid of dying so close to the end.' And from the German side, on 18 October, Crown Prince Rupprecht wrote that his troops were no longer dependable, and artillery was being lost 'from lack of horses'.

At last, at 11 a.m. on 11 November 1918, the guns fell silent. It was on the western front that the war had been won, but how had these allied victories come about? The answers are reasonably simple, and are listed in order of importance. First, the cumulative effects of attrition on the German army had been critical, for they could afford to lose fewer soldiers than the allies. The allied offensives of 1916 and 1917 had played their part in fatally weakening the German army. Then, ironically, the German army never recovered from their own spring 1918 offensives, where their best men were lost, and which undermined German morale once and for all. Further German losses in 1918 led to a total of around 1.76 million casualties between 21 March and 11 November, including a large number of Germans unwilling to go on fighting. The German army actually ran out of men, while the allies were continually increasing manpower through the American build-up. The German army was defeated through attrition and exhaustion.

The second reason for allied victory was the overwhelming allied superiority in technology and material. Whether in artillery, ammunition supplies, tanks, planes, Lewis guns, rifle grenades, machine guns, food supplies, rail lines, or even horses, the allies were irresistibly superior. Even before the

German spring offensives, the German army on the western front could mount only 14,000 total guns against 18,500 allied guns, 3,760 planes versus 4,500, and 10 tanks against 800. Perhaps the key weapon in 1918 was artillery, and here there was no shortage of allied ammunition, as one British official historian wrote: 'for every shell the enemy sent over, he received ten or twenty back. In the bombardments . . . of the summer and autumn of 1918, the British artillery dominated to such an extent that the enemy retaliation was largely blind.' Thus the greatest twenty-four-hour expenditure of shell during the war by the BEF occurred between 28 and 29 September 1918, when 945,052 rounds were fired. In the French army in midsummer, the average daily shell expenditure of the 75-mm. field gun was 280,000 per day. The German army was simply worn down by allied material superiority.

Then, if a turning point can be found in 1918, it was the French counter-offensive at the Marne, followed by the Amiens offensive. Here are the origins of the third reason for victory, namely, tactical change. Now the French and British armies perfected the art of combined-arms warfare, using surprise, unregistered artillery barrages, effective counter-battery fire, plus tanks, planes, and the infantry in open formations. Despite this, better tactics did not prevent heavy casualties; indeed they were more severe than is generally acknowledged. From 1 July to 15 September, the French army lost 7,000 officers and nearly 272,000 men. British casualties from August to

The 42nd Battalion (Royal Highlanders of Canada) approach the outskirts of Mons on 10 November 1918, as civilians escape. Despite this orderly scene, the Germans strongly defended the city. But by daybreak on 11 November, Canadian troops reached the centre of Mons, and heard then that an armistice had been reached for 11 a.m.

Artillery was the major killer of the war and its heavier calibres—like this 15-inch howitzer—its most decisive weapon. Most artillery fire was indirect, that is to say that batteries could not see their targets. Much of France was resurveyed to enable accurate shooting from maps, and aerial observation, flash spotting and sound ranging allowed the guns to fire without preliminary registration.

October were around 300,000. As an example of comparative severity, the Canadian Corps, between August and November, suffered 30,089 casualties in 1916, largely at the Somme; 29,725 in 1917, largely at Passchendaele; and 49,152 in 1918. Therefore 1918 may well have seen the hardest fighting of the war even as allied forces used the new combined-arms tactics.

Finally, what were the relative achievements of the allied armies in 1918 on the western front? During this period, the BEF captured 188,700 prisoners and 2,840 guns; the French army captured 139,000 prisoners and 1,880 guns; the AEF captured 43,300 prisoners and 1,421 guns; and the Belgian army captured 14,500 prisoners and 474 guns. These final statistics may fairly represent the respective 1918 contributions to victory of the main allied armies in France.

CHAPTER 22

The Peace Settlement

ZARA STEINER

T

he Paris Peace Conference was officially opened on 18 January 1919. **The peace**
Delegations from thirty-seven nations from different continents **conference**
crowded into the French capital still living under wartime conditions.
Large numbers of unofficial representatives and supplicants thronged the
hotel corridors and a press corps over 500 strong appeared to record the proceedings for world consumption. Woodrow Wilson's Fourteen Points had
caught the European imagination and the American president was the hero
of the hour. War-weary people welcomed the prospects of peace and prosperity embodied in the American dream. Peace had returned to the western
fronts but elsewhere the fighting continued. The defeat and collapse of three
great empires created conditions of anarchy and revolution in their former
territories. Neither old Russia nor the Soviet Union was present at the peacemaking, though, like Banquo's ghost, the threat of a Bolshevik tide over
Europe hovered over the peace table. Old and new states seized neighbouring territories. Civil war raged in Russia and in its borderlands. Where allied
troops were still in place, the peace could be enforced, but large parts of
Europe were left beyond the victors' reach.

Despite a good deal of pre-conference preparation in London, Washing-
ton, and Paris, the actual organization of the meetings was chaotic. The
Council of Ten, with two representatives of the major victor powers, Britain,
France, Italy, Japan, and the United States, proved too unwieldy and in mid-
March an informal Council of Four emerged with Lloyd George, Georges
Clemenceau, Woodrow Wilson, and Vittorio Orlando, the least influential of
the four, conferring on the main issues to be decided. In an *ad hoc* and piece-

Facing: President
Wilson signing the
peace in the packed
Hall of Mirrors, Trianon
Palace, Versailles,
28 June 1919. With little
ceremony or dignity,
the Germans signed
first and then the other
Delegates.

meal manner, assisted by commissions, committees, and personal advisers, the 'Big Three' took the major decisions embodied in the peace treaties.

It was due to the prestige and popularity of Woodrow Wilson and the allied recognition of the importance of American power that the plenary conference at its second meeting set up a commission, under Wilson's chairmanship, to consider the proposed League of Nations. The Covenant, based on an Anglo-American draft, created an institutionalized form of collective action by the sovereign states to keep the peace and, as a secondary concern, to encourage international co-operation for social and economic welfare. Intended to replace the failed balance of power, the heart of the new system lay in Articles 10 and 11 calling on League members to respect and preserve the territorial integrity and political independence of all other member states and to make war or the threat of war against any state a matter for concern and action for the League. Articles 12 to 17 described the procedures and sanctions that could be taken against an aggressor. War was not outlawed but delayed for three months so that international opinion could be mobilized. The Covenant embraced the ideals of a 'collective security system', a term used only in the 1930s, but did not create a super-state and was intended to operate in a world of sovereign nations.

From its inception, the League, though a success at the ideological box office, proved unacceptable to those who would have to make the system work. The American Senate rejected the Covenant and the Treaty of Versailles in which it was contained. The Wilsonian institution failed to attract the support of either the British or French governments. Lloyd George, anxious to assuage the strong pro-League currents in Britain, embraced the League but had little affection for it and used other means of personal diplomacy to achieve his aims. The French wanted a strengthened victors' council backed by a permanent military force. Unable to prevail, a thoroughly sceptical Clemenceau, without any confidence in the power of international opinion, placed his hopes in securing more tangible guarantes of French security. The incorporation of the Covenant in each of the Paris peace treaties and the temporary exclusion of the ex-enemy nations identified the new institution with the victors' peace and the status quo, fuelling the German sense of Wilson's 'betrayal' and intensifying Soviet hostility towards the new institution.

Whether a collective security system could have worked at all is highly questionable but the subsequent behaviour of the member states underlined its fundamental weaknesses even before it became established and was tested. The creation of the League, seen by many people as the chief achievement of the conference, became, none the less, a new feature of the international order and left its mark on both statesmen and their publics. The promise of disarmament and collective protection against aggression gave substance to the Wilsonian claims of a war to end all wars. Unfortunately, like the balance of power, the new system relied on deterrents and on the willingness, in the last resort, of the states to fight to enforce it.

With the Covenant in place, the main tasks of peacemaking could begin. The Treaty of Versailles signed on 28 June 1919 in the Hall of Mirrors at Versailles, five years to the day since the assassination of Franz Ferdinand, was the most important of the five peace treaties concluded in Paris.

Clemenceau, Lloyd George, and Woodrow Wilson, as well as their fiercely Germanophobe publics, held Germany responsible for the war and insisted on punishment. No one believed that Germany could be destroyed but none was prepared for a 'soft peace'. Like Clemenceau, Lloyd George thought the war a 'crime against humanity', while Woodrow Wilson's conception of justice, contrary to German expectations, contained a strong punitive element. Conciliation could only follow punishment. Beyond these shared assumptions, the three leaders differed dramatically in their aims. The 78-year-old Clemenceau was singularly focused on the future security of France and sought guarantees that would protect his country against its more populous and economically powerful neighbour. He wanted a peace structure that would readjust the pre-war balance between Germany and France in the latter's favour. Ever the supreme realist, he knew this could not be achieved without American and British underwriting. Lloyd George, having secured Britain's major naval and colonial aims at German expense before the conference opened, was concerned not just with the punishment of Germany

The Treaty of Versailles

293

but with the future stability of continental Europe. While acknowledging France's claims for security, he sought a 'just peace' that the Germans could accept. There were to be no new sources of enmity created by the peace, no new Alsace-Lorraines that would serve as provocations for future wars. Too harsh a peace would destabilize the German government and bring revolution and impoverishment. Britain needed the return of a prosperous Germany to the concert of Europe if it were to pursue its paramount imperial and economic ambitions. The prime minister, in his element in Paris, sought to broker a peace that would eventually establish a continental balance of power that Britain would not be called upon to maintain. The key to Woodrow Wilson's thinking lay in the creation of the new League of Nations. A democratic and pacific Germany would be welcomed into the League and into the liberal world trading system which was its economic equivalent. If Wilson had been a better negotiator, he might have secured a more liberal treaty, but he proved willing to sacrifice some of the principles enunciated in the Fourteen Points in the confident belief that the League would correct the mistakes of the peacemakers.

The Treaty of Versailles represented a victory for the French demands for security modified in the face of British concerns for continental stability and Wilson's preoccupation with self-determination and the League of Nations.

Allied officers trying to get a view of the proceedings in the Hall of Mirrors. The rooms and terraces were crammed with people from the many delegations represented at the peace conference.

This was not a 'Carthaginian peace', as J. M. Keynes asserted in his brilliant, highly influential, and misleading polemic *The Economic Consequences of the Peace*, published in 1919. Germany was not dismembered nor was its capacity for revival destroyed. The country remained basically intact and potentially, given the disappearance of the empires on its borders, the most powerful state on the continent. The treaty terms were harsh but not unduly so given the length and destructiveness of the war and the completeness of the allied victory.

Clemenceau won a number of his key objectives. Germany was disarmed; its army restricted to 100,000 men and its navy reduced to little more than a coastal defence force. It was not permitted any military aircraft. It suffered territorial losses, some 13 per cent of its pre-war territory, between 6.5 and 7 million people, and all of its overseas territories. On its northern and western frontiers, apart from the loss of Alsace-Lorraine and the Saarland, the territorial changes were modest, with three small territories ceded to Belgium and a small strip of northern Schleswig given to neutral Denmark after a plebiscite. In the east, the losses were more considerable and included Memel, Danzig, a small part of Upper Silesia to Czechoslovakia, and, after a much disputed plebiscite, two-thirds of the rest of Upper Silesia to Poland. It was the territories lost to the reconstituted Poland which were the most repugnant to many Germans and judged in 1919 as the most objectionable part of the treaty.

Clemenceau, who considered the territorial changes, apart from the disarmament provisions, the most important gains for France, was forced to compromise over the Rhineland, the Saar, and the Polish frontiers. He had to abandon, mainly due to Lloyd George's opposition, his demand for the detachment of the Rhineland from Germany, considered by Marshal Foch as the key to France's future security. After a considerable struggle, he settled for a demilitarized left bank and strip on the right bank of the river and a fifteen-year allied occupation of this demilitarized zone. Provision was made for withdrawals in five-year intervals tied to German execution of the treaty terms. Lloyd George, highly suspicious of French hegemonic ambitions in the region, argued that the detachment of the Rhineland from Germany would make impossible the re-establishment of any equilibrium in Europe. He engineered the deal by which Clemenceau's retreat would be compensated by parallel Anglo-American guarantees to France in case of unprovoked German aggression. It was not untypical of the prime minister's tactics that at the last moment the British offer was made contingent on American ratification. When the Senate rejected the treaty, the British guarantee lapsed. The French spent most of the inter-war period seeking a replacement. Clemenceau recognized the dangers at the time and pressed for concessions that would prolong occupation or provide for re-occupation should the Germans fail to fulfil their treaty or reparation obligations. None the less, even before the much desired guarantee lapsed, his retreat over the Rhineland was sharply criticized in France. None of the Big Three was happy with the compromise, which unusually in this treaty involved some measure of enforcement.

Clemenceau also lost the battle over the Saarland in the face of President Wilson's strong objections to its annexation by France. It was Lloyd George who convinced the reluctant president to accept a compromise. Germany ceded sovereignty of the Saarland to the League of Nations and the ownership of its valuable mines to France. A plebiscite would be held in fifteen years; if the Saarlanders voted to rejoin Germany, they would have to repurchase the mines from France. Whether the French object was to gain a major economic advantage at German expense or to revive pro-French sentiment in the hope of regaining the territory, or possibly both, the bargain gave Clemenceau less than he wanted but more than Wilson was willing to concede.

The dispute over the Polish borders was fought out mainly between Clemenceau and Lloyd George. The French had taken up the Polish cause for entirely practical reasons. With the collapse of the tsarist state and the success of the Russian Revolution, France looked to the creation of a large and strong Poland as an essential part of its 'barrière de l'est' intended to contain Germany expansionism and the spread of Bolshevism. Wilson's thirteenth point endorsed the concept of an independent Poland with access to the sea. Like a later president in another great war, Wilson had an important bloc of Polish-Americans to satisfy, but he also believed in the need to reconstitute Poland and was sympathetic to the Polish cause. Lloyd George was a reluctant convert to Polish independence and his latent anti-Polish sentiments were fanned by the aggressive behaviour and the inflated demands made by the Polish statesmen in Paris. He felt that that the creation of a large Poland involving the incorporation of relatively large numbers of Germans was a recipe for future disaster. This was one of the few cases where the prime minister rejected the recommendations of the territorial committees and was able, with Wilson's grudging consent, to make some changes in their proposals. Danzig became an autonomous state under League control but incorporated within the Polish customs area and its foreign policy placed under Polish control. During the June debates over the final revisions of the draft treaty, Lloyd George managed to arrange for the plebiscite in Upper Silesia. The Polish problem was complicated by the unstable situation along Poland's eastern frontiers. Only a Polish–Soviet war and the Treaty of Riga of March 1921 settled the Russo-Polish border. Poland, by far the largest of the successor states and inevitably a multinational country, included 260 square miles of German territory. East Prussia, the heartland of *Junker* power, was isolated from the rest of Germany by the newly created 'Polish Corridor' consisting of parts of Poznań and West Prussia and giving Poland access to the sea. Germany would lose 3 million people, not all of German stock, and an additional number when Upper Silesia was divided in 1922. Not only did many Germans refuse to accept the new Polish settlement but subsequent British governments believed that the future revision of the eastern frontiers

was inevitable. Neither the prohibition of *Anschluss* at French insistence, nor the agreed incorporation of the German-speaking Sudetenlanders into Czechoslovakia, aroused the same passions as Poland. These decisions were hardly in accord with the principles of self-determination or popular sovereignty, but British and American protests were muted or non-existent and German feelings less engaged over the former subjects of Austria-Hungary than their own.

The peacemakers, as was to be expected after the new kind of war they had fought, were acutely aware of the economic dimensions of the settlement. Germany was deprived of more than 10 per cent of its pre-war resources, including basic raw materials, and subjected to commercial and economic restrictions, mainly of a temporary nature. The latter formed part of a broader French strategy to improve France's position at German expense but proved acceptable to the British and Americans. Most unexpectedly, the allied reparation demands became the most difficult and contentious problem faced by the Big Three. Wilson, with no demands to make, wanted German liability for war costs strictly limited to damage done to civilians and their property, and secured a pre-conference agreement along these lines. In Paris he sought a reasonable sum to be set and paid within a fixed period of time. At the same time, the president rejected as totally unacceptable allied

The first members of the German delegation arrive at Vaucresson, near Versailles. They were presented with the terms of the draft treaty on 7 May and permitted only to make 'practical suggestions' in writing.

demands that reparations and the $10.3 billion allied debt owed to the United States be linked, thereby weakening the American bargaining position. Both Clemenceau and Lloyd George, who faced greater domestic pressure over reparations than any other question, were intent on securing the restitution demanded by their publics. Paradoxically, in view of their later quarrels, it was Britain rather than France which swelled the reparation bill by insisting that pensions be included in the overall sum and Lloyd George rather than Clemenceau who rejected compromise demands that were within the realm of the possible. Lloyd George backed the astronomical figures proposed by his personally appointed delegates even when warning at Fontainebleau in March of the dire consequences of demanding too much from the Germans. Though Clemenceau's advisers were divided in their views, the French would have preferred either the continuation of allied wartime agreements or a war debt settlement to a high reparation bill: they even tried, unsuccessfully, for a broader reparation and industrial arrangement with the Germans which would have benefited France without the difficulties involved in a transfer of reparation funds. None the less, between the French determination to secure the compensation due them and the British effort to secure as large a share of the indemnity as possible, the sums demanded of Germany became impossibly high. Unable to reach agreement

A group of British naval officers leaving Reims Cathedral after inspecting the extensive physical damage inflicted by the Germans. In the foreground are the archbishop of Reims and Vice Admiral Sir Arthur Leveson.

on either war costs or Germany's capacity to pay, the three leaders agreed to postpone any decision until 1921 when an inter-allied commission would settle the issue. In the interim Germany was to pay 20,000 gold marks ($5 billion) in cash and kind. Wilson was defeated in his attempt to secure an overall fixed sum and a thirty-year time limit on payments.

The reparation clauses were denounced in Germany and created consternation in the American and British delegations, provoking in the latter case Keynes's condemnatory book. The decision for postponement was a major error of judgement. Lloyd George hoped this would satisfy the immediate public demand for high reparations while providing time for tempers to cool and more rational terms to emerge. Instead, with the American withdrawal from the peace settlement, postponement produced prolonged arguments between France and Britain and a continual battle with the Germans, who were determined to pay as little as they could. Reparations became the post-peace battleground, and the symbol and even the reality of the Franco-German struggle for the future control of Europe.

Another major error in the reparation section of the treaty, Article 231, had equally damaging consequences for its enforcement. In a treaty designed to embody the principles of nationalism, the so-called war guilt clause was bound to provoke and enrage the Germans. Following an American recommendation, the article was intended to distinguish between Germany's moral responsibility for the war and its consequences, thereby satisfying allied domestic opinion, and its limited legal liability for reparations. The Germans used the charge that Germany and her allies (the clause was included in each of the Paris peace treaties) bore the sole responsibility for the war to attack not only the reparation clauses but also the ethical basis of the whole treaty. In a short time, the attack won the support of large sections of the public in Britain and the United States. Inadvertently, the peacemakers provided the Germans with a powerful weapon to undermine the moral justification of the peace.

With the exception of Orlando, the Council of Four took less interest in the settlements of south-eastern Europe and tended to accept the recommendations of the territorial committees in drawing up the new frontiers. Both the British and the Americans strongly supported the application of the principles of self-determination while France favoured the creation of strong successor states as part of its 'eastern barrier' that was to provide a substitute for the lost Russian alliance. As in the German case, nationality could not be adopted as the only guide in drawing up frontiers. There were wartime promises to Italy, Romania, and Greece to be honoured or ignored; the Italian demands for the northern frontier on the Brenner Pass and its conflicts with Yugoslavia over Dalmatia and Istria proved the most disputatious and divisive of these quarrels. A disappointed Orlando returned home to face the charge of having signed a 'mutilated peace'. The peacemakers, moreover, were not responsible for the 'balkanization' of east central Europe, which

The settlement of south-eastern Europe

took place before the conference met. They could only ratify the results of national revolutions and sort out frontiers and quarrels. Three new states, Czechoslovakia, Poland, and Yugoslavia, were in existence before 1919. Along Russia's western and southern borders, seven other states claimed their independence, Finland, Estonia, Latvia, Lithuania, and the more short-lived republics of Georgia, Azerbaijan, and Armenia. After continuous debate, it was agreed to do nothing about the Soviet Union. Allied troops were withdrawn from Russian territories but the door to talks was neither opened nor shut. The nightmares of Bolshevik revolutions outside Russia, given reality in Budapest, began to subside during the conference but the fear remained. Given Russia's absence from the peace conference, the civil war, and the border conflicts, there could be no decisions about frontiers in the east.

The Treaty of Saint-Germain-en-Laye with Austria, 10 September 1919, the Treaty of Neuilly with Bulgaria, 27 November 1919, and the Treaty of Trianon with Hungary on 4 June 1920 were concluded after Wilson and Lloyd George had left Paris and were dealt with by the lesser lights. The three treaties, modelled on the Treaty of Versailles, contained the Covenant of the League of Nations, and similar war responsibility, reparation, and disarmament demands. In distinction to the German treaty, each recognized the kingdom of the Serbs, Croats, and Slovenes (the name Yugoslavia became official only in 1929) and contained provisions providing protection for ethnic, religious, and linguistic minorities. Austria became little more than a rump state with a population of 8 million people and a highly precarious economic future. Forbidden *Anschluss*, the Austrian boundary with Germany followed pre-war lines. Italy and the successor states benefited from the divisions of her former territories. The Hungarian treaty was delayed because of the Bela Kun revolution of 21 March 1919 and the inability of the peacemakers to decide what to do about it. It was only after the Romanians, acting independently, occupied the capital and were eventually persuaded to leave that a final settlement with the Hungarians could be concluded. Hungary lost two-thirds of its pre-war territory and one-third of its Magyar population as well as many other nationalities over which it had so ruthlessly ruled. Though more economically viable than Austria, Hungary suffered from the fragmented way in which its settlement evolved. Czechoslovakia, Yugoslavia, and Romania each benefited at its expense. Not only did Hungary become one of the most bitter enemies of the peace settlement but the Hungarian minorities beyond its borders felt deeply aggrieved and kept the flames of revisionism alive. The Bulgarians, too, felt hard done by in ethnic terms, though, apart from the loss of Thrace to Greece, which blocked Bulgarian access to the sea, relatively little territory was lost. The Treaty of Neuilly was unique in that an actual sum for reparations was included, £90 million, later to be much reduced.

Great Power interests, strategic and economic, and wartime promises to allies were not the only reasons why the principles of self-determination

could not be consistently applied. The experts on the territorial committees had to consider economic and strategic viability as well as ethnic loyalties if the new states were to survive. Few in 1919, or at any time after, fully appreciated the racial complexity of eastern Europe. It was impossible to draw boundaries to conform to national lines. More people than before 1914 lived under governments of their own nationality but many of the dissatisfied nationalities in the old empires became the dissatisfied minorities of the new states. It is to their credit that, apart from the Turco-Greek exchange, few in 1919 considered the forced movement of populations. The triumph of national principles fed nationalist and revisionist movements among the discontented, and new conflicts between neighbours were actually created by the peace treaties. The League of Nations mechanism contained in the minority treaties, which Poland, Czechoslovakia, Yugoslavia, Romania, and Greece were obliged to sign, represented a first step towards the recognition of national rights but could not guarantee them. The establishment of democratic forms of government in the successor states proved all too short-lived and where they survived, as in Czechoslovakia, they did not lead to the redress of minority greviances. While the treaties provided opportunities for economic integration, nationalist currents blocked co-operation to the detriment of all.

In 1919, the British and French empires reached their zenith. Self-determination was not extended to the extra-European world, though some recognition was given to the responsibilities of the rulers to those they ruled. The mandates solution represented a nod in the Wilsonian direction; at best

British press correspondents watching allied topographers drawing the new territorial boundaries of post-1919 Europe. Trentino, a mainly Italian-speaking part of Austria-Hungary, was given to Italy, fulfilling the allied promises of 1915.

Turkey and the Treaty of Sèvres

it broadened rather than challenged the basis of colonial rule. The Japanese effort to include a racial equality clause in the Covenant was opposed by the United States as well as Britain. It is true that the new emphasis on national-ist principles had its effects in India and Egypt, in the new mandates, and in China, where the grant of Shantung to Japan on 4 May produced one of the first demonstrations of Chinese nationalism and the Chinese rejection of the Treaty of Versailles. In Turkey, the Nationalists, ably led by Mustafa Kemal, thwarted allied plans for the division of the Turkish heartland and established their own republic. Despite the roles of the United States and Japan in Paris, the extra-European settlements were distinctly European in their spirit and content.

The Treaty of Sèvres, signed on 10 August 1920, was the last, the most complicated, and the shortest-lived of the treaties of Paris. It marked a high point in European imperialism of the most old-fashioned kind and repre-sented a vast extension of British power and influence. The completeness of the Ottoman collapse, disputes between would-be heirs, and divided coun-sels in London explain why the peace was so delayed. The long-time lapse proved fatal for Britain's inflated ambitions and Greek dreams of a 'Greater Greece'. In March 1919 when the Italians, thwarted over Fuimi, threatened to take Smyrna, the Greeks, supported by the philhellene Lloyd George, occupied the port and eastern Thrace. It was the action at Smyrna that sparked the successful Kemalist resistance movement in the summer of 1919.

The Treaty of Sèvres confirmed Turkey's loss of all its Arab lands and their division between Britain and France. The Hijaz, now named Saudi Arabia, became independent under Sherif Hussein of Mecca. After fierce quarrels between Lloyd George and Clemenceau which poisoned Anglo-French rela-tions for years to come, it was agreed that Iraq (Mesopotomia) and Palestine would be British mandates, and Syria and Lebanon French. The Balfour Declaration, endorsing a 'national home' for the Jews in Palestine, was included in the mandatory terms despite earlier British promises to the Arabs and the French. The British won control of Mosul with the French given a 25 per cent share of the oilfields. This division of the spoils of war was not challenged by the nationalists though relations between Britain and France, their mandates, and the independent states remaining under their influence were stormy. An imposed settlement left a troublesome legacy.

With regard to the rest of Turkey, the drafters of the Treaty of Sèvres ignored the success of the Kemalists and reduced Turkey-in-Europe to a shadow of itself. Constantinople remained under Turkish sovereignty but most of its European territories were handed over to the Greeks along with the two Aegean islands. Anatolia was partitioned, with a separate agreement recognizing Italian and French special interests. An independent Armenia was created and an autonomous Kurdistan recognized. The Straits would be open both in peace and war to ships of all countries except as the Council of the League of Nations decided otherwise. The allied powers would control the entire finances of the country and the hated capitulatory regime was confirmed and extended.

Such terms could not be enforced. Mustafa Kemal defeated the Greeks in 1922 and exploited the disunity of the allies to his advantage, cancelling French and Italian claims and leaving the British alone to defend Constantinople against the Nationalists. In October 1922, Lloyd George gave way and agreed to Kemal's demand for a new peace treaty. With the British withdrawal of troops from the Caucasus, Kemal joined in a partnership with the Soviet Union. Azerbaijan, Armenia (divided between the two powers), and Georgia came under Soviet rule. The new Turkish treaty was signed at Lausanne on 24 July 1923. Turkey was freed from all capitulations, reparations, and military limitations except for a small demilitarized zone along the Straits. It regained possession of eastern Thrace, İzmir (Smyrna), and some of the Aegean islands. Under Kemal's leadership, Turkey became a force for stability in the the region. The Treaty of Lausanne, the only peace treaty to be negotiated, was the most successful and enduring of the peace settlements.

The Paris peace treaties were a disappointing end to a struggle of such proportions and such length. Marshal Foch was all too right when he said, 'This is not peace; it is an Armistice for twenty years.' It is commonly claimed that the Treaty of Versailles was too harsh to conciliate Germany and too soft to restrain it. There was no way Germany could be punished and conciliated. It is difficult to believe that any allied peace would have been acceptable to the Germans, who refused to face the reality of their defeat. It could be argued that, despite the American absence, if the French and British had stood together, the treaty might have been enforced; instead the former demanded strict compliance and the latter wanted appeasement and revision. The lack of harmony among the victors and the strength of revisionist movements on both sides of the war divide turned the treaty into an uneasy truce which lasted until Hitler's attack on the territorial status quo. The unique claims for a 'just peace' were undermined by the sometimes specious arguments used to cloak the victors' demands and the misjudgements made in justifying these demands in the treaty. Such clauses provided the arguments used to question the treaty's legitimacy in Germany and abroad. Many of the weaknesses of the settlement were due less to utopian hopes than to the realities of the situation left by the war. The old balance of power was destroyed and could not be restored. Germany was defeated but remained potentially strong. The French were left too weak to maintain the artificial balance of 1919 without assistance. Britain preferred to restore Germany to the European concert than to underwrite the French. The peripheral and ambiguous roles of the United States and the Soviet Union contributed to the instabilities of the settlement. It would take decades and another war before their potential strength was translated into actual power. Pre-war questions were left undecided while the war itself eroded the already unravelling European order. Far from being utopian, the peacemakers recognized and responded to the

A temporary settlement only

strength of the nationalist movements in Europe if not beyond. The national frontiers drawn at Paris lasted until 1938–9 and even then, with some notable changes, survived the periods of both Nazi and Soviet domination. The most recent upheavals in Europe bear witness to the persistence of nationalist aspirations. Even with regard to the League of Nations, the peacemakers were not just utopian dreamers. The impulse to create institutionalized forms of international co-operation is with us still despite the disappointments and failures of the last decades. Contemporary events suggest a more qualified judgement of the peace treaties than that offered by past generations of historians.

CHAPTER 23

Memory and the Great War

MODRIS EKSTEINS

You lie still, chum,' I sez to 'im, 'you'll be all right presently.' An' 'e jes
gives me one look, like 'e were puzzled, an' 'e died.
(Frederic Manning, *The Middle Parts of Fortune*)

The Great War has haunted our century; it haunts us still. It continues to
inspire imaginative endeavour of the highest order. It invites pilgrimage and commemoration surrounded by palpable sadness. Eighty
years after the war, 'The Last Post', intoned every evening at the Menin Gate
in Ypres, still summons tears. We wish it all had not happened.

We associate the war with the loss of youth, of innocence, of ideals. We are
inclined to think that the world was a better and happier place before 1914.
If our century has been one of disjunction and endless surprise rather than of
the mounting predictability many expected at the last *fin-de-siècle*, the Great
War was the greatest surprise of all. The war stands, by most historical
accounts, as the portal of entry to our century of doubt and agony, to our dissatisfaction.

Its extremes of emotion, both the initial jubilation and subsequent despair,
are seen as a preface to the politics of extremism that took hold in Europe in
the aftermath; its mechanized killing is regarded as a necessary prelude to
the even greater ferocity of the Second World War and to the Holocaust; its
assault on the values of the Enlightenment is seen as a nexus between inde-
terminacy in the sciences and the aesthetics of irony. Monty Python might

never have lived had it not been for the Great War. The war unleashed a floodtide of forces that we have been unable ever since to stem. 'Lord God of Hosts, be with us yet, Lest we forget—lest we forget!' How in the world, Mr Kipling, are we to forget?

The enthusiasm surrounding the outbreak of war many described as a social and spiritual experience beyond compare. Engagement was the hallmark of the day. 'We have', wrote Rupert Brooke, 'come into our heritage.' The literate classes, and by then they were the literate masses—teachers, students, artists, writers, poets, historians, and indeed workers, of the mind as well as the fist—volunteered *en masse*. School benches and church pews emptied. Those past the age of military service enrolled in the effort on the home front.

Words, literary words, visible on the page, flowed as they had never flowed before, in the trenches, at home, and across the seven seas. The Berlin critic Julius Bab estimated that in August 1914 50,000 German poems were being penned a day. Thomas Mann conjured up a vision of his nation's poetic soul bursting into flame. Before the wireless, before the television, this was the great literary war. Everyone wrote about it, and for it.

Not surprisingly, the Great War turned immediately into a war of cultures. To Britain and France, Germany represented the assault, by definition barbaric, on history and law. Brutality was Germany's essence. To Germany, Britain represented a commercial spirit, and France an emphasis on outward form, that were loathsome to a nation of heroes. Treachery was Albion's name. Hypocrisy was Marianne's fame.

A middle-class war But the war was also an expression of social values. The intense involvement of the educated classes led to a form of warfare, certainly on the western front, characterized by the determination and ideals of those classes. Trench warfare was not merely a military necessity; it was a social manifestation. It was to be, in a sense, the great moral achievement of the European middle classes. It represented their resolve, commitment, perseverance, responsibility, grit—those features and values the middle classes cherished most.

> And here for dear dead brothers we are weeping.
> Mourning the withered rose of chivalry,
> Yet, their work done, the dead are sleeping, sleeping
> Unconscious of the long lean years to be.

Those lines from the *Wykehamist*, the journal of Winchester College, of July 1917 evoked both the passing of an age and the crisis of a culture.

'The bourgeoisie is essentially an effort,' insisted the French bourgeois René Johannet. The Great War was essentially an effort too. The American writer F. Scott Fitzgerald would call the war on the western front 'a love battle—there was a century of middle-class love spent here. All my beautiful lovely safe world blew itself up here with a great gust of high-explosive love.' Fitzgerald's 'lovely safe world' was one of empire, imperial ideas, and impe-

rial dreams. It was a world of confidence, of religion, and of history. It was a world of connections. History was a synonym for progress.

Fuelled initially by Horatian ideals—*dulce et decorum est pro patria mori*—taught in all the grammar schools, *lycées*, and gymnasia of Europe and then driven by a stubbornness that in Britain was appropriately called bottom, the war of attrition decimated the old aristocracy and much of the intelligentsia of Europe. Ten million would die. Twenty million would be mutilated. In the front lines casualties were highest among officers, called upon to lead by example, and by corollary among soldiers who had left their liberal professions, such as teaching and the law, to become warriors. For these men chances of survival for more than a few weeks, without death or at least injury, were small. The scions of those families looked to for moral leadership and political authority were mowed down, gassed, and blown to bits: Asquiths, Bethmann Hollwegs, Moreau-Nélatons, Roosevelts. Artists and writers, too, died in droves: Franz Marc, Umberto Boccioni, August Macke, Henri Gaudier-Brzeska, Alain-Fournier, Isaac Rosenberg, Georg Trakl, Edward Thomas, Charles Péguy, Wilfred Owen. Because of its staggering cost in talent and tradition, the war was bound to provoke a furore of secondary wars, political, social, moral—a re-examination of the very foundations of civilization and society.

After the wave of celebratory traditionalism that accompanied the outbreak of war had subsided, that re-examination began, at first slowly, cautiously. During the war it had to remain, of necessity, largely private. In 1916 Henri Barbusse did publish a widely read novel, *Le Feu* (Under Fire), denouncing

The Hood Battalion before departure to Gallipoli, April 1915. Rupert Brooke, the poet, stands second from left in the second row; beside him, third and fourth along, are the composers W. Denis Browne and F. S. Kelly. The scholars Patrick Shaw and Charles Lister also belonged to the Battalion. All five died in the war.

Language and the war

307

the war, but it was more his broader perspective on the war and less his con-demnation of it that first interested readers. The poet-warrior Siegfried Sas-soon, influenced by Barbusse, attempted a demonstrative protest against the war, but then was drawn back to join his comrades in the front lines. His introspective and charged poetry initially reached only a small circle. Like-wise, the pyrotechnics of the Dada crowd in neutral Zurich, where Tristan Tzara, Richard Huelsenbeck, Hugo Ball, and other exiles parodied every-thing, including themselves, had at first little resonance. But the questioning had begun, of all sorts of fundamental issues: reason, honour, duty, patrio-tism, beauty, class, love, art. And, above all, authority.

In this questioning, the integrity of language seemed to break first. Words seemed so remote, syntax so helpless, when confronted by the urgency, the unpredictability, of actual experience. As a result, Tristan Tzara issued in-structions on how to write a poem: cut words from a newspaper and put them in a bag, shake the bag, and remove the words one by one. *Voilà le poème!* One needed a new word for mud, said John Masefield, a new word for death, said Louis Mairet, a new word for war, said Beverley Nichols. 'Only the names of places had dignity,' concluded Ernest Hemingway, the American writer who served with the Italians in the war.

Because of the failure of imagination and hence language to contain ex-perience, the soldiers of the Great War felt that they possessed a secret, 'a secret', said Charles Carrington, 'that can never be communicated'. If lan-guage becomes unstable, how does one communicate? What remains of the social contract? What happens to law and authority? The old ideas simply lost their validity, like punctured tyres. 'Heroes', said Osbert Sitwell, 'became bores.' And when the crisis of expression had reached a new plateau in the next war, Virginia Woolf decided that 'the wordless are the happy'.

Most combatants recited the platitudes of their society—Isaac Rosenberg called them 'second-hand phrases'—to the end. Dying soldiers mouthed the prayers taught them in infancy, 'Gentle Jesus, meek and mild.' For some the war remained 'ripping good sport', or so at least they claimed in their letters home. The war was fought on the basis of values and assumptions drummed into its participants through systems of universal education and other institu-tions of state. Put to the test the old values held—they held for more than four long years, everywhere, except in Russia. But the seeds of doubt had been planted.

The crisis of expression was to be more immediate in cultures that lost the war, Germany in particular, or that felt, like Italy, that they were denied the appropriate spoils of victory. In these societies the experience of the war, its mystical implications, took precedence over articulated meaning. Here the war had spiritual, instead of rational, essence. The war, said many Germans right from the start, was a question of spiritual liberation. When such logic was carried forward in the face of defeat, the upshot was a celebration of experience instead of purpose and result. In this situation the ancient pro-verb that necessity knows no law could readily become the guide to conduct.

Grief, and her twin, sadness, dominated the mood of the 1920s. The make-shift battlefield cemeteries, with their ramshackle crosses, were turned to beautiful order. New concentration cemeteries were created. Headstones were erected, monuments built. 'Silent cities', Kipling called the cemeteries. The iconography was of course traditional. To help them in choosing an inscription for the headstone of their loved one, British families received a booklet of suggestions drawn from the Bible and from the classics of English literature. Inspired by their serene order and glorious flowers, the poet Edmund Blunden called the British and empire cemeteries 'the poetry of that high action' that was the war; 'the dead speak yet through achievement of beauty.'

A variety of attempts, by among others the Michelin firm in France and the Pickfords travel agency in Britain, to turn the battlefields into tourist sites immediately after the war had little success. But gradually visitors began to come in search of the resting places of those dear to them. The pilgrimages reached a high point in 1928–9, before the onset of the great depression. In the summer of 1928 the British Legion organized a huge pilgrimage to Ypres, with close to 15,000 participants. The visitors' books at the Menin Gate memorial to the missing contain over 8,000 signatures for the month of July and almost 15,000 for the month of August. By then the Germans, initially

Commemoration

Crowds gather at Vimy Ridge, July 1936, for the dedication of the Canadian memorial. Designed by W. S. Allward, it is the most venturesome of all the memorials along the western front. The fiercely contested ridge overlooks the Douai Plain and coal-fields of northern France. The craters in the foreground remain a feature of the memorial park to this day.

prohibited, then discouraged from visiting France and Belgium, had started coming too. Official speeches all reiterated the moral purpose of the war: on the allied side, to preserve liberty and dignity through duty and sacrifice; on the German side, as General Hindenburg said at the dedication of the Tannenberg memorial in 1927, 'to defend the Fatherland'. 'With clean hearts we marched . . . with clean hands we fought.' A carapace of piety surrounded the war and its dead.

War literature

One mourned, but at the same time, one tried, *pace* Kipling, for the sake of sanity, to forget. Robert Graves and T. E. Lawrence had an agreement that they would not discuss the war. Stanley Casson, the ex-serviceman and archaeologist, was in a similar mood: 'We talked of almost everything else.' Regimental histories were written. A few memoirs appeared and the odd novel: A. P. Herbert, C. E. Montague, Ernst Jünger, Roland Dorgelès, R. H. Mottram, e. e. cummings (for cummings even capital letters had lost their authority). Jünger had considerable success in Germany. *In Stahlgewittern* (Storm of Steel), with its celebration of primordial violence, first appeared in 1920 and was reprinted regularly after that, but the print runs, of 5,000 or 6,000 copies at a time, were still modest. The romance of war was ever present in Ernest Raymond's *Tell England*, first published in 1922; it too had yearly, though again small, printings through the 1920s. Everyone waited for the great war novel, the one that would put everything into proper Homeric perspective. Everyone but the publishers, that is. Those with an eye on profits, during a decade of mass unemployment when the book business suffered, assumed that the public had no interest in the war. Indicators of public taste confirmed this view. A poll of 300,000 British cinema-goers in August 1927 revealed that they were not at all attracted by war films or even by historical films in general. Sentimentality, in the guise of 'society drama', was what they wanted. There were twenty-two films that year with *Love* in their title: among them *Love on the Beach*, *Love at the Crossroads*, *Betty Peterson's Love*, and even *Bloody Love*.

There seemed to be little time for books during that first decade after the war. The cinema, motor cars, aeroplanes—excitement and bustle of any sort seemed preferable to a quaint activity like reading. A new frenzy seized mass culture. Much of the inspiration—the syncopated rhythms of jazz, the gin-swilling flappers, the Charleston—seemed to come from America or other frontier lands. Elders were appalled, by the images, the sounds, the language. Both young and old were apt to attribute the new morality, with its heightened sensuality, to the influence of the war.

As the physical landscape of war recovered, as travel to the former war zones in Belgium and northern France became easier, and as the cemeteries came to dominate the visit to the western front, many ex-servicemen felt that they were losing their war. The war was being corrupted not only by time, but also by sentimentality, vulgarity, and ignorance. Gerhard Schinke, a German, journeyed to Flanders in 1927. He was shocked by how the countryside had

revived but even more upset at how Ypres had commercialized the war. In addition to a profusion of manufactured souvenirs for sale in shops, children on the street offered to sell him rusted weapons, helmets, grenades, and tunic buttons. A former captain with the Royal Fusiliers remarked that 'the Cloth Hall of Ypres must rank close to Niagara as one of the world's most-photographed sights'. The novelist Christopher Isherwood visited Ypres on 11 November 1935 to pay his respects to his father who had been killed in the salient in 1915. Isherwood, too, was taken aback by the vulgarity: 'The town is certainly "for ever England"', he wrote in his diary—'the England of sordid little teashops, faked souvenirs and touts'.

If traditional political authority was questioned dramatically after 1918, as civil war raged in Russia and broke out intermittently in other parts of Europe, old forms of expression in the arts were also considered inadequate. An often wild experimentalism took hold in the visual arts, music, drama, and literature. Artists used brushes and paint as if they were revolvers and bombs. Marcel Duchamp affixed a moustache to the *Mona Lisa* and called this art. To one exhibition he submitted a urinal, calling it *The Fountain*. It was, he

Ruins of Ypres, 1915, with the famous Cloth Hall and Grote Markt. On seeing these ruins J. W. Gamble wrote home: 'It is really a wonderful sight—weird, grotesque, and desolate of course—but most interesting. I expect the place will be flooded with sightseers and tourists after the war, and they will be amazed by what they see.'

311

said, the one object he could think of that was most likely to be disliked. Composers conjured up the sounds of mental anguish. Theatre producers and directors sought to change the world. A mood of anger and violence permeated the arts. The French poet Louis Aragon was excited by an image of destruction—by 'the splendid and chaotic heap | Which is easily produced with a church and some dynamite'. And the outwardly gentle British poet Stephen Spender ended his verse play *Trial of a Judge* with the lines: 'And the aerial vultures fly | Over the deserts which were cities. | Kill! Kill! Kill! Kill!'

A new type of artist-intellectual had appeared in the wake of the war, *l'homme engagé*, for whom the word and the deed, previously considered distinct, began to blend. Intellectuality became an event. The French writer André Malraux was perhaps the best representative of this genus, a man who created his literary image through action. 'I want to leave a scar on the world,' one of his characters says. One admiring critic of Malraux would call his books *livres-cicatrices*, scar-books.

There is here the thrill of vitality beyond morality, life beyond good and evil. 'I plunge my gaze into the eyes of passing women, fleeting and penetrating as a pistol shot, and rejoice when they are forced to smile,' wrote the war veteran Ernst Jünger in his book *Der Kampf als inneres Erlebnis* (War as Inner Experience). For him the spiritual side of war was as important as the physical. For him the Great War continued after the armistice, after the peace treaty; that war never left him. He regarded its destructive-creative energy as a beacon for the future.

André Breton, the surrealist, spoke of the 'crisis of the object'. But, as the ideas of Sigmund Freud suggested, there was a 'crisis of the subject' too. Psychoanalytic theory had a special importance in the search for a new reality and Freud became a household name in the 1920s. And while Albert Einstein distanced himself from all attempts to link his theory of relativity with the new artistic forms, the wider public was not loath to make a connection between modern art and relativity. 'Mathematics', declared the poet William Carlos Williams in 1921, alluding to the impact of science, 'comes to the rescue of the arts.' The role of the Great War in all of this was that, in a manner far more comprehensive, it too, like Freud and Einstein, had destroyed absolutes and thus made the public more receptive to new ideas.

Ruminating in 1915 on the mainsprings of art and especially on the effect of the war on literature, John Galsworthy had predicted great 'internal stress' in Britain. 'That stress', he had written in the *Times Literary Supplement*, 'will most likely have a more ultimate and powerful influence upon literature than the war itself. If there is to come any startling change, it should be five or ten years after the war rather than one.' At the end of the 1920s, a decade of political instability, economic turmoil, unemployment, and many other indignities, Galsworthy's prediction materialized: the emotional storm broke. The war moved once again to the very centre of public attention, put there, however, as Galsworthy foresaw, by more immediate concerns that seized on the Great War as the great agent.

Erich Maria Remarque's novel *Im Westen nichts Neues* (All Quiet on the Western Front) was at the heart of the commotion. Serialized in a Berlin newspaper in late 1928, it appeared in book form in January 1929. Within months the 31-year-old Remarque was the world's most famous author. By 1930 twenty-eight translations had appeared and world sales approached 4 million copies. From late 1928 into the early 1930s war books dominated the lists of publishers, books by Robert Graves, Edmund Blunden, Siegfried Sassoon, Richard Aldington, Ernest Hemingway, Ludwig Renn, Arnold Zweig. R. C. Sherriff's play *Journey's End* ran for 594 consecutive performances in London and by the end of 1929 had been staged in twelve different countries. A rash of war films appeared too: among them G. W. Pabst's *Westfront 1918*, Herbert Brenon's *The Case of Sergeant Grischa*, and Lewis Milestone's rendition of Remarque's novel for Universal Studios. Released in the spring of 1930 the film version of *All Quiet* played to packed houses throughout the world. It was to be accorded the Academy Award for best picture of the year.

This 'war boom' used the war to voice contemporary anxiety. At the same time, however, it did more to shape the popular image of the Great War than any work by historians before or since. Its most successful works, Remarque's *All Quiet*, Graves's *Good-bye to All That*, Zweig's *The Case of Sergeant Grischa*, and Hemingway's *Farewell to Arms*, denounced the war as a futile slaughter, a monstrous injustice, a political and social catastrophe. Progress and purpose, all those bloated words with their putrid aspirates, consisted of nothing but foul-smelling vapour—reminding him, said Hemingway, of the stockyards of Chicago. Only individual resilience and an elementary camaraderie had meaning in this hell, tragic meaning at that. The ordinary soldier, the unknown warrior, the nameless, faceless victim, became the symbol of this war. The anti-hero took the place of the hero, in a world devoid of socially significant will. Wilfred Owen, the young poet who had been killed a week before the armistice, had said of his work: 'The poetry is in the pity.' The same could be said of Remarque's more prosaic intentions a decade later. The new hero of the 1920s was the vagabond misfit Charlie Chaplin, who strolled through life buffeted and baffled by it.

If the war boom reflected the mood of the 1920s more accurately than that of the war, much of the public accepted these books and films as accurate depictions. When the American novelist William Faulkner wrote in 1931, 'America has been conquered not by the German soldiers that died in French and Flemish trenches, but by the German soldiers that died in German books,' he was pointing to the enormous power of fiction in influencing attitudes and values. Novelists and filmmakers have played a far more important role in developing our century's historical imagination than have historians. That, too, was a result of the Great War.

The thrust of this 'mud and blood literature' angered many. To not a few veterans and bereaved families the suggestion that the war had been in vain and their loved ones merely victims—sons murdered by fathers—was sacri-

lege. Because of a number of references to bodily functions in the books by Remarque and Graves, the whole genre was dismissed by some as the 'lavatory school' of war literature. In Britain and the dominions there was widespread sentiment that this was a foreign genre. 'I did not think that I should ever live to read books written by my own countrymen which are like the dirty work done by enemy propagandists,' said a clergyman at armistice celebrations in Folkestone in 1929. The war had been fought specifically against foreign perversity, and here was this alien depravity influencing home-grown youth again.

But in Germany, too, there was opposition to Remarque and his sort. His success came at a crucial point in Germany's post-war history, the year of the tenth anniversary of the Versailles Treaty, the latter with its painful war guilt clause, and a year when the German economy slumped badly. The deepening economic crisis was to become a worldwide phenomenon but Germany was hit particularly hard. It was the passivity of Remarque's soldiers that the Nazis, who moved into the national spotlight in 1929–30 with massive electoral gains, despised. Many of them, including Adolf Hitler, were ex-servicemen to whom the spiritual achievement in war was all important. They denounced Remarque and his confrères and they protested, with violent demonstrations, against the Berlin showing in December 1930 of Hollywood's version of Remarque's novel. The government at the time, a fragile coalition of moderates led by the Centrist Heinrich Brüning, capitulated to right-wing pressure and worked successfully to have the film banned on grounds that it was hostile to Germany.

After Hitler's accession to power in January 1933, the political polarization of Europe gained pace. At both political extremes, the image of the soldier as helpless victim was unwelcome. For both fascists and communists, the soldier was an agent of revolution. But the theory was deflated by collective memory. When war broke out again in 1939, there was no cheering, not even in Berlin.

The memory of the Great War had hung like a dense cloud over the inter-war era, never more depressingly than in the international negotiations in 1938–9 over German territorial claims. The tone of the literature, drama, and films of the war boom had suggested that the Great War had not been worth the cost. 'Another great war for many years to come would seem . . . to be impossible,' the British *Army Quarterly* had editorialized in April 1930. For Adolf Hitler, by contrast, the war had been, as he put it in *Mein Kampf*, 'the greatest and most unforgettable time of my earthly experience'. Still, this celebration of violent will notwithstanding, Hitler did not expect the war he got in 1939 and even in his inner circle there was no gladness.

Despite the moral statement inherent in their declaration of war against Germany in September 1939, after the invasion of Poland, neither France nor Britain showed the slightest desire to fight. France fell. Britain fought on largely because of Hitler's appalling military and political miscalculations.

Facing: Hollywood's Universal Pictures began filming *All Quiet on the Western Front* at the Irvine Ranch in California on 11 November 1929. E. M. Remarque's best-selling novel and Lewis Milestone's award-winning film have had a greater influence in shaping public views of the Great War than the work of any historian.

The memory of the war since 1945

Some of the old rhetoric was trotted out again, but the propaganda effort in this war was very different from that in the previous one. This was a tenacious struggle for survival, not a civilizing mission.

The horror, devastation, and scope of the Second World War overwhelmed the western imagination. The acute moral dilemmas and agonies evoked by revelations of genocide, by saturation bombing of cities, and by the use, at the end, of atomic weapons made the heavy artillery, submarines, tanks, and even the gas cylinders of the First World War seem like toys. The Great War receded into the mists of memory as a rather primitive and unsophisticated affair.

As, in the second half of the 1940s, hot war turned to cold, the historical importance of Hitler, Stalin, Churchill, and Roosevelt seemed so much greater than that of Kaiser Wilhelm, Tsar Nicholas, and even President Wilson, let alone premiers Lloyd George or Clemenceau. As the world split into ideological camps and as the prospects of a nuclear Armageddon became increasingly real, the Great War became correspondingly less great. The Second World War appeared to represent a far greater divide than the First.

However, in the 1960s our perspective on our century began once again to change. A new wave of irony linked up with the earlier adversarial temper of the 1920s. The success of the satirical revue *Oh What a Lovely War!* and a burgeoning black humour suggested, against the backdrop of the Vietnam War, connections to Dada and the cabaret wit of Berlin during the Weimar years. Moreover, historians began to point to the continuities between the

The charter of the Imperial (after 1960 Commonwealth) War Graves Commission bids it to maintain the cemeteries in perpetuity. Each headstone bears the badge of service or national emblem, the name, rank, and decorations of the soldier, and, at the base, an inscription. Graves of the unidentified are designated by the words 'Known Unto God'. Here a mason re-engraves a headstone.

two world wars. The notion appeared that the years 1914–45 constituted the Thirty Years War of the twentieth century—in essence a civil conflagration among the peoples of Europe.

The dream, still premature in the first years after the Great War, of significant tourism to the battlefields finally became a reality in the 1960s. Who visits the battle sites and the graves of the First World War dead these days, in Flanders, at Vimy, on the Somme, at Verdun? And why do they come? The proportion of pilgrims, people with a family connection to the war, is still high. Time and time again, in the visitors' books at cemeteries, one encounters the comment, often from Australians, New Zealanders, South Africans, Canadians: 'Found at last, granddad.' Tour groups are plentiful. Visits by school classes are frequent. But casual visitors may in fact now be the majority.

The commentary in the visitors' books is, as a result, often platitudinous or sentimental. Political, nationalistic, and ideological reactions are frequent. The Dutch, the Belgians, and the Scandinavians seem most likely to express pacifist sentiments; the British to cite poetry; the Americans to be colloquial. Pervading most of the comments, however, is an extraordinarily high level of emotion. It is clear from the visitors' books that the Great War engages us still. At the New Irish Farm cemetery an Australian writes: 'Glad to have visited here. Life's ambition.'

There is something about the trench experience of the First World War—the intensity, the unpredictability, the bewilderment, the horror, and indeed the intimation of futility—that speaks across the century. We admire the commitment, the remarkable stamina, that soldiers displayed. A part of us may even regret that this kind of fortitude—as F. Scott Fitzgerald asserted back in the 1930s—will probably never be seen again in the western world. But did the war make the world a better place? In social, political, and ideological terms, it is hard to imagine any worse outcome, at least in the short term. In 1915 Galsworthy wrote: 'Those of us who are able to look back from thirty years hence on this tornado of death will conclude with a dreadful laugh that if it had never come the state of the world would be very much the same.' By 1945—those thirty years hence—Galsworthy was no longer with us; the tornado of death, however, was. There was no dreadful laugh. There was only dreadful silence.

And yet, one might argue that, in its implosive and disintegrative power, the Great War—and it will forever retain that name—did have a positive side. By subverting context it liberated text. By undermining old authority, it released creativity. It threw us all back upon ourselves. In that sense it was and remains the great emancipatory adventure-experience of the modern age, open to all, involving all, democratic, symbolic, and inescapable. It is the representative event of our century.

We wallow in that war, 'the greatest of all human contentions', as Winston Churchill called it. Its agony is with us still. We cannot forget, nor can we ever truly comprehend.

FURTHER READING

Correlli Barnett, *The Swordbearers* (London, 1963).

Hugh Cecil and Peter Liddle (eds.), *Facing Armageddon: The First World War Experienced* (London, 1996).

C. R. M. F. Cruttwell, *A History of the Great War, 1914–1918* (2nd edn, London, 1936).

Cyril Falls, *The First World War* (London, 1960).

Marc Ferro, *The Great War, 1914–1918* (London, 1973).

B. H. Liddell Hart, *A History of the World War 1914–1918* (London, 1934).

Bela K. Kiraly, Nandor F. Dreisziger, and Albert A. Nofi (eds.), *East Central European Society in World War I* (Boulder, Colo., 1985).

Allan R. Millett and Williamson Murray (eds.), *Military Effectiveness, i: The First World War* (Boston, 1988).

Keith Robbins, *The First World War* (Oxford, 1983).

David Stevenson, *The First World War and International Politics* (Oxford, 1987).

J. M. Winter, *The Experience of World War I* (London, 1988).

Austria-Hungary

Mark Cornwall (ed.), *The Last Years of Austria-Hungary 1908–1918* (Exeter, 1990).

Manfried Rauchensteiner, *Der Tod des Doppeladlers: Österreich-Ungarn und der Erste Weltkrieg* (Graz, 1993).

Leo Valiani, *The End of Austria-Hungary* (London, 1973).

Britain

J. M. Bourne, *Britain and the Great War 1914–1918* (London, 1989).

G. J. De Groot, *Blighty: British Society in the Era of the Great War* (London, 1996).

Trevor Wilson, *The Myriad Faces of War: Britain and the Great War 1914–1918* (Oxford, 1986).

J. M. Winter, *The Great War and the British People* (London, 1985).

France

Jean-Jacques Becker, *The Great War and the French People* (Leamington Spa, 1985).

Jean-Baptiste Duroselle, *La France et les Français 1914–1920* (Paris, 1972).

Germany

Michael Geyer, 'German Strategy in the Age of Machine Warfare, 1914–1945', in Peter Paret (ed.), *Makers of Modern Strategy from Machiavelli to the Nuclear Age* (Oxford, 1986).

Holger Herwig, *The First World War: Germany and Austria-Hungary 1914–1918* (London, 1996).

Peter Graf von Kielmansegg, *Deutschland und der Erste Weltkrieg* (Stuttgart, 1980).

Fritz Klein *et al.*, *Deutschland im Ersten Weltkrieg* (3 vols., Berlin, 1968–9).

Italy

Giorgio Rochat, *L'Italia nella Prima Guerra Mondiale* (Milan, 1976).

J. A. Thayer, *Italy and the Great War: Politics and Culture 1870–1915* (Madison, 1964).

General

By state

Russia

Michael T. Florinsky, *The End of the Russian Empire* (New Haven, 1931).

W. Bruce Lincoln, *Passage through Armageddon: The Russians in War and Revolution 1914–1918* (New York, 1986).

Bernard Pares, *The Fall of the Russian Monarchy: A Study of the Evidence* (London, 1939).

United States of America

E. M. Coffman, *The War to End All Wars: The American Military Experience in World War I* (Madison, 1968).

David Kennedy, *Over Here: The First World War and American Society* (New York, 1980).

Ronald Schaeffer, *America in the Great War: The Rise of the War Welfare State* (New York, 1991).

1. The Origins of the War

Luigi Albertini, *The Origins of the War of 1914*, ed. and trans. Isabella Massey (3 vols., London, 1952–7).

Volker Berghahn, *Germany and the Approach of War in 1914* (2nd edn, London, 1993).

Richard Bosworth, *Italy and the Approach of the First World War* (London, 1983).

Arden Bucholz, *Moltke, Schlieffen and Prussian War Planning* (New York, 1951).

R. J. W. Evans and Hartmut Pogge von Strandmann (eds.), *The Coming of the First World War* (Oxford, 1988).

'The First World War, 1914–1918', in Donald Kagan, *On the Origins of War and the Preservation of Peace* (New York 1995).

Fritz Fischer, *War of Illusions: German Policies from 1911 to 1914*, trans. Marian Jackson (London, 1975).

Imanuel Geiss, *July 1914: The Outbreak of the First World War: Selected Documents* (London, 1967).

David G. Herrmann, *The Arming of Europe and the Making of the First World War* (Princeton, 1996).

James Joll, *The Origins of the First World War* (2nd edn, London, 1992).

John F. V. Keiger, *France and the Origins of the War* (London, 1983).

Paul Kennedy (ed.), *The War Plans of the Great Powers, 1880–1914* (London, 1979).

H. W. Koch (ed.), *The Origins of the First World War: Great Power Rivalry and German War Aims* (2nd edn, London, 1984).

D. C. B. Lieven, *Russia and the Origins of the First World War* (London, 1983).

Ernest R. May (ed.), *Knowing One's Enemies: Intelligence Assessment before the Two World Wars* (Princeton, 1984).

Steven E. Miller (ed.), *Military Strategy and the Origins of the First World War* (Princeton, 1985).

Jack Snyder, *The Ideology of the Offensive: Military Decision Making and the Disasters of 1914* (Ithaca, NY, 1984).

Zara Steiner, *Britain and the Origins of the War* (London, 1977).

Samuel R. Williamson, Jr., *Austria-Hungary and the Origins of the First World War* (London, 1991).

—— *The Politics of Grand Strategy: Britain and France Prepare for War, 1904–1914* (2nd edn. rev. London, 1990).

Keith Wilson (ed.), *Decisions for War, 1914* (London, 1995).

2. The Strategy of the Central Powers

Holger Afflerbach, *Falkenhayn: Politisches Denken und Handeln im Kaiserreich* (Munich, 1994).

J. Andrassy, *Diplomacy and the World War* (London, 1921). A survey from the Austro-Hungarian point of view.

Bertrand Auerbach, *L'Autriche et la Hongrie pendant la guerre* (Paris, 1925).

Theobald Bethmann Hollweg, *Betrachtungen zum Weltkriege*, vol. ii (Berlin, 1922). Unavoidably special pleading but revealing.

Karl E. Birnbaum, *Peace Moves and U-boat Warfare: A Study of Imperial Germany's Policy towards the United States, April 18, 1916–January 9, 1917* (Stockholm, 1958).

Stephan Burian, *Drei Jahre aus der Zeit meiner Amtsführung im Kriege* (Berlin, 1923). Biased but interesting.

Franz Conrad von Hötzendorf, *Aus meiner Dienstzeit*, vols. iii–v (Vienna, 1922–5).

Gordon A, Craig, 'The World War I Alliance of the Central Powers in Retrospect: The Military Cohesion of the Alliance', *Journal of Modern History* (September 1965), 336–45.

Erich Falkenhayn, *General Headquarters 1914–1916 and its Critical Decisions* (London, 1920).

L. L. Farrar, *Divide and Conquer: German Efforts to Conclude a Separate Peace, 1914–1918* (Boulder, Colo., 1978).

——*The Short-War Illusion: German Policy, Strategy and Domestic Affairs August–December 1914* (Santa Barbara, 1973)

Fritz Fischer, *Germany's Aims in the First World War* (New York, 1967).

W. W. Gottlieb, *Studies in Secret Diplomacy during the First World War* (London, 1957). Focuses on the first two years.

Karl Heinz Janssen, *Der Kanzler und der General: Die Führungskrise um Bethmann Hollweg und Falkenhayn, 1914–1916* (Göttingen, 1967).

Konrad H. Jarausch, *The Enigmatic Chancellor: Bethmann Hollweg and the Hubris of Imperial Germany* (New Haven, 1972). Nuanced but basically sympathetic.

Arthur J. May, *The Passing of the Habsburg Monarchy, 1914–1918* (Philadelphia, 1966).

Gerhard Ritter, *The Schlieffen Plan* (London, 1958).

——*The Sword and the Sceptre: The Problem of Militarism in Germany*, vol. iv (London, 1973). Critical of the military, more apologetic of the civilians.

Gary W. Shanafelt, *The Secret Enemy: Austria-Hungary and the German Alliance, 1914–1918* (Boulder, Colo., 1985)

Gerald E. Silberstein, *The Troubled Alliance: German-Austrian Relations, 1914 to 1917* (Lexington, Ky., 1967).

Wolfgang, Steglich, *Bündnissicherung oder Verständigungsfrieden: Untersuchungen zu dem Friedensangebot der Mittelmächte vom 12. Dezember 1916* (Göttingen, 1958). A sympathetic handling.

Z. A. B. Zeman, *A Diplomatic History of the First World War* (London, 1971). Particularly good on personalities.

J. J. Becker, *1914: Comment les Français sont entrés dans la guerre* (Paris, 1977).

Marc Bloch, *Memoirs of War, 1914–1915*, trans. C. Fink (Ithaca, NY, 1980).

Walter Bloem, *The Advance from Mons* (London, 1930).

J. M. Craster, *'Fifteen Rounds a Minute': The Grenadiers at War, 1914* (London, 1976).

Anthony Farrar-Hockley, *Death of an Army* (London, 1967).

John Horne and Alan Kramer, 'German "Atrocities" and Franco-German Opinion, 1914: The Evidence of German Soldiers' Diaries', *Journal of Modern History*, 66 (1994), 1–33.

John Keegan, *Opening Moves: August 1914* (New York, 1971).

Lyn Macdonald, *1914* (New York, 1987).

3. Manœuvre Warfare

Bradley Meyer, 'Operational Art and the German Command System in World War I' (Ph.D. dissertation, Ohio State University, 1988).

Douglas Porch, 'The Marne and After: A Reappraisal of French Strategy in the First World War', *Journal of Military History*, 53 (1989), 363–86.

Dennis Showalter, *Tannenberg: Clash of Empires* (Hamden, Conn., 1991).

Major General Sir Edward Spears, *Liaison 1914* (London, 1930).

Norman Stone, *The Eastern Front, 1914–17* (London, 1975).

Sewell Tyng, *The Campaign of the Marne, 1914* (Oxford, 1935).

Karl Unruh, *Langemarck: Legende und Wirklichkeit* (Koblenz, 1986).

4. The Strategy of the Entente Powers

C. Andrew and A. S. Kanya-Forstner, *France Overseas: The Great War and the Climax of French Imperial Expansion* (London, 1981).

K. M. Burk, *Britain, America and the Sinews of War 1914–1918* (London, 1985).

K. J. Calder, *Britain and the Origins of the New Europe, 1914–1918* (Cambridge, 1976).

G. H. Cassar, *The French and the Dardanelles* (London, 1971).

G. R. Conyne, *Woodrow Wilson: British Perspectives, 1912–1921* (London, 1992).

D. Dutton, 'The Balkan Campaign and French War Aims in the Great War', *English Historical Review*, 94 (1979), 97–113.

W. B. Fest, *Peace or Partition: The Habsburg Monarchy and British Policy 1914–1918* (London, 1978).

D. French, *British Strategy and War Aims, 1914–16* (London, 1986).

—— *The Strategy of the Lloyd George Coalition* (Oxford, 1995).

J. Gooch, 'Soldiers, Strategy and War Aims in Britain, 1914–1918', in B. Hunt and A. Preston (eds.), *War Aims and Strategic Policy in the Great War* (London, 1977), 21–40.

F. H. Hinsley (ed.), *British Foreign Policy under Sir Edward Grey* (Cambridge, 1977).

K. Neilson, *Strategy and Supply: The Anglo-Russian Alliance, 1914–1917* (London, 1984).

J. Nevakivi, *Britain, France and the Arab Middle East 1914–1920* (London, 1969).

R. Rhodes James, *Gallipoli* (London, 1965).

V. H. Rothwell, *British War Aims and Peace Diplomacy 1914–1918* (Oxford, 1971).

D. Stevenson, *French War Aims against Germany, 1914–1919* (Oxford, 1982).

N. Stone, *The Eastern Front 1914–1917* (London, 1975).

J. K. Tanenbaum, *General Maurice Sarrail, 1856–1929: The French Army and Left-Wing Politics* (Chapel Hill, NC, 1974).

S. R. Williamson, *The Politics of Grand Strategy: Britain and France Prepare for War, 1904–14* (Cambridge, Mass., 1969).

D. R. Woodward, *Lloyd George and the Generals* (Newark, NJ, 1983).

5. The Balkans, 1914–1918

G. F. Abbott, *Greece and the Allies, 1914–1922* (London, 1922). Although old still a useful summary both of the political aspects of the internal struggles in Greece and of Greece's complex relations with the warring sides.

John Clinton Adams, *Flight in Winter* (Princeton, 1942). A detailed account of the Serbian retreat in 1915.

Vasile Alexandrescu, *Romania in World War I: A Synopsis of Military History* (Bucharest, 1985).

Grigore Antipa, *L'Occupation ennemie de la Roumanie et ses conséquences économiques et sociales* (New Haven, 1929).

Victor Atanasiu et al., *România cin anii primului râzboi monmdial* [Romania during the First World War] (Bucharest, 1987). Clogged with Ceaușescuist gibberish but contains much detail.

Richard J. Crampton, *Bulgaria 1878–1918: A History* (New York, 1983).

Georgi T. Danailov, *Les Effets de la guerre en Bulgarie* (New Haven, 1932).

Marcel Dunan, *Le Drame balkanique de 1915. L'Automne serbe; notes d'un témoin avec une carte en couleurs* (Paris, 1932).

Cyril Falls, *Military Operatons, Macedonia* (2 vols., London, 1933–5). The official history.

Wolfgang-Uwe Friedrich, *Bulgarien und die Mächte: Ein Beitrag zur Weltkriegs- und Imperialismusgeschichte* (Wiesbaden, 1985).

Keith Hitchins, *Rumania 1866–1947* (Oxford, 1994).

Hristo Hristov, *Voinishkoto vûstanie, 1918g* [The Military Rising of 1918] (Sofia, 1961). Despite its ideological content has useful information on the supply problem for the Bulgarian army and on civilian privations.

George B. Leontaritis, *Greece and the First World War: From Neutrality to Intervention, 1917–1918* (New York, 1990). In two parts, the first dealing with the domestic front and the second with war aims.

A. Lulchev, *Septemvriiski dni 1918g* [September Days, 1918] (Sofia, 1926). Recollections of the collapse of the Bulgarian war effort by a Bulgarian general.

Alan Palmer, *The Gardeners of Salonika* (London, 1965).

Michael Boro Petrovich, *A History of Modern Serbia 1804–1918*, vol. ii (New York, 1976).

Vasil Radoslawoff, *Bulgarien und die Weltkrise* (Berlin, 1923). Provides 'official' line for Bulgaria's entry into the war by the prime minister who was responsible.

J. Swire, *Albania: The Rise of a Kingdom* (London, 1929).

G. E. Torrey, 'Romania in the First World War: The Years of Engagement', *International History Review*, 14 (1992), 462–79

—— 'The Rumanian Campaign of 1916: Its Impact on the Belligerents', *Slavic Review*, 39 (1980), 27–43.

Gen. St. Toshev, *Deistvie na III armiya v Dobrudja prez 1916g* [The Third Army in the Dobrudja in 1916] (Sofia, n.d.). By a leading Bulgarian participant.

T. Vlahov, *Otnosheniya mezhdu Bûlgariya i Tsentralnite Sili prez vionite, 1912–1918* [Relations between Bulgaria and the Central Powers, 1912–1918] (Sofia, 1957). A basically reliable diplomatic history.

Feroz Ahmad, *The Making of Modern Turkey* (London, 1993). **6. Turkey's War**

A. J. Barker, *The Neglected War: Mesopotamia 1914–1918* (London, 1967).

Fahri Belen, *Birinci Cihan Harbinde Turk Harbi* [The Turkish War during the First World War] (5 vols., Ankara, 1963–7).

Wolfdieter Bihl, *Die Kaukasus-Politik der Mittelmächte* (Vienna, 1975).

Briton C. Busch, *Britain, India, and the Arabs, 1914–1921* (Berkeley, 1971).

George H. Cassar, *The French and the Dardanelles* (London, 1971).

Ahmed Emin, *Turkey in the World War* (New Haven, 1930).

Isaiah Friedman, *Germany, Turkey, and Zionism, 1897–1918* (Oxford, 1977).

Ulrich Gehrke, *Persien in der deutschen Orientpolitik während des Ersten Weltkrieges* (2 vols., Stuttgart, 1960).

Paul G. Halpern, *The Naval War in the Mediterranean, 1914–1918* (London, 1987).

Richard G. Hovannisian, *Armenia on the Road to Independence, 1918* (Berkeley, 1967).

Firuz Kazemzadeh, *The Struggle for Transcaucasia, 1917–1921* (New York, 1951).

Marian Kent (ed.), *The Great Powers and the End of the Ottoman Empire* (2nd edn, London, 1996).

N. G. Korsun, *Pervaya mirovaya voina na Kavkazkom fronte* [The First World War on the Caucasian Front] (Moscow, 1946).

Maurice Larcher, *La Guerre turque dans la guerre mondiale* (Paris, 1926).

Hermann Lorey (ed.), *Der Krieg in den tërkischen Gewässern* (2 vols. Berlin, 1928–38).

Frederick J. Moberly, *Operations in Persia, 1914–1918* (London, 1987).

Carl Mühlmann, *Das deutsch-türkische Waffenbündnis im Weltkrieg* (Leipzig, 1940).

——*Der Kampf um die Dardanellen 1915* (Oldenburg, 1927).

Christopher Pugsley, *Gallipoli: The New Zealand Story* (Auckland, 1984).

E. K. Sarkisyan, *Ekspansionistkaya politika Osmanskoy Imperii v Zakavkaze* [The Expansionist Policy of the Ottoman Empire in Transcaucasia] (Erevan, 1962).

Ulrich Trumpener, *Germany and the Ottoman Empire, 1914–1918* (Princeton, 1968).

Frank G. Weber, *Eagles on the Crescent: Germany, Austria and the Diplomacy of the Turkish Alliance 1914–1918* (Ithaca, NY, 1970).

Erik J. Zürcher, *The Unionist Factor* (Leiden, 1984).

——*Turkey: A Modern History* (London, 1993).

7. The War in Africa

Michael Crowder, 'The First World War and its Consequences', in A. Adu Boahen (ed.), *General History of Africa*, vii: *Africa under Colonial Domination 1880–1935* (London, 1985), 283–311.

——and Jide Osuntokun, 'The First World War and West Africa', in J. F. Ade Ajayi and Michael Crowder (eds.), *History of West Africa*, vol. ii (2nd edn. London, 1987), 546–77.

T. R. H. Davenport, *South Africa: A Modern History* (4th edn. London, 1991), ch. 10.

Myron Echenberg, *Colonial Conscripts: The Tirailleurs Sénégalais in French West Africa, 1857–1960* (London, 1991), ch. 3.

Albert Grundlingh, *Black Men in a White Man's War: South African Blacks and the First World War* (Braamfontein, 1986).

Geoffrey Hodges, *The Carrier Corps: Military Labor in the East African Campaign of 1914 to 1918* (Westport, Conn., 1986).

Journal of African History, 19/1 (1978), special issue on Africa and the First World War.

Sir Charles Lucas, *The Empire at War*, vols. i–iv (London, 1921–4).

Marc Michel, *L'Appel à l'Afrique: Contributions et réactions à l'effort de guerre en AOF (1914–1919)* (Paris, 1982).

Charles Miller, *Battle for the Bundu: The First World War in East Africa* (London, 1974).

Jide Osuntokun, *Nigeria in the First World War* (London, 1979).

Melvin Page (ed.), *Africa and the First World War* (London, 1987).

Andrew Roberts (ed.), *The Cambridge History of Africa*, vii: *1905–1940* (Cambridge, 1986).

8. The War at Sea

Patrick Beesly, *Room 40: British Naval Intelligence, 1914–1918* (London, 1982).

N. J. M. Campbell, *Jutland: An Analysis of the Fighting* (London, 1986). Particularly important for gunnery and damage inflicted.

Julian S. Corbett and Henry Newbolt, *History of the Great War: Naval Operations* (5 vols. in 9, London, 1920–31). Subject to the caution that this was the semi-official history written when the major leaders were still alive and had the opportunity to influence the work.

James Goldrick, *The King's Ships Were at Sea: The War in the North Sea August 1914–February 1915* (Annapolis, 1984).

Andrew Gordon, *The Rules of the Game: Jutland and British Naval Command* (London, 1996).

Paul G. Halpern, *The Mediterranean Naval Situation, 1908–1914* (Cambridge,

Mass., 1971); *The Naval War in the Mediterranean, 1914–1918* (London, 1987); and *A Naval History of World War I* (Annapolis, 1994).

Holger H. Herwig, '*Luxury Fleet*': *The Imperial German Navy, 1888–1918* (London, 1980).

Roger Keyes, *The Naval Memoirs* (2 vols., London, 1934–5). Essential for the 1915 Dardanelles campaign and Zeebrugge raid in 1918.

Nicholas A. Lambert, 'British Naval Policy, 1913–1914: Financial Limitation and Strategic Revolution', *Journal of Modern History*, 67 (1995), 595–626.

Arthur J. Marder, *From the Dreadnought to Scapa Flow: The Royal Navy in the Fisher Era, 1904–1919* (5 vols., London, 1961–70). A magisterial study although certain areas, particularly on the pre-war period, are now subject to revision.

George Nekrasov, *North of Gallipoli: The Black Sea Fleet at War, 1914–1917* (Boulder, Colo., 1992).

Tobias R. Philbin, *Admiral von Hipper: The Inconvenient Hero* (Amsterdam, 1982).

Stephen Roskill, *Earl Beatty: The Last Naval Hero* (London, 1980).

Lawrence Sondhaus, *The Naval Policy of Austria-Hungary, 1867–1918: Navalism, Industrial Development and the Politics of Dualism* (West Lafayette, Ind., 1994).

Jon Tetsuro Sumida, *In Defence of Naval Supremacy: Finance, Technology and British Naval Policy, 1889–1914* (Boston, 1989).

V. E. Tarrant, *Jutland: The German Perspective* (Annapolis, 1995). Quotes extensively from the German official history of 1925.

David F. Trask, *Captains and Cabinets: Anglo-American Naval Relations, 1917–1918* (Columbia, Mo., 1972).

Michael Wilson, *Baltic Assignment: British Submarines in Russia, 1914–1919* (London, 1985).

John Winton, *Convoy: The Defence of Sea Trade, 1890–1990* (London, 1983).

W. Arnold-Forster, *The Blockade, 1914–1919; before the Armistice—and after* (Oxford, 1939). **9. Economic Warfare**

L. M. Barnett, *British Food Policy during the First World War* (London, 1985).

A. C. Bell [Historical Section, Committee of Imperial Defence], *A History of the Blockade of Germany and the Countries Associated with her in the Great War, Austria-Hungary, Bulgaria, and Turkey, 1914–1918* (London, 1937 [but classified until 1961])

Lothar Burchardt, 'The Impact of the War Economy on the Civilian Population of Germany during the First and Second World Wars', in Wilhelm Deist (ed.), *The German Military in the Age of Total War* (Leamington Spa, 1985).

K. M. Burk, *Britain, America and the Sinews of War, 1914–1918* (London, 1985).

W. M. Carlgren, *Neutralität oder Allianz: Deutschlands Beziehungen zu Schweden in den Anfangsjahren des Ersten Weltkrieges* (Stockholm, 1962).

J. W. Coogan, *The End of Neutrality: The United States, Britain, and Maritime Rights 1899–1915* (Ithaca, NY, 1975).

M. M. Farrar, *Conflict and Compromise: The Strategy, Politics and Diplomacy of the French Blockade, 1914–1918* (The Hague, 1974).

C. E. Fayle, *The War and the Shipping Industry* (Oxford, 1927).

J. A. Grohmann, *Die deutsche-schwedishe Auseinandersetzung um die Fahrstrassen des Öresunds im Ersten Weltkrieg* (Boppard am Rhein, 1974).

F. W. Hirst, *The Political Economy of War* (London, 1916).

R. Hough, *The Great War at Sea 1914–1918* (Oxford, 1983).

B. D. Hunt and A. Preston (eds.), *War and Strategic Policy in the Great War* (London, 1977).

P. Kennedy (ed.), *The War Plans of the Great Powers, 1880–1914* (London, 1979).

J. Kocka, *Facing Total War: German Society, 1914–1918* (Cambridge, Mass., 1984)

[English translation of *Klassengesellschaft im Krieg: Dt. Sozialgeschichte 1914–1918* (Göttingen, 1973)].

Joe Lee, 'Administrators and Agriculture: Aspects of German Agricultural Policy in the First World War', in J. M. Winter (ed.), *War and Economic Development* (Cambridge, 1975).

B. J. C. McKercher, *Esme Howard: A Diplomatic Biography* (Cambridge, 1989).

Robert G. Moeller, *German Peasants and Agrarian Politics, 1914–1924: The Rhineland and Westphalia* (Chapel Hill, NC, 1986).

H. Newbolt, *History of the Great War: Naval Operations*, vol. v (London, 1931).

B. Nolde, *Russia in the Economic War* (New Haven, 1928).

A. Offer, *The First World War: An Agrarian Interpretation* (Oxford, 1989).

M. C. Siney, *The Allied Blockade of Germany 1914–1918* (Ann Arbor, 1957).

A. Spindler, *Der Handelskrieg mit U-Booten* (Berlin, 1932).

G. Stolper, *Das Mitteleuropäische Wirtschaftsproblem* (Leipzig, 1919).

C. P. Vincent, *The Politics of Hunger: The Allied Blockade of Germany* (Athens, Oh., 1985).

10. Economic Mobilization

T. Balderston, 'War Finance and Inflation in Britain and Germany, 1914–1918', *Economic History Review*, 2nd series, 42 (1989), 222–44.

Gerd Hardach, *The First World War 1914–1918* (London, 1977). An overview of the economic history of the war.

Austria-Hungary

Eduard Marz, *Austrian Banking and Financial Policy: Creditanstalt at a Turning Point, 1913–1923* (London, 1984).

James Robert Wegs, 'Austrian Economic Mobilization during World War I: With Particular Emphasis on Heavy Industry' (Ph. D dissertation, University of Illinois, 1970).

Britain

R. J. Q. Adams, *Arms and the Wizard: Lloyd George and the Ministry of Munitions* (London, 1978).

Kathleen Burk (ed.), *War and the State: The Transformation of British Government, 1914–1919* (London, 1982).

History of the Ministry of Munitions (12 vols., London, 1921–2).

E. Victor Morgan, *Studies in British Financial Policy 1914–25* (London, 1952).

France

Arthur Fontaine, *French Industry during the War* (New Haven, 1926).

John Godfrey, *Capitalism at War: Industrial Policy and Bureaucracy in France 1914–1918* (Leamington Spa, 1987).

Gaston Jèze and Henri Truchy, *The War Finance of France* (New Haven, 1927).

Germany

Robert B. Armeson, *Total Warfare and Compulsory Labor: A Study of the Military-Industrial Complex in Germany during World War I* (The Hague, 1964).

Gerald D. Feldman, *Army, Industry and Labor in Germany 1914–1918* (Princeton, 1966).

——*The Great Disorder: Politics, Economics and Society in the German Inflation, 1914–1922* (New York, 1993).

Italy

Douglas J. Forsyth, *The Crisis of Liberal Italy: Monetary and Financial Policy, 1914–1922* (Cambridge, 1993).

Russia

Peter Gatrell and Mark Harrison, 'The Russian and Soviet Economies in Two World Wars: A Comparative View', *Economic History Review*, 2nd series, 46 (1993), 425–52.

Alexander M. Michelson, Paul N. Apostol, and Michael W. Bernatzky, *Russian Public Finance during the War* (New Haven, 1928).

Lewis H . Siegelbaum, *The Politics of Industrial Mobilization in Russia, 1914–17: A Study of the War-Industries Committees* (London, 1983).

S. O. Zagorsky, *State Control of Industry in Russia during the War* (New Haven, 1928).

United States of America

Kathleen Burk, *Britain, America and the Sinews of War, 1914–1918* (Boston, Mass., 1988).

Charles Gilbert, *American Financing of World War I* (Westport, Conn., 1970).

General

Richard Evans, *Comrades and Sisters: Feminism, Socialism and Pacifism in Europe 1870–1945* (Brighton, 1987). Good comparative history.

M. R. Higonnet, J. Jenson, S. Michel, and M. C. Weitz, *Behind the Lines: Gender and the Two World Wars* (New Haven, 1987).

Richard Wall and Jay Winter (eds.), *The Upheaval of War* (Cambridge, 1988). See in particular Wall on the effect of war on families, Patrick Friedenson on France, Ute Daniel on German women, Deborah Thom on England, and Richard Sieder on life in Vienna.

Julie Wheelwright, *Amazons and Military Maids: Women who Dressed as Men in Pursuit of Life, Liberty and Happiness* (London, 1989). This book has a great deal of information on both Flora Sandes and the Russian women's battalions.

(margin note) 11. Women, War, and Work

Britain

Gail Braybon, *Women Workers in the First World War* (London, 1989). Largely about attitudes to women workers amongst unions, employers, and government. Not much about women themselves, but this was to some extent remedied by *Out of the Cage: Women's Experiences in Two World Wars* (London, 1987), written jointly with Penny Summerfield.

Diana Condell and Jean Liddiard, *Working for Victory? Images of Women in the First World War 1914–1918* (London, 1987). A wonderful collection of the Imperial War Museum's photographs of women, with good captions.

Cate Haste, *Rules of Desire; Sex in Britain: World War 1 to the Present* (London, 1992). This puts the effects of the war into perspective, and is a useful antidote to the kind of generalizations about sexual morality and women's 'new sexual freedom' that one often finds in more general books.

Nosheen Khan, *Women's Poetry of the First World War* (Brighton, 1988).

Deborah Thom, 'Tommy's Sister: Women at Woolwich in World War 1', in Raphael Samuel (ed.), *Patriotism: The Making and Unmaking of British Identity* (London, 1989).

France

Jean Jacques Becker, *The Great War and the French People* (Oxford, 1985).

Patrick Friedenson, *The French Home Front 1914–18* (Oxford, 1992).

Steven Hause, *Women's Suffrage and Social Politics in the French Third Republic* (Princeton, 1984).

James McMillan, *Housewife or Harlot: The Place of Women in French Society 1870–1940* (Brighton, 1981).

Susan Pederson, *Family, Dependence and the Origins of the Welfare State: Britain and France, 1914–1945* (Cambridge, 1993).

Germany
Richard Bessel, *Germany after the First World War* (Oxford, 1993).
Ute Frevert, *Women in German History* (Oxford, 1989).
Robert Weldon Whalen, *Bitter Wounds: German Victims of the Great War* (Ithaca, NY, 1984). Although much of this is about ex-servicemen, there is quite a lot of material here about war widows.

Russia
Rose L. Glickman, *Russian Factory Women* (Berkeley and Los Angeles, 1984). About working-class women before the war. Unfortunately there are very few books about women's role in the war itself, as this has taken second place to the revolutionary period of 1917.
S. O. Zagorsky, *State Control of Industry during the War* (New Haven, 1928).

United States of America
Maurine Weiner Greenwald, *Women, War and Work* (Ithaca, NY, 1990). The similarities with Britain are marked, yet there is the added dimension of race as well as sex stereotyping at work.

12. The Challenge to Liberalism

Austria-Hungary
Barbara Jelavich, *Modern Austria: Empire and Republic* (Cambridge, 1987).
Arthur May, *The Passing of the Hapsburg Monarchy, 1914–1918* (2 vols., Philadelphia, 1966).
Joseph Redlich, *Austrian War Government* (New Haven, 1929).
Z. A. B. Zeman, *The Break-Up of the Habsburg Empire, 1914–1918* (London, 1961).

Britain
Cameron Hazlehurst, *Politicians at War July 1914 to May 1915: A Prologue to the Triumph of Lloyd George* (London, 1971).
A. J. P. Taylor, *Politics in Wartime* (London, 1964).
John Turner, *British Politics and the Great War* (New Haven, 1992).

France
Majorie Farrar, *Principled Pragmatist: The Political Career of Alexandre Millerand* (London, 1991).
P. J. Flood, *France 1914–1918: Public Opinion and the War Effort* (New York, 1989).
John Keiger, *Raymond Poincaré* (Cambridge, 1997).
Jere Clemens King, *Generals and Politicians: Conflict between France's High Command, Parliament and Government, 1914–1918* (Berkeley, 1951).
David Newhall, *Clemenceau: A Life at War* (New York, 1992).
Catherine Slater, *Defeatists and their Enemies: Political Invective in France, 1914–1918* (Oxford, 1981).

Germany
K. Epstein, *Matthias Erzberger and the Dilemma of German Democracy* (Princeton, 1959).
Konrad Jarausch, *The Enigmatic Chancellor: Bethmann-Hollweg and the Hubris of Imperial Germany* (New Haven, 1973).
Martin Kitchen, *The Silent Dictatorship: The Politics of the German High Command under Hindenburg and Ludendorff, 1916–1918* (London, 1976).
J. Kocka, *Facing Total War: German Society 1914–1918* (Leamington Spa, 1984).
James N. Retallack, *Notables of the Right: The Conservative Party and Political Mobilization in Germany, 1876–1918* (London, 1979).
Gerhard Ritter, *The Sword and the Sceptre*, vols. iii and iv (London, 1973).

Arthur Rosenberg, *The Birth of the German Republic 1871–1918* (New York, 1962).

Hans-Ulrich Wehler, *The German Empire 1871–1918* (Leamington Spa, 1985).

Italy
D. J. Forsyth, *The Crisis of Liberal Italy 1914–1922* (Cambridge, 1993).

Christopher Seton-Watson, *Italy from Liberalism to Fascism, 1870–1925* (London, 1967).

J. Thayer, *Italy and the Great War: Politics and Culture, 1870–1915* (Madison, 1964).

J. Whittam, *The Politics of the Italian Army* (London, 1976).

Russia
Bernard Pares, *The Fall of the Russian Monarchy* (London, 1939).

Raymond Pearson, *The Russian Moderates and the Crisis of Tsarism 1914–1917* (London, 1977).

Hans Rogger, *Russia in the Age of Modernisation and Revolution* (London, 1983).

United States of America
Arthur S. Link, *Woodrow Wilson and the Progressive Era* (New York, 1954).

Seward W. Livermore, *Politics is Adjourned: Woodrow Wilson and the War Congress 1916–1918* (Middletown, Conn., 1966).

John A. Thompson, *Reformers and War: American Progressive Publicists and the First World War* (Cambridge, 1987).

13. Eastern Front and Western Front

Shelford Bidwell and Dominick Graham, *Fire-Power: British Army Weapons and Theories of War 1904–1945* (London, 1982).

J. E. Edmonds, *History of the Great War: Military Operations France and Belgium* (14 vols., London, 1922–48).

A. H. Farrar-Hockley, *The Somme* (London, 1964).

Paddy Griffith, *Battle Tactics of the Western Front* (New Haven, 1994).

Alistair Horne, *The Price of Glory: Verdun 1916* (London, 1962).

Jackson Hughes, *The Monstrous Anger of the Guns* (Cambridge, forthcoming).

Geoffrey Jukes, *Carpathian Disaster* (London, 1971).

John Keegan, *The Face of Battle* (London, 1976).

Alfred Knox, *With the Russian Army 1914–1917* (London, 1921).

Lyn Macdonald, *They Called it Passchendaele* (London, 1978).

Kenneth Macksey, *Vimy Ridge* (London, 1972).

Martin Middlebrook, *The First Day on the Somme* (London, 1971).

William J. Philpott, *Anglo-French Relations and Strategy on the Western Front, 1914–18* (Basingstoke, 1996).

Robin Prior and Trevor Wilson, *Command on the Western Front* (Oxford, 1992).

——*Passchendaele, the Untold Story* (New Haven, 1996).

Gunther Rothenberg, *The Army of Francis Joseph* (West Lafayette, Ind., 1976).

Len Smith, *Between Mutiny and Obedience: The Case of the French 5th Infantry Division during World War One* (Princeton, 1994).

E. L. Spears, *Prelude to Victory* (London, 1939).

Norman Stone, *The Eastern Front 1914–1917* (London, 1975).

John Terraine, *Douglas Haig: The Educated Soldier* (London, 1963).

Tim Travers, *The Killing Ground* (London, 1987).

14. Mutinies and Military Morale

Tony Ashworth, *Trench Warfare, 1914–1918: The Live and Let Live System* (London, 1980).

Stéphane Audoin-Rouzeau, *Men at War 1914–1918: National Sentiment and Trench Journalism in France during the First World War* (Providence, RI, 1992).

Anthony Babington, *For the Sake of Example* (London, 1983). Inadequate study of military justice system in British army. Should be supplemented by Pugsley.

John Baynes, *Morale: A Study of Courage: The Second Scottish Rifles at the Battle of Neuve Chapelle, 1915* (London, 1967). Professional officer's perspective on problems of unit cohesion and combat motivation.

Ian F. W. Beckett and Keith Simpson (eds), *A Nation in Arms: A Social Study of the British Army in the First World War* (Manchester, 1985).

Richard Bessel, *Germany after the First World War* (Oxford, 1993).

Gladden Dallas and Douglas Gill, *The Unknown Army: Mutinies in the British Army in World War I* (London, 1985).

Wilhelm Deist, 'The Military Collapse of the German Empire: The Reality behind the Stab-in-the-Back Myth', *War in History*, 3 (1996), 186–207.

John Ellis, *Eye-Deep in Hell: Trench Warfare in World War I* (New York, 1976).

J. G. Fuller, *Troop Morale and Popular Culture in the British and Dominion Armies 1914–1918* (Oxford, 1990). Shows how provision of sports and music-hall-style entertainments kept the blues away from the British.

Paul Fussell, *The Great War and Modern Memory* (Oxford, 1975). Influential study of alleged discontinuous character of modern warfare.

Richard Holmes, *Firing Line: The Behaviour of Men in Battle* (London, 1985).

Daniel Horn, *Mutiny on the High Seas: The Imperial German Naval Mutinies of World War I* (London, 1973).

John Horne (ed.), *State, Society and Mobilization in Europe during the First World War* (Cambridge, 1997).

John Keegan, *The Face of Battle: A Study of Agincourt, Waterloo and the Somme* (London, 1976).

Eric J. Leed, *No Man's Land: Combat and Identity in World War I* (New York, 1979). Implausible study of supposed mass alienation of troops due to requirements of new technological battlefields.

Philippe Masson, *La Marine française et la Mer Noire 1918–1919* (Paris, 1982).

Evan Mawdsley, *The Russian Revolution and the Baltic Fleet* (London, 1978).

Guy Pedroncini, *Les Mutineries de 1917* (Paris, 1967).

Christopher Pugsley, *On the Fringe of Hell: New Zealanders and Military Discipline in the First World War* (Auckland, 1991).

Antoine Prost, *In the Wake of War: Les Anciens Combattants and French Society, 1914–1939* (Providence, RI, 1993). Emphasizes salience of republicanism in outlook of the French soldier.

Luc Schepens, *Albert Ier et le gouvernement Broqueville 1914–1918* (Brussels, 1983).

Leonard V. Smith, *Between Mutiny and Obedience: The Case of the Fifth Infantry Division during World War I* (Princeton, 1994).

Alan K. Wildman, *The End of the Russian Imperial Army: The Old Army and the Soldiers' Revolt* (Princeton, 1980).

——*The End of the Russian Imperial Army: The Road to Soviet Power and Peace* (Princeton, 1987).

15. War Aims and Peace Negotiations

K. J. Calder, *Britain and the Origins of the New Europe, 1914–1918* (Cambridge, 1976).

A. Dallin et al., *Russian Diplomacy and Eastern Europe, 1914–1917* (New York, 1963).

R. K. Debo, *Revolution and Survival: The Foreign Policy of Soviet Russia, 1917–1918* (Toronto, 1979).

L. L. Farrar, *Divide and Conquer: German Efforts to Conclude a Separate Peace, 1914–1918* (New York, 1978).

F. Fischer, *Germany's Aims in the First World War* (English edn., London, 1967).

H. W. Gatzke, *Germany's Drive to the West: A Study of Western War Aims during the First World War* (Baltimore, 1950).

W. W. Gottlieb, *Studies in Secret Diplomacy during the First World War* (London, 1957).

M. Kent (ed.), *The Great Powers and the End of the Ottoman Empire* (London, 1984).

T. J. Knock, *To End All Wars: Woodrow Wilson and the Quest for a New World Order* (New York, 1992).

N. G. Levin, *Woodrow Wilson and World Politics: America's Response to War and Revolution* (New York, 1968).

D. Lloyd George, *War Memoirs* (6 vols., London, 1933–6).

A. J. Mayer, *Political Origins of the New Diplomacy, 1917–1918* (New Haven, 1959).

H. C. Meyer, *Mitteleuropa in German Thought and Action, 1815–1945* (The Hague, 1955).

G. Ritter, *The Sword and the Sceptre: The Problem of Militarism in Germany* (English edn., 4 vols., London, 1969–73). A reply to Fischer.

V. H. Rothwell, *British War Aims and Peace Diplomacy, 1914–1918* (Oxford, 1971).

C. M. Seymour (ed.), *The Intimate Papers of Colonel House* (4 vols., London, 1926–8).

C. J. Smith, *The Russian Struggle for Power, 1914–1917: A Study of Russian Foreign Policy during the First World War* (New York, 1956).

G.-H. Soutou, *L'Or et le sang: Les Buts de guerre économiques de la Première Guerre mondiale* (Paris, 1989). An important corrective to Fischer.

D. Stevenson, *French War Aims against Germany, 1914–1919* (Oxford, 1982).

——— *The First World War and International Politics* (paperback edn., Oxford, 1991). The best overview.

J. W. Wheeler-Bennett, *Brest-Litovsk: The Forgotten Peace, March 1918* (London, 1938).

Stéphane Audoin-Rouzeau, *La Guerre des enfants* (Paris, 1994).

Maurice Bardèche and Robert Brasillach, *The History of Motion Pictures*, trans. Iris Barry (New York, 1938).

Annette Becker, *La Guerre et la foi: De la mort à la mémoire* (Paris, 1994).

Kevin Brownlow, *The War, the West and the Wilderness* (New York, 1979).

Charles Chaplin, *My Autobiography* (New York, 1964).

E. A. Demm, 'Les Thèmes de la propagande allemande en 1914', *Guerres mondiales et conflits contemporains*, 150 (1988), 3–16.

Karel Dibbets and Bert Hogenkamp (eds.), *Film and the First World War* (Amsterdam, 1994).

Denis Gillford, *Chaplin* (New York, 1974).

Adolf Hitler, *Mein Kampf* (Munich, 1926).

Marie-Monique Huss, 'The Popular Postcard and French Pronatalism in the First World War', in R. Wall and J. M. Winter (eds.), *The Upheaval of War: Family, Work and Welfare in Europe 1914–1918* (Cambridge, 1988).

Harold Lasswell, *Propaganda and the Great War* (Cambridge Mass, 1971; 1st edn. 1927).

Charles T. Maland, *Chaplin and American Culture: The Evolution of an Image* (Princeton, 1989).

A. G. Marquis, 'Words as Weapons: Propaganda in Britain and Germany during the First World War', *Journal of Contemporary History*, 13 (1978), 467–98.

J. A. Moses, 'State, War, Revolution and the German Evangelical Church, 1914–18', *Journal of Religious Studies*, 17 (1992), 47–59.

16. Propaganda and the Mobilization of Consent

George Mosse, *Fallen Soldiers: Reshaping the Memory of the World Wars* (New York, 1990).
Michael Sanders and Philip Taylor, *Propaganda and the First World War* (London, 1983).
Kenneth E. Silver, *Esprit de Corps: The Art of the Parisian Avant-Garde and the First World War, 1914–1925* (London, 1989).
James Duane Squires, *British Propaganda at Home and in the United States from 1914 to 1917* (Cambridge, Mass., 1935).
J. M. Winter, *Sites of Memory, Sites of Mourning* (Cambridge, 1995).
D. G. Wright, 'The Great War, Government Propaganda and English "Men of letters"', *Literature and History*, 7 (1978), 70–100.

17. Socialism, Peace, and Revolution

John Cammett, *Antonio Gramsci and the Origins of Italian Communism* (Stanford, 1969).
Isaac Deutscher, *Trotsky*, i: *The Prophet Armed, 1879–1921* (Oxford, 1954).
Leo Haimson and Giulio Sapelli (eds.), *Strikes, Social Conflict and the First World War* (Milan, 1991).
Georges Haupt, *Socialism and the Great War: The Collapse of the Second International* (Oxford 1972).
John Horne, *Labour at War: France and Britain, 1914–1918* (Oxford, 1991). A comparative study of the distinctive labour and socialist reformism that emerged during the war.
Karl Kautsky, *The Dictatorship of the Proletariat* (1918: English translation, 1919; new edn., Ann Arbor, 1964). A contemporary critique of Bolshevism by the key theoretician of the pre-war German Social Democratic Party and of the Second International.
David Kirby, *War, Peace and Revolution: International Socialism at the Crossroads, 1914–1918* (London, 1986).
Diane Koenker and William G. Rosenberg, *Strikes and Revolution in Russia, 1917* (Princeton, 1989).
Annie Kriegel, *Aux origines du communisme français, 1914–1920* (2 vols., Paris, 1964).
David Mandel, *The Petrograd Workers and the Fall of the Old Regime* (London, 1983) and *The Petrograd Workers and the Soviet Seizure of Power* (London, 1984).
Susanne Miller, *Burgfrieden und Klassenkampf (die deutsche Sozialdemokratie im Ersten Weltkrieg)* (Düsseldorf, 1974).
David Morgan, *The Socialist Left and the German Revolution: A History of the German Social Democratic Party, 1917–1922* (Ithaca, NY, 1975).
J. Peter Nettl, *Rosa Luxemburg* (Oxford, 1969).
Richard Pipes, *A Concise History of the Russian Revolution* (London, 1995).
Christophe Prochasson, *Les Intellectuels, le socialisme et la guerre, 1900–1938* (Paris, 1993).
John Reed, *Ten Days that Shook the World* (1919: new edn. London, 1977). A classic, engaged account of the October Revolution.
Jean-Louis Robert, *Les Ouvriers, la patrie et la révolution: Paris 1914–1919* (Besançon, 1995).
Gary Steenson, *Karl Kautsky, 1854–1938: Marxism in the Classical Years* (Pittsburgh, 1978).
Jay Winter, *Socialism and the Challenge of War: Ideas and Politics in Britain* (London, 1974).
Chris Wrigley (ed.), *Challenges of Labour: Central and Western Europe, 1917–1920* (London, 1993).

American Battle Monuments Commission, *American Armies and Battlefields in Europe: A History, Guide, and Reference Book* (Washington, 1928).

Daniel R. Beaver, *Newton D. Baker and the American War Effort, 1917–1919* (Lincoln, 1966).

Paul R. Braim, *The Test of Battle: The American Expeditionary Forces in the Meuse-Argonne Campaign* (Newark, Del., 1987).

Robert Lee Bullard, *Personalities and Reminiscences of the War* (Garden City, NY, 1925).

Kathleen Burk, *Britain, America, and the Sinews of War, 1914–1918* (Boston, 1984).

Edward M. Coffman, *The Hilt of the Sword: The Career of Peyton C. March* (Madison, 1966).

Robert D. Cuff, *The War Industries Board: Business–Government Relations during World War I* (Baltimore, 1973).

Harvey A. DeWeerd, *President Wilson Fights his War: World War I and the American Intervention* (New York, 1968).

John Dickinson, *The Building of an Army: A Detailed Account of Legislation, Administration and Opinion in the United States, 1915–1920* (New York, 1922).

Robert H. Ferrell, *Woodrow Wilson and World War I, 1917–1921* (New York, 1985).

Historical Section, Department of the Army, *United States Army in the World War, 1917–1919* (17 vols., Washington, 1948).

Mary Klachko with David F. Trask, *Admiral William Shepherd Benson: First Chief of Naval Operations* (Annapolis, Md., 1987).

Hunter Liggett, *A. E. F.: Ten Years Ago in France* (New York, 1928).

Peyton C. March, *The Nation at War* (Garden City, NY, 1932).

Rod Paschall, *The Defeat of Imperial Germany 1917–1918* (Chapel Hill, NC, 1989).

Frederic L. Paxson, *America at War: 1917–1918* (Boston, 1939).

John J. Pershing, *My Experiences in the World War* (2 vols., New York, 1931).

Donald Smythe, *Pershing: General of the Armies* (Bloomington, Ind., 1986).

David F. Trask, *Captains and Cabinets: Anglo-American Naval Relations 1917–1918* (Columbia, Mo., 1972).

—— *The United States in the Supreme War Council: American War Aims and Inter-Allied Strategy, 1917–1918* (Middletown, Conn., 1961).

—— *The AEF and Coalition Warmaking, 1917–1918* (Lawrence, Kan., 1993).

18. The Entry of the USA into the War

Robert B. Asprey, *The German High Command at War: Hindenburg and Ludendorff Conduct World War I* (New York, 1991).

Cyril Falls, *The Battle of Caporetto* (London, 1966).

Bruce I. Gudmundsson, *Stormtroop Tactics: Innovation in the German Army, 1914–1918* (New York, 1989).

Holger H. Herwig, *The First World War: Germany and Austria-Hungary 1914–1918* (London, 1997).

Peter Kilduff, *Germany's First Air Force 1914–1918* (London, 1991).

Martin Kitchen, *The Silent Dictatorship: The Politics of the German High Command under Hindenburg and Ludendorff, 1916–1918* (New York, 1976).

Timothy T. Lupfer, *The Dynamics of Doctrine: The Changes in German Tactical Doctrine during the First World War* (Fort Leavenworth, Kan., 1981).

Martin Middlebrook, *The Kaiser's Battle, 21 March 1918: The First Day of the German Spring Offensive* (London, 1978).

Erwin Rommel, *Infantry Attacks* (Toronto, 1990).

Martin Samuels, *Command or Control? Command, Training and Tactics in the British and German Armies, 1888–1918* (London, 1995).

—— *Doctrine and Dogma: German and British Infantry Tactics in the First World War* (Westport, Conn., 1992).

19. The German Victories, 1917–1918

G. C. Wynne, *If Germany Attacks: The Battle in Depth in the West* (London, 1940).

David T. Zabecki, *Steel Wind: Colonel Georg Bruchmüller and The Birth of Modern Artillery* (Westport, Conn., 1994).

20. The War in the Air

Charles Christienne *et al.*, *Histoire de l'aviation militaire française* (Paris, 1980).

Malcolm Cooper, *The Birth of Independent Air Power: British Air Policy in the First World War* (London, 1986).

K. N. Finne, *Igor Sikorsky: The Russian Years*, ed. Carl Bobrow and Von Hardesty, trans. Von Hardesty (Washington, 1987).

Peter Fritzsche, *A Nation of Fliers: German Aviation and the Popular Imagination* (Cambridge, Mass., 1992). Well-done cultural study.

Peter M. Grosz, George Haddow, and Peter Schiemer, *Austro-Hungarian Army Aircraft of World War I* (Mountain View, Calif., 1993).

Richard P. Hallion, *Rise of the Fighter Aircraft, 1914–1918* (Annapolis, Md., 1984).

Robin Higham and Jacob W. Kipp, *Soviet Aviation and Air Power: A Historical View* (Boulder, Colo., 1977).

Felix P. Ingold, *Literatur und Aviatik: Europäische Flugdichtung, 1909–1927* (Basel, 1978). Comprehensive study of continental literature.

Lee Kennett, *The First Air War, 1914–1918* (New York, 1991).

Peter H. Liddle, *The Airman's War 1914–18* (Poole, 1987). Anecdotal and illustrated.

Maurer Maurer (ed.), *The U.S. Air Service in World War I* (4 vols., Washington, 1978–9). A comprehensive documentary collection.

John H. Morrow, Jr., *German Air Power in World War I* (Lincoln, Nebr., 1982). Study of military–industrial relationships.

——*The Great War in the Air: Military Aviation from 1909 to 1921* (Washington, 1993).

Michael Paris, *Winged Warfare: The Literature of Aerial Warfare in Britain, 1859–1917* (Manchester, 1992).

Dominick A. Pisano, Thomas J. Dietz, Joanne M. Gernstein, and Karl S. Schneide, *Legend, Memory and the Great War in the Air* (Seattle, 1992).

Walter Raleigh and H. A. Jones, *The War in the Air*, vols. i–vi (Oxford, 1922–37). The British official history.

Douglas H. Robinson, *The Zeppelin in Combat: A History of the German Naval Airship Division, 1912–1918* (London, 1962).

Herschel Smith, *A History of Aircraft Piston Engines* (Manhattan, Kan., 1986 [1981]).

Piero Vergnano, *Origins of Aviation in Italy, 1783–1918* (Genoa, 1964). Spare.

Denis Winter, *The First of the Few: Fighter Pilots of the First World War* (London, 1982). Excellent study of British aviators.

S. F. Wise, *Canadian Airmen and the First World War: The Official History of the Royal Canadian Air Force*, vol. i (Toronto, 1980).

Robert Wohl, *A Passion for Wings: Aviation and the Western Imagination, 1908–1918* (New Haven, 1994). Magnificent cultural history.

21. The Allied Victories, 1918

Daniel Dancocks, *Spearhead to Victory: Canada and the Great War* (Edmonton, 1987).

Wilhelm Deist, 'The Military Collapse of the German Empire: The Reality behind the Stab-in-the-Back Myth', *War in History*, 3 (1996), 186–207.

Sir James E. Edmonds, *Military Operations, France and Belgium, 1918*, vols. ii–v (London, 1937–47).

Hubert Essame, *The Battle for Europe: 1918* (London, 1972).

Col. T. Bentley Mott (trans.), *The Memoirs of Marshal Foch* (New York, 1931).

Barrie Pitt, *1918: The Last Act* (London, 1962).

Robin Prior and Trevor Wilson, *Command on the Western Front: The Military Career of Sir Henry Rawlinson, 1914–1918* (Oxford, 1992).

Leonard V. Smith, *Between Mutiny and Obedience: The Case of the French Fifth Division during World War I* (Princeton, 1994).

John Terraine, *To Win A War: 1918, the Year of Victory* (London, 1978).

David Trask, *The AEF and Coalition Warmaking, 1917–1918* (Lawrence, Kan., 1993).

Tim Travers, *How the War Was Won: Command and Technology in the British Army on the Western Front, 1917–1918* (London, 1992).

David T. Zabecki, *Steel Wind: Colonel Georg Bruchmüller and the Birth of Modern Artillery* (Westport, Conn., 1994).

22. The Peace Settlement

M. L. Dockrill and J. P. Goold, *Peace without Promise: Britain and the Paris Peace Conferences, 1919–1923* (London, 1981).

I. Floto, *Colonel House in Paris: A Study of American Policy at the Paris Peace Conference, 1919* (Aarhus, 1973).

P. Helmreich, *From Paris to Sèvres: The Partition of the Ottoman Empire and the Paris Peace Conference of 1919–20* (1974).

M. Kent (ed.), *The Great Powers and the End of the Ottoman Empire* (London, 1984).

J. M. Keynes, *The Economic Consequences of the Peace* (London, 1920).

A. Lentin, *Guilt at Versailles: Lloyd George and the Pre-History of Appeasement* (London, 1984).

A. J. Mayer, *Politics and Diplomacy of Peacemaking: Containment and Counter-revolution at Versailles, 1918–19* (London, 1968).

H. Nicolson, *Peacemaking* (London, 1933).

G. Schulz, *Revolutions and Peace Treaties, 1917–1920* (London, 1972).

H. Schwabe, *Woodrow Wilson, Revolutionary Germany and Peacemaking 1918–19: Missionary Diplomacy and the Realities of Power*, trans. R. and R. Kimber (Chapel Hill, NC, 1985).

A. Sharp, *The Versailles Settlement: Peacemaking in Paris, 1919* (Basingstoke, 1991).

J. M. Thompson, *Russia, Bolshevism and the Versailles Peace* (Princeton, 1966).

A. Walworth, *Wilson and his Peacemakers: American Diplomacy at the Paris Peace Conference, 1919* (London, 1986).

23. Memory and the Great War

Omer Bartov, *Murder in our Midst: The Holocaust, Industrial Killing, and Representation* (New York, 1996).

Richard Bessel, *Germany after the First World War* (Oxford, 1993).

Alan Borg, *War Memorials* (London, 1991).

Hugh Cecil, *The Flower of Battle: British Fiction Writers of the First World War* (London, 1995).

Christopher Coker, *War and the Twentieth Century: A Study of War and Modern Consciousness* (London, 1994).

Richard Cork, *A Bitter Truth: Avant-Garde Art and the Great War* (New Haven, 1994).

Tim Cross (ed.), *The Lost Voices of World War I* (London, 1988).

Geoff Dyer, *The Missing of the Somme* (London, 1994).

Modris Eksteins, *Rites of Spring: The Great War and the Birth of the Modern Age* (New York, 1989).

Paul Fussell, *The Great War and Modern Memory* (Oxford, 1975).

Adrian Gregory, *The Silence of Memory: Armistice Day, 1919–1946* (Oxford, 1994).

Samuel Hynes, *A War Imagined: The First World War and English Culture* (London, 1990).

John Keegan, *The Face of Battle: A Study of Agincourt, Waterloo and the Somme* (London, 1976).

George L. Mosse, *Fallen Soldiers: Reshaping the Memory of the World Wars* (New York, 1990).

Peter Parker, *The Old Lie: The Great War and the Public-School Ethos* (New York, 1987).

Daniel Pick, *War Machine: The Rationalisation of Slaughter in the Modern Age* (New Haven, 1993).

Antoine Prost, *In the Wake of War: Les Anciens Combattants and French Society* (Oxford, 1992).

Kenneth E. Silver, *Esprit de Corps: The Art of the Parisian Avant-Garde and the First World War, 1914–1925* (London, 1989).

Denis Winter, *Death's Men: Soldiers of the Great War* (London, 1978).

J. M. Winter, *Sites of Memory, Sites of Mourning: The Great War in European Cultural History* (Cambridge, 1995).

Robert Wohl, *The Generation of 1914* (London, 1979).

MAPS

1. Europe in 1914

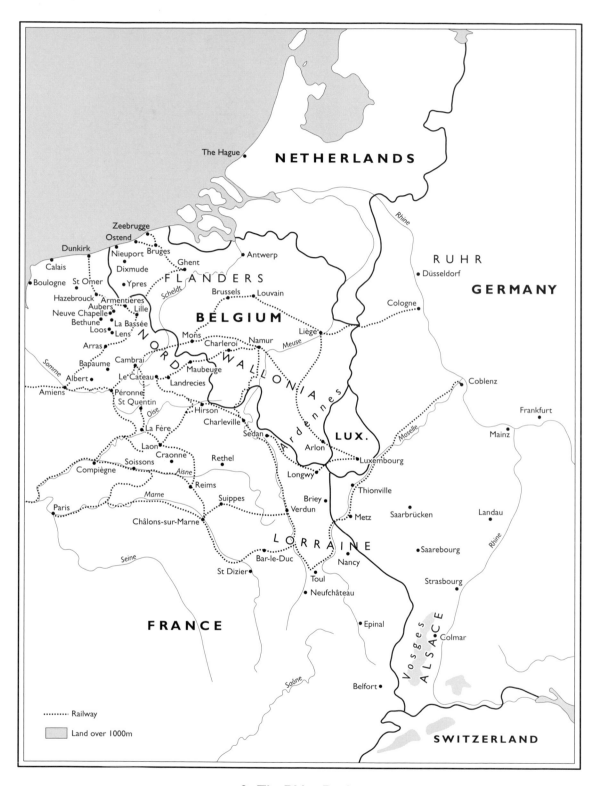

2. The Rhine Basin

3. The Adriatic

4. Eastern Europe

Land over 1000m

Vilna

Minsk

Königsberg

Danzig

Tannenberg

Niemen

Dnieper

Narew

Posen

Warsaw

Brest-Litovsk

Pripet Marshes

Lodz

Kiev

Breslau

Oder

Vistula

Cracow

Tarnow

Przemysl

Gorlice

San

Lemberg

Dniester

Bug

Bratislava

Vienna

Danube

Prut

Budapest

Brasov

Sibiu

Sava

Cernavoda

Bucharest

Constanza

Belgrade

Drina

Morava

Danube

Sarajevo

Nish

Varna

Vranja

Stara Zagora

Sofia

Cattaro

Drin

Skopje

Plovdiv

Uskub

Shtip

Struma

Durazzo

Bitola

Constantinople

Tirana

Salonica

Gallipoli

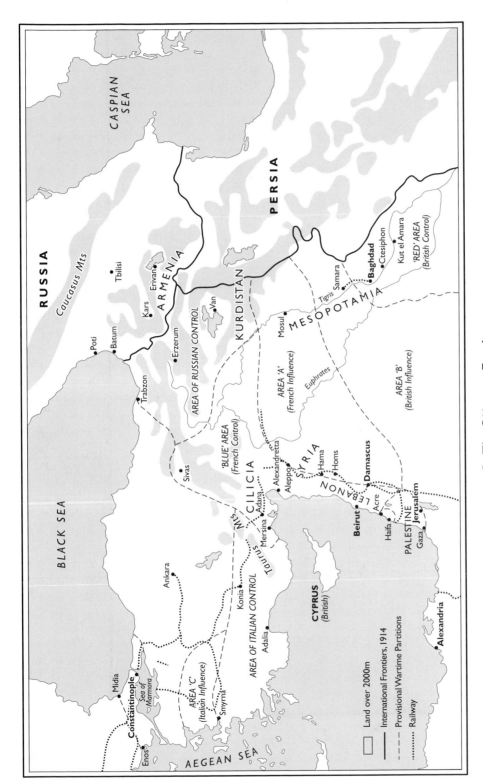

5. The Ottoman Empire

RUSSIA

CASPIAN SEA

PERSIA

ARMENIA

Caucasus Mts

Tbilisi

Erivan

Kars

KURDISTAN

Van

AREA OF RUSSIAN CONTROL

Poti

Batum

Erzerum

Trabzon

Mosul

MESOPOTAMIA

Tigris

Samara

Baghdad

Ctesiphon

Kut el Amara

'RED' AREA (British Control)

AREA 'A' (French Influence)

Euphrates

AREA 'B' (British Influence)

Sivas

'BLUE' AREA (French Control)

CILICIA

Alexandretta

Aleppo

SYRIA

Hama

Homs

Damascus

Adana

LEBANON

Taurus Mts

Mersina

Beirut

Acre

Haifa

PALESTINE

Gaza

Jerusalem

Ankara

Konia

Adalia

AREA OF ITALIAN CONTROL

CYPRUS (British)

Alexandria

BLACK SEA

Midia

Constantinople

Sea of Marmora

AREA 'C' (Italian Influence)

Smyrna

Enos

AEGEAN SEA

☐ Land over 2000m

— International Frontiers, 1914

- - - Provisional Wartime Partitions

···· Railway

343

**6. Europe after the
First World War**

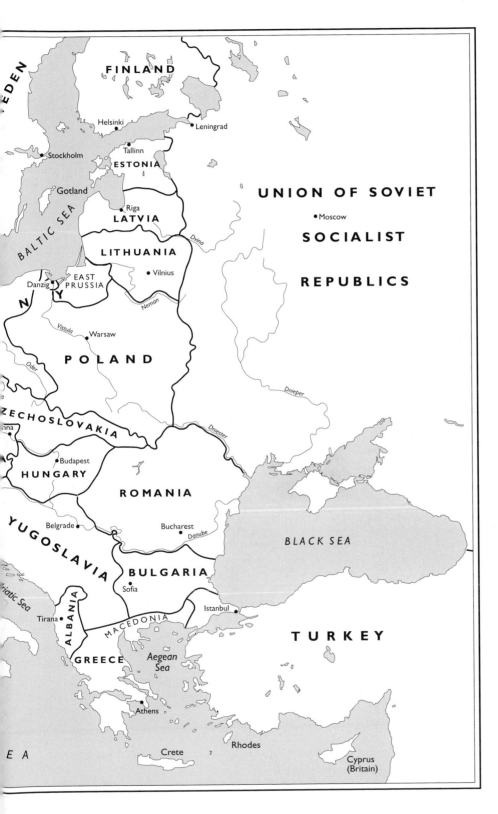

FINLAND

Helsinki • •Leningrad

Stockholm• •Tallinn
ESTONIA

Gotland

BALTIC SEA

•Riga
LATVIA

LITHUANIA

•Vilnius

Danzig EAST
PRUSSIA

Vistula •Warsaw

Oder

POLAND

CZECHOSLOVAKIA

•Budapest

HUNGARY

ROMANIA

Belgrade•

YUGOSLAVIA

•Bucharest
Danube

UNION OF SOVIET

•Moscow

SOCIALIST

REPUBLICS

Dvina

Neman

Dnieper

Dniester

BLACK SEA

BULGARIA

Sofia•

ALBANIA

Tirana •

MACEDONIA

Istanbul•

TURKEY

Adriatic Sea

GREECE

Aegean
Sea

•Athens

E A

Crete

Rhodes

Cyprus
(Britain)

345

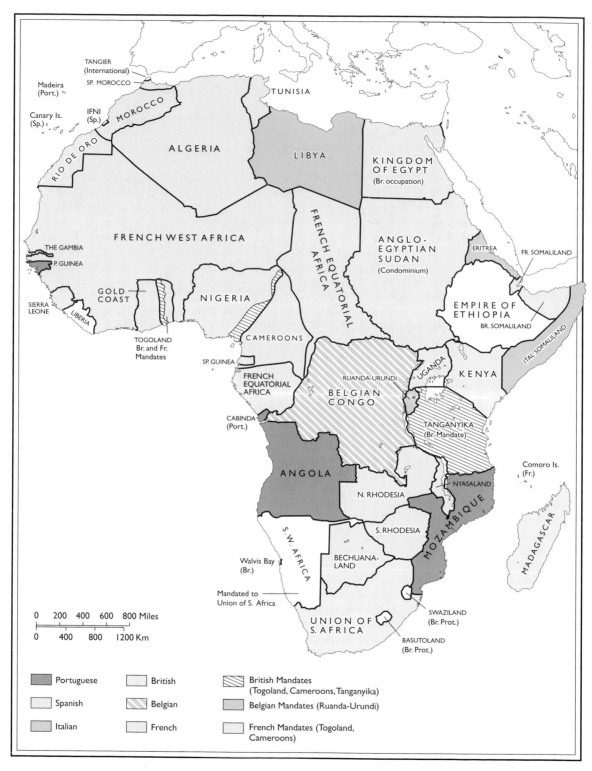

7. Africa after the First World War

ILLUSTRATION SOURCES

The editor and publishers wish to thank the following who have kindly given permission to reproduce the illustrations on the following pages:

IWM = Imperial War Museum
BDIC = Bibliothèque de Documentation Internationale Contemporaine, Nanterre & Paris

9   Hulton Getty
10   IWM HU68062
14   bpk, Berlin 1997
17   Suddeutscher Verlag Bilderdienst
18   Ullstein Bilderdienst
22   Hulton Getty
23   IWM Q81763
26   IWM Q113409
27   bpk, Berlin 1997
31   IWM Q113409
34   Hulton Getty
39   © photo Musée de l'Armée, Paris
40   Jüdisches Museum, Frankfurt & Stadtische Kunsthalle Recklinghausen
43   IWM Q57228
47   © photo Musée de l'Armée, Paris
50   IWM Q11719
51   IWM Q49378
52   Illustrated London News Picture Library
54   Roger-Viollet
57   IWM Q51019
58   Roger-Viollet
62   Roger-Viollet
65   Hulton Getty
66   IWM Q87148
67   IWM Q52316
70   IWM Q32256
71   IWM Q52325
73   IWM Q32309
74   IWM Q52237
76   IWM Q87289
78   IWM Q87148
80   Ullstein Bilderdienst
82   Hulton Getty
83   bpk, Berlin 1997
85   Ullstein Bilderdienst
86   Armin Wegner/Yves Ternon
87   Corbis-Bettman/UPI
89   IWM Q55382
91   IWM Q59314
92   Cape Town Archives Repository
93   IWM Q15370
94   Bundesarchiv, Koblenz
95   copyright reserved
97   Cape Town Archives Repository
98   South African National Museum of Military History
104   IWM Q19668
105   IWM Q63704
112   IWM Q63046
113   IWM Q53021
115   (top) IWM Q18794
        (bottom) IWM SP 634
117   IWM Q48241
118   IWM Q19668
119   IWM Q3214
121   Historisches Archiv Krupp, Essen
123   IWM Q3214
125   Käthe Kollwitz, Germany's Children are Hungry © DACS 1998; © Elke Walford, Hamburg/Hamburger Kunsthalle
127   British Library, Newspaper Library
128   IWM Q20875
131   Ullstein Bilderdienst
132   IWM Q110883
134   IWM/Camera Press London
136   Archives Larousse-Giraudon
138   Ginner, The Filling Factory, National Gallery of Canada, Ottawa
140   Illustrated London News Picture Library
143   Heeresgeschichtliches Museum, Vienna
144   Kharbine-Tapabor
146   IWM/Camera Press, London
149   IWM Q30679
153   IWM Q28014
154   IWM Q20666
156   IWM Q30679
158   IWM Q19134

159   IWM Q5958
160   IWM Q5950
163   IWM PIC685
166   © Harlingue-Viollet/Roger-Viollet
172   IWM Q57040
174   Hulton Getty
176   IWM PIC685
179   IWM Q10711
180   IWM Q54534
184   IWM Q754
186   IWM Q1142
187   Pierre Bonnard, *Village en ruine aux environs de Ham* © ADAGP, Paris and DACS, London 1998 & BDIC
189   IWM Q10711
191   David King Collection
192   WA78/3/15 National Archives of New Zealand, Head Office Wellington (War Archives, 2 Battalion Canterbury Regiment, WA Series 78)
193   IWM Q81092
195   Süddeutscher Verlag Bilderdienst
198   David King Collection
201   IWM Q2953
204   IWM Q23883
209   Jiji, Tokyo
213   IWM Q23883
216   First National, courtesy Kobal
217   Musée d'histoire contemporaine, Paris
219   Musée d'histoire contemporaine, Paris
220   Musée d'histoire contemporaine, Paris
222   First National, courtesy Kobal
227   Hoover Institution Archives, Stanford
230   J. Vigne/BDIC
232   Hoover Institution Archives, Stanford
234   Ullstein Bilderdienst
238   Novosti, London
239   Bara-King/National Archives

241   Süddeutscher Verlag Bilderdienst
244   Bara-King/US National Archives
248   Bara-King/US National Archives
250   AKG
253   Bara-King/US National Archives
255   Bara-King/US National Archives
260   IWM Q55479
261   Bara-King/US National Archives
263   IWM Q55010
265   Library of Congress
268   Roger-Viollet
269   Library of Congress
270   Royal Air Force Museum P15256
272   bpk, Berlin 1997
273   Royal Airforce Museum P168
275   Michelin
278   IWM Q9326
279   IWM Q10797
282   IWM C02969
283   IWM Q11218
285   IWM Q9326
286   IWM CO3369
289   IWM CO3624
290   IWM EAUS 921
293   IWM Q14997
294   Hulton Getty
305   National Archives of Canada/PA-803934
307   IWM Q71074
309   National Archives of Canada/PA-803934
311   IWM Q50941
314   Universal, courtesy Kobal
316   Martin Middlebrook

In a few instances we have been unable to trace the copyright holder prior to publication. If notified, the publishers will be pleased to amend the acknowledgements in any future edition.

Picture research by Sandra Assersohn.

INDEX

Monmouth 108–9
Monro, Charles 88
Mons 43, 259, 289
Montagu, E. S. 176–7
Montague, C. E. 310
Montdidier 260, 263
Montenegro 16, 66, 68–9, 71–2, 79
Monty Python 305
Moon 256
morale 118, 191, 196, 199–202
Morane aircraft 269
Morgan, J. P. 130
Morhange 42
Morocco 10–13, 55, 94–5, 101–2, 266
mortars 141, 193, 257
Moscow 238
Mosul 88, 90, 302
Mottram, R. H. 310
Mozambique 95
Mudros armistice 90
Müller, Hermann 176–7
Müller, Karl von 108
munitions production 4, 6, 72–3, 116, 121, 123, 137–46, 229, 288–9
Murmansk 246
Muş 85
mutinies 3, 64, 114, 118, 182, 188, 196–202, 209

Nablus 90
Nancy 263
Narotch, lake 180
Narva 259
Nash, Paul 245
nationalism 7, 13, 101–2, 165–7, 194, 215, 299–304
Naval War Council 245
Neajlov river 74
Netherlands Overseas Trust 124
Neuilly, treaty of 300
neutrality 2, 114, 121, 123–4, 128–31
Neuve Chapelle 51, 59
New Armies 53, 56
New Zealand 56, 108, 317
Nicholas II, tsar 21, 62, 316
Nichols, Beverley 308
Nicolson, Arthur 15
Nielson, Asta 224
Niemen river 48
Nieuport aircraft 269
Niger 95
Nigeria 93, 96
Nikolai Nikolaevich, Grand Duke 84
Nish 67, 69
Nivelle, Robert 64, 172, 174, 187–8, 196, 256
North sea 104–7, 111, 116–17, 122
Northcliffe, Alfred Harmsworth, Lord 265
Northern Patrol 106
Norway 243
Noyon 261, 263
Nungesser, Charles 271
Nur-ed-Din, Yusef 87
Nuri bey 86
Nürnberg 108

Nyasaland 95, 98, 100

Oderzo 264
Odessa 79
Oh What a Lovely War! 316
Ohrid lake 72
oil 77
Oise river 248, 262
Orlando, Vittorio-Emanuele 174, 176–7, 291, 299
Orpen, William 176–7
Ösel 110, 256
Ostend 117, 205
Ostrovo 75
Ottoman empire 2, 3, 7, 10, 14, 30–2, 37, 56–7, 61, 66, 68, 70, 74, 80–91, 94–6, 106, 113–14, 125, 135, 137, 178, 208, 212
    see also Turkey
Otranto 108
Otranto, strait of 112, 117, 243
Ourcq river 45
Owen, Wilfred 307, 313

Pabst, G. W. 313
pacifism 151–2, 168, 173, 229, 233, 237, 317
Padua 264
Painlevé, Paul 172, 210
Palestine 81–3, 89–90, 95, 117, 243, 302
Pankhurst, Emmeline 152
pan-Turanianism 80
Paris 43–5, 55, 262–3, 279
Paris:
    allied economic conference 123, 173, 208, 211
    peace conference, *see* peace
Parker, Gilbert 224–5
Pašić, Nikolai 15, 19, 176–7
Passchendaele 3, 174, 190, 256, 290
Pathfinder 107
peace 6, 176–7, 252, 291–304
peace negotiations 29, 31–4, 36–7, 49, 61, 147, 206–7, 209–11, 221, 231–2, 240
'peace resolution' 210, 213
Peck, Cy 281
Péguy, Charles 307
Peralba, monte 258
Péronne 260–1
Pershing, John J. 244, 247–51, 262
Persia 85, 87–8, 94
Persian gulf 55
Pétain, Philippe 64, 174, 188, 261–2, 273, 276, 279
Petrograd 63, 109, 197–8, 232–4, 256
Philippeville 106
Piave river 258, 263–4, 288
Picardy 249, 252
Pichon, Stephen 176–7
Pickford, Mary 223
Pickfords 309
pilgrimages 309, 317
Pirot 69
plan XVII 28, 40–1

Ploesti 76
Plumer, Herbert 188, 190
Pohl, Hugo von 35, 111, 114
Poincaré, Raymond 13, 18, 233, 241
Pola 114
Poland 13, 36, 48–50, 68, 206–10, 213, 215, 254, 295–6, 300–1
Pont Arcy 263
poppies 277
porters 97–9
Portugal 178
    in Africa 93–6, 100, 102
Potiorek, Oskar 67
Poznań 49, 296
press 52
Princess Royal 109
Princip, Gavrilo 9–10
Pripyat marshes 600
propaganda 3, 52, 94, 148–9, 154, 181, 196, 216–26, 244
Przemyśl 47
Pskov 259
psychoanalysis 312
Putnik, Radomir 67

Quéant 284
Queenstown 114, 242

'race to the sea' 46
racism 302
Radoslavov, Vasil 68–9, 78–9
railways 83–4, 146–7, 153, 255, 259
Rathenau, Walther 139, 177
Rauf, Hüseyin 90
Ravenna 197
Rawlinson, Henry 185, 281–2, 287
Raymond, Ernest 310
reconnaissance aircraft 267–8, 275
Red sea 83
refugees 47
Reims 256, 262, 266, 279, 298
religion 101, 218–19
    see also Catholicism; Islam; Jews
Remarque, Erich Maria 313–15
Renault, Louis 141, 267, 275
Renn, Ludwig 313
reparations 297–300
revolution 3, 77, 170, 178, 209, 231–3, 236, 308
    German 125, 132–3, 170, 178, 199–200, 214–15, 236–7
    Hungarian 300
    Russian 32, 37–8, 63, 85, 114, 131, 169–70, 181–2, 197, 199, 209, 212, 217, 231–6, 256
    war as opportunity for 178, 227, 230
Rhineland 96, 208–9, 215, 295
Rhodesia, Northern 94, 100
Rhodesia, Southern 102
Ribot, Alexandre 166, 172, 210–11
Richtofen, Manfred von 271–2
Riddell, George 176–7
Rif 102
Riga 53, 256, 296
Riga, gulf of 110
Robertson, William 64, 174